VOLUME 633

THE ANNALS

of The American Academy of Political and Social Science

PHYLLIS KANISS, *Executive Editor*

The Child as Citizen

Special Editor:

FELTON EARLS
Harvard University

SAGE

Los Angeles | London | New Delhi
Singapore | Washington DC

The American Academy of Political and Social Science

202 S. 36th Street, Annenberg School for Communication, University of Pennsylvania, Philadelphia, PA 19104-3806; (215) 746-7321; (215) 573-2667 (fax); www.aapss.org

Origin and Purpose. The Academy was organized December 14, 1889, to promote the progress of political and social science, especially through publications and meetings. The Academy does not take sides in controverted questions, but seeks to gather and present reliable information to assist the public in forming an intelligent and accurate judgment.

Meetings. The Academy occasionally holds a meeting in the spring extending over two days.

Publications. THE ANNALS of The American Academy of Political and Social Science is the bimonthly publication of the Academy. Each issue contains articles on some prominent social or political problem, written at the invitation of the editors. These volumes constitute important reference works on the topics with which they deal, and they are extensively cited by authorities throughout the United States and abroad.

Membership. Each member of the Academy receives THE ANNALS and may attend the meetings of the Academy. Membership is open only to individuals. Annual dues: $94.00 for the regular paperbound edition (clothbound, $134.00). Members may also purchase single issues of THE ANNALS for $18.00 each (clothbound, $27.00). Student memberships are available for $52.00.

Subscriptions. THE ANNALS of The American Academy of Political and Social Science (ISSN 0002-7162) (J295) is published bimonthly—in January, March, May, July, September, and November—by SAGE Publications, 2455 Teller Road, Thousand Oaks, CA 91320. Periodicals postage paid at Thousand Oaks, California, and at additional mailing offices. POSTMASTER: Send address changes to The Annals of The American Academy of Political and Social Science, c/o SAGE Publications, 2455 Teller Road, Thousand Oaks, CA 91320. Institutions may subscribe to THE ANNALS at the annual rate: $788.00 (clothbound, $889.00). Single issues of THE ANNALS may be obtained by individuals who are not members of the Academy for $142.00 each (clothbound, $160.00). Single issues of THE ANNALS have proven to be excellent supplementary texts for classroom use. Direct inquiries regarding adoptions to THE ANNALS c/o SAGE Publications (address below).

All correspondence concerning membership in the Academy, dues renewals, inquiries about membership status, and/or purchase of single issues of THE ANNALS should be sent to THE ANNALS c/o SAGE Publications, 2455 Teller Road, Thousand Oaks, CA 91320. Telephone: (800) 818-SAGE (7243) and (805) 499-0721; Fax/Order line: (805) 375-1700; e-mail: journals@sagepub.com. *Please note that orders under $30 must be prepaid.* For all customers outside the Americas, please visit http://www.sagepub.co.uk/customerCare.nav for information.

Printed on acid-free paper

THE ANNALS

Editorial Office: 202 S. 36th Street, Philadelphia, PA 19104-3806
For information about membership* (individuals only) and subscriptions (institutions), address:
SAGE Publications
2455 Teller Road
Thousand Oaks, CA 91320

For SAGE Publications: Allison Leung (Production) and Lori Hart (Marketing)

From India and South Asia,
write to:
SAGE PUBLICATIONS INDIA Pvt Ltd
B-42 Panchsheel Enclave, P.O. Box 4109
New Delhi 110 017
INDIA

From Europe, the Middle East,
and Africa, write to:
SAGE PUBLICATIONS LTD
1 Oliver's Yard, 55 City Road
London EC1Y 1SP
UNITED KINGDOM

*Please note that members of the Academy receive THE ANNALS with their membership.
International Standard Serial Number ISSN 0002-7162
International Standard Book Number ISBN 978-1-4129-9585-6 (Vol. 633, 2011) paper
International Standard Book Number ISBN 978-1-4129-9586-3 (Vol. 633, 2011) cloth
Manufactured in the United States of America. First printing, January 2011.

Please visit http://ann.sagepub.com and under the "More about this journal" menu on the right-hand side, click on the Abstracting/Indexing link to view a full list of databases in which this journal is indexed.

Information about membership rates, institutional subscriptions, and back issue prices may be found on the facing page.

Advertising. Current rates and specifications may be obtained by writing to The Annals Advertising and Promotion Manager at the Thousand Oaks office (address above). Acceptance of advertising in this journal in no way implies endorsement of the advertised product or service by SAGE or the journal's affiliated society(ies) or the journal editor(s). No endorsement is intended or implied. SAGE reserves the right to reject any advertising it deems as inappropriate for this journal.

Claims. Claims for undelivered copies must be made no later than six months following month of publication. The publisher will supply replacement issues when losses have been sustained in transit and when the reserve stock will permit.

Change of Address. Six weeks' advance notice must be given when notifying of change of address. Please send the old address label along with the new address to the SAGE office address above to ensure proper identification. Please specify the name of the journal.

THE ANNALS
OF THE AMERICAN ACADEMY OF POLITICAL AND SOCIAL SCIENCE

Volume 633 January 2011

IN THIS ISSUE:

The Child as Citizen

Special Editor: FELTON EARLS

Introduction

INTRODUCTION

Children: From Rights to Citizenship

By
FELTON EARLS

This article introduces the themes of children's rights and citizenship and surveys the authors' contributions to this volume of *The Annals*. The volume marks the 20th anniversary of the United Nations General Assembly's adoption of the Convention on the Rights of the Child (CRC). As the most widely ratified of all human rights covenants, adoption of the CRC represents a landmark achievement in the history of childhood. Yet there remains a noticeable gap in its implementation. The United States has not ratified the CRC. The contributions to this volume take the CRC as a starting point along the path of achieving functional citizenship for children. Issues of child protection, political maturity, deliberative democracy, and intergenerational nondomination are covered. Several examples of empirical research on children's participation in social and political matters are provided. Recommendations are made to advance the case of child citizenship over the near term. This includes the need to urge the United States to ratify the CRC.

Keywords: Convention on the Rights of the Child (CRC); ratification; intergenerational citizenship

On November 9, 2009, a group of scholars assembled at the House of the American Academy of Arts and Sciences (AAAS) in Cambridge, Massachusetts, to refine and possibly to expand their notions of children as citizens. The meeting, staged as a workshop to prepare for this volume of *The Annals*, provided a moment to consider the connection

Felton Earls is a professor of social medicine at Harvard Medical School and a professor of human behavior and development at Harvard School of Public Health. His interests span child mental health, epidemiology, and human rights. From 1990 to 2005, he was the principal investigator for the Project on Human Development in Chicago Neighborhoods, a multilevel, longitudinal study on the causes and consequences of children's exposure to violence. His current project, the Ecology of HIV/AIDS and Child Mental Health in Tanzania, is a community-level randomized control trial aimed at strengthening children's capacity to promote community health in the context of the HIV/AIDS epidemic.

DOI: 10.1177/0002716210383637

between our understanding of childhood as a vitally important period in the life cycle and the advancement of democratic principles and institutions. The American Academy of Political and Social Science (AAPSS) sponsored the workshop. The date, setting, and sponsorship carry separate and combined significance. The date marked the 20th anniversary of the United Nations (UN) General Assembly's passage of the Convention on the Rights of the Child (CRC). The setting of the AAAS represented an auspicious place to reflect on the ideals of democracy, since its founders intended this institution to provide a forum to serve the democratic interests of the nation. Sponsorship by the AAPSS, which has a long history of examining concerns related to the welfare of children, presented an opportunity to publish the proceedings of this deliberation in *The Annals*. The convergence of time, setting, and patronage culminated in this volume, which offers a broad reflection on the achievements, deficiencies, and future possibilities of the CRC at a turning point in the history of childhood. The contributors provide a robust intellectual foundation to guide the realization of citizenship for children.

Thinking seriously about the special nature of childhood can be traced to the Enlightenment. Rousseau (1979), in particular, considered childhood a period of innocence and mutability, which evoked sentiments that children were deserving of protection and education. Over the next two centuries, steady progress was made in improving the welfare of children. (See this volume's appendix for key events establishing children's rights.) In the industrialized nations, survivorship has increased through discoveries in medicine and public health; universal public education has become the norm; and systems of social welfare, juvenile justice, and child protection have strengthened the integrity of family life and childhood. In the effort to reduce global disparities in health and well-being, only moral and political constraints prevent such knowledge from being shared with the developing world.

The Convention on the Rights of the Child

The UN General Assembly adopted the CRC in November 1989, and it entered into force in September 1990. Within a decade, 193 of the 195 member states of the UN had ratified the CRC. Only the United States and Somalia stand apart. Although it does not mention child citizenship—the focus of this volume—the CRC follows an uncompromising path along which citizenship, with its rights and obligations, can be envisioned. The universal standards articulated in the CRC date back to the Geneva Declaration of the Rights of the Child that the League of Nations adopted in 1924. Following the passage of the Universal Declaration on Human Rights in 1948, the issue of human rights for children resurfaced in the 1958 Declaration of the Rights of the Child and in several UN covenants (UNICEF 2009).

Prompted during the International Year of the Child in 1979, the UN Commission on Human Rights established an "Open-Ended Working Group" to produce a legally binding human rights treaty for children. Consulting widely with governments and nongovernmental organizations (NGOs) and including the testimonies of children representing themselves, drafting of the treaty took a decade to complete. The product is a far-reaching manifesto that, in its fifty-four provisions, includes forty-one articles covering the entire range of civil, political, social, cultural, and economic rights and thirteen articles that establish the basis for monitoring and implementation. Once the General Assembly adopted the CRC as international law, individual governments signed and eventually ratified the CRC. Ratification formally binds a government to meet the obligations and responsibilities that the treaty espouses. Each ratifying country establishes a special committee to monitor the interpretation and implementation of the CRC in that country. The World Summit for Children; the World Declaration on the Survival, Protection, and Development of Children; and the Plan of Action for Implementing the World Declaration on the Survival, Protection, and Development of Children all quickly followed the adoption of the CRC. More recently, additional events have occurred to maintain the CRC's vitality, including the addition of two optional protocols and a special meeting of the General Assembly to review progress on the CRC.

Despite its universal status, the celebration of the CRC's 20th anniversary was not a significant event in the United States or in many other parts of the world. Many informed people remain either unaware of the CRC's existence or consider it utopian rhetoric. Does it matter that children have rights? How can children be citizens if they are thought to be too immature to vote? Children's welfare is naturally in the hands of authority figures. After all, that is why they must have parents and guardians. Such attitudes are prevalent in any discussion on giving autonomy and responsibility to children. In one way, children acquire the status of a citizen by virtue of being born in a state, but the truth is that they are not fully citizens until they are old enough to vote, serve in the military, or hold public office.

Childhood is the last frontier in the articulation of rights for special groups. But unlike the women's suffrage campaign and the civil rights movement, children have not demanded human rights. For the most part, they have not struggled or risked their lives in war and civil disobedience. When they have, as in the Soweto uprising in South Africa and the National Movement of Street Boys and Girls in Brazil, the world took fleeting notice and moved on. It seems paradoxical that it was against this rather bland and largely disinterested background that the CRC has achieved such universal status.

The CRC has become an essential tool to improve conditions for children around the world (Himes 1995). Many ratifying countries have incorporated its values into their national plans, programs, and legislation to secure the rights of children in a variety of areas, including education and health care. In the area of juvenile justice, El Salvador, Peru, and Bolivia enacted new justice codes for children, based on the CRC. Mexico, Pakistan, and Tunisia also modified laws to afford greater protection to young offenders. France moved to give children the right to express their views in court. Vietnam reviewed its judicial processes, amended all legal documents related to juvenile justice, and has since discussed establishing a juvenile court. In Rwanda, UNICEF and the International Committee of the Red Cross have used provisions of the CRC as the basis for their program to transfer some of the children accused of genocide and murder out of the overcrowded adult prisons and into rehabilitation centers.

The CRC's articulation of four cardinal principles is central to its understanding. These principles are articles intended to represent underlying themes that link to and coordinate all the other articles. These four principles advance the participation of children in society; cite the provision of resources required for their survival and well-being; and specify their protection from discrimination, neglect, and abuse. Furthermore, the CRC requires that governments make decisions and allocate resources according to the "best interests of the child" (UN General Assembly 1989, Article 3).

The articles specifying the participatory rights are arguably the most important in the pursuit of children's citizenship. These rights represent the radical turn in our notion of children's interests and capacities and more generally in their status in society. Article 12 has special importance, as it recognizes the right of a child to express his or her views freely in matters affecting him or her and ensures that those views are given due weight in accordance with the child's maturity. This article also has the status of a "principle" as it pertains to all other CRC articles. Four other articles considered "participation rights" give substance to the agency and capacities, not simply the vulnerability and dependency, of the child. These four articles include Article 13, which acknowledges the child's right to freedom of expression, to seek, receive, and impart information; Article 14, which specifies the right of the child to freedom of thought, conscience, and religion; Article 15, which recognizes the rights of the child to freedom of association and to freedom of peaceful assembly; and Article 17, which guarantees the child's access to information and material, especially those aimed at the promotion of his or her social, spiritual, and moral well-being and physical and mental health. These rights carry the promise of legitimately engaging children in the civic and political functions of their communities and governments.

The United States and the CRC

The United States was a major participant in establishing the momentum to draft the CRC. After its adoption at the UN, the U.S. Committee for UNICEF spurred a national campaign to persuade the Bush and Clinton administrations and the House and Senate to sign and ratify the treaty. The effort was partially successful. President Bill Clinton eventually signed the CRC but left office without getting it ratified. He did manage to sign the two optional protocols to the unratified CRC, one that prohibits military service for children under age 18 and another that criminalizes child prostitution and pornography. The signing of these protocols was done without fanfare and was largely ignored in the mainstream media. President George W. Bush put the CRC before the Senate, which, in turn, failed to advance the CRC.

Ratification, which mandates a two-thirds majority vote in the Senate, would represent a powerful endorsement of the principles of provision and participation that so uniquely distinguish the CRC. By obligating itself to the CRC, the United States would be required to monitor the well-being of children and implement policies and programs to improve their lives.

Although the prospects for ratification appear remote, it is useful to consider reasons for resistance, since without establishing children as rights-holders, there is little utility in advancing their pathway to citizenship. Prior to the Supreme Court's decision in *Roper v. Simmons* in 2005 to render the death penalty unconstitutional for juvenile offenders, this sanction had been a major legal obstacle. There remain several additional impediments to U.S. ratification. First, the Convention on the Elimination of All Forms of Discrimination against Women is often cited as the nation's top priority among human rights treaties.[1] There are other international charters forming a queue for ratification in the Senate. Second, there is reluctance in some quarters to ratify the CRC, because it would interfere with the rights of parents by granting children freedom of expression and the right to representation in court. The CRC also touches on health care issues in ways that can be negatively interpreted by groups opposed to abortion or universal health care coverage. Third, according to Article VI of the U.S. Constitution, international law can supersede federal and state statutes. However, it is important to note that ratification of the CRC can be achieved without agreeing to all its clauses. States are allowed to introduce reservations when provisions of the CRC prove incompatible with existing law.

One of the few groups promoting the CRC in the United States is the Child Welfare League of America (CWLA). With the CWLA's leadership, a core group of child advocates convened the first meeting of the Campaign for U.S. Ratification of the CRC in August 2002. Participants focused on efforts needed to build a national coalition. Out of this effort, the campaign has grown to encompass membership from two hundred organizations and academic institutions.[2]

Citizenship: National and Global

Citizenship is a cluttered term. A variety of connotations and aspirations are embraced in its definition. In approaching this volume, no attempt was made to precisely delimit the terms *citizen* or *citizenship*. The authors' concerns were rooted in the meaning of national citizenship, where issues of birthright, taxation, voting, and patriotism define its essence (Abowitz and Harnish 2006). Exclusion as a nonmember is as sharply drawn as inclusion. More often than not, the benefits of membership have been hard-won, leaving a legacy of struggle as the basis for national identity. The principles and values of national citizenship are codified and enforced through a legal system. But over the course of the twentieth century, nation-states ceased to be the sole arbiter of rights and citizenship. The term *global citizen* has become indiscriminately inclusive. The values of respect for others and the situations characterized by international migration, common security, and the protection of natural resources are the platforms that inspire the emergence of global citizenship. These aspirations are weakly enforced through international laws and codes that depend almost exclusively on moral suasion for enforcement. Global citizenship is granted by decree and remains diffuse and uneven in its manifestations. Yet as reflected in international agencies, corporations, and the ever-growing electronic media, global citizenship is on course to rival nationality as the predominant determinant of our freedoms and well-being.

The authors presumed the historical, legal, and ethical aspects of the CRC to be the common ground for thinking about the movement from rights to citizenship. While couched in universalistic rhetoric, the CRC identifies nation-states as duty-bearers and children as rights-bearers. But citizenship is more than geopolitical identity and entitlements. Having the motivation and capacity to voice one's opinions and preferences in mutually respectful ways represents the highest level of democratic achievement (Marshall 1950). The willingness to communicate, especially with a diverse set of agents, is a crucial step toward the achievement of collective well-being. Political maturity should be defined as having the skills to assess and act with others to attain the common good. Even if children are denied access to electoral processes, they do have opinions and preferences and capacities for deliberation and social action.

Sissela Bok, in *Common Values* (1995, 59), pinpoints the following quote from Charles Darwin's *Descent of Man* (1871, 100–101), which asserts the fundamental human quality embodied in citizenship.

> As man advances in civilization, and small tribes are united into larger communities, the simplest reason would tell each individual that he ought to extend his social instincts and sympathies to all members of the same nation, though personally unknown to him. This point being reached, there is only an artificial barrier to prevent his sympathies extending to the men of all nations and races.

What are these artificial barriers to citizenship: nationality, ethnicity, gender, religion? For the theme of this volume, it is age. Yet childhood is a developmental phase of overwhelming potential for enhancing democratization.

The Organization of This Volume

The contributions to this volume consider how history, philosophy, science, education, law, and policy deal with children as active and capable members of society. The first six articles cover historical background, legal issues, and policy matters (Fass, Van Bueren, Maurás, Rizzini, Bartholet, and Hernandez, Denton and Blanchard). Two articles introduce theory-based considerations on child citizenship (Bohman and Rehfeld). Five are concerned with the challenges of implementation from the standpoints of developmental social science and practice (James, Torney-Purta and Amadeo, Hart and Atkins, Carlson and Earls, and Fonseca and Bujanda). These clusters were introduced more to achieve a sense of procedure than to impose a structure on the ideas and activities presented in this volume.

Paula Fass presents a historical analysis of how the definition of a progressive childhood, developed in the nineteenth century as a result of the antislavery movement, concerns about poverty, and public health advances, confronted the challenges that resulted from the civilian casualties of war in the twentieth century. Notions of protection provided the foundation on which the notion of child rights was introduced in the League of Nations and continued to evolve during the twentieth century up to the time of the adoption of the CRC. The context in which children's rights evolved was fueled by the active involvement of women, the growing influence of NGOs on policy, the active expansion of the welfare state in countries such as Sweden and its strategic role in postwar diplomacy, and less sentimental and more purposeful images of children capable of definitive social action.

As a member of the open-ended working group that formulated the CRC, Geraldine Van Bueren explicitly acknowledges its utopian aspirations (as opposed to protection of rights in catastrophic situations). She presents a decidedly optimistic viewpoint on its achievements and future. This promising perspective not only enhances discourse on the place of children in society but makes empirical claims as well (i.e., that the CRC sets the stage for saving millions of children's lives under age five). She outlines a path over which the CRC is poised to advance the idea of multigenerational and global citizenship.

Marta Maurás, a member of the UN Committee on the Rights of the Child—the body organized to monitor implementation and oversee interpretation of the CRC—presents insights, especially from the Latin American context, that show how the CRC is becoming situated in a normative and policy context. She suggests that an initial emphasis on legal reforms to adapt national law to the CRC needs now to give space to changes in other important areas of public action, including that of children. She argues that implementation of the rights of children can be a lever for more equitable, open, and progressive societies, through comprehensive systems of social protection that not only protect but also promote social integration, provide expansion of opportunities, and open spaces for dialogue.

Brazil provides a vivid case study of the difficulties of translating legislation into enhanced outcomes for children. A bill of rights for children and adolescents was installed in the country's new constitution. Irene Rizzini reports on the challenges of putting into practice these laws and obligations. The chronic imbalance of power that structurally persists in the society represents the most significant problem to implementation. Reflecting this disparity, rampant violence and drug trafficking remain uncontrolled. Yet progress is being made through a governing structure of more than five thousand Child Rights Councils distributed throughout the country. Children are referred to as citizens in the national discourse, and significant gains have been made in improving health and education and in reducing child labor.

When it comes to recognizing children's rights, the United States lies at the opposite end of the international spectrum from Brazil. There is no legal framework obligating the government to recognize and support children's social, cultural, economic, and participatory rights. Elizabeth Bartholet, a legal scholar, indicates a variety of ways in which the CRC can advance child well-being in the United States, most notably through recognizing children as full rights-bearing individuals, providing greater protection against maltreatment, and challenging the dominance of parental rights. She also considers the potential for ratification of the CRC to have a negative impact. She argues that the CRC presents risks to children because key provisions limit adoption, especially international adoption, and thus limit unparented children's prospects for finding nurturing homes. Accordingly, she recommends ratification with reservations, rejecting the CRC provisions restricting transracial and international adoption.

Donald Hernandez, a social demographer, and his coauthors provide a dynamic picture of the compositional changes well under way in the United States, reflecting the ascendancy of poorer minorities becoming the majority. They argue that the productivity and attitudes of the younger generation toward sustaining the social and economic security of an aging population (a particular challenge in the United States and other postindustrial nations) should strengthen the resolve to advance the rights and welfare of children. Against the grain of socioeconomic indicators for health, education, and income, they provide an analysis of how specific articles of the CRC should inform policies to ensure economic growth and sustainability.

From the stance of a political philosopher, James Bohman explores the consequences of subordinating the current generation in terms that interfere with the capacity to exercise rights of children that reflect their long-term interests. Freedom from domination, or nonmastering interference, should be the position of parents, teachers, and policy-makers. Bohman posits that intergenerational democracy must be developed as a means to encourage the older population to act as trustees for the younger generation. Yet to accomplish this objective, there is a need for a fundamental change in the public perception of and attitudes toward children. He defines capability failure as the lack of opportunity structures for children to exercise rights in a climate of subordination. This results in the unfairness of having a present generation disregard future generations, as exemplified in the threats of global warming.

Political scientist Andrew Rehfeld is concerned that the CRC is already cast in a guardianship role, without offering a sufficient foundation to promote children's political maturation and its expression. Because the CRC provides for no voice in legislative processes, he argues that it fails the test of democratization and the defense of citizenship. Rehfeld carefully defines political maturity and proposes institutional designs for children's political expression, including fractional voting, electoral constituencies, and political budgets for children. His recommendation is to cultivate child citizenship through the design of political institutions. In the process, he warns against relying on schools as the setting in which to best achieve this kind of competence.

Closely linked to Bohman's and Rehfeld's arguments is the explicit concern with voting that Daniel Hart, a developmental psychologist, introduces. He notes that the current state of psychological science understudies adolescent development, specifically in the domains relevant to citizenship, membership, and genuine participation in society. Age-graded empirical evidence is provided in support of the position that adolescents at age 16, but not before this, have the political maturity and civic mindedness to vote as responsibly as young adults. The importance of lowering the voting age gains momentum given the reality that the interests of young people are easily overshadowed by an aging population.

Judith Torney-Purta and Jo-Ann Amadeo begin their article with a review of studies on the political socialization of children, covering the past half century. Their international research, with samples of adolescents drawn from twenty-nine countries, produces the sobering evidence that the majority of young adolescents across all regions surveyed are prepared only moderately well for exercising the rights and responsibilities of citizenship. In this article, they provide examples of programs that deliberately seek to establish democratic climates for children in their everyday lives, starting at ages 10 and 11. If arranged properly, such niches for development can provide an apprenticeship model of citizenship development through legitimate, emergent participation.

Sociologist Allison James offers a constructivist perspective on childhood. With this framework, she contrasts a diminished definition of child citizenship that exists in Great Britain with a more complete version that exists in Norway. Adjusting the focus from a national level to the everyday lives of children, James describes the attitudes and behaviors of adult medical personnel toward children in the microcosm of a children's hospital. Her findings of sometimes dismissive and demeaning attitudes among the hospital caregivers indicate the wide gap that exists between rights language and everyday adult behavior. Generalizing from the microcosm to the society at large, James concludes that despite Great Britain's ratification of the CRC, the society is still not yet ready fully to respect children as citizens.

Mary Carlson and Felton Earls trace how their international experiences have fostered theoretical depth and scientific rigor. While informed by child rights, their work takes the CRC as an incomplete framework. Philosophical and developmental theories are required to complete the construction in which children practice deliberative citizenship. They report on a structural intervention, known as the Young Citizens Program, which was evaluated in a community-level randomized control trial designed to promote community competence in controlling the AIDS epidemic in Tanzania. Results demonstrate how new channels of intergenerational communication were opened and the community mobilized around a stigmatized disease.

The Young Citizens Program inspired the final article in this volume, by Clotilde Fonseca and Maria Eugenia Bujanda. Based in one of the stronger democracies in the world—Costa Rica—the Deliberative Capabilities in School-Age Children Program is designed to enhance critical thinking and communicative and analytical skills in efforts to prioritize and solve social and political problems. The unique and innovative aspects of this program are its adaptation of digital technology in school-based computer labs. From these labs, located throughout the country, children have formed a digital network in which they exchange opinions and preferences and devise and monitor action plans.

The collected wisdom stemming from these articles yields a refreshing synergy of understanding and some guarded optimism about policies and practices related to children becoming engaged in the civil and political lives of their communities. No author here thinks of the CRC as useless rhetoric. Rather, it marks a landmark achievement in the history of childhood and sets in motion the inclusion of children as national and global citizens.

Moving Forward

In the history of establishing rights and citizenship, 20 years is a short time. While the 20th birthday of the CRC was not heralded on television news programs in the United States and around the world, that it is a step removed from universal ratification is significant. It is all too easily taken for granted that the struggle for universal human rights moves in an upward spiral. While some skepticism is warranted when asked to believe that the claims made in human rights treatises are nonnegotiable and irreversible, it is likely that the CRC will serve as a foundation for the advancement of children's well-being over the short course of the next 20 years. During this period, it will be essential that the path from rights to citizenship be examined from the collective perspectives of the humanities, political and social sciences, and policy development.

Our expectation is that this volume will facilitate a continual and critical inquiry into why "junior" citizenship matters as much as senior citizenship does. Do citizens live longer and experience greater well-being than noncitizens? As the status and expectations of citizenship are extended to children, will their health, education, and behavior be improved? Will racial and ethnic disparities in health and education outcomes be reduced? Will child citizenship result in stronger and more stable democracies, greater trust and confidence in public institutions, higher voter turnouts, and better-informed and more skillful deliberations on matters of public interest? These are all-important questions that should provide an inspiration for innovative and bold new work in the social and political sciences.

Much of what is advanced in this volume is intergenerational in nature. Focusing on the child automatically brings in adults and concerns about social and political stability and improvement. Child rights, the last station along the human rights succession, may be the most fundamental, for there is no other period of the life cycle that offers such openness, mutability, and enthusiasm. The beneficiaries of children's citizenship should start with the child and extend to the environment and society that they share with adults.

Moving forward is challenging. First, it does make a difference, domestically and internationally, for the United States to ratify the CRC. The current administration should be cajoled to give priority to this goal. Training curricula designed for professionals who work with children and adolescents are needed to foster a climate of equality and respect among adults and children. Parents and caregivers need models to emulate in this respect. Voting patterns of the youngest enfranchised age groups need analysis, interpretation, and dissemination. Supportive efforts and designated spaces within government entities must be created for political maturity to be nurtured. Policy-makers, teachers, and providers of human services should prepare for a society characterized by a new demographic majority of children and families. Finally, bold new efforts are needed to engage children as citizens in places where democratic ideals are besieged. All too often, these are places where young people are already at the forefront of movements for change.

There has been considerable progress in the science of child development over the past century. Theories and complex research designs have been directed toward increasing our understanding of the cognitive, social, and emotional components of human behavior. This knowledge has led to a greater understanding of children as members of families and society. Over this same period, children and adolescents have become socially and politically isolated. Alienation of youth has been associated with everything from crime and violence to antiwar and democratization movements. While it must remain an empirical question, the constructive engagement of the young in society carries the promise of enhancing the practice of democracy and fostering environmental protection and human security.

Notes

1. See www.unicef.org/crc/index_30229.html.
2. See http://childrightscampaign.org/crcindex.php.

References

Abowitz, Kathleen, and Jason Harnish. 2006. Contemporary discourses on citizenship. *Review of Educational Research* 76 (4): 653–90.

Bok, Sissela. 1995. *Common values*. Columbia, MO: University of Missouri Press.

Darwin, Charles. 1871. *The descent of man and selection in relation to sex*. London: J. Murray.

Himes, James, ed. 1995. *Implementing the Convention on the Rights of the Child: Resource mobilization in low-income countries*. The Hague: Martinus Nijhoff.

Marshall, Thomas H. 1950. *Citizenship and social class and other essays*. New York, NY: Cambridge University Press.

Rousseau, Jean-Jacques. 1979. *Emile or on education*. Trans. Allan Bloom. New York, NY: Basic Books.

UN General Assembly. 1989. Convention on the Rights of the Child. Res. 45/25. New York, NY: United Nations. Available from www.un.org/documents/instruments/docs_en.asp (accessed 8 August 2010).

UNICEF. 2009. State of the worlds' children special edition: Celebrating 20 years of the Convention on the Rights of the Child. Available from www.unicef.org/publications (accessed 9 August 2010).

A Historical Context for the United Nations Convention on the Rights of the Child

The United Nations (UN) Convention on the Rights of the Child (CRC) was a by-product of international commitments to human rights, but its history lies in the complex and contradictory developments of the twentieth century, when elevated expectations regarding the welfare of children confronted the realities of war. In the late nineteenth century, material conditions and reform efforts redefined the lives of children in the Western world and created new sentiments about childhood and investments in children's progress. World Wars I and II exposed children's acute vulnerability and the myth of inevitable progress. After each of these wars, defining what was owed to children and how best to meet their needs was part of larger international negotiations regarding power and prestige. Throughout this period, the involvement of women, a new Swedish presence in international diplomacy, and the growing role of nongovernmental organizations (NGOs) affected what would become a rearticulation of child welfare and protection and a more active commitment to children's rights.

Keywords: children's welfare; war; nongovernmental organizations; women; photography; schooling; poverty; child rearing

By
PAULA S. FASS

The desire to articulate the rights and needs of children in universal terms has accompanied the growing importance of international organizations and universal charters throughout the twentieth century. Thus the immediate sequence of events that led to the creation of the 1989 Convention on the Rights of the Child (CRC) can be quickly and efficiently described. The first legally binding treaty was signed in 1919, when the International Labor Organization adopted conventions prohibiting children from working in hazardous conditions. Then, in 1924, the League of Nations adopted the nonbinding Declaration of Geneva to protect children's rights. After World War II, human rights ideals, inscribed into the United Nations (UN) Charter (Article I) and the Universal Declaration of Human Rights in 1948—which was not legally binding—established the basis for defining the

DOI: 10.1177/0002716210382388

rights of children in full and legally binding ways. As a result, in 1959, the UN adopted the Declaration of the Rights of the Child, the immediate predecessor of the CRC, though it expressed a much more restricted conception of rights than would finally emerge when the General Assembly adopted the CRC in 1989 (Cohen 2002). In between these two dates, the UN had announced the Year of the Child in 1979 to mark the twentieth anniversary of the original declaration.

This seemingly smooth account of the "history" of the CRC in stepwise progression actually takes us through 70 of the most tumultuous, violent, and deadly years in human history. The story begins with the conclusion of World War I (at least in Western Europe) and the continent's recovery from the killing fields of "the Great War." It then proceeds through the death camps, fire bombings, and atomic bombs of World War II and takes us finally to the downfall of the Berlin Wall and the liberation of Eastern Europe from Communism and the subsequent strife and displacements in the Balkans. A deeper, fuller, and more nuanced understanding of the history of the CRC requires that we stop more often to examine the historical landscape and that we understand the longer-term developments of which the CRC was an expression.

Historians tend to go back quite a distance to understand events and developments (Alaimo 2002).[1] But I want to focus here, instead, on the twentieth century and the tensions and contradictions that had, by the middle of the century, emerged between Western ideals and expectations and the realities of the treatment of children and to examine how these contributed to the eventual annunciation of the CRC in terms of the rights of children. Those "rights" have become familiar to us over the past 20 years since they were first set forth in 1989 as a balance between viewing the child as the object of caretaking who requires various services and protections from adults and the rights of the child to act fully in his or her capacity as a person. Throughout most of the century, it was the former rights—to be cared for and protected—that defined the ideals that international institutions adopted. These rights to protection were closely associated with the welfare and well-being of children through most of the century, certainly during the first 50 years, and it was these rights that both the League of Nations and the initial 1959 Declaration of the Rights of the Child emphasized.

To understand why the CRC did not simply evolve from the earlier League of Nations Declaration of Geneva, it is important to acknowledge that by the middle of the twentieth century, child advocates recognized the harms that had been done to children after a period of elevated expectations about our abilities to protect them. Because the apparent progress made in the West to protect children's welfare turned out to be quite illusory and our solicitude inadequate, a firmer, more rights-based approach came to the fore.

Paula S. Fass, Margaret Byrne Professor of History at the University of California, Berkeley, is the author of Children of A New World: Society, Culture, and Globalization *(New York University Press 2007) and* Kidnapped: Child Abduction in America *(Oxford University Press 1997), among other books, and the editor of* The Encyclopedia of Children and Childhood in History and Society *(Gale 2004). Her memoir,* Inheriting the Holocaust, *was published in 2009 by Rutgers University Press.*

By the late nineteenth century in the Western world, the situation and setting for child welfare had changed enormously as a result of several factors. New medical breakthroughs in antisepsis made birth less dangerous, and public health measures regarding clean water and sanitation reduced the threat of many waterborne diseases that led to childhood diarrhea (still today a widespread killer of young children), while also reducing the tolls taken by typhus and cholera. Vaccinations for diphtheria significantly undercut this once common and deadly childhood illness. More effective forms of birth control made it possible to better avoid conception, which, as most Western observers came to realize, could have positive consequences for the children born into smaller families. There was generally a sense that science and medicine were taking huge steps forward with great benefits to children (Meckel 2004).

These developments, however, were uneven. Some Western societies such as the United States, Sweden, Germany, and France outpaced others in the Western Hemisphere and Eastern and Southern Europe. And almost everywhere, divides between rural and urban parts of even the most advanced countries continued. Nevertheless, there was room for optimism, and the growing emphasis on public health and the potentials for government in advancing the well-being of its citizens most often found expression in legislation and organizations aimed at children and the improvement of the life of the child. Indeed, throughout the West, nationalism was most strongly articulated around goals for a nation's children as these seemed to secure both the identity of the state and its future (Cunningham 1995, 114–70). In this view, the state continued, and sometimes compensated for, the caretaking and protection that children had a right to expect in their families and communities.

Inquiries into the nature and consequences of the poverty of children accompanied these views. Manifest deprivation became less tolerated by middle-class do-gooders who aspired to have all children, not just the privileged, benefit from the advances taking place. And those who looked to national aims believed that progress required that all the nations' children be brought up to a basic level. As a result, they began to articulate children's needs and rights in universal terms. In the United States, child savers looked to rescue children from the ills associated with poverty, exploitative industry, the dangers of the streets, and parents' inadequate attention.[2] By the early twentieth century, good middle-class reformers were cognizant that the abuse of children and child neglect often resulted from deprivation, rather than from malign intent, and this changed the larger social conversation to include more demands for government funds for efforts such as mothers' pensions and other family supports (Gordon 1988; Lindenmeyer 1997; Skocpol 1992). At the same time, labor organizations demanded higher family wages so that children could be more adequately provided for (Glickman 1997).

Reformers moved vigorously to include underserved populations in the new benefits that middle-class children were already enjoying. In the United States and England, social settlements attended to immigrants and the inner-city poor, while organizations such as the Baron de Hirsch Fund spread new ideas about child welfare and effective domestic caretaking among poor Jewish coreligionists in Eastern Europe. In many places, Societies for the Prevention of Cruelty to Children were investigating the poor and threatening parents into more careful forms of child protection (Gordon 1988). While these organizations often still blamed parents' immorality for their conditions, they began to recognize that poverty itself was hardly the children's fault. Above all, reformers looked to schools as tools to create better lives for children, as convenient arenas in which services could be provided, and above all, as an alternative to exploitative work and the streets. Almost everywhere in the West, schooling became compulsory and attendance obligatory.

Wherever industry had taken root, anti-child-labor ideas and, in some cases, avid campaigns against child labor spread throughout Western Europe and the United States. It should not be surprising that the first truly international efforts and a binding international treaty centered on protecting children from hazardous work, since child labor was a banner that bound Western reformers together and was often the entering wedge for many child-centered reforms in the West. Even in the early twentieth century, many observers recognized that this "protective" legislation was not without its problems, since it usually involved serious intrusion into family authority and often caused friction with the very populations it aimed to serve. Very few, however, questioned its aim—to improve the lives of children—since almost no one thought that children might have other views or goals.[3]

The emphasis on schooling, as I have suggested, paralleled these attempts to remove children from hazardous labor. Schooling became the ideal setting for the child, and school attendance became compulsory through most of Western Europe and the United States. Even in many Eastern and Southern European countries, such as Poland and Italy, schools became an expression of nationalist aims that made them increasingly compulsory for at least limited periods in children's lives. Schools set new standards for literacy, as well as for a child's well-being, as the child was seen as able to grow and fulfill his or her potential, while education ensured citizenship and habits of work and regularity. Schools also instituted new standards for bodily care. In countries such as Sweden, the United States, and France, schools became important venues for information regarding hygiene and nutrition and provided sites for measurements of heights and weights and medical and dental inspections. In the United States, school-based visiting nurses brought this information into the homes of slum dwellers, while various state fairs and healthy baby contests brought information to rural areas (Lovett 2007). Healthy child life was now seen as a social objective, and this called for rigorous sanitary standards and their enforcement. Nutrition also became an important front in this campaign. Free lunches (and sometimes breakfasts) were introduced in schools, and clean milk campaigns became common in American cities. Thus, gradually, what had once been the privileges of the few—schooling, hygiene, nutrition, and medical attention—were seen as the right of all children (Heywood 2001, 134–56).

By the early twentieth century, the middle classes, everywhere, turned their attention to elevating and universalizing standards for child welfare. Many educated women created new roles for themselves or entered into existing roles in innovative arenas such as social work and public health to oversee the welfare of the population—especially children (Muncy 1991; Lindenmeyer 1997; Odem 1995). In the United States, this process and reform goals were accelerated by journalists such as Jacob Riis, who alerted the general public to the dangers of poverty and abuse within the society and called on all Americans to pay attention to the welfare of the society's children. In books (accompanied by captivating photographs) such as *How the Other Half Lives* (1890) and, even more to the point, *The Children of the Poor* ([1892] 1971), Riis and others made poor children and the hazards they posed to the society a central front in efforts aimed at social change and progress.

If the emphasis on sturdy minds and healthy bodies was the public face of the new expectations for children, the private face was also changing rapidly. While the state sought to create healthy citizens, mothers increasingly were led to believe, from the language that psychologists and other developmental specialists used, that they could raise children who were well-balanced and well-adjusted. In the United States, proper child rearing became a passion by the 1920s, as middle-class mothers turned to advice from new specialists who were informed by Freudian or Watsonian behaviorist theories (see Fass 1977). *Parents Magazine* was established and grew by leaps and bounds, while the publicly funded Children's Bureau distributed millions of pamphlets, guiding mothers to better child care at low costs, to women from less privileged homes (Grant 1998; Stearns 2003). This passion for improving child care and children's lives was perfectly expressed in John Watson's dedication in his child-rearing tract: to "the first mother who raises a happy child" (Watson 1928, dedication page).

Parents' desires for the best and latest information, informed by science and expertise, were often met with confusing and even contradictory advice (Hulbert 2003), but the aims are an important reminder of how widespread the optimism about child life was. By the early twentieth century, American mothers especially, but parents elsewhere in the West as well, began to turn to the expressive and progressive possibilities for their children and were hopeful that childhood could be a fulfilling time. Less physically hazardous, more protected and well nurtured, childhood now became a period in which mothers and nations believed that they could turn out happy and productive young citizens. This belief was expressed in, for example, the interest in progressive education (Fass 1989; Cremin 1961; Ravitch 1983) and other institutional venues, such as summer camps and kindergartens, in which the innocence of childhood was preserved and the child could be valued in individual terms (Paris 2008; Chudacoff 2007). Indeed, schooling, to which the state turned to create citizens, also became an arena with great potential for liberating a child's creativity and individuality, and parents, as well as reformers, often saw it in these terms.

Thus, when Ellen Key proclaimed the "Century of the Child" from "the Strand," her perch above Lake Vadstena in Sweden in 1900, she had every reason to expect that a continuing improvement would proceed with the unfolding century and that progressive nations and progressive mothers, especially, would protect their children and enhance their lives.[4]

Then, in less than a decade and a half, the evidence began to roll in—not from Africa and Latin America, as it tends to do today, but from the heart of Europe. And it came with a drum roll of war. World War I was a shocking experience in the West, not only because of the huge battlefield losses of young men[5] when armies collided, but also because of the subsequent futile war of attrition in which disease and despair eventually settled on armies dug into their trenches. But the shock did not stop with the solider. Behind the front lines, the vulnerability of the civilian population was dramatically exposed, as women and children became actual as well as symbolic victims of war. The bayoneting of infants in Belgium by helmeted German soldiers became a prominent image in war posters and one with some significant influence on American policy (Little 2009). But even this terrible image was overshadowed toward the end of the war by the evidence of starving children throughout Europe. As war took its toll on noncombatants, special problems arose in places in the east, such as Serbia and Poland. The war was also agonizingly long, and embargoes and starvation became conscious strategies of participant nations (Little 2009).

The journalists and photographers who viewed the events of 1914 to 1918, as well as their audiences, were primed to see this suffering and feel outraged by the pains of children as a result of the heightened expectations that I have discussed. These expectations had formed a basis for a new sentimental attachment to children, just as the growing sentiments regarding childhood served as stimulants for improvement (Zelizer 1985).[6] What observers may have been willing to overlook during the Napoleonic campaigns a century earlier became unbearably visible in this revised emotional context. At the same time, war too had changed. The direct targeting of civilian populations became a more "normal" part of twentieth-century warfare, obscuring earlier distinctions between military and civilian arenas. Children had become more explicitly victimized, while they also became more often the objects of sentimental perspectives. As Dominique Marshall has pointed out, Herbert Hoover became the prime figure and the most significant proponent in the effort to feed the children of Europe, first through the Committee for Belgian Relief (1914–1917); then, after the armistice in 1919, through the American Relief Administration; and then through an entirely private venture, the European Children's Fund, at the end of 1919. "These agencies contributed to the feeding of more than 10 million children. . . . After the Americans entered the war, no other program for relief for allied civilians achieved the popularity of the efforts on behalf of children" (Marshall 2002, 185). Hoover hoped to increase American prestige in the world, as well as its visibility as a world power, through these efforts. It was perfectly logical in this context that when the League of Nations sought to define human rights, it included children among the populations it set out to define and protect.

This confluence of spreading sensibilities, visibility, and active targeting of civilians in World War I was, I believe, the initial setting for what would become a new commitment in the twentieth century to an international ideal of defining the rights of children. And contemporary organizations put in place just those ideas about protection that had defined progressive views about children. When, subsequently, World War II exposed a landscape of even greater destruction and horror in which children died in millions—the direct targets of belligerents and the subjects of inhuman "scientific" experiments, as well as collateral damage—the field for proclaiming the need for a children's charter of some kind became obvious. The experiences of World War II also illuminated some of the limitations of earlier views of protection, since no amount of sentiment had been able to shelter children from intentional injury. Children could not simply rely on being protected because they were children and had a "right to childhood" in the words of the United States Children's Bureau (Lindenmeyer 1997). They needed to be treated in their full humanity and not just as subordinate and dependent subjects, since they had been targeted along with everyone else. It was their humanity, not their childhood, to which they had a right and to which new international commitments should have been directed.

While the two wars were the overwhelming facts on the ground that collided with the elevated optimism that opened the century, the way these facts were engaged also had important influences on the particular history of the CRC. Among the factors that, I believe, strongly influenced the final product, three deserve some attention: (1) the role of NGOs, (2) the emergence of Sweden as an international influence in matters of civilian relief and assistance, and (3) the role of women.

The role of NGOs. In the context of the brutal and dehumanizing experience of these two Europe-centered wars, the first NGOs to protect child populations took shape. As already noted, the efforts by Herbert Hoover to feed Europe's children through three such privately organized groups began these efforts during and shortly after World War I. But others soon emerged. Some were associated with antiwar sentiments and took over where Hoover's activities had left off. Perhaps the most conspicuous and important was the Save the Children Fund—whose mission was to assist children whose lives had been devastated by war—founded by Eglantyne Jebb, a vocal antiwar activist, and her sister Dorothy Buxton in England in 1919 (Nehlin 2009, 12–13). The organization took over from the Red Cross the ideal of using humanitarian sympathies, and such an approach spread rapidly after the organization was announced at the International Women's Association of Peace and Freedom, which met in Zurich that same year. Radda Barn, Save the Children's Swedish affiliate, was quickly created thereafter in 1920, through the efforts of Anna-Lenah Elgstrom and Margit Levinson. A year later the French created their own affiliate, L'Union Internationale de Secours aux Enfants (UISE) (Nehlin 2009, 13). When the League of Nations was organized, it created a Child Welfare Committee, of which Eglantyne Jebb became a member (Marshall 2002, 191).

Radda Barn is especially interesting because the antiwar sentiments behind the original founding were elaborated in Sweden as official policy. As a nation that remained neutral during World War II, Sweden's Save the Children affiliate was able to grow through the long period of child crisis that defined that war while others were handicapped by wartime commitments. From an initial membership of 904 in 1941, Radda Barn had 15,000 members by 1944, making it a significant group domestically and a serious presence in Europe in the period after the war. By 1947, its membership had ballooned to 47,000, as the postwar years made the plight of Europe's children abundantly clear. Throughout this period, women dominated the board of the organization (Nehlin 2009, 14, 16).

The role of Sweden. Initially, after the war, Sweden viewed its own role as largely limited to providing assistance to other "Nordic" countries, and it was reluctant to venture further to assist Europe's children more generally. But as its potential and prominence grew and the wider needs became glaring, Sweden's sense of obligation expanded. This was in part a result of public relations efforts by Sweden's leaders, who tried to compensate for the nation's neutrality during the war and its shameful violation of this policy when it provided assistance to Nazi Germany during the war (in terms of loans and troop movements across its territories) (Nehlin 2009, 17–19). With this background in mind, members of Swedish society, including the king, became committed to playing a special role in Europe's reconstruction. Thus, for example, Folke Bernadotte (a national hero and a member of one of Sweden's most prominent families) noted that "relief to foreign countries" through the Red Cross was "the most primary and necessary task" after the war. "The reason for this is more than anything else the goodwill that . . . Sweden would gain by making an active and grand contribution" (Nehlin 2009, 41–42). As Sweden looked to compensate in world esteem for its less than heroic behavior during the war, activities in the international arena became a prominent part of its postwar strategy. Goodwill efforts on behalf of children were especially desirable, and Radda Barn had been growing to meet that challenge. Despite considerable jockeying for position within and among various Swedish organizations in terms of who should control relief, eventually, as Ann Nehlin, a historian of the organization, noted, "The Swedish government's interests in redeeming its inactivity on the side of the allies created possibilities—a space to act within—for Radda Barn" (Nehlin 2009, 81).

Whatever complex set of motives and visions underwrote its efforts, Sweden's subsequent prominence on behalf of children in the immediate post–World War II world and then into the middle of the century projected that small country on the outskirts of Europe firmly into the center of various international organizations. The UN and its associated organizations made Sweden an unexpectedly significant force in subsequent efforts to define the rights and needs of children.

Among the UN efforts on behalf of children that emerged from the war, the UN International Children's Emergency Fund (UNICEF) is likely the most prominent. Given its founding date, December 1946, and the prominent Swedish role in postwar relief efforts, it was hardly surprising that Sweden was asked both to contribute to UNICEF financially and to be represented on its executive committee (Nehlin 2009, 86–91). Indeed, by the 1950s, Sweden had become closely identified with international organizations and with international assistance to children, and its views, perspectives, and personnel became important to efforts on behalf of children.

Thus Sweden, whose reformers in the early twentieth century were committed to a better life for children at home, became, by the late twentieth century, active in setting models for children's rights in an international context. Sweden, and the Scandinavian countries generally, by the 1960s and 1970s had become notable as locales in which the active participatory rights of children became prominent in both policies and rhetoric (Sandin forthcoming). Indeed, in contemporary Sweden, the CRC is not only taken seriously but often influences the shape of domestic legislation (Sandin forthcoming). Far more than in other places, such as the United States, where the protection of children became prominent in the early twentieth century, Sweden, Norway, and Finland have moved toward a much more active vision of the rights of children. In the Swedish case, this view is both emblematic and ironic. The country in Europe whose own children had been protected from the violence and destruction of two devastating wars became both a witness to and an active agent in defining how children could best be served.

The role of women. Throughout the twentieth century, women were drawn to international actions on behalf of children—as with the origins and continuing activities of the Save the Children organizations—as a natural extension of their activities at home. In the United States, for example, women moved into the public household to act on behalf of children and saw this as both a respectable extension of their gender roles and necessary for social well-being. Many became involved internationally because of their antiwar sentiments and their rejection of extreme nationalist perspectives; others increasingly turned to international organizations to promote women's rights. After World War I, women's rights advocates, such as Alice Paul in the United States, turned to international fora and proclamations to define their rights most comprehensively in terms that they believed they could not be accorded in their individual nations. International efforts on behalf of children also grew naturally from this perspective (Hill 1999).

Finally, in considering the factors that have contributed historically to the creation of the CRC, it is useful to think about how vital images of children in need, and especially as victims of war, have been in the twentieth century. Just as photography helped to make citizens aware of and impelled to react to child abuse and poverty in the late nineteenth and early twentieth centuries, photography and newsreels in World War I and movies by World War II, as well as other media later in the century, have brought the terrible costs of war into popular consciousness. In the nineteenth century, the sentimentalization of childhood turned poor or abused children into objects of pity and even objects of sensational exploitation.[7] This trend continues. Visual images of children from around the world in need of hare lip repairs are a familiar sight in newspapers everywhere in the West. International organizations and NGOs of all kinds use photographs of children to encourage contributions and adoptions. Great photojournalists, such as Sebastiâo Salgado, provide photo tours of the lives of children dislocated and disoriented by war, conflict, and economic change (Fass 2007, 219–20).

I am not sure that we can see any great progression in these photographic depictions. Most still rely on our sentimental visions of the child's innocence, beauty, and vulnerability. They are hardly witness to a newer emphasis on strong children or on children's autonomous rights in the twentieth-first century. But visual portrayals of children have made them sympathetic subjects. Anthropologist Tobias Hecht has suggested that this attention has often made children aware of the power that they exert over the viewers, and this self-awareness has encouraged them to use and manipulate their own appeal. If this is the case, then photography has helped to encourage children's own agendas and provide them with an indirect means to exercise serious agency (Hecht 1998, 2006).

In providing this capsule history of the context for the CRC, my examination has several times alluded to the ironic or unexpected in the path to contemporary children's rights. It is important to bear this in mind in understanding how the CRC took its final form. Sweden, for example, was hardly the first place one would have looked for leadership after a war in which its record of heroic assistance could not withstand scrutiny. Before that, Herbert Hoover's remarkable record of assistance to the child victims of war and starvation after World War I was obtained by a man who, as president of the United States, was unable to respond to the needs of his own depression-ravaged people and who gave assistance to Europe at least in part to shed positive light on America's new importance in the world. Women in many societies acted on behalf of children to increase their public roles as protectors of the young. After the late nineteenth century, as I have suggested, acting on behalf of children, who had become objects of sentimental attachment among respectable people, was a safe way for adults and societies to appeal for prestige and international regard. By that time, the very helplessness of children had made them emblems of altruistic and humanistic goals. Similarly, photographs of children meant to make them objects of caretaking have, in some cases, turned them into active subjects who use their portrayal toward active control. The road to children's rights has been a winding and unpredictable one, wending its way through matters that touch on power politics, the re-creation of gender roles, and aesthetics of the twentieth century.

The growing recognition by the 1980s that even in acting on their behalf, children could remain the voiceless objects of exploitation and potentially misused may help us to understand why and how the UN commission that began in earnest to revise the initial statement on children's rights provided the new document with more bones (if not more teeth). In asserting the positive rights of participation and the view that children could and should act for themselves (in some contexts), the 1989 document acknowledged the limitations that bedeviled earlier charters and statements on behalf of children—the limitations of dependency. Two world wars plus the violence and hazards of the world since the 1970s have made empowerment of children an obvious challenge. In the words of one historian, "It has been estimated—and estimates are all that can be offered—that 150 million children have been killed in war and civil war since the 1970s, around the world, and another 150 million crippled or maimed" (Stearns 2006, 112).

Beyond death and maiming, the modern world has become aware of how many children are victims of sexual violence, how many are left orphaned by diseases such as HIV/AIDS, and how many are recruited to become murderers and rapists. One wonders what is left of innocence in this light or what use innocence can possibly be to these children.

All of this has become especially clear as a result of the shrinking of the globe since the 1970s and 1980s and the increasing penetration by journalists, photographers, NGO personnel, and others who have made the world's children familiar to observers everywhere. With their innocence so exposed, it has also become clear that children are not only victims, but they can and do act on their behalf and that of others, as they have in wars in South Africa and Central America (Fass 2007). This has underlined the limitations of the Western view of children. Globalization has drawn distant places and their children closer to the West, not just as colonial dependents or to be tutored in the ways of the West, but as peoples and places with their own strengths and lessons. Steadily, but not without resistance, the Western picture of helpless children—carefully constructed a hundred years ago to appeal more to its adult observers than to its participants—has given way to a sturdier portrait of children surviving and acting with purpose (see Kincaid 1998). In that sense, the West's exposure to children in other places has been instructive. Westerners have learned to see children as more than sentimental objects of concern.

As Western sentimentality confronted children's complex lives and experiences around the world, the older view of children's needs has become insufficient in defining what children require and what they should be understood to have as basic rights. Thus, when the original 1959 UN Declaration came up for revision in 1979 (the year that the UN designated as the "International Year of the Child"), the original document that saw children as "objects" of services was augmented with a new emphasis on the child's sturdier expressive rights. We should not be confused or misled, however. Even a better-structured and more sophisticated instrument of rights does not necessarily translate into embodied experience. But as a statement of purpose and a guide to ideals, it is a much better axe to wield in the world.

A century ago, a new devotion to children's welfare and optimism about their future initially set the groundwork for outrage at the vulnerabilities of children in war in the early twentieth century and formed the background to the international efforts on behalf of children. That devotion has now been supplemented by very real and painful experiences. In the past 20 years, the CRC has sought not only to protect children through its provisions from the terrible costs of future conflicts, but to empower them so that they can now express their views and potentially make their own distinct contributions to decisions that could determine their fate. Certainly, this, too, is optimistic and hopeful and grounded in a continuing devotion to children's welfare. But in facing that future today, one that contains many hazards and ever new instruments of death, children should have every possible tool in their own defense.

Notes

1. A good place to begin this is Kathleen Alaimo (2002, 1–23).

2. Among the most prominent was Jane Addams, founder of Hull House and an unusually effective proponent; see her *The Spirit of Youth in the City Streets* ([1909] 1972). See also Jacob Riis, *The Children of the Poor* ([1892] 1971). Many historians have looked at the phenomenon of "child saving." One of the most interesting and well-known is Linda Gordon, *Heroes of Their Own Lives: The Politics and History of Family Violence, Boston 1880–1960* (1988).

3. This point is made clearly in David Nasaw, *Children of the City: At Work and at Play* (1985). Nasaw shows how work was sometimes something that children chose and benefited from, while reformers never saw it this way.

4. Ellen Key was known throughout the West for her crusading efforts on behalf of children in the early twentieth century. Her book, *The Century of the Child*, was published in Swedish in 1900 and translated into English in 1909. Key's book has often been invoked and her title even more so. See, for example, Judith Sealander, *The Failed Century of the Child: Governing America's Young in the Twentieth Century* (2003, 1).

5. For the common perception that World War I destroyed a generation, see Robert Wohl, *The Generation of 1914* (1979).

6. The foundational text for understanding sentimentalization of childhood is Viviana A. Zelizer, *Pricing the Priceless Child: The Changing Social Value of Children* (1985).

7. For the role of paintings and illustrations in creating a sentimental view of childhood, see Anne Higonnet, *Pictures of Innocence: The History and Crisis of Ideal Childhood* (1998). For the exploitation of pictures of ragged children in earlier times, see Seth Koven, *Slumming: Sexual and Social Politics in Victorian London* (2006).

References

Addams, Jane. [1909] 1972. *The spirit of youth in the city streets*. Urbana, IL: University of Illinois Press.

Alaimo, Kathleen. 2002. Historical roots of children's rights in Europe and the United States. In *Children as equals: Exploring the rights of the child*, eds. Kathleen Alaimo and Brian Klug, 1–23. Lanham, MD: University Press of America.

Chudacoff, Howard P. 2007. *Children at play: An American history*. New York, NY: New York University Press.

Cohen, Cynthia Price. 2002. United Nations Convention on the Rights of the Child: Developing international norms to create a new world for children. In *Children as equals: Exploring the rights of the child*, eds. Kathleen Alaimo and Brian Klug, 49–72. Lanham, MD: University Press of America.

Cremin, Lawrence A. 1961. *The transformation of the school: Progressivism in American education, 1876–1957*. New York, NY: Knopf.

Cunningham, Hugh. 1995. *Children and childhood in Western society since 1500*. London: Longman.

Fass, Paula S. 1977. *The damned and the beautiful: American youth in the 1920s*. New York, NY: Oxford University Press.

Fass, Paula S. 1989. *Outside in: Minorities and the transformation of American education*. New York, NY: Oxford University Press.

Fass, Paula S. 2007. *Children of a new world: Society, culture, and globalization*. New York, NY: New York University Press.

Glickman, Lawrence B. 1997. *A living wage: American workers and the making of consumer society*. Ithaca, NY: Cornell University Press.

Gordon, Linda. 1988. *Heroes of their own lives: The politics and history of family violence, Boston 1880–1960*. New York, NY: Viking.

Grant, Julia. 1998. *Raising baby by the book: The education of American mothers*. New Haven, CT: Yale University Press.

Hecht, Tobias. 1998. *Children in the streets: Street children of northeast Brazil*. Cambridge: Cambridge University Press.

Hecht, Tobias. 2006. *Afterlife: An ethnographic novel*. Durham, NC: Duke University Press.

Heywood, Colin. 2001. *A history of childhood: Children and childhood in the West from medieval to modern times*. Cambridge: Polity.

Higonnet, Anne. 1998. *Pictures of innocence: The history and crisis of ideal childhood*. New York, NY: Thames and Hudson.

Hill, Diane. 1999. International law for women's rights: The equality treaties campaign of the National Woman's Party and reactions of the U.S. State Department and the National League of Women Voters (1928–1938). PhD diss., University of California, Berkeley.

Hulbert, Ann. 2003. *Raising America: Experts, parents and a century of advice about children*. New York, NY: Knopf.

Key, Ellen. 1909. *The century of the child*. New York, NY: G. P. Putnam.

Kincaid, James R. 1998. *Erotic innocence: The culture of child molesting*. Durham, NC: Duke University Press.

Koven, Seth. 2006. *Slumming: Sexual and social politics in Victorian London*. Princeton, NJ: Princeton University Press.

Lindenmeyer, Kriste. 1997. *"A right to childhood," The U.S. Children's Bureau and child welfare, 1912–46*. Urbana, IL: University of Illinois Press.

Little, John Branden. 2009. Band of crusaders: American humanitarians, the Great War, and the remaking of the world. PhD diss., University of California, Berkeley.

Lovett, Laura L. 2007. *Conceiving the future: Pronatalism, reproduction, and the family in the United States, 1890–1938*. Chapel Hill, NC: University of North Carolina Press.

Marshall, Dominique. 2002. Humanitarian sympathy for children in times of war and the history of children's rights, 1919–1959. In *Children and war: A historical anthology*, ed. James Marten, 184–203. New York, NY: New York University Press.

Meckel, Richard. 2004. Infant mortality. In *The encyclopedia of children and childhood in history and society*, vol. 2, ed. Paula S. Fass, 474–78. Farmington Hill, MI: Gale.

Muncy, Robyn. 1991. *Creating a female dominion in American reform, 1890–1935*. New York, NY: Oxford University Press.

Nasaw, David. 1985. *Children of the city: At work and at play*. New York, NY: Oxford University Press.

Nehlin, Ann. 2009. Exporting visions and saving children: The Swedish Save the Children Fund. *Linköping Studies in Arts and Science* 494:12–13.

Odem, Mary E. 1995. *Delinquent daughters: Protecting and policing adolescent female sexuality in the United States, 1885–1920*. Chapel Hill, NC: University of North Carolina Press.

Paris, Leslie. 2008. *Children's nature: The rise of the American summer camp*. New York, NY: New York University Press.

Ravitch, Diane. 1983. *The troubled crusade: American education, 1945–1980*. New York, NY: Basic Books.

Riis, Jacob. 1890. *How the other half lives: Studies among the tenements of New York*. New York, NY: Charles Scribner's Sons.

Riis, Jacob. [1802] 1971. *The children of the poor*. New York, NY: Arno Press.

Sandin, Bengt. Forthcoming. From difference to similar: Childhood and welfare in Sweden, 1945–2000. In *Reinventing childhood in the post World War II world*, eds. Paula S. Fass and Michael Grossberg. Philadelphia, PA: University of Pennsylvania Press.

Sealander, Judith. 2003. *The failed century of the child: Governing America's young in the twentieth century*. Cambridge: Cambridge University Press.

Stearns, Peter N. 2003. *Anxious parents: A history of modern childrearing in America*. New York, NY: New York University Press.

Stearns, Peter N. 2006. *Children in world history*. New York, NY: Routledge.

Skocpol, Theda. 1992. *Protecting soldiers and mothers: The political origin of social policy in the United States*. Cambridge, MA: Harvard University Press.

Watson, John B. 1928. *Psychological care of infant and child*. New York, NY: W. W. Norton.

Wohl, Robert. 1979. *The generation of 1914*. Cambridge, MA: Harvard University Press.

Zelizer, Viviana A. 1985. *Pricing the priceless child: The changing social value of children*. New York, NY: Basic Books.

Multigenerational Citizenship: The Importance of Recognizing Children as National and International Citizens

By
GERALDINE VAN BUEREN

This article discusses the author's concept of multigenerational citizenship, arguing that for citizenship to be relevant for children, there needs to be a more flexible and relational approach to citizenship. Tom Paine's theories are expanded upon, by examining the increasing acceptance, by both international and regional fora in both political and human rights, of a child's autonomy in bringing complaints to a human rights body. The article examines the recent developments in the move toward establishing a complaints mechanism under the Convention on the Rights of the Child (CRC) and argues that this is an important element of international child citizenship. The article also examines the progress made in national courts toward child citizenship, which has helped to change the international consensus on providing an international remedy for breaches of child citizenship rights. The article compares the growing acceptance of children as international citizens by the European Court of Human Rights and under the specially designed African Charter on the Rights and Welfare of the Child's complaints mechanism. Because of all these developments, the author rejects the assumption that regeneration is needed to reenergize the international social movement for children as citizens, arguing that such pessimism is an oversimplification of both the achievements and failures of the CRC.

Keywords: United Nations; children; communication procedure; child citizenship

The Emergence of Citizenship as Multigenerational

Throughout history the concept of citizenship has been a work in progress, generally moving in a more inclusive direction. Indeed,

Geraldine Van Bueren is a barrister and professor of international human rights law in Queen Mary College at the University of London and is a visiting fellow at Kellogg College, Oxford. She was one of the original drafters of the United Nations Convention on the Rights of the Child and was a recipient of UNICEF's Child Rights Lawyer Award. She also serves as a commissioner on the UK's Equality and Human Rights Commission.

DOI: 10.1177/0002716210383113

when the movement has been retrogressive—with the refusal in the United States to implement the Fourteenth Amendment to all Americans or confiscation of citizenship from Jews in Germany and from South African citizens during apartheid—it can be seen as a warning sign of even graver violations of human rights. Hence, citizenship and human rights have a symbiotic, although not exclusive, relationship.[1]

According to Dahrendorf (1974), there is "no more a dynamic social figure in modern history than the citizen"; yet at the time of the drafting of the Convention on the Rights of the Child (CRC), children, if conceptualized at all as citizens, were regarded as passive citizens. Children were, and to some extent still are, similar in status to the *metiokas* of ancient Greece, "the alien residents who had some but not all the attributes of citizenship" (Van Bueren 1998, 26).

Bellamy, Castiglione, and Santoro (2004, 6–7) discuss three approaches to the facets of citizenship. Citizenship is identified with, first, the possession of individual rights; second, a reciprocal relationship through membership of a national community; and third, economic and political participation. A fourth facet, however, is developing, which is essential in a globalized world, and that is the capacity to act on one's own behalf and on behalf of others internationally and, in particular, before international bodies.

All four facets of citizenship are equally important to children, as is the reconfiguration of citizenship as multigenerational. By reconfiguring citizenship as multigenerational,[2] space is created for moving toward a concept of citizenship that also embraces childhood. Historically, children have been measured against adult models of citizenship. Such a flawed approach assumes that competence and biological age are always correlative (see Archard 2003), but as Bauböck (1995, 214) recognizes, for citizens, the concept of a right does not necessarily imply that its bearer must be seen as an agent "fully capable of communicating those of her own needs and interests."

The development of multigenerational citizenship is the latest stage in the evolution of citizenship from the Athenian exclusion of, *inter alia*, women and slaves (Aristotle 2008),[3] to the inclusion of women in the twentieth century.[4] Since the almost universal adoption of the CRC,[5] any plausible legal or political theory ought to consider multigenerational citizenship's impact upon citizenship theories.

Multigenerational citizenship, like citizenship itself, at least in the terms of social contract theory, carries with it the implementation of both rights and responsibilities. Rights and responsibilities of citizenship are a means for children to directly increase their participation in both the national and global societies. Indeed, de facto child citizenship responsibility already occurs in, for example, the increasing number of child-headed households. But without a de jure recognition of their citizenship responsibilities, children become more vulnerable and not less. For child-headed households, access to social security payments and to legal identity documents are essential for their education and survival and that of their young families, yet frequently such access is only granted upon reaching adulthood (Sloth-Nielsen 2005).

Childhood responsibilities are key to multigenerational citizenship, including the voluntary assumption of the duty to contribute to public policy decisions.

However, the performance of rights ought not to be contingent upon children's performance of their duties. This is one of the reasons why the too broadly drafted articles on child parental obedience in both the African Charter on Human and Peoples' Rights (Organization of African Unity 1981, Article 29)[6] and the African Charter on the Rights and Welfare of the Child (Organization of African Unity 1990, Article 31)[7] are widely criticized. They belong to an era when democracy was a rare phenomenon in Africa, rather than the contemporary continental shift toward democratic government.[8] The voluntary assumption of responsibilities for children, such as in child parliaments, helps to enhance rather than to undermine children's enjoyment of their rights. Progress toward active international citizenship for children, however, in part has been impeded by the lack of opportunities in many states for children to engage with political systems and processes. If it were reasoned that children could not contribute to domestic public policy, the possibility of children contributing to global policy would appear remote.

In the tail end of the past century and in the first decade of this century, there has, however, been a slow evolution toward child democratic citizenship in the creation of child parliaments. Hence, an increasing number of nation-states have established children's parliaments, even in nation-states that have comparatively poor infrastructures. In West and Central Africa, children's parliaments have been established in nation-states including Benin, Burkina Faso, Cameroon, Côte d'Ivoire, The Gambia, Guinea, Liberia, Mali, Niger, Senegal, and Togo. In addition, in Sierra Leone there is also the National Children's Forum. These parliaments are woven into the national political structure, with the majority falling under the Ministries of Social Affairs or the Ministries for Women and Children. Their electoral processes are mostly organized in partnership with decentralized ministry offices and with civil society (Plan International 2009).

These are still relatively new ideas, and to dismiss such initiatives as tokenism or without effective power is to ignore the historical evolution of nascent parliaments, such as those in England before the English Civil War, which began with very weak powers.

Children's parliaments can be important spaces to allow children to practice multigenerational democracy and political participation and thus also to develop their skills and contribute at an international level. However, there needs to be more strategic thinking to secure a wider pool from which to elect child parliamentarians[9] and more innovative ways of creating more child-initiated policies to avoid the risk of children merely following adults' political agendas. In addition, even though children's parliaments can act as consultative bodies for governmental decision-making or actively influence governmental policy and practice, much more needs to be done to formalize their political contribution. Several countries have acknowledged that children's parliaments have been highly influential on national policy debates concerning children. The governments of Guinea and Liberia, for example, have adopted a national children's code, which owes much to the effective advocacy of their children's parliaments. In Cameroon, the children's parliament argued successfully for the eradication of compulsory fees for primary education and for a raise in salary for government employees (Plan International 2009).

These successes ought to be stressed, as all too often the focus is on the dangers of children implementing their political rights as citizens. As Hart recognizes, children are a readily available "army" of concern that can be easily seduced into involvement in a movement that is really not "their own" (Hart 1997). However, education for democratic citizenship minimizes such risks.

In 2010, the Council of Europe adopted a recommendation on the Council of Europe Charter on Education for Democratic Citizenship and Human Rights Education. The recommendation defines education for democratic citizenship as

> education, training, awareness-raising, information, practices and activities which aim, by equipping learners with knowledge, skills and understanding and developing their attitudes and behaviour, to empower them to exercise and defend their democratic rights and responsibilities in society, to value diversity and to play an active part in democratic life, with a view to the promotion and protection of democracy and the rule of law. (Council of Europe 2010)

The recommendation has no minimum age limit, and it specifically focuses on the role of states to support youth organizations in providing such education (Plan International 2009, para. 10). Although the focus of the recommendation is on national citizenship, it clearly has implications for children as citizens of the world. Hence, the responsibility facet of multigenerational citizenship ought not to be feared both by those who traditionally support children's rights and by those who are nervous about child citizenship.

Rights and the noncontingent performance of responsibilities can help to develop a sense of community. Multigenerational citizenship has the advantage of emphasizing the duality of citizenship. "Duality" in the sense of a citizen holding both individual rights and community rights of interdependence—an increasingly important facet in this era of human rights and climate change. This even extends to recognizing the exercise of child citizenship responsibilities. The Philippine Supreme Court applauded children who sought to protect their community against deforestation, defining their responsibilities as extending to protect the rights of generations yet unborn (see *Minors Oposa et al. v. Fulgencio S. Factoran, Jr. et al.* 1993). The *Minors Oposa* judgment is a stronger endorsement of the principle incorporated in Agenda 21, which was adopted at the Rio Conference on Environment and Development. In a nonbinding law, Agenda 21 weakly called for "possible participation of youth of both genders, by 1993," in environmental decision-making processes at all levels (United Nations [UN] Department of Economic and Social Affairs 1992, chap. 25).[10] Hence, multigenerational citizenship regards childhood as contributing positively to citizenship rather than undermining it. Therefore, citizenship theories, post-CRC, need to be sufficiently flexible to encompass child development rather than competency. Child development is a dynamic child-focused concept resting upon the evolving capacities of the child, whereas competency is static. As Flekkøy and Kaufman (1997, 48) argue, if competency were the sole determinant, then "many adults would also be excluded."[11]

Childhood and Emerging International Citizenship

Multigenerational citizenship conceptualizes children as both national and international citizens. International child citizenship or citizenship of the world (the terms are used interchangeably here) as well as national citizenship are concepts that offer a lot of potential for children, not only for children who, in breach of the CRC, remain stateless (UN General Assembly 1989, 1966)[12] but for all children regardless of nationality.

The inclusion of children's entitlements in the writings of Tom Paine ought to prompt a reconsideration of his contribution to the development of multigenerational citizenship[13] and to consider whether children, as well as Tom Paine himself, are citizens of the world. Tom Paine was one of the earliest advocates in the West for children's educational and social security entitlements. Paine, as far back as the eighteenth century, advocated for all children to be entitled to schooling and for the authorities to grant to the poor four pounds annually for children under 14—not an inconsiderable sum for the eighteenth century. In addition, he advocated that women should receive twenty shillings on the birth of a child (Paine 1792, 142, 150).[14] These he described as "not of the nature of a charity but of a right" (Paine 1792, 40). His concern for the socioeconomic entitlements of children preceded that of Eglantyne Jebb, the original drafter of the League of Nations Declaration of the Rights of the Child, by 133 years.[15]

Within multigenerational citizenship, the development of the child as a citizen of the world as well as a citizen of a nation-state is a concept that is the opposite of John Quincy Adams's unjustifiable description of Paine as having "no country, no affections that constitute the pillars of patriotism" (Hawke 1974, 33). The slow emergence of children as citizens of the world recognizes that there is a global concern for the community of the child, which augments, rather than detracts from, national commitments. Hence, cosmopolitan, strangely used by some as a term of insult, literally means citizen of the world.[16]

Nevertheless, despite the writings of Tom Paine, children remained largely invisible on the international agenda prior to the CRC. One of the important achievements of the CRC is that children are no longer always falling through the safety net of international protection and are also slowly emerging as "citizens of the world."[17] The rights in the CRC have a transnational facet—they are guaranteed by the specialized agencies of the UN, such as the World Health Organization and the International Labor Organization, and other bodies of the UN, such as the UN Children's Fund and the UN High Commissioner for Refugees. The rights are also guarded by international nongovernmental organizations (NGOs).

As the Inter-American Court of Human Rights (2002) has recognized, there is now a "new juridical order" for children's rights, and states have to legislate in accordance with this new juridical order. This new juridical order also has consequences for the global political order of citizenship.

Although Tom Paine's rights of the child and Eglantyne Jebb's Declaration of the Rights of the Child valuably described children as rights holders, neither went so far as to envisage children as participants in determining their own autonomy. It was, however, this dynamic vision of child citizenship that underlay much of the rationale for the first generally binding human rights treaty for children: the CRC. Ironically, though, the CRC does not expressly enshrine a duty on states to promote active child citizenship beyond a duty in Article 29(d) in relation to the goals of education.[18]

The CRC was the first global human rights treaty in which children participated in some of the drafting. Thus, for the first time, the global community, as represented by the UN, acknowledged the value not only of children speaking on their own behalf but also as citizens of the world, speaking on behalf of their global counterparts. The work of children ranged from speaking directly to the open-ended working group of the Commission on Human Rights entrusted with drafting the CRC, to lobbying against the death penalty, and to signing an international petition seeking to exclude children's participation in armed conflict. Although child participation was more ad hoc than structured and occasional rather than comprehensive, the majority of the children's interventions were successful. Australia acknowledged that speeches from indigenous Canadian children were the catalyst for Australia's dropping its opposition to the inclusion of children's indigenous rights in the CRC.[19] Amnesty International worked with American schoolchildren successfully to urge delegates to include the prohibition of the death penalty (see Van Bueren 1995). It was only in the area of armed conflict that children's views were disregarded, although some of these concerns were later incorporated in the optional protocol to the CRC on the involvement of children in armed conflict (UN General Assembly 2000).[20]

Overcoming the Obstacles to Multigenerational Citizenship

The twin inclusion in the CRC of the best interests of the child and of the evolving capacities of the child is significant for multigenerational citizenship. The concepts provide an ideology that affirms that it is in the best interests of both children and the state for policies and mechanisms to be adopted that allow for greater participation of child citizens in society as children grow older and mature. Prior to the CRC, the traditional focus of national and regional jurisprudence, as well as international instruments on the best interests of the child as a principle governing all actions concerning children, related to child access and custody,[21] maintenance,[22] and adoption,[23] circumstances focusing principally on parents, families, and their alternatives.[24] The CRC's reworking of the best interests of the child principle to extend to the public as well as the private sphere implies that best interests are as equally applicable as a matter of international law to children's economic, social, and cultural rights as to their civil rights. In essence, the best interests of the child, which originated as a compassionate self-limiting power upon adult discretion, has become transformed by the CRC into an expression of child legal affirmative action.

The CRC also opened the door to effective multigenerational citizenship through Articles 12 and 13 and their emphasis on child-focused participation. This emphasis is an attempt to break the cycle of disadvantage—a less than full implementation of the right to expression leads to a lesser right to de facto participation, which is disempowering, diluting the concept of child citizenship even further. Article 12 of the CRC, therefore, refers expressly to "all matters," which implies that the state has a legal duty to create mechanisms that allow children to participate in all levels of decision-making in accordance with their evolving capacities. Participation implies access to public policy formation and, thus, the strengthening of the membership of a community.

Education is a means of making child citizens' participation effective; this is the reason behind Cullen's argument that the right to education is "primarily an individual right" but that education also has a "social function of developing people as full citizens of their society" (Cullen 1993, 143). Paradoxically, however, the historical invisibility of children as citizens has been reinforced by the great clarions of human rights in England, the United States, and France. The Bill of Rights 1686, the Virginia Declaration of Rights 1776, the American Declaration of Independence 1776, and the Declaration of the Rights of Man 1789 omitted any provision on the right to education. Yet Mary Wollstonecraft (2001) recognized the importance of education, both as a right and as a means of obtaining rights. This is one of the reasons for the status of the right to education as a nonderogable right in a number of human rights treaties and why the CRC provides so much detail on the goals of education.

The gradual untying of the link between citizenship and direct economic contribution and the creation, in a small but growing number of democratic states, of a link between citizenship and socioeconomic entitlement are of particular potential benefit for the development of the concept of child citizenship. A broader concept of multigenerational citizenship is beginning to develop, which includes not only civil and political rights but also socioeconomic rights, creating a legal basis for asserting child citizens' right of equal access to resources (see Stalford 2000, 113).

Children, however, suffered from a double disadvantage caused by the operation of two distinct ideologies: (1) the resistance of law to take seriously its capacity for the strategic alleviation of poverty as a legal cause of action and (2) the capacity of children as evolving citizens and rights-holders in the economic and social spheres. The economic facets of national citizenship are frequently conceptualized as exclusively adult. This common but erroneous perception fails to consider that economic and social rights are not only commodities but also essential for the right to live as citizens in security and dignity: a right that is as pertinent for children as it is for adults. Children's and adults' sharing of the economic and social facets of citizenship stamps citizenship in the twenty-first century as multigenerational.

According to the UN, civil, political, economic, social, and cultural rights are all equal and interdependent (UN 1993), and their application to multigenerational citizenship implies that children require access to public policymaking not only through legislatures but also through the courts. However, to do so, a longstanding myth requires debunking: the myth that the separation of powers requires as much judicial deference for children as it does for adults. The post-CRC world, which constitutes the new child juridical order, requires a consideration, from the child citizen's perspective, of the separation of the powers of the courts, the legislature, and the executive—an important perspective that is lacking in Montesquieu (1748) and other classical authorities.

The classical paradigm of the separation of powers argues that democratic legislatures and executives have primary responsibility for the expenditure of resources, because if resources are not distributed in ways that are acceptable to the majority, then the democratically elected party may not be reelected. Hence, the courts become the "least dangerous" branch of government, because they possess neither the power of "the purse" (legislative power) nor the "the sword" (executive power) (Hamilton 1788). The powers ascribed to the legislature rest upon the bedrock of universal suffrage; however, in most countries, children remain disenfranchised.[25] Hence the need, at the very least, for child legislatures. However, because the separation of powers has operated effectively for adults, there has not been any criticism of the way that the powers are divided to render children invisible. The courts have even defended children's disenfranchisement. The District of Columbia Circuit Court of Appeals rejected the argument that children are politically powerless, because such impotence is

> not measured solely in terms of access to the ballot box, for the broad array of laws and government programs dedicated to protecting and nurturing children—combined with the large number of voters who are parents who are otherwise concerned about children—belies the argument that children and their needs cannot attract the attention of the legislature. (*Hedgepeth v. Washington Metropolitan Area Transit Authority et al.* 2004)

However, the same arguments could have been used in the nineteenth century in relation to women, particularly if the court's use of the word "parents" is substituted with "husband."

Some may seek to argue that legislatures are democratically accountable to children through their parents, who vote; however, this excludes several groups of children, including orphans and child-headed households. In addition, to maintain that parents are enfranchised on their behalf and also on behalf of their children is unsustainable, as there is an absence of any required consultation or proxy. The nature of the democratic voting process is that enfranchisement is personal, individual, and confidential. Therefore, within the majority of democratic separation of powers paradigms, children suffer from a democratic deficit, as children are the only group who almost universally do not vote or participate directly in the democratic process.[26] Under the classical approaches to the separation of powers, children fall into a vacuum, with these theories failing them.

For child citizens living in poverty, this failure carries with it particularly harsh consequences, as the judiciary, normally responsive to parental child abuse, have through self-denying traditions generally regarded themselves as unable to act on behalf of children abused where the state apportions too few resources. The theory that the legislature makes the law and apportions resources, while the courts generally interpret the law and do not question apportionment beyond the issues of irrationality and unreasonableness, has resulted not in the safeguarding of the separation of powers for child citizens but in the absence of powers. For effective multigenerational citizenship to be established, the immutability of the historic division of the separation of powers requires further scrutiny (see Van Bueren 2008b, 237–73).

In the case *Certification of the Constitution* (1996), the South African Constitutional Court observed that the separation of powers is neither a fixed nor a rigid doctrine. Specifically in relation to social justice entitlements, the court observed that "it cannot be said that . . . task is conferred upon the courts so different from that ordinarily conferred upon them by bills of rights, that it results in a breach of separation of powers" (para. 78).

However, in relation to child citizens, this "no bright lines" theory requires further development. For multigenerational citizenship, there is an additional conceptual element since there is something inherent in the separation of powers that demands a greater role for the courts, as children are the only group of citizens who are not only disenfranchised but to whom the primacy of the best interest principle attaches as a binding principle of both international law and of national law. In applying the universal principle of best interests to states, where children under 18 are disenfranchised, the separation of powers requires that the courts have to be vigilant in ensuring that all the rights of the child, including their social justice rights, are protected, so as to fill the lacuna in the separation of powers toward child citizens. An important consequence of the no bright lines approach is to include child citizens in the separation of powers paradigm, because the legal duties imposed upon the judiciary by the principle of the best interests[27] imply that the redress of structural child inequality becomes an appropriate legal question for the courts as well as an electoral political quest. Relying on governments' political promises or reliance only upon governments to fully implement the concluding observations of the UN Committee on the Rights of the Child has so far not proven successful—child poverty has increased in the majority of OECD nation-states since the adoption of the CRC. Political target setting for reductions in child poverty, without the safety net of an international child complaints mechanism, risks the continuing image of children as the means to a fairer society in the future. Multigenerational citizenship, in contrast, conceptualizes that children have sufficient legal capacity to ensure a socially just society that is enjoyed while they are still children. This has occurred in a growing number of nations, including Brazil, Chile, India, the Philippines, and South Africa. Children have won socioeconomic rights cases, including cases on the rights to nutrition (see *PULC v. Union of India and Others* 2001), to housing (*Government of the Republic of South Africa and Others v. Grootboom and Others* 2000), and to a sustainable environment. Without the recognition that the separation of powers in democratic states requires reconceptualizing to protect effectively poorer child citizens, the concept of multigenerational citizenship will not reach its full potential in enhancing the lives of all children.

Progress and the International Social Movement for Child Citizenship

Although a treaty that took almost a decade to draft may be criticized,[28] that period of time did allow for ideas to mature and gave sufficient space and time for more governments to reflect on and embrace a more child-focused approach to the meaning of citizenship. However, the CRC has a significant lacuna in relation to the concept of child citizenship; the CRC omits procedures whereby children can challenge their governments' decisions concerning citizenship. In addition, although several treaty bodies have the jurisdiction to receive complaints from children, their respective mandates remain limited,[29] and such a scattered and non-child-focused approach has limited the potential for developing a coherent and comprehensive approach to child citizenship. The CRC, therefore, perhaps unwittingly, helps to perpetuate a lesser image of the child as an international citizen. Even in refusing to consider an interstate complaints mechanism, whereby states can bring actions to the UN Committee on the Rights of the Child, the CRC limits the concept of children as world citizens and therefore as of equal concern to the world.

If a gauge were necessary to measure how far the international social movement for children has progressed in its attitude toward child citizenship, a valuable gauge would be civil societies' attitudes around the world about developing a complaints mechanism,[30] diplomatically referred to as a communications measure, to be used by children to protect their rights under the CRC. During the 1980s not only were states against such a mechanism but so were the majority of NGOs (the latter is not very well known). The majority of nation-states and NGOs opposed a draft joint proposal from the International Commission of Jurists and Amnesty International, which I had the privilege of representing, on three grounds. Hence, for children, the Latin maxim of "*ubi ius, ibi remedium*" ("where rights exist, redress is possible") was reinterpreted to mean that redress would only be possible if adults took action on children's behalf.

The first objection was that a petitioning or complaints mechanism would damage children's rights, because it would introduce an element of complaint when so much more had been achieved in the drafting procedure based on consensus. It was believed that state self-reporting and the UN Committee on the Rights of the Child's scrutiny of states' reports and technical advice and assistance were sufficient (see UN General Assembly 1989, Articles 43–45). Although never stated expressly, such an objection harkened back to the era when it was believed that children's objections to a particular law or policy would be better represented indirectly and mediated through adults exercising citizenship on children's behalf. Although the UN Committee on the Rights of the Child considerably expanded the role of child participation in the reporting process, the lack of direct access has impeded the progress of moving toward active multigenerational citizenship, which also incorporates children.

The second objection, which was more understandable in the historical context of the 1980s, was that the CRC not only enshrined civil and political rights but also economic, social, and cultural rights. The latter three, it was argued, were inherently nonjusticiable and, therefore, inappropriate for any complaints mechanism. Such objectors could point to the absence of petitioning mechanisms in global treaties protecting socioeconomic rights as well as the few states that allowed their citizens access to the courts litigating socioeconomic rights violations. In the twenty-first century, however, in addition to regional treaties, procedures allowing for individual complaints have been incorporated into all the other core international human rights treaties.[31] These allow petitioning of socioeconomic rights so that the nonjusticiability issue disappears, at least on the international level.

The third objection was that the CRC protects children's rights in armed conflicts and that complaints mechanisms had never before been extended to victims of armed conflicts. It was also argued that complaints mechanisms were Western and not part of a universal tradition. Nation-states, it was erroneously argued, particularly in Africa, had a long tradition of improvement through building a consensus rather than the formal taking of complaints. However, within a year of the UN adopting the CRC, the Organization of African Unity, as it was then known,[32] adopted in 1990 its own general regional treaty on children's rights called the African Charter on the Rights and Welfare of the Child. This not only enshrines a petitioning mechanism allowing children to petition on civil, political, economic, social, and cultural rights, but it also creates a petitioning mechanism that allows children to petition the African committee on violations of children's rights in peacetime and in times of armed conflicts. These objections imply that there is an acceptance that citizenship rights are, as a matter of law, lost in situations of armed conflict. Although it is often the case that de facto citizenship rights are lost in situations of conflict, this is very different from accepting a de jure loss of citizenship. Hence, by clinging to old conceptions of Africa, armed conflicts, and child citizenship, at least on a de jure level, the majority of CRC drafters created the arbitrary situation in which children in Africa have better de jure protection of their citizenship rights than those in other parts of the world.

Additional objections have been raised to proposals for drafting a communication or complaints procedure since the CRC has entered into force. The first objection has been that because of the vulnerable status of children, there is a risk that children may be manipulated when submitting a complaint. However, there no evidence of this becoming a problem with applications submitted by children to the European or Inter-American Courts of Human Rights, both of which have a substantial history of considering complaints from children. Nor is there any evidence of such manipulation before any of the UN human rights bodies, including the Human Rights Committee or the Committee on the Elimination of All Forms of Discrimination against Women.

There is a serious issue concerning the length of proceedings and the consequences for an application if a child reaches majority and adulthood before the UN Committee on the Rights of the Child decides on a communication. However, the problem is overstressed. The issues are the subject matter of the complaint at the time of receipt and whether it will still be relevant to public policy or national legislation for children living in the applicant's state after the child submitting the application reaches majority.

Two objections have also been raised that are common to all human rights treaties. The first concern is the risk of forum shopping by complainants. However, this can be easily avoided, as the majority of States Parties to the European Convention on Human Rights, for example, have lodged a reservation to Article 5, paragraph 2(a), of the optional protocol to the International Covenant on Civil and Political Rights (UN General Assembly 1966), which limits the Human Rights Committee's competence to examine complaints that the European Court of Human Rights has already examined. Other treaty bodies are prohibited by the terms of the treaty from examining communications that relevant international organs have already decided.

The second objection is that of delay due to an overburdening of the UN Committee on the Rights of the Child. However, as this is an issue raised in relation to all human rights bodies, it is not a reason for denying one group in the global community access to a communications procedure, particularly as pending cases vary from treaty to treaty, with some having little delay (see UN General Assembly 2010a).[33]

The Consequences of Recognizing Children as International Citizens

Recognizing that children are both citizens of a nation-state and of the global community helps to justify the need for an international remedy to be enshrined in the CRC. This is particularly important for children who live in parts of the world where such mechanisms do not exist, not even for violations of the civil and political rights of adults and children. Asia, where the majority of children live, has no regional human rights machinery to which children or adults can petition. Neither the Council of Europe (see Van Bueren 2008a) nor the Organization of American States has a single general children's rights charter equivalent to the African Union's (AU's) Charter on the Rights and Welfare of the Child (see Van Bueren 2008a). Whether a child has recourse to a remedy on an international level depends upon whether the child is within the AU or living elsewhere; this produces an arbitrary and irrational result. This lack of universal equity in procedural access hinders the development of children as citizens of the world.

Even for children living in nations within the Council of Europe, the European Convention on Human Rights was not designed to protect them as a group, and this lack of focus on the child is reflected in both the language of the European Convention and in a number of unsatisfactory judgments (see Van Bueren 2008a). The European Convention does not even expressly enshrine the general principle of the best interests of the child. Ironically, the first express reference to children in the European Convention on Human Rights is to a provision that provides grounds for depriving children of their liberty rather than protecting it (see Van Bueren 2008a). This is not to argue that the concept of multigenerational citizenship has been wholly neglected under the European Convention on Human Rights—this is clearly not the case—but to assert that the European Convention was never intended to be a child-focused treaty. Therefore, it would be unrealistic to expect the European Court of Human Rights to go beyond its jurisdiction to better protect multigenerational citizenship.

Although the status of the decisions that the UN Committee on the Rights of the Child makes will be that of recommendations and not, as with the European Court of Human Rights, binding judgments, a communications procedure will assist in the development of international citizenship for children. The advantage of having the UN Committee on the Rights of the Child receive communications is that the complaints will be judged by those with direct experience with children's rights and whose focus is the development of child citizenship. A successful complaint against one nation-state would not only benefit children living in that nation-state but would set a standard that other states would have to meet to avoid similar complaints. In this way, the complaints procedure would serve both as a deterrent and as a catalyst for implementing minimal standards, at the very least, in child citizenship.

The decisions of the UN Committee on the Rights of the Child will also have a persuasive value for similar cases raised before national courts and in regional fora. In this way there would be a circular process for increasing the implementation of the rights of children. Similarly, decisions of the UN Committee, although recommendatory only, will provide a catalyst for changes in legislatures.

A communications procedure will also provide an opportunity for the UN Committee on the Rights of the Child to provide fuller and better-reasoned opinions. Therefore, the concept of child citizenship will gain more respect among states. There have been cases, for example, concerning the physical punishment of children in schools in the United Kingdom, where the European Court of Human Rights found the United Kingdom not to be in violation and the Committee on the Rights of the Child found the United Kingdom to be in breach (Van Bueren 2008a). It is difficult to persuade a nation-state to adopt a more progressive approach when it has two conflicting opinions from different international bodies. The recommendation from the UN Committee on the Rights of the Child provided very little reasoning even though it contradicted the earlier decision of the European Court of Human Rights and extended the prohibition on physical punishment to intrafamilial physical punishment. A more fully reasoned opinion would be more persuasive, opening the door to more reasoned arguments comparing the prohibition of physical punishment on adult citizens and questioning the reason for retaining such punishment for child citizens. Indeed such an approach has been recognized by the committee, at least in regard to its General Comment 8, which provides much reasoning and analysis of the different justifications for child physical punishment as well as a statement on the international law.

The actual negotiations over the procedures to be included in any communications mechanism will also impact the development of how child citizenship operates on a formal level. It would be a loss of opportunity if the complaints mechanism for the CRC were simply to replicate the communications mechanisms of other treaties, without taking into account the special needs of child citizenship. Neither the International Covenant on Civil and Political Rights (UN General Assembly 1966) nor the Convention on the Elimination of All Forms of Discrimination against Women (UN General Assembly 1979) offers appropriate models. At the time of writing, no girl under the age of 18 has won her case under the Convention on the Elimination of All Forms of Discrimination against Women; although there are decisions that have been helpful to children. The procedures of the International Covenant on Civil and Political Rights takes insufficient account of a child's best interests (Van Bueren 1995).

Creating a complaints mechanism would also focus attention on the issue of children as citizens of the world and the degree to which others share an interdependent responsibility to protect child citizens' rights. Although the communication procedure would be international, if it were sufficiently flexible and child-sensitive, it would help to focus attention on how to make child citizenship more relevant to vulnerable children, who often are allowed to fall through the safety net of child citizenship protection. One issue that will require constructive and novel approaches is how an international complaints mechanism can be accessible to the world's most vulnerable child citizens, including the most impoverished children and children living and working in the streets and beyond the normal reach of formal structures. As with all other international legal tribunals, children will not have access to an international communication procedure until all effective domestic remedies have been exhausted. Existing national children and human rights institutions, including national commissions and ombudsmen offices, will need to develop innovative approaches to securing access to and the trust of the most vulnerable children. In so doing, comparative best practice will be invaluable.

One of the reasons for the success of the South African Bill of Rights is that there is a broad standing—NGOs, individuals, and groups are able to bring cases—creating a network of support for the most vulnerable in the community (see Republic of South Africa 1996, sec. 38). Allowing civil society, as well as nation-states, to bring actions against nation-states is essential for the full development of multigenerational citizenship.

The formal details of citizenship are usually accessible only to adults, although the CRC and other international laws on children place a duty on nation-states to make their provisions available in child-friendly versions. Judgments and rulings, even when considering aspects of child citizenship, rarely appear in a child-friendly format. The development of child citizenship requires that the decisions of the UN Committee on the Rights of the Child on a child complaint be published in a form that would be child-sensitive. This is not only so that the child or child victims can understand but also, in this era of international child citizenship, so that children globally are able to understand judgments concerning their own rights and statuses. The test for measuring progress in the development of international child citizenship will be the extent to which children participate in the formulation of a child complaints mechanism, ad hoc, as with the drafting of the original CRC, or in a truly representative manner.

An Open-Ended Working Group and a Child-Sensitive Communication Mechanism

Anniversary celebrations have often been used strategically to progress children's rights. Indeed, the original proposal to draft a binding treaty on children's rights was accepted in 1979, the International Year of the Child. Diplomatically, a rejection of the proposal in such a year would have been very difficult. The UN Committee on the Rights of the Child recognized in General Comment 5 that children's special and dependent statuses create substantive difficulties for them in pursuing remedies for breaches of their rights (UN Committee on the Rights of the Child 2005). This was further developed by the chairperson of the committee, expressing in her oral report to the General Assembly that the development of a communications procedure for the CRC would significantly contribute to the overall protection of children's rights. The UN Committee on the Rights of the Child has endorsed the idea on a number of occasions, including at the 10th anniversary of the CRC and more recently in the buildup to the 20th anniversary (UN Committee on the Rights of the Child 1999). Hence, the occasion of the 20th anniversary of the CRC made it possible for a resolution to be adopted without a vote at the Human Rights Council—the successor body to the Commission on Human Rights—to establish an open-ended working group of the Human Rights Council to explore the possibility of elaborating an optional protocol to the CRC to provide a communications procedure complementary to the reporting procedure under the CRC (UN General Assembly 2009). The council recognized that in many nation-states, national remedies are inadequate, but even where national remedies are effective, children still have the same overwhelming case for gaining an international communications mechanism, alongside those created for other international human rights treaties for other groups traditionally subjected to discrimination.

It is too soon to assess what weight will be given to active child participation. The General Assembly has recognized, inter alia, that the full enjoyment of the rights of the child to be heard and to participate require adults to adopt an appropriate child-centered attitude, listening to children and respecting their rights and individual points of view, which would include the drafting of a communications procedure (UN General Assembly 2010b).

At its first meeting, on December 16, 2009, the working group elected Drahoslav Štefánek from Slovakia as its chairperson-rapporteur. The chairperson was nominated by a core group of member states, including Chile, Egypt, Finland, France, Kenya, the Maldives, Slovakia, Slovenia, Thailand, and Uruguay, which all have supported the initiative for a new optional protocol on a communications procedure (UN General Assembly 2010a).

It is, however, clear that an opportunity was lost when states rejected the proposal to incorporate a communications procedure into the main body of the CRC rather than in an additional and optional protocol. This may have meant that the communication procedure would have been similar to the approach that the amended European Convention on Human Rights used.[34] However, despite being optional, many advantages will follow. The development of an effective and accessible international procedure will, where necessary, highlight the need for and may stimulate the development of effective remedies for violations of the rights of the child at local, national, and regional levels. Similarly, the decisions by the UN Committee on the Rights of the Child on individual and group cases ought to mean that the body of jurisprudence that it develops will assist in the interpretation of children's rights that national and regional courts and tribunals make. Even the process of drafting and adopting an international communications procedure for the CRC may encourage the development of appropriate national remedies for children.

At present, not all ombudsman for children have the power to investigate complaints; nor do the majority of ombudsmen in Europe have the jurisdiction to take legal action on behalf of children, either nationally or before regional human rights bodies. A communications procedure under the CRC may offer opportunities to strengthen the powers of national child ombudsmen.

The lack of a communications procedure in the CRC has, on occasion, resulted in national and regional courts interpreting children's rights in limited ways. However, for the jurisprudence of the UN Committee on the Rights of the Child to maximize its potential as a dynamic catalyst for the development of children's rights, it is necessary that the procedures of the committee are child-sensitive. The UN Guidelines on Justice in Matters Involving Child Victims and Witnesses of Crime (UN Economic and Social Council 2005, IV, 9(d)) define *child-sensitive* as "an approach that balances the child's right to protection and that takes into account the child's individual needs and views." It is also clear that for a complaints mechanism to be child-sensitive, it should be designed so that its procedures are tailored both in line with the CRC and with the general comments of the UN Committee on the Rights of the Child, particularly with its most recent general comment on the right to be heard. General Comment 12 ranges from an analysis of how states give due weight to a child's maturity, to the necessity of having complaint procedures that should ensure that children are confident that using them will not expose them to risk of violence or punishment (UN Committee on the Rights of the Child 2009).

A child-sensitive, international complaints mechanism will also require a range of methods for submitting a communication. The Inter-American Commission on Human Rights, for instance, can receive online petition forms. Such an approach could be extended to allow for the possibility of sending audio or audiovisual materials. A number of international bodies and offices are developing child-sensitive procedures. The special rapporteur on the sale of children, child prostitution, and child pornography, for example, is developing a child-friendly version of the letter of allegation form, and the International Criminal Court has accepted more than four hundred drawings from children from Darfur, which it may use as evidence of genocide. This is consistent with the CRC, which provides that a key element of the child's right to freedom of expression is the child's choice of the medium of expression.

A key element of child-sensitive communications procedures is that they take into account a child's sense of time and are processed accordingly. Since the CRC was born, there has been a rapid development of best practices concerning children's access to child-sensitive justice and to effective remedies. This means that the drafting of a child-sensitive communications procedure could be accomplished within a short period of time.

Conclusion

Multigenerational citizenship, with its flexible approach to citizenship, is attractive because it also creates links not only between children in different states but between other groups in the global community who have also been wrongfully relegated to passive citizenship roles, in particular the aged and those living with disabilities. The recognition of the achievements of the international social movement for child citizenship is therefore critical. However, academic fora focusing on human rights issues are universally hesitant about acknowledging the achievements of a particular international law. Instead, scholastic energies are understandably focused either on matters of wrongful commission or omission. To acquire an accurate picture of how the CRC has enhanced multigenerational citizenship, account must also be taken of the positive impacts of the CRC. These range from the utilization of the CRC to ensure that child citizens are able to access the health resources of a state, which has resulted since 1990 in the saving of 10 million children's lives under the age of five;[35] to the formal creation of child-focused courts around the globe; and to the enfranchisement of child citizens, who are voting in both local and national elections in a small but increasing number of states.[36]

It is also clear that what were once considered radical notions—"child citizenship" and "children's rights"—have in the past two decades become more accepted in states that are party to the CRC. It may be that there are different attitudes toward the achievements and state of the international social movement for children's rights in States Parties to the CRC. The United States, although it signed the CRC in 1990, has still, 20 years later, not ratified it.[37] Such differences in attitudes are to be expected. Energetic national movements for the incorporation of the CRC into national law[38] and widening the powers of children's rights commissioners[39] have no chance of even beginning in a state that has yet to ratify.

This is not to deny the failings of the CRC, in particular, in relation to child refugees and asylum seekers and to children in detention in many nations. Such failings are reflections of commonly held images, which still persist despite the CRC, of who falls within and who falls outside of child citizenship and the de facto, although not de jure, limitations of the best interests principle. The CRC was never intended to be a universal cure for all the violations of the rights of child citizens. However, the many successes of civil society in its formulation and in the pace of ratifications continue to energize many nations and much of civil society in seeking to improve the implementation of the world's charter for child citizens.

Notes

1. The test for human rights protection is a jurisdictional one and not that of citizenship. If it were otherwise, a state would be at liberty to remove citizenship from a person and thereby violate fundamental human rights.

2. This also has advantages for older persons, and there is an international social movement under way to persuade the United Nations to draft and adopt a treaty on the rights of older persons.

3. According to Aristotle's definition, children were not citizens, since they did not share "in the administration of justice and in offices" (Aristotle 2008, 101).

4. Some nations, including Kuwait, still excluded women as political citizens, and not every canton in Switzerland enfranchised women until late in the twentieth century.

5. Somalia and the United States are the only two nations that have not ratified the CRC.

6. Article 29 states that "the individual shall also have the duty: 1. to preserve the harmonious development of the family and to work for the cohesion and respect of the family; to respect his parents at all times, to maintain them in case of need."

7. Article 31 states that "every child shall have responsibilities towards his family and society, the State and other legally recognized communities and the international community. The child, subject to his age and ability, and such limitations as may be contained in the present Charter . . ."

8. This is not to deny the entrenched nature of some dictatorial regimes in Africa.

9. As Plan International (2009) observes, although there is no standard practice for their elections in most countries, elections appear to depend heavily on schools to reach young voters, which excludes out-of-school children. There are also varying practices with regard to voter eligibility, often drawing on children's school performance. Age ranges for active and passive rights to vote in children's parliaments also vary significantly, though an active right to vote seems to be mostly determined by age 16 and above. Efforts have been made in most countries in West Africa to ensure that an equal number of boys and girls are elected into office. In Senegal, for example, the participation criteria for the children's parliament require a broad representation of children, including children in and out of school, with disabilities, affected by HIV, and so on. However, few parliaments in the region have children with disabilities as members.

10. UNICEF launched, in 1996, the Child Friendly Cities Initiative, which promotes children's participation in local government.

11. Although Flekkøy and Kaufman (1997) were arguing against competency in relation to rights, the same applies to citizenship.

12. Article 7 of the CRC provides that "States Parties shall ensure the implementation of these rights [rights to a name, nationality, and to know and be cared for by parents] in accordance with their national law and their obligations under the relevant international instruments in this field, in particular where the child would otherwise be stateless." See also Article 8. A complaint has been lodged with the African Committee of Experts submitted by the Justice Initiative on behalf of Nubian children in Kenya who are stateless as a result of the Kenyan government's refusal to grant them nationality. The African Charter on the Rights and Welfare of the Child in Article 24(3) states that "States Parties . . . shall undertake to ensure that their Constitutional legislations recognize the principles according to which a child shall acquire the nationality of the State in the territory of which he has been born if, at the time of the child's birth, he is not granted nationality by any other State in accordance with its laws."

13. His contributions were at both ends of the age spectrum.

14. He advocated this approach more than a century before the country of his birth introduced such benefits.

15. The League of Nations adopted the first Declaration of the Rights of the Child in 1924.

16. From the Greek "*kosmopolitai*."

17. This was an epithet that was attributed to Tom Paine but was also a concept that Diogenes used.

18. Article 29(d) calls for "the preparation of the child for responsible life in a free society, in the spirit of understanding, peace, tolerance, equality of sexes, and friendship among all peoples, ethnic, national and religious groups and persons of indigenous origin."

19. Author's notes taken during the drafting of the CRC.

20. The General Assembly adopted this optional protocol and opened it for signature, ratification, and accession on May 25, 2000. It entered into force on February 12, 2002.

21. International instruments include The Hague Convention on the Civil Aspects of International Child Abduction (Hague Conference 1980) and the Inter-American Convention on the International Return of Children (Fourth Inter-American Specialized Conference on Private International Law 1989a). Domestic examples of jurisprudence from the United States and the United Kingdom include *Troxel v. Granville* (2000), where paternal grandparents petitioned for visitation with children born outside of marriage; and *Re L (Removal from Jurisdiction: Holiday)* (2001), where a holiday providing the child with an opportunity to meet his extended family in the United Emirates was in the best interests of the child but the court requested a deposit of £50,000 for his return.

22. International instruments include the Inter-American Convention on Support Obligations (Fourth Inter-American Specialized Conference on Private International Law 1989b), and an example of domestic jurisprudence from South Africa includes *Bannatyne v. Bannatyne and Another* (2002).

23. The international instruments include The Hague Convention on the Protection of Children and Cooperation in Respect of Intercountry Adoption (Hague Conference 1993) and the United Nations Declaration on Social and Legal Principles Relating to the Protection and Welfare of Children, with Special Reference to Foster Placement and Adoption Nationally and Internationally (UN General Assembly 1986). Domestic jurisprudence from South Africa and the United States includes *Fraser v. Children's Court, Pretoria North and Others* (1997), in which a prohibition on foreigners adopting was held to be unconstitutional; and *Lofton v. Dept Child Family Services* (2004), in which homosexual foster parents and guardians challenged the constitutionality of a Florida law prohibiting homosexuals from adopting children.

24. The focus has not been exclusively on the family and its replacement. Cases concerning education, for example, have also considered the application of the best interests of the child. See *Christian Education South Africa v. Minister of Education* (2000), in which the prohibition of physical punishment in educational settings was upheld.

25. There are a few exceptions, including Brazil and Nicaragua. See Van Bueren (forthcoming).

26. Prisoners are another group that does not participate in the democratic process, with exceptions, such as South Africa. However, prisoners are not able to benefit from the principle of best interests.

27. I have discussed how the principle of best interests has evolved into a principle of *jus cogens*, recognized by international law as binding on all states, regardless of whether or not they are parties to the CRC. See Van Bueren (2008b).

28. However, such a period of time is not unduly lengthy in the light of the drafting of other treaties.

29. Due to the limited mandate, only 2 to 2.5 percent of the complaints that the treaty bodies considered related to children.

30. As of December 8, 2009, 601 organizations had signed a petition calling for such a mechanism. See www.crin.org/petitions/petition.asp?petID=1007.

31. Three such treaties discussed in this article include the Convention on the Elimination of All Forms of Discrimination against Women (UN General Assembly 1979), the International Convention on the Protection of the Rights of All Migrant Workers and Members of Their Families (UN General Assembly 1990), and the Convention on the Rights of Persons with Disabilities (UN General Assembly 2006).

32. The Organization of African Unity is now the African Union.

33. In regard to the Human Rights Committee, the secretariat indicated that approximately 430 cases were pending. Approximately 100 cases are registered each year, and an equal number of final decisions are adopted each year. The Committee against Torture has 85 cases pending before it, and approximately

400 cases have been registered under the latter committee's procedures since the early 1990s. The Committee on the Elimination of Racial Discrimination and the Committee on the Elimination of All Forms of Discrimination against Women have very few cases registered. At the time of writing, the new Committee on the Rights of Persons with Disabilities does not yet have any registered individual communication.

34. The European Convention on Human Rights now has a communication procedure as an integral part of the treaty. Originally states could have been party to the convention without having to recognize the right of individual petition.

35. New survey figures reported by UNICEF as of this writing show solid progress, with worldwide child deaths at a record low of 9.7 million per year—down from almost 13 million in 1990. See UNICEF (2007).

36. These include Brazil and Nicaragua.

37. The United States has been criticized for its failure to ratify. Such criticism, however, has to be balanced against the records of Burma, Equatorial Guinea, and North Korea, all of which have ratified the CRC.

38. ROCK (Rights of the Child UK) in the United Kingdom is one example of an organization calling for incorporation into national laws.

39. CRAE (Children's Rights Alliance in England), for example, has called for the widening of these powers.

References

Archard, David. 2003. *Children: Rights and childhood.* New York, NY: Routledge.

Aristotle. 2008. *Politics*. Trans. Benjamin Jowett and ed. H. W. C. Davis. New York, NY: Cosimo Classics.

Bannatyne v. Bannatyne and Another. 2002. CCT 18/02 (ZACC 31).

Bauböck, Rainer. 1995. *Transnational citizenship: Membership and rights in international migration*. Brookfield, VT: Edward Elgar.

Bellamy, Richard, Dario Castiglione, and Emilio Santoro. 2004. *Lineages of European citizenship: Rights, belonging, and participation in eleven nation-states*. New York, NY: Palgrave.

Certification of the Constitution of the Republic of South Africa. 1996. CCT 23/96 (ZACC 26).

Christian Education South Africa v. Minister of Education. 2000. CCT 4/00 (ZACC 11).

Council of Europe, Committee of Ministers, 120th Session. 2010. Recommendation on the Council of Europe Charter on Education for Democratic Citizenship and Human Rights Education. CM/Rec (2010)7.

Cullen, Holly. 1993. Education rights or minority rights? *International Journal of Law, Policy and the Family* 7 (2): 143–77.

Dahrendorf, Ralf. 1974. Citizenship and beyond: The social dynamics of an idea. *Social Research* 41 (4): 673–701.

Flekkøy, Målfrid Grude, and Natalie Hevener Kaufman. 1997. *The participation rights of the child: Rights and responsibilities in family and society*. London: Jessica Kingsley.

Fourth Inter-American Specialized Conference on Private International Law. 1989a. Inter-American Convention on the International Return of Children. Organization of American States Treaty Series 70. Washington, DC: Organization of American States. Available from www.oas.org/juridico/english/treaties/b-53.html (accessed 14 July 2010).

Fourth Inter-American Specialized Conference on Private International Law. 1989b. Inter-American Convention on Support Obligations. Organization of American States Treaty Series 71. Washington, DC: Organization of American States. Available from www.oas.org/juridico/english/treaties/b-54.html (accessed 14 July 2010).

Fraser v. Children's Court, Pretoria North and Others. 1997. CCT 31/96 (ZACC 1).

Government of the Republic of South Africa and Others v. Grootboom and Others. 2000. CCT 11/00 (ZACC 19).

Hague Conference on Private International Law. 1980. Hague Convention on the Civil Aspects of International Child Abduction. Available from www.unhcr.org/refworld/docid/3ae6b3951c.html (accessed 14 July 2010).

Hague Conference on Private International Law. 1993. Hague Convention on the Protection of Children and Co-operation in Respect of Intercountry Adoption. Available from www.unhcr.org/refworld/docid/3ddcb1794.html (accessed 14 July 2010).

Hamilton, Alexander. 1788. The Federalist no. 78. *Independent Journal*. Washington, DC: The Judiciary Department. Available from www.constitution.org/fed/federa78.htm (accessed 14 July 2010).

Hart, Roger. 1997. *Children's participation: The theory and practice of involving young citizens in community development and environmental care*. London: Earthscan.

Hawke, David Freeman. 1974. *Paine*. New York, NY: Harper & Row.

Hedgepeth v. Washington Metropolitan Area Transit Authority et al. 2004. 386 F.3d 1148 (DC Cir.).

Inter-American Court of Human Rights. 2002. *The legal status and human rights of the child*. Advisory Opinion OC-17/2002. San José, Costa Rica: Inter-American Court of Human Rights.

Lofton v. Dept Child Family Services. 2004. 358 F.3d 804.

Minors Oposa et al. v. Fulgencio S. Factoran, Jr. et al. 1993. G.R. no. 101083 (Philippine Supreme Court).

Montesquieu, Charles. 1748. *The spirit of laws*. Geneva: Barillot.

Organization of African Unity (OAU). 1981. African Charter on Human and Peoples' Rights. OAU Doc. CAB/LEG/67/3. Addis Ababa, Ethiopia: OAU.

OAU. 1990. African Charter on the Rights and Welfare of the Child. OAU Doc. CAB/LEG/24.9/49. Addis Ababa, Ethiopia: OAU.

Paine, Thomas. 1792. *Rights of man: Being an answer to Mr. Burke's attack on the French Revolution*. Albany, NY: Charles R. & George Webster.

Plan International. 2009. Children as active citizens: Addressing discrimination against children's engagement in political and civil society processes. Paper presented at the 20th anniversary on the Convention of the Rights of the Child, 8–9 October 2009. Geneva.

PUCL v. Union of India and Others. 2001. Writ Petition (Civil) 196. (Supreme Court of India).

Re L (Removal from Jurisdiction: Holiday). 2001. 1 FLR 241.

Republic of South Africa. 1996. Bill of Rights. In Constitution of the Republic of South Africa, 1245–67. Pretoria: Government of the Republic of South Africa.

Sloth-Nielsen, Julia. 2005. Of newborns and nubiles: Some critical challenges to children's rights in Africa in the era of HIV/Aids. *International Journal of Children's Rights* 13 (1): 73–85.

Stalford, Helen. 2000. The citizenship status of children in the European union. *International Journal of Childrens Rights* 8 (2): 101–31.

Troxel v. Granville. 2000. 530 U.S. 57.

United Nations (UN). 1993. Vienna Declaration. World Conference on Human Rights. 14–25 June 1993. Vienna, Austria.

UN Committee on the Rights of the Child. 1999. *Report on the 22nd Session of the Committee on the Rights of the Child*. UN Doc. CRC/C/90. Geneva: UN.

UN Committee on the Rights of the Child. 2005. *General measures of implementation of the Convention on the Rights of the Child*. General Comment no. 5, UN Doc. CRC/GC/2003/5. Geneva: UN.

UN Committee on the Rights of the Child, Fifty-first Session. 2009. *The right of the child to be heard*. General Comment no. 12. UN Doc. CRC/C/GC/12. Geneva: UN.

UN Department of Economic and Social Affairs, Division for Sustainable Development. 1992. Children and youth in sustainable development. In *Agenda 21*. Adopted at the United Nations Rio Conference on Environment and Development, 3–14 June. Rio de Janeiro, Brazil.

UN Economic and Social Council. 2005. *Guidelines on justice in matters involving child victims and witnesses of crime*. UN Doc. ECOSOC Res. 2005/20. New York, NY: UN.

UN General Assembly. 1966. International Covenant on Civil and Political Rights. UN Doc. A/6316. New York, NY: UN.

UN General Assembly. 1979. Convention on the Elimination of All Forms of Discrimination against Women. UN Doc. A/34/46. New York, NY: UN.

UN General Assembly. 1986. Declaration on Social and Legal Principles Relating to the Protection and Welfare of Children, with Special Reference to Foster Placement and Adoption Nationally and Internationally. UN Doc. A/RES/41/85. New York, NY: UN.

UN General Assembly. 1989. Convention on the Rights of the Child. UN Doc. A/44/49. New York, NY: UN.

UN General Assembly, Forty-fifth Session. 1990. International Convention on the Rights of All Migrant Workers and Members of Their Families. UN Doc. A/45/49. New York, NY: United Nations.

UN General Assembly, Fifty-fourth Session. 2000. Optional protocols to the Convention on the Rights of the Child on the involvement of children in armed conflict and on the sale of children, child prostitution and child pornography. UN Doc. A/RES/54/263. New York, NY: UN.

UN General Assembly, Eleventh Session. 2009. Open-ended working group on an optional protocol to the Convention on the Rights of the Child to provide a communications procedure. UN Doc. A/HRC/11/L.3. New York, NY: UN.

UN General Assembly, Thirteenth Session. 2010a. Report of the open-ended working group to explore the possibility of elaborating an optional protocol to the Convention on the Rights of the Child to provide a communications procedure. UN Doc. A/HRC/13/43. New York, NY: UN.

UN General Assembly, Sixty-fourth Session. 2010b. *Rights of the child*. UN Doc. A/RES/64/146. New York, NY: UN.

UNICEF. 2007. Press release: Child deaths fall below 10 million for first time. New York, NY: UNICEF.

Van Bueren, Geraldine. 1995. *The international law on the rights of the child*. New York, NY: Springer.

Van Bueren, Geraldine. 1998. Children's rights: Balancing traditional values and cultural plurality. In *Children's rights and traditional values*, eds. Gillian Douglas and Lelsie Sebba, 15–30. Hampshire, UK: Dartmouth.

Van Bueren, Geraldine. 2008a. *Child rights in Europe: Convergence and divergence in judicial protection*. Strasbourg, France: Council of Europe.

Van Bueren, Geraldine. 2008b. The separation of powers and the international legal status of the best interest of children in assisting domestic courts to protect children's economic and social rights. In *Rights of the child proceedings of the international conference*, eds. Tara M. Collins, Rachel Grondin, Veronica Piñero, Marie Pratte, and Marie-Claude Roberge, 237–73. Montreal: Wilson and Lafleur.

Van Bueren, Geraldine. Forthcoming. *The international law on the rights of the child*. 2nd ed.

Wollstonecraft, Mary. 2001. *A vindication of the rights of woman*. New York, NY: Penguin Books.

Public Policies and Child Rights: Entering the Third Decade of the Convention on the Rights of the Child

By
MARTA MAURÁS

After 20 years of implementation of the Convention on the Rights of the Child (CRC), it is increasingly clear that states bear the responsibility to promote, guarantee, respect, and fulfill the realization of children's rights by all members of the national and international communities. An initial emphasis on legal reforms to adapt national law to the CRC—absolutely necessary but not sufficient—needs to give space to changes in other important areas of public action: economic policy and financing; social policy and administration; and public participation, including that of children. Enforcement and justiciability of rights need to be addressed today to face questions about public policy, systems, and institutions in the long term. The evolution of social policies in Latin America and the Caribbean, from neoliberal policies to systems of social protection, illustrates that only a comprehensive and equity-based view of social and economic policy, underpinned by the four principles of children's rights (nondiscrimination, best interests of the child, survival and development, and the right to be heard), will satisfy the requirements for implementation of the CRC.

Keywords: child rights; public policies; justiciability; participation; social compact; social protection

With the Convention on the Rights of the Child (CRC) adopted in 1989, the concept of children took a radical turn: girls and boys ceased to be regarded as objects of protection and became recognized as subjects of rights. This clear-cut distinction has huge implications

Marta Maurás, a Chilean sociologist, is an expert in social policy, human rights, and international relations. She is member of the United Nation Committee on the Rights of the Child. In 2008, she was the special envoy for UNICEF to Latin America. Between 2005 and 2007, Maurás was secretary of the Economic Commission for Latin America and the Caribbean. Before that, she served in the office of UN Secretary General Kofi Annan. Between 1974 and 1998, she served with UNICEF in different technical and managerial positions, including regional director for Latin America and the Caribbean. She has also held teaching positions at Universidad Católica de Chile and Pontificia Universidad Católica de Rio de Janeiro.

DOI: 10.1177/0002716210382993

on the way states conduct business (as it has for families, communities, and children). It is increasingly clear that states bear the responsibility to promote, guarantee, respect, and fulfill the realization of children's rights by all members of national and international communities.

In 20 years of the CRC's existence, along with the other eight human rights treaties, much has happened in terms of state responsibility, both influenced by and influencing human rights implementation. This article reviews changes in the public sphere brought about by the introduction of a new human rights paradigm for public policy—that is, children have rights.

It makes the case that an initial emphasis on legal and normative reforms to adapt national law to the CRC needs to give space to changes in other important areas of public action, such as economic policy and financing; social policy and administration; and public participation, including that of children, leading to the enforcement of their rights.

The article reviews the evolution of social policies in the case of Latin America and the Caribbean, ranging from the liberal and neoliberal policies (neoconservative, from another point of view) to systems of social protection, to conclude that only a systemic view of social policy, underpinned by the four principles of children's rights (nondiscrimination, best interests of the child, survival and development, and the right to be heard), will satisfy the requirements of implementation of the CRC. It also reviews the work of the United Nation (UN) Committee on the Rights of the Child and makes some general recommendations for review given the new challenges.

The Law

Following an unprecedented rush to ratification, covering all countries except two,[1] the first two decades of the CRC's life have been greatly devoted to finding the juridical and normative expressions required to actually implement its provisions. Legislative activity was most intense in the 1990s to try to define within the legal frameworks of most member states what was meant by "children's rights."

Old legislation was reviewed and new laws were passed in most cases dealing with Article 3 (best interests of the child) and Article 12 (right of the child to be heard), the new pillars of this children's rights approach. To abandon the welfare paradigm, many countries undertook reforms of their penal codes or the so-called "minors"[2] codes designed in the nineteenth and early twentieth centuries to "protect" children—mostly the poor or those in "especially difficult circumstances." This was the case, in particular, in countries within the civil law tradition (García-Mendez 2010).

Despite these achievements, very few cases of an integral or holistic application of the CRC to national law can be found even today. The most paradigmatic example of such a comprehensive piece of legislation is the Brazilian Statute on the Child and the Adolescent passed in July 1990 as a culmination of the 1980s process leading the country to restore democracy after military rule. Other examples of a unified body of child law exist in Egypt, Kenya, Mozambique, Nigeria, Sierra Leone, South Africa, Tanzania, Tunisia, and Vietnam.

By now, a second generation of legislative reform has begun to emerge, with some countries reviewing and reforming legislation passed immediately after the CRC came into effect. Sometimes this has happened to reflect a better understanding of child rights, for example in Mozambique, which raised the marriage age to 18 for both boys and girls.

In other countries, retrogressively, as recently in some Central American countries, there is a trend toward reducing the age of criminal responsibility of children and increasing sentences against children in conflict with the law. This change is a reaction by some political leaders and legislators to an increased perception of insecurity in the society, which leads to a distorted image of "high criminal activity" by children (despite evidence to the contrary that shows that children are victims more than victimizers) and the application of unsuccessful policies of "high-handedness" (*mano dura*) (see UNICEF 2007; Maurás 2008; Organización de los Estados Americanos y Comisión Interamericana de Derechos Humanos 2009). Yet it is encouraging to note that such actions are not being taken without debate and resistance, as, for example in El Salvador, where legislation to this effect was passed by Parliament in early 2010 but vetoed by the president of the republic.

Still other states are failing entirely to translate international obligations on human rights into national law or are simply not implementing existing laws. Save the Children Fund's (SCF) recent review of legislation in thirteen countries with the highest infant mortality rates in the world found a clear link between legislation and demonstrated political commitment on child survival. In Niger and Afghanistan, two countries that have no legislation to tackle the intermediate causes of child mortality, the governments lacked any clear strategy to prevent children from dying. Meanwhile Brazil and Egypt, which are both on track to reach Millennium Development Goal (MDG) 4—a two-thirds reduction in under-five mortality by 2015—have used legal reform to underpin their efforts (Save the Children 2010, 2).

The UN Committee on the Rights of the Child, the international body of experts created to monitor the CRC (Article 43), has placed much emphasis on legislative reform. Many of its members were and continue to be lawyers and doctors in law and human rights, in particular. One of the tests that the committee uses to assess the application of the CRC when reviewing a member state's report is—without prescribing an optimal legislative framework—whether the different courts have adopted decisions quoting the provisions of the CRC. With this test, the committee aims to determine the enforcement and justiciability (meaning the competence of a court, once a right is recognized as part of law, to enforce and adjudicate on it) of economic, social, and cultural rights, along with civil and political rights.

In 2009, as part of its review for the 20th anniversary of the CRC, UNICEF looked at the state of legislation in fifty-two countries (UNICEF 2009). Of these, two-thirds had incorporated the CRC into national law, and their courts had adopted decisions quoting its provisions. One-third of the fifty-two had incorporated into their national Constitution the provisions, or some provisions, of the CRC, and some countries had adopted new or reformed child codes.

Monitoring the impact of existing legislation will do much to make laws more effective. Yet it is increasingly clear to legislators, policy-makers, academics, and activists that to leave behind discriminatory and authoritarian forms of relating to children that impede the full exercise of their rights, the law is absolutely necessary but not sufficient. Legislation can help to preserve progressive policies (including institutions and resources) despite changes in government[3] and can provide civil society a powerful tool for advocacy and demands for action, but it will not by itself push further implementation of the CRC. The conclusion is that enforcement and justiciability of rights are issues that need to be addressed and that doing so leads to questions regarding public policy.

Interestingly, recent case studies that the Pan American Health Organization (PAHO) and WHO presented to a technical consultation on health and child and adolescents' rights, which WHO, SCF, World Vision, and UNICEF organized in Geneva, Switzerland, in May 2010, describe how the Ministries of Health in Guatemala and Honduras requested technical assistance from PAHO to support their argument that the CRC and the committee's concluding observations obligate states to pass legislation. In the case of Guatemala, Parliament established "the legal capacity of adolescents to consent to HIV/AIDS treatment without parental consent, access of young people to HIV services and treatment, voluntary testing, and family planning methods"; and in Honduras, the Supreme Court ruled that there was the need to provide adolescents "access to emergency contraception" (Vasquez and Morlachetti 2010).

Both these events set a new stage in the use of the CRC and of the concluding observations of the committee in policymaking by states (and in advocacy by WHO). One can deduce from them that for the law to be applied, two interlinked factors are required: on one hand, a true understanding of the profound cultural change implied by the CRC and, on the other, public policies and programs that frame state and civil society actions based on children and adolescent rights.

Therefore, while continuing to improve the normative and legislative national frameworks, there is a need to move more rigorously with analysis, action, and communication into the policy, resource allocation, and institutional/administrative environments required to make children's rights a reality in all countries. Therein lie the challenges as we enter the third decade of the CRC.

Linking Public Policies and Child Rights

Development policies and human rights belong to two different, albeit complementary, paradigms. The human development paradigm aims to improve human capacities and quality of life; the human rights paradigm, to improve freedom and equality (UNDP 2000). These paradigms need to be brought together, or they risk running in separate tracks: the hard reality of needs and the "soft" aspiration of rights.

When defining priorities, actions, and mobilizing for rights, the difference between the "top-down" design that public institutions (duty bearers) use and the "bottom-up" approach that the subjects of rights (rights bearers) use—in particular children—makes it difficult for public policies and human rights to meet coherently in the public sphere. If rights and human development complement each other, then public policies, laws, and mechanisms of protection of rights (juridical, administrative, and financial) must coordinate under the umbrella of a comprehensive policy and a common strategy.

When examining the effect of social and economic policies on poverty reduction and social integration, the UN Economic Commission for Latin America and the Caribbean (ECLAC/CEPAL) has been making the case over a decade that three dimensions need to be present:[4]

- high and sustained economic growth to generate more and better jobs and a strengthened taxation system;
- an integrated and effective social policy that can impact the determinants of access to employment (equal capabilities and opportunities) and provide the compensation mechanisms for the poorest and most vulnerable; and
- a sense of belonging by way of a social and intergenerational contract, generating social agreements based on rights, including the solidarity mechanisms to finance social protection and security.

Economic growth

After a long period of recession and increased poverty (the so-called "lost decade of the 1980s" and the "difficult 1990s"), Latin America has had, since 2000, better indicators of economic growth and better-shaped social policies that have decreased poverty to 33 percent of the total population in 2008—a success experienced by almost all countries in the region. Yet the effects of the ongoing global economic crisis threaten to redress once more the progress that has been made.

This is an all-too-familiar scenario in the region where, in the recent past, repeated crises (the big debt crisis in the 1980s and several smaller ones in the 1990s, including the effects of the Asian crisis) have delayed poverty reduction. The 1980 GDP per capita of US$3,620.00 per year and poverty levels of 40.5 percent worsened over the next 15 years because of economic crises. Poverty only started to diminish close to 1994 when GDP per capita was able to return back to 1980 levels. The poverty level decreased to 39.8 percent in 2005, when GDP increased to US$4,000.00 per year. Due to population growth, it was only in 2006 that the number of poor people became slightly lower than in 1990, that is, 194 million poor and 71 million extremely poor (see CEPAL 2009a, 2009b, 2009c; World Bank 2009).

Since 2000, sustained—albeit moderate—growth, prudent fiscal policy, and moderately increased social investments (countercyclical policies) lowered the poverty rate to 33 percent by 2008. Nevertheless, ECLAC/CEPAL forecast an upward trend (9 million additional poor people, of which 5 million are extremely poor), with GDP estimated to decrease by only 1.8 percent in 2009 due to the most recent wave of global financial and economic crises.

Only six countries (Argentina, Brazil, Chile, Ecuador, Mexico, and Panama) had, by 2008, reached the level required to halve poverty by 2015, as agreed upon in the MDGs. Employment has been increasing somewhat, but indications are that remittances have been affected by the global crisis, decreasing between 2008 and 2009 by 10 to 15 percent. In addition, the Latin American tax base is much lower than in most other regions of the world (except for Southeast Asia), with an average of 18 percent of GDP and no progress in sight.

These financial gaps occur against the permanent backdrop of acute inequalities in the region—the most unequal in the world, with an average Gini coefficient in 2007 of 0.5 (only sub-Saharan Africa and East Asia average more than 0.4, with the rest of the world being much lower). While income inequality has been a constant feature in Latin America, it started to slowly decline from 2002 to 2007. As Cornia has pointed out, "A continuation of fiscally prudent distributive and redistributive policies should preserve most of the income inequality gains recorded in recent years. Changes can be attributed to external shocks and changes in macroeconomic, educational and social domestic policies since the left-of-center wave of governments hit the region. An important factor . . . was the rise in public social expenditure" (Cornia 2010).

Inequality does not only exist in terms of distribution of income but also as imbalances in social outcomes by gender and age, social origin, and place of residence, such as reduced calorie intake despite economic growth in some countries or more unemployment for women than for men. Social segregation and discrimination are prevalent, and authoritarian streaks appear in retrogressive legislation. Violence, in the form of physical or psychological punishment and bullying and sexual abuse, against children and women has become a reality in schools and within families and is featured daily in the media.

Integrated and effective social policy

A brief review of the evolution of social policy in Latin America illustrates progress made and also shows the challenges and opportunities for the realization of human rights, particularly child rights.

A great deal of innovation in social policy has taken place in Latin America. For example, conditional cash transfer programs aimed at disadvantaged groups were born in this region. The first, Bolsa Escola in Brazil, was the country's response to poverty and the need to put children in school. It has been followed today by much more massive and complex social protection programs in Brazil as well as in many other countries in the region and in other regions.[5] More recently, a variety of policies to tackle the 2008 economic crisis have included consumer subsidies, unemployment subsidies, social security, job generation, as well as the protection of poor families; some of these policies have had a notable gender and life cycle focus. More important, social public spending has not been decreased during the recent crises and has moved from US$318 per capita in 1990 and 1991 to US$819 per capita in 2008 (CEPAL 2009b).[6] Yet a third of the population is still under the poverty line, and child mortality levels are behind the MDG target of halving mortality by 2015 in more than half of the countries.

There is a need, therefore, to articulate a comprehensive framework of social policy that goes beyond simply being a tool to reduce poverty and compensate for the inequalities and imbalances that the market operations generate. To advance toward more cohesive societies and democratic states requires what is now being called "comprehensive systems of social protection." This system is a wise combination of economic, social, cultural, and environmental public policies, underpinned by human rights, all of which reinforce each other and are aimed at building egalitarian and open societies. Everywhere in the world today, the dilemma facing governments is to find a human rights–based balance among economic growth, social progress, and environmental sustainability. Latin America and the Caribbean are no exception.

The typology that Raczynsky and Serrano (Serrano 2005) propose on the functions of social policy—understood as the organized action of the state in the social sphere—is useful for the analysis here. The functions of the state include (1) provision of assistance and protection, (2) promotion of well-being, (3) realization of social rights, and (4) generation of a social space of belonging. These are not mutually exclusive. They have not developed in a linear way in Latin America or elsewhere, but jointly and progressively they can lead to an active state that guarantees rights.

In the early twentieth century in Europe and in the Americas, assistance and protection were the first manifestations of a state's systemic action, aimed at the growing working class linked to industrialization and urban life. This action marked, in effect, the appearance of labor rights, later linked to the idea of ensuring minimum standards of living for lower-income groups. Up to this point, social policy or "social protection" had been understood only in terms of leveling differences, without aiming at equalizing opportunities, a concept that evolved later.

Welfare is another function that the welfare states in Europe typified. The state in this case was in charge of generating opportunities through the expansion of labor rights and universal access to health and education. Such an approach was forward-looking and essentially linked to sector policies. However, the welfare approach came under heavy questioning and was replaced by a neoliberal model, focusing more on assistance and protection than on social integration and expansion of opportunities. Now, the pendulum has begun to swing back to more complex concepts of welfare and social protection. Today, these concepts are understood to mean the recognition of social rights through public services and benefits, both universal and selective, using equity criteria for their application and targeting the most disadvantaged.

Realization of social rights is not a new agenda in social policy, but in the context of a global economy that has been generating persistent exclusion throughout several "adjustment" periods, often accompanied by social and political crises, the core principles of the human rights agenda—the rights to dignity, life, equality, and work—emerge strongly.

A sense of belonging

The last function of this typology is the generation and preservation of social spaces of belonging. Social policy, according to this function, is not just a list of benefits from the state to the people but the ability to share and socially construct values of integration and equality in a given national or subnational community. The market logic does not allow for this space of belonging, and states inspired only by it will not be able to construct social cohesion and welfare without introducing dialogue and encouraging the full exercise of citizenship. Contemporary social policy implies public commitments—widely known and subject to public control—between citizens and state institutions.

In Latin America, highly centralized and hierarchical state institutions and agents still prevail. At the same time, progress in building democracy in the past 30 years, along with the spread of global information and communication technology and universal access to basic education, has created a more demanding citizenship, more conscious about its rights and making the case for their enforcement. The "Penguins' Revolution" in Chile in 2007 (so called because of the blue and white uniform of secondary students) was the first acute crisis of Michelle Bachelet's presidency and resulted in a shift in the focus of government priorities toward quality education, financing, open administrative and school regimes, and other education issues. Dialogue and debates are still far from being part of the generalized practice for policy- and decision-makers, and their sustainability (in Chile and elsewhere) needs to be tested as governments change.

New Challenges for the Application of the CRC

As seen from the example of Latin America, new challenges for the application of the CRC are using the rights of children as a lever for more equitable, open, and progressive societies and creating "comprehensive systems of social protection" that not only protect but also promote social integration and provide expansion of opportunities to all and open spaces for dialogue.

The four core principles of the CRC, rights unto themselves, can guide policy design and implementation. They constitute a "litmus test" of progressive public policy to implement child rights.

The first principle comprises nondiscrimination and universality and their interdependence (Article 2). In other words, public policies aimed at children, with human rights approaches, need to cover all rights for all girls, boys, and adolescents in a country, along their life cycle as children.

The second principle involving the best interests of the child (Article 3) implies a horizontal view of all policies and of all subjects of policies and a distribution of resources in the best interests of the child to the maximum extent possible. This means that it is today (not tomorrow) that all the resources available need to be used in a progressive way, and universal public policies for children need to be adopted. A real test of good governance would be to apply the best interest of the child to public policy and resource distribution in general.

The third principle is survival and development or the right to be alive and lead a life of evolving and growing capacities (Article 6). Applying this principle requires paying attention to the outcome of policies, programs, and services. Therefore, what matters, from a public policy point of view, is not the quantity and quality of services but their result, for example, in lowering infant mortality.

The last principle is the right to be heard (Article 12), which requires creating a systematic practice of consulting children and listening to them in matters that affect them. It implies the state's obligation to produce an environment for this—for families, teachers, social workers, judges, security forces, politicians, and many others to be able to hear children's views and to create the spaces for communications (see UN Committee on the Rights of the Child 2009).[7]

Realizing the importance of elaborating on the enforcement of rights as a state responsibility, the UN Committee on the Rights of the Child (2003) issued General Comment 5, expanding on Article 4 of the CRC, which deals with the adoption of all administrative, legislative, and other measures to realize child rights to the maximum extent possible; and on dissemination (Articles 42 and 44).This general comment covers a vast spectrum of state action from legislation, national strategy, administration, decentralization, and coordination to budget formulation, data and statistics collection, and training. It builds on the Plan of Action for Implementing the World Declaration on the Survival, Protection, and Development of Children (UNICEF 1990) and on the document that the UN General Assembly's special session on children issued in 2002, among others.

A critical analysis reveals that the thinking behind the general comment from the UN Committee on the Rights of the Child was still framed in top-down planning and was not yet incorporating a holistic or systemic view of policy based on human rights and equity financing. The committee acknowledged the difficulty of the task by stating that it "probably will formulate later more detailed general observations on the different elements [of the general measures of implementation]" (UN Committee on the Rights of the Child 2003, Preamble).

Along this line, the committee held in 2007 a Day of General Discussion (UN Committee on the Rights of the Child 2007), where the question of investing in children through the national budget (and international cooperation) was explored in more detail. The committee's concluding observations of States Parties' reports since this discussion in 2007 have begun to reflect expanded knowledge, new practices, and updated technologies on budget management aimed at realizing children's rights.

A virtuous cycle of "monitoring-reporting-learning-recommending-applying-monitoring" by the committee and a state on policymaking for children's rights, using the States Parties' report, is thus generated and can be further improved. As planning processes and methods evolve in countries and national and international research provides evidence on the effectiveness of these methods, there will continue to be a need to review and revise committee guidelines on general measures of implementation. At least four areas in need of continued review can be identified (see Sheahan 2010).

The first area to review on an ongoing basis is legislation to proceed with the incorporation of the CRC into the respective national body of law. A bottom-up approach to legislative reform is to be encouraged, driven by public concerns and an increasing consensus for the protection of children linked to broader policy. For example, evidence that UNICEF and the United Nations Population Fund collected in Senegal and The Gambia on female genital mutilation suggests that legislative measures banning harmful practices must be developed, taking into consideration the social, cultural, political, and historical context onto which they are superimposed. Otherwise, reactions may be negative, such as continuing with the practice of female genital mutilation in secrecy or hiring unqualified practitioners to perform it. At the same time, mechanisms need to be established to test all new legislation against the CRC and ensure and evaluate its enforcement. Such mechanisms should include the withdrawal of reservations[8] stipulated by states at the time of the state's ratification.

Data and statistics for planning, monitoring, and evaluating policy and programs constitute a second area for continual review. An ongoing task is to review and revise indicators of child rights realizations in the different areas that the CRC covers. States need to strengthen statistical systems, ensuring the production of national- and subnational-level disaggregated data by age group, gender, ethnic group, socioeconomic status, and other appropriate categories, keeping in line with international standards to ensure quality and comparability. Research on specific issues regarding implementation is also required, especially on emerging issues such as the environment and migration. The ultimate aim is to ensure evidence-based public action for children's rights.

Participatory planning for social policy is a third area to review. Ongoing state reform processes are necessary entry points to examine and improve the area of participation. For example, countries where there have been radical constitutional reforms—such as Ecuador and Bolivia, where indigenous peoples' collective rights and participation have been brought to the fore in normative and policy terms—will need to be followed up closely to help to formulate comprehensive policies and enforce child rights. In all cases, issues of decentralization and local management are critically in need of being better studied to ensure civil societies', communities', and children's participation in planning and, thus, to generate the social agreements that would give sustenance to comprehensive public policies.

The assessment of gender policies across economic, social, and environmental dimensions is also essential. These policies should not be confined to cash transfers or to day-care centers, important as they are for the family, especially in crisis periods. Such policies should aim at supporting women to lead fulfilled lives, starting from childhood, and to balance work and family responsibilities for both women and men.

The allocation of resources for children's rights is a fourth area that needs continued evaluation. The committee has recommended that States Parties increase allocations for children's rights, to protect allocations from shifts in priorities or changes in revenue, to manage resources more efficiently to achieve established targets and evaluate impact, to use track indicators, and to ensure participation in decision-making about resource allocation. Yet in general, States Parties do not quantify resources spent on children, nor are they able to demonstrate how priorities get set in resource allocation. Work that UNICEF, UNDP, and the World Bank are doing to build strategic budgets that can lay out priorities, monitor, and evaluate impact on children is crucial. Likewise, there is a need to improve the dialogue between the committee and States Parties in regard to equity financing in general (based on a redistributive taxation system) and financing for children's rights specifically, including solidarity financing of social protection. Simply calling for States Parties to draw up national plans of action on children's rights (as the committee is currently doing, following its General Comment 5) does not satisfy the requirement for these plans to form comprehensive protection policies that are supported by the national budget and in which children figure centrally.

A sterling example of the implementation of such a broad policy is San Juan Province in Argentina (Ministerio de Desarrollo Social 2010), where, in 2004, a comprehensive policy on children, adolescents, and the family was adopted, based on public dialogue with civil society (including the business sector and labor unions) and a political compact between the nation, the province, and the municipalities. On the legal side, a provincial law for the integral protection of children and adolescents was passed (San Juan Province 2004), based on the CRC and was later reformed to conform to the subsequent National Law 26.061 on a "System for the Integral Protection of Children" (Congress of Argentina 2005). On the political side, a "Pact for Children" was drawn up, defining standards for municipal responsibility in the province to protect and guarantee the rights of girls, boys, and adolescents. On the technical and financial sides, a policy to deconcentrate resources in favor of municipalities has supported the establishment in all nineteen districts of directorates or bureaus for children and the family. In addition, in 2009, a law on family violence was promulgated (San Juan Province 2009) and mechanisms established to prevent violence, protect victims, and prosecute perpetrators. Likewise, the Penal Code is being reformed to establish a system of juvenile justice, based on guarantees that the CRC and other international law set out.

The impact on children of such an articulation of a comprehensive policy is beginning to be seen. San Juan, being a small and fairly underdeveloped province, has had no case of severe malnutrition in five years. School matriculation has increased by 25.6 percent, and dropout rates have decreased. San Juan is on its way to lowering infant mortality to a single digit, a historic landmark, if achieved. It has deinstitutionalized twelve hundred children under 16 and created a program to provide them with family alternatives, supported by counselors, social workers and other trained professionals, and subsidies. Children and adolescents meet every year to discuss human rights and democracy, and an experimental human rights curriculum has been introduced in schools.

Finally, in the international scene, enforcement will remain incomplete if the CRC continues to be the only human rights treaty without a communication and complaints mechanism.[9] The Human Rights Council has established a working group to draft an optional protocol to the CRC to create the appropriate international forum for individual complaints from girls, boys, adolescents, and/or their representatives who are seeking justice and reparation. This should go a long way in stimulating States Parties' realization of child rights.

In conclusion, the bridge between public policies and child rights is being constructed. The CRC is the normative framework of a new human rights paradigm for public policy, that is, children's rights.

Its enforcement has brought about changes in the public sphere with an initial emphasis on legal and normative reforms to adapt national law to the CRC. Changes in other important areas of public action, such as economic policy and financing, social policy and administration, and public participation, especially for children, leading to the enforcement of children's rights, have also been occurring to different degrees and are being reported by States Parties to the UN Committee.

As social policies evolve—from the so-called neoliberal policies (with a conservative value system) to comprehensive systems of social protection that aim to balance economic growth with equity development concerns—only a comprehensive view, underpinned by the four principles of children's rights, will satisfy the requirements for the implementation of human and children's rights.

The CRC as a mandatory international instrument, spelling out the rights of children and adolescents, is clearly linked to difficult processes of democratization of a society and within the family. The profound cultural transformation that requires changes in the relationship between parents, children, and the state, and between parents and children, where children are subjects of rights, needs to be sustained by a legal framework as well as by the implementation of policies, plans, and institutions truly inspired by the CRC—not a minor issue for policy-makers and for society at large.

Notes

1. To date, 193 UN General Assembly members have ratified the CRC. The United States and Somalia remain as the only two members who have not. The United States has ratified the CRC's two optional protocols on children in armed conflict and on the sale of children, child prostitution, and child pornography.

2. Influenced by the CRC, the term *minor* (still used in Europe and the United States) in Latin America derogatorily denotes a child or adolescent who is seen as a threat to public safety, mostly stigmatized by virtue of being poor, in conflict with the law, or abandoned by his or her family. In most of the region, the phrase "boys, girls, and adolescents" is replacing "minor."

3. A case in point is legislation passed in the Chilean Congress during the last months of President Michelle Bachelet's government (2006–2010) to convert into law the successful program and system for the Integral Protection of Children known as "Chile Crece Contigo" (Congress of Chile 2009).

4. Growth with equity has been the *leit motif* of ECLAC/CEPAL policy recommendations to governments since the late 1990s. CEPAL's annual publications and special studies have made the case for a new social contract, including a fiscal pact to ensure equity financing of public policies, as well as updating economic and social data to support such financing.

5. UNICEF Regional Offices in South Asia and East Asia and the Pacific have been engaged in the analysis of the evolution of social and economic policies in these regions and have abundant literature on the subject.

6. Dollar amounts expressed in 2000 U.S. dollars, for an average in twelve countries.

7. A "general comment" by the UN Committee on the Rights of the Child is the distillation of pronouncements in the form of conclusions and recommendations on States Parties' reports regarding

particular articles of the CRC that, in the committee's judgement, require clarification according to the times, new knowledge, and new experiences. A "Day of General Discussion" may be the prelude to such general comments. To date, the committee has issued twelve general comments.

8. Reservations are objections by a state to a specific provision of a treaty; they do not impede action and can be withdrawn at any time.

9. See Van Bueren's article in this volume.

References

CEPAL. 2009a. *Balance preliminar de las economías de América Latina y el Caribe* [Preliminary overview of the economies of Latin America and the Caribbean]. Santiago, Chile: División de Desarrollo Económico, CEPAL.

CEPAL. 2009b. *Inversión extranjera en América Latina y el Caribe* [Foreign direct investment in Latin American and the Caribbean]. Santiago, Chile: CEPAL.

CEPAL. 2009c. *Panorama social de América Latina* [Social panorama of Latin America]. Santiago, Chile: CEPAL.

Congress of Argentina. 2005. Comprehensive Protection Bill of Rights: Girls, Boys, and Adolescents. Law 26.061. Buenos Aires, Argentina: Congreso de la República Argentina.

Congress of Chile. 2009. Chile Crece Contigo. Law 20.379. Santiago, Chile: Congreso de Chile.

Cornia, Andrea. *Recovery with a human face*. In UNICEF "Recovery with a human face" network [e-discussion]. New York, NY: UNICEF. Available from http://sites.google.com/site/recoverywithahumanfacenetwork (accessed 28 May 2010).

García-Mendez, Emilio. 2010. De las relaciones públicas al neomenorismo: 20 años de Convención Internacional de los Derechos del Niño en America Latina (1989–2009). In *Revista Criminología, de Cuadernos de Doctrina y Jurisprudencia Penal*. Buenos Aires, Argentina: Editorial Ad Hoc. Available from www.surargentina.org.ar/10_-_mayo_-_EGM_-_20_anos_CDN.pdf (accessed 22 July 2010).

Maurás, Marta. 2008. La Adolescencia y la Juventud en las Políticas Públicas de Iberoamérica [Adolescents and youth in the public policies of Ibero America]. *Revista FORO Chile 21* Año 8–N°77.

Ministerio de Desarrollo Social, República Argentina. 2010. Aplicación de la Convención de los Derechos del Niño. Lista de Cuestiones relacionadas al Examen del Tercer Informe Periódico. Presented to the Committee on the Rights of the Child, 15 April. Geneva.

Organización de los Estados Americanos y Comisión Interamericana de Derechos Humanos. 2009. *Informe sobre Seguridad Ciudadana y Derechos Humanos*. OEA/Ser.L/V/II. Doc. 57. Washington, DC: Comisión Interamericana de Derechos Humanos.

San Juan Province. 2004. Full Protection of the Rights of All Children and Adolescents. Law no. 7338. San Juan, Argentina: Chamber of Deputies of the Province of San Juan.

San Juan Province. 2009. Family Violence Act. Law no. 7943. San Juan, Argentina: Chamber of Deputies of the Province of San Juan.

Save the Children. 2010. *Why law matters for children's survival*. Policy Brief. London: Save the Children. Available from www.savethechildren.org.uk/en/54_11022.htm (accessed 22 July 2010).

Serrano, Claudia. 2005. *Claves de la política social para la pobreza*. Proyecto FONDECYT no. 1040260. Consultora Asesorías para el Desarrollo. Available from www.asesoriasparaeldesarrollo.cl/files/claves_politica_social_para_la_probreza.pdf.

Sheahan, Frances, for Save the Children. 2010. *Preventing the preventable: An analysis of CRC concluding observations on the right to survival*. Oslo, Norway: Save the Children.

UNDP. 2000. *Human development report 2000*. New York, NY: United Nations Publications.

UNICEF. 1990. *Plan of action for implementing the World Declaration on the Survival, Protection, and Development of Children*. New York, NY: UNICEF.

UNICEF. 2007. *El Impacto de las Armas Pequeñas en los Niños y Adolescentes en Costa Rica, El Salvador, Jamaica y Trinidad y Tobago* [The impact of small arms on children and adolescents in Costa Rica, El Salvador, Jamaica, and Trinidad and Tobago]. New York, NY: UNICEF.

UNICEF. 2009. *Celebrating 20 years of the Convention on the Rights of the Child*. The State of the World's Children, Special Edition. New York, NY: UNICEF.

United Nations (UN) Committee on the Rights of the Child, Thirty-fourth Session. 2003. *General measures of implementation of the Convention on the Rights of the Child*. General Comment no. 5. UN Doc. CRC/GC/2003/5. Geneva: UN.

UN Committee on the Rights of the Child, Forty-sixth Session. 2007. *Day of general discussion on "Resources for the Rights of the Child—Responsibility of States."* Geneva: UN.

UN Committee on the Rights of the Child, Fifty-first Session. 2009. *The right of the child to be heard*. General Comment no. 12. UN Doc. CRC/C/GC/12. Geneva: UN.

UN General Assembly, Twenty-seventh Special Session. 2002. *A world fit for children*. UN Doc. A/RES/S-27/2. New York, NY: United Nations.

Vasquez, Javier, and Alejandro Morlachetti for Pan American Health Organization/World Health Organization. 2010. Case study—Monitoring and evaluation. National follow-up to CRC concluding observations and recommendations for Guatemala and Honduras. Presented at the Technical Consultation on the Practical Application of the Convention on the Rights of the Child to Advance Child and Adolescent Health in Countries, 10–11 May 2010. Geneva.

World Bank. 2009. *World development report 2009: Spacial disparities and developmental policy*. Washington, DC: World Bank.

The Promise of Citizenship for Brazilian Children: What Has Changed?

By
IRENE RIZZINI

This article explores the ideas behind the promise of citizenship to children in Brazil. The human rights of children has become a very important issue in Brazil. This has been especially true since the inclusion of Article 227 in the 1988 Constitution referring to children's rights and the approval of the Statute on the Child and the Adolescent in 1990, less than a year after the ratification of the United Nations Convention on the Rights of the Child (CRC). The article examines the changing discourse connected to what was promised and what the law actually accomplished. The conclusion focuses on some of the most relevant improvements affecting children's lives and some of the remaining challenges Brazilians face in the attempt to keep the promises made in the Constitution and the statute.

Keywords: citizenship; children's rights; law; implementation; public policies

Since the approval of the Statute on the Child and the Adolescent in 1990 (Brasil 1990), less than a year after the ratification of the United Nations (UN) Convention on the Rights of the Child (CRC), children's rights have become an important issue in Brazil. Before these events, Brazil had gone through 20 years of

Irene Rizzini is a professor and a researcher at the Pontifical Catholic University of Rio de Janeiro, Brazil, and director of the International Center for Research on Childhood (CIESPI). She served as president of Childwatch International Research Network from 2002 to 2009. She held the visiting chair in Brazilian cultural studies at the Helen Kellogg Institute for International Studies at the University of Notre Dame in 2006 and was appointed a John Simon Guggenheim Memorial Foundation fellow in 2008. She is the author and editor of several books, among them Disinherited from Society: Street Children in Latin America *(Editora Universitaria Santa Ursula 1995);* Children and the Law in Brazil—Revisiting the History (1822–2000) *(Editora Universitaria Santa Ursula 2002);* Globalization and Children *(coedited with Natalie Hevener Kaufman) (Kluwer Academic 2002);* The Lost Century: The Historical Roots of Public Policies on Children in Brazil *(Editora Cortez 2008, 2nd ed.);* The Art of Governing Children: The History of Social Policies, Legislation and Child Welfare in Brazil *(Editora Cortez 2009, 2nd ed.).*

DOI: 10.1177/0002716210383950

brutal military dictatorship, and the country was eager to see the institutionalization of democratic practices on many fronts. In the 1980s, there was a burst of social mobilization aimed at the recognition of people's rights. In 1988, Brazil completely reformulated its Constitution (Brasil 1988) to promulgate the Citizens' Constitution (*a Constituição cidadã*), as it became known, which focused on the detailed rights of all citizens.

Interestingly, children became one of the most powerful targets of these social movements, especially marginalized children. So-called "street children" (children who were visible as they spent their days on the street) became a particular focus of attention,[1] representing clear evidence of the lack of social justice in the country.

The new Constitution had one article totally dedicated to children's rights. Article 227 of the Constitution became a symbol of the struggle to improve children's lives and a major driving force for the intense mobilization that took place in the coming years. The introduction to Section 227 of the Constitution states,

> It is obligatory that the family, society and the state assure the child and adolescent as an absolute priority of the right to life, health, nutrition, education, leisure, a professional training, culture, dignity, respect and liberty, and to living together in a family and community, also to place them in safety from every form of negligence, discrimination, exploitation, violence, cruelty and oppression.[2]

There was a new sense of hope that things could indeed change, and the possibility of change was clearly associated with the idea of citizenship—a hope that was expressed in the popular motto "*de menor a cidadão*": from minor to citizens. In Brazil, the term *menor* includes, in addition to the notion of a young person, the sense of a child or young person who is seen as a threat to public safety. So the term carries some of the same stigma attached in English to the terms *abandoned* and/or *delinquent* children. The term in Portuguese implies, moreover, that these are children who should be subject to some kind of official intervention. *De menor a cidadão* was often used in Brazil in the 1990s, particularly by advocates, to mark the struggle to recognize that all children, including poor children, had rights as citizens.

This article explores the ideas behind the promise of citizenship to children in Brazil. It discusses what the 1990 federal law on the child and the adolescent promised, the changing discourse connected to what was promised, and what the law actually accomplished. The conclusion focuses on some of the most relevant improvements affecting children's lives and some of the remaining challenges that we face in the attempt to keep the promises made in the Constitution and the statute.

The Promise in Law

As the CRC was being framed and debated, the Brazilian Congress, still working on strengthening the new democracy, passed the Statute on the Child and the Adolescent (Brasil 1990).[3] The framers of the Brazilian legislation were aware of the international debates on children's rights, and the legislation reflected some of those debates. The major conceptual change embedded in the legislation was that children were to be the "subject of rights" as citizens. The underlying rationale of the laws relating to children was changed from *Doutrina da Situação Irregular* (principles for children in irregular situations), a phrase that reinforced the stigma of the poor, abandoned, or delinquent children, to *Doutrina da Proteção Integral*, the principle of promoting full protection for all children.

This shift in the paradigm, led by the legal community, started in Brazil and spread rapidly to other countries in Latin America. References to the Doctrine of Full Protection appear in textbooks in various parts of the continent. Similar ideas and practices were finding their way in proposals to implement the idea and adopt the new conceptions of childhood in such places as exemplified in this text published in Mexico:

> The Doctrine of Full Protection . . . constitutes an interdisciplinary theoretical construct . . . which takes the shape of something that enables us to respond to the demands of various social actors—among whom are minors—in the sense that the construct modifies institutional structures from the position of new concepts of childhood and new adopted ideas. (Beristáin and Campos 2006, 16)[4]

Another key element of the statute was the provision that mandated the creation of Children's Rights Councils at the federal, state, and municipal levels. The Children's Rights Councils are mandated to develop, elaborate, and monitor the implementation of key policies on children that the responsible public departments or secretariats in the so-called System for Guaranteeing Rights (*Sistema de Garantia de Direitos*) are then to adopt and implement. In theory, this provision creates an unprecedented balance or "parity" between government and civil society as membership is equally divided between the two sectors. The reality of this theory is discussed later in this article.

The ratification of the CRC gradually has had a major impact on the history of childhood in the twentieth century. Despite the many struggles in implementing the law, the new concept that children were entitled to human rights has become firmly established in the past few decades. The same can be said about the CRC's impact on the Brazilian statute and the implications of that law in Brazil. Encompassing both broad and specific provisions, the Statute on the Child and the Adolescent includes this new concept of children in its articles.

> Article 3. Without prejudice to the full protection treated in this Law, the child and adolescent enjoy all the fundamental rights inherent to the human person and, by law or other means, are ensured of all opportunities and facilities so as to entitle them to physical, mental, moral, spiritual and social development, in conditions of freedom and dignity.
>
> Article 4. It is the duty of the family, community, society in general and the public authority to ensure, with absolute priority, effective implementation of the rights to life, health, nutrition, education, sports, leisure, vocational training, culture, dignity, respect, freedom and family and community living.

Article 18. It is the duty of all to watch over the dignity of the child and adolescent, preserving them from any inhuman, violent, terrorizing, vexing or coercive treatment.

Article 19. Every child or adolescent has the right to be raised and educated in the midst of his family and, exceptionally, in a foster family, in such a way as to ensure family and community life in an environment free of the presence of persons dependent on narcotic substances.[5]

Similar to the CRC, some of the statute's articles can be considered so broad that they become utopian. Notwithstanding this utopian element, there is general agreement in Brazil that these laws played an important role in establishing new parameters for action and in encouraging significant changes in social attitudes. Whatever Brazilians' or non-Brazilians' view of this utopian element, it is clear that the statute, building on the Constitution, deliberately takes a much broader view of human rights than constitutions that are mainly concerned with due process of law.

While we should not underplay the difficulties of even beginning to implement some of these rights, the statute represents a fundamental shift in the legal and rights frameworks for children, and that shift is a necessary condition for change on the ground. As Kaufman and I said in an earlier article,

> Even at the level of the national state, law cannot transform society over night. It can, however, set forth an expectation of governmental as well as non-governmental behavior and these expectations can in turn legitimize policies and programs which contribute to changing attitudes and actions. Normally, some attitudes have changed in order to bring about a change in law and the law can then provide a basis for moving forward that particular set of values. (Kaufman and Rizzini 2009, 425)

The Changing Discourse

Children as "subjects of rights"

Perhaps the most important change in the discourse on children, which occurred rapidly, was the understanding that all children have rights. The expression *crianças são sujeitos de direitos*—children are subjects of rights—was repeated over and over by advocates of this new idea. One consequence of the new legal language and rhetoric was that the distinction between *children* and *menores* became unacceptable in a short period, at least in public discourse. Indeed, the word *menores* and the phrase *minor in irregular situations* became politically incorrect. The discourse of protecting *abandoned and delinquent children* that predominated in the nineteenth and twentieth centuries, up to the 1980s, shifted to a discourse of guaranteeing and protecting children's rights, with an understanding that these rights are comprehensive and cover all crucial aspects of a child's life.

In this new dialogue of rights, there has been an increasing awareness about the need to provide equal opportunities for all children and to protect especially those who are most vulnerable. One of the best-known sections of the statute is Article 19, quoted above, which specifies the right that children and adolescents have to be raised in their own families and communities. Article 23 goes on to say that "the lack or shortage of material resources is not sufficient reason for the loss or suspension of paternal power."[6] This provision is important because lack of such resources was a regularly used reason to take children away from their parents before the 1990 law.

Another key provision is that there can be no deprivation of freedom, unless a child or adolescent is caught in an illegal act or by written order of the competent judicial authority (Article 106).[7] Before the statute, young people could be arrested just on suspicion and sent to institutions for their "reeducation and rehabilitation" (Rizzini 2008). Obviously not all children were so treated. This "punishment" was reserved for those whom the authorities deemed dangerous and children who were poor, black, or of mixed race, who were much more likely to be regarded with suspicion.

Children are citizens

Another promise that was part of the idea that children were entitled to human rights was the notion that children were citizens. The idea of equal rights was used to emphasize that children had rights *similar to other citizens*. In addition, not instead of, they had special protections because they were "in the special condition of development" (*em condição especial de desenvolvimento*) (Statute, Article 15). The power of the motto *de menor a cidadão* had the political effect of reaffirming that children were indeed citizens of Brazil. These ideas might sound simple or even banal 20 years after the law was passed, but they are ideas that were inconceivable before that event.

The notion of children as citizens is now commonplace in the international discourse on children's rights. It may still, however, be problematic in some countries (Taylor and Smith 2009; Rizzini, Thapliyal, and Butler 2009). It is, perhaps, less complicated in Brazil, a country that has a different history of immigration than, for example, the United States. With very little immigration in the past 30 years, the issue of citizenship is not complicated by the presence of large numbers of undocumented or underdocumented residents as is the case in the United States. In other words, the use of *citizen* or *citizenship* does not immediately raise the issue of residents who are not citizens or are undocumented. Another difference with other countries is that the question of citizenship in Brazil goes beyond a discussion of children and young people to people in general. Brazil is a country where many adults throughout history did not feel they were respected as citizens (Carvalho 2005). This feeling is still quite present in contemporary society. In consequence, the notion of citizenship is a potent rallying cry for the less powerful.

An important aspect behind the idea of a child as a citizen is that children, similar to any other people, should be respected and valued as members of Brazilian society. Another key part of the concept is that citizenship applies equally to young, disadvantaged people who have for a long time in Brazil's history not even been regarded primarily as human beings but instead and foremost as slaves, delinquents, or vagrants (Filho 1996). Take, for example, these statements from two young people who lived on the streets of Rio.[8] Priscila, 17 years old, said, "How I would like to be seen? I only want them to see me as a person. . . . Only as a person. Because everyone is a child of God, everyone regardless of their attitude. . . ." Sabrina, a 15-year-old, stated, "We are also people, aren't we? It does not matter what a person is or is not—it is still a person. I think that everybody deserves a chance" (see Rizzini et al. 2003; Rizzini, Butler, and Stoecklin 2007).

The demography of Brazil is one reason for the emphasis on children as citizens. Brazil has 60 million people under the age of 18, and half the population is under 24. More than half of young children ages one to three live in families that are poor. Therefore, the general development of the idea of citizenship for everyone is made even more urgent by the fact that young people are such a huge percentage of the population and that a large proportion of the rising generation is growing up in conditions of poverty, poor education, and probable exclusion from mainstream society.

The change in the law relating to children is clear and dramatic. But changes in law are a necessary, but not a sufficient, condition for changes in children's lives.

What Has Changed? Improvements in the Condition of Children

It is important to recognize that there have been some major improvements in the condition of children in the past 20 years. These improvements are a direct consequence of all the discussions about rights. Listed below are some of the most dramatic changes.

- Between 1990 and 2007, the infant mortality rate declined from 49 to 20 per 1,000 live births.
- Between 1998 and 2008, the percentage of children at grade level increased from 8.3 to 30.5 percent for children in the bottom income quintile and from 17.5 to 42.7 percent for children in the second lowest income quintile.
- Between 1998 and 2008, the percentage of households with per capita family incomes (the most common indicator of income in Brazil) of less than half a minimum salary declined from 32.4 to 22.6 percent.
- In the same period, the proportion of nine-year-olds who could not read or write declined from 14.2 to 7.8 percent.
- Between 1993 and 2005, the percentage of young people 10 to 15 years of age in the workforce declined from 23.7 to 12.8 percent, an important victory in the national and international campaigns against child labor (Brazilian Institute of Geography and Statistics 2007).

By any measure, these are major changes that are the necessary foundation for the many remaining challenges.

Remaining Challenges

The condition of Brazil's children is necessarily embedded in the conditions of the broader society. Some of the challenges that Brazil faces for improving the condition of children's lives are structural, and some of these structural challenges are as resistant to change as any of the specific challenges to improving the lives of children. The following are among the most important of the structural challenges.

- Brazil still has one of the most inequitable distributions of income in the world. This situation is caused in part by the fact that in the sixteenth century vast tracts of land or hereditary captaincies were granted to a diverse group of bureaucrats, merchants, and petty nobility who had some connection to the crown (see Fausto 1999, 11–13). These captaincies could not be sold or partitioned. Until the passage of the 1988 Constitution, Brazil did not have a systematic land distribution policy.
- The informal economy represents 40 percent of the gross domestic product and half of all urban employment. Workers in the informal sector lack the most basic protections and benefits.
- In 1950, 8 percent of Rio's population lived in slums or *favelas*. That figure is now estimated at between 20 and 30 percent. Living in a *favela* means constant violence, overcrowding, high levels of noise and stress, discrimination, and physical separation from the major metropolitan job markets.
- There are insufficient mechanisms for the implementation and monitoring of the extensive rights contained in the law.
- Some key actors including the police do not recognize the guaranteed rights of people including children if they are poor or nonwhite.

Another issue, widely disseminated through the media, is that the violence from drug traffickers, unofficial militias, and the police contribute to high homicide rates. In the past few years there has been an epidemic of crack cocaine use among young people. Even very young children are addicted. There are no figures about the extent of the problem, but it is highly visible in the communities, schools, and streets. The public health authorities recognize that they do not know how to deal with the problem.

These structural challenges inhibit the practical extension of the rights to children established in the law. In addition to the structural challenges, there are specific challenges relating to children. These include

- a persisting perception that all unattended, low-income children are a menace and that remedial efforts on their behalf are a waste of time;
- the fact that key actors, including the various police forces, insist that low-income children are dangerous and a threat to the social and economic order, particularly those on the streets;
- the fact that some children on the streets carry guns and engage in robbery and assault;

- the explosion of crack cocaine among children and youth;
- the continuing practice of "solving the problem" by occasionally sweeping the streets of poor children and removing them to shelters or juvenile justice facilities; and
- an inability to tackle the issue of vulnerable children at its source by improving the condition of poor children in low-income areas and the slums in which they live before they lose their connection to home, school, and their community.

The combination of the structural and specific challenges leaves many children extremely vulnerable. A frightening example of this vulnerability is the rate of homicide for youth. Indicators from the Ministry of Health in 2006 show that there has been a significant increase in the homicide rate from 1996 to 2006 in all regions. In Rio, the homicide rate for 16- and 17-year-olds is 94 per 100,000 (nationally it is 32 per 100,000). The rate for black and colored youth is more than 300 per 100,000 (SIM/DATASUS 2006).

Strategies for Implementing Rights

There is no doubt that an incredible transformation has taken place in perceiving children and their role in society, including in the family, school, and other settings. It is equally apparent that the implementation of those rights is in its earliest stages. One of the strategies for implementation, the creation of Children's Rights Councils, is embedded in the Statute on the Child and the Adolescent. There are Children's Rights Councils in practically all municipalities of the country, more than five thousand of them in all. A description of a recent attempt to use this strategy in Rio de Janeiro will give some indication of the practical struggles to implement children's rights.

The reality of the Children's Rights Councils

As stated earlier, Children's Rights Councils are mandated by federal law to develop, elaborate, and monitor the implementation of key policies on children, which are then to be adopted and implemented by the responsible public departments or secretariats in the so-called system for guaranteeing children's rights. This provision created in theory an unprecedented balance or parity between government and civil society as membership in the councils is equally divided between the two sectors.[9]

Until recently, the Children's Rights Council in Rio had adopted policies on two issues: children in shelters and the sexual exploitation of children. Both sets of policies are generally regarded as being stronger in their theoretical framework than they are on concrete, protective provisions. Indeed, it is probably fair to say that there was no deliberate provision made for their implementation, a lacuna that indicates the lack of political interest or pressure for their enforcement.

In 2008, however, the council began deliberations on policies for children living on the streets, children who are constantly exposed to poor health, violence, separation from school and community, and arbitrary police and vigilante power. These children, in short, are the most visible examples of the denial and violation of rights.

The council formally adopted the policy in June 2009, having survived a change in mayoral administrations in January 2009 and in key positions beyond the mayoralty. The council's policy is, arguably, more concrete, and therefore potentially more capable of implementation, than the policies on children in shelters and the sexual exploitation of children.

The policy is stated in a nineteen-page document, much of which sets out the key national and international agreements that guarantee specific and wide-ranging rights to children and youth. The document also contains key data, much of which were provided by the International Center for Research on Childhood (CIESPI) to set the specific problem of children on the streets in the context of vulnerable children in general. This is one of the first times that the council made such a deliberate and extensive use of existing data and research in the development of its policies. These data include rates of poverty, school achievement, teenage pregnancy, and violent deaths. These data were included in the policy statement to underline the fact that children who ended up on the streets came, in general, from very vulnerable situations and that this contemporary vulnerability had deep antecedents in the history of the Portuguese settlement, the empire, and the republic. This section of the document stresses, in particular, the history of slavery, the massively unequal distribution of income, and the long history of the denial of basic rights to much of the population.

The inclusion of these data was also seen as a reminder to the council, once it had completed its work on street children, to pay attention to the more general harms that many low-income children in Rio face. Such research on the demography of vulnerable children might at some point indicate which low-income children are particularly likely to end up on the streets and so permit prevention strategies for these specific children. It is not clear, however, that moving from the regular daily life of a low-income community to a life on the streets is a predictable event.

The key component of the policy document is a set of specific instructions to specific city departments or secretariats on their actions toward street children. For example, the Secretariat of Education is instructed to include street children on the list of priority children for vacant places in child care centers and to make sure that older street children get placed in various educational programs. The Secretariat of Sports and Leisure must reserve places in municipally sponsored youth sports for street children. The Secretariat of Health and Civil Defense must promote the attendance of street children at public health clinics and work out strategies to prevent the spread of key communicable diseases among this population. The Municipal Guard, one of the local police forces and a group with a reputation of being deeply hostile to street children, has to train its officers in how to protect these children's rights. The Municipal Street Cleaning Company

(COMLURB), whose employees come across street children in their daily work, has similarly to instruct those employees in street children's rights. The policy also includes provisions for the responsibilities of civil society. These include the responsibilities of keeping the issue of street children in the public view and of proposing and monitoring the use of resources to assist these children. All of these organizations are also instructed to encourage and guarantee the participation of children and youth in the implementation of the policy.

Reflections on the Council's Process

Its successes

The council's work in constructing a policy on street children was, in significant ways, a success. In the first place, the policy that the council approved was based on a deliberate analysis of a range of existing data and research. The process involved considerable input from both the relevant municipal secretariats and key representatives of civil society. The policy document included concrete and detailed instructions to a number of public bodies and some continuing responsibilities for organizations of civil society.

A key to the council's success was the early decision to establish a "working group" (Grupo de Trabalho or GT) within the council that had the responsibility of drafting the policy. The GT respected the important principle of having equal representation of the public and nonprofit sectors, which federal law established for the council. The council's knowledge of the day-to-day realities of street children was enhanced by involving other nonprofit organizations that were actively engaged with street children in the GT's discussions. While the involvement of civil society organizations respected the principle of equal participation, the presence of the public bodies was necessary for the passage of the policy.

The meetings of the GT and of the council also permitted an exchange of information and viewpoints that led to a greater degree of a shared and deeper understanding about the problem and possible solutions. The key agreement, only achieved after a great deal of discussion, was a working definition of "children in the situation of the streets." There was also a series of discussions on the divisive issue of how, in general, such children should be regarded, the central division between seeing children as "subjects of rights" and children who should be subject to forceful control. But whatever those tensions (and they were certainly not fully resolved), the final policy document came down clearly on the side of regarding street children as first and foremost the subjects of rights.

The Rio Children's Network (Rede Rio Criança), a civil society group, was a member both of the council and of the GT, and through its work, the voices of street children were brought into the process of developing the policy. In April 2009, the network organized a major debate among street children and youth on the issue of their rights relating to education. This debate involved about sixty children. The debate widened into other areas of their lives, and the results of the discussion were summarized and presented to the GT.

While the establishment of the policy and the process to do so was a success, the policy encountered major difficulties along the way, some of which are likely to impede its implementation.

Its challenges

A "Municipal Fund for Children and Youth" exists in Rio's budget. Before the council's work on street children began, there was a major dispute in the council about this budget line's inadequate funding. There was also a major dispute about how the funds should be spent. After major debates, essentially among the representatives of civil society and of the public sector, the council voted in 2008 and 2009 for a policy approving funds specifically for assisting street children. But the municipal council, the final public budget authority in Rio, did not include the 2009 recommendations in the municipal budget. Without budget provisions, the policy cannot be implemented, so the budget decisions in the Rights Council and the Municipal Council will be critical in future years (Princeswal and Caldeira 2010).

Another source of tension between the two groups represented in the council was the different reaction of the public sector representatives to initiatives that the secretariats they represented proposed and initiatives that civil society groups proposed. When a public proposition was on the table for discussion, the public officials showed up in force. When a civil society proposal was on the agenda, the public sector representatives often failed to respond to requests for key data about existing programs or delayed the discussion to future meetings. In addition, representatives of some of the key secretariats were not senior enough to be part of the executive teams in their departments. This meant that they lacked knowledge of important aspects of their departments' work and the status to commit on behalf of their departments. This lack of senior representation will also be a problem for implementation.

Despite the data the CIESPI provided to the council, the council still lacked some basic information. Some of the secretariats were also unable to provide accurate information about the various services that they were currently providing. Such a critical lack of knowledge meant it was difficult to assess the levels of service or the gap between current and needed services and to measure the implementation of the new plan.

There was a particular difficulty associated with the timing of the council's process. As mentioned above, in January 2009, mayoral elections were held in Rio. As the elections approached, two considerations cast a cloud over the deliberations of the GT. First, senior officials in the secretariats were becoming lame ducks as it became clearer that the mayoral candidate of the current ruling party was losing ground. Second, the civil society members of the council were concerned that if a policy were finally approved prior to the election, the new mayor and his appointees would be reluctant to implement the policies of the former mayor. This second fear was reinforced when the new mayor, from a different party than the former mayor, returned to the policies of "cleaning the streets" in his first few days in office. In consequence of this political calendar and the fact that some important presentations and discussions had not yet occurred, in November 2008, the GT made the decision not to present a final draft of the policy to the council until a few months into the new administration.

The Challenges of Implementing Such Policies

It is clear from the foregoing analysis that the implementation of the policy is going to be a challenging task. A number of key actors, including the various police forces that operate in Rio de Janeiro, believe that unattended poor children are, first and foremost, a threat to social and economic order and should be treated as such. At the very least, this attitude—now sanctioned by the current policy—results in the occasional sweeping of street children into shelters, the criminal justice system, or poorer neighborhoods. At its worst, such a viewpoint sanctions the use of excessive force against such children, including killing of street children by on-duty policemen and the murder of children and youth by the militias of off-duty public officials who operate in some of Rio's low-income neighborhoods. These actions are justified by reference to the small minority of street children who carry guns and engage in robbery and assault. The public officials who hold this view of the problem see little point in assisting street children to improve their lives, let alone granting them their constitutional and legal rights.

The normal difficulties that result when public sector bodies need to cooperate, along with the added challenge of benefiting from the participation of civil society organizations, complicate the development, implementation, and monitoring of the policy's many goals. Cooperation between the public sector and the nonprofit sector is a special challenge in Brazil, where the history of such cooperation as it is today only dates back to the end of the dictatorship. The most current manifestation of this struggle in relation to the policy on street children is the council's public sector members' reluctance to fulfill one of the provisions in the policy to establish a monitoring committee to check whether the policy is actually being implemented.

All this said, the fact that there now exists a broad, yet specific, policy to help street children to attain their rights, and that this policy is set in the clear context of their constitutional and legal rights, is a major step forward. Without the more accurate statement of the problem in the policy document, and without the clear agenda for change, change would be at best partial, fragmentary, and haphazard.

Conclusion

No one who lived under the dictatorship would underestimate the changes that the return to democracy brought to Brazil. While Brazil has not yet gone through the open process of truth commissions that, for example, occurred in Chile and South

Africa, it is in political terms a fully functioning democracy with extremely efficient and open elections. Indeed, voting is mandated, and there are a variety of penalties for failing to vote. The Constitution and the statute on the child contain a broad range of conceptual and concrete guarantees that provide for positive freedoms as well as negative freedoms.[10] These freedoms were lacking even in theory to individuals, including children, under the dictatorship. The two critical legal documents, the Constitution and the statute, make it clear that all Brazilians, including children, are entitled to those rights and that children are citizens.

I have sketched out some of the shortcomings in the implementation of these rights. I have also pointed out that in addition to the difficulties of implementing rights-related legislation in any country, Brazil has the special challenge of the newness of its democracy and the lack of experience in the strategies, practices, and monitoring of the implementation of children's rights. As one more example of the problem, public budgets in Brazil are opaque. It is almost impossible to find out in concrete detail what sums of money have been allocated to what detailed line item in the federal, state, or municipal budgets. It is hard to monitor the practical implementation of children's rights without knowing how much money is supposed to be spent on what aspects of implementation and how much money has already been spent.[11]

The legal existence of rights and the lack of implementation of the rights of child citizens, particularly poor children, exist together. The former should be and is the essential foundation for the latter. The latter has yet to be built.

Notes

1. The notion in the 1970s that street children actually lived on the streets was corrected in the following decades as research that the International Center for Research and Policy on Childhood and others conducted revealed that most of these children in fact circulated between sleeping at home, with relatives and friends, and in shelters or detention centers (Rizzini 1986).

2. This provision appears in Title VIII, Chapter 7, Section 227 of the Brazilian Constitution as adopted in 1988 and amended in 1996. See http://pdba.geogretonw.edu/Constitutions/Brazil/english96.html (accessed 28 March 2010).

3. Democratic government was restored in Brazil in a series of steps in the mid-1980s.

4. For other references to the legal shift in paradigms at the time of the ratification of the CRC frequently found in Latin American manuscripts, see Costa (1991), Pilotti (1994), Méndez (1998), Baratta (1992), Belfoff (1999), and Cillero and Madariaga (1999).

5. See www.eca.org.br/ecai.htm (accessed 17 March 2010).

6. Ibid.

7. Ibid.

8. The young people were interviewed in Rio de Janeiro, October 2001.

9. Note that CIESPI is currently involved in a research project, which Brazilian and European sources fund, to monitor the process of the Rio Council's work on children of the streets and assist the council members by providing them with relevant research on street children and children in situations of vulnerability in urban Brazil. CIESPI is also monitoring the work of councils in the municipalities of eight other states as part of the same funded research. The author is grateful for the dedicated work of two associates, Paula Caldeira Sampalo and Marcello Princeswal, respectively cocoordinator and researcher, in the project and to Malcolm Bush, from Chapin Hall, University of Chicago, who serves as a consultant to CIESPI and to the project. His long-term dialogue with the author as well as his insights and comments on this article were a precious contribution.

10. "Negative liberty is the absence of obstacles, barriers, or constraints. One has negative liberty to the extent that actions are available to one in this negative sense. Positive liberty is the possibility of acting—or the fact of acting—in such a way as to take control of one's life and realize one's fundamental purposes." This definition is taken from the Stanford Encyclopedia of Philosophy at http://plato.stanford.edu/entries/liberty-positive-negative/ (accessed 29 March 2010). A full description of the two concepts can be found in Berlin (1969).

11. For a full description of this problem, see Sadeck (2005).

References

Baratta, Alessandro. 1992. *La situación de la protección del niño en América Latina*. Buenos Aires: UBA/Centro de Estudios Avanzados y Pibes Unidos.

Belfoff, Mary. 1999. Protección integral de los derechos del niño y de la situación irregular; un modelo para armar y otro para desarmar. In *Justifica y derechos del niño*. Santiago, Chile: UNICEF/Ministerio Chileno de Justicia.

Beristáin, Antonio, and Marta Campos. 2006. *Protocolo teórico-metodológico para la verificación del grado de protección legislativa de los derechos de la infancia en Mexico*. Mexico City: Universidad Autonoma Metropolitana/UNIFEM.

Berlin, Isaiah. 1969. Two concepts of liberty. In *Four essays on liberty*. London: Oxford University Press.

Brasil. 1988. Constituição da República Federativa do Brasil. Brasília, Brazil: Distrito Federal.

Brasil. 1990. Estatuto da Criança e do Adolescente. Lei N.0 8.069.

Brazilian Institute of Geography and Statistics. 2007. *Pesquisa nacional de domicílio (Household Survey)*. Rio de Janerio: Brazilian Institute of Geography and Statistics.

Carvalho, José Mutilo de. 2005. *Cidadania no Brasil: O longo caminho*. Rio de Janeiro: Civilização Brasileira.

Cillero, Miguel, and Hugo Madariaga. 1999. La reforma legislativa en la década de los noventa. In *Infancia, derecho y justicia*. Santiago, Chile: Universidad de Chile/UNICEF.

Costa, Antonio Carlos Gomes da. 1991. *Aventura pedagógica. Caminos y descaminos de una acción educativa*. Brasília, Brazil: UNICEF.

Fausto, Boris. 1999. *A concise history of Brazil*. Cambridge: Cambridge University Press.

Filho, Walter Fraga. 1996. *Mendigos, moleques e vadios na Bahia do século XIX*. São Paulo, Brazil: HUCITEC.

Kaufman, Natalie Henever, and Irene Rizzini. 2009. Closing the gap between rights and the realities of children's lives. In *Handbook of childhood studies*, eds. Jens Qvortrup, William Corsaro, Michael-Sebastian Honig, and Gill Valentine. New York, NY: Palgrave Macmillan.

Méndez, Emilio García. 1998. *Infância–de los derechos y de la justicia*. Buenos Aires: Editores del Puerto.

Pilotti, Francisco. 1994. *Infancia em riesgo social y políticas sociales em Chile*. Montevideo, Uruguay: Instituto Interamericano del Nino, Organización de los Estados Americanos.

Princeswal, Marcelo, and Paula Caldeira. 2010. *Processos de construção da política pública para crianças e adolescentes em situação de rua no município do Rio de Janeiro*. Rio de Janeiro: CIESPI.

Rizzini, Irene. 1986. *A geração da rua*. Rio de Janeiro: CESPI/EDUSU.

Rizzini, Irene. 2008. *O século perdido*. 2nd ed. São Paulo, Brazil: Editora Cortez.

Rizzini, Irene, Udi Mandel Butler, Alexandre Soares, Paula Caldeira, and Aline Martins. 2003. *Vida nas ruas*. Rio de Janeiro: Edições Loyola.

Rizzini, Irene, Udi Mandel Butler, and Daniel Stoecklin, eds. 2007. *Life on the streets*. Sion, Switzerland: Institut Universitaire Kurt Bösch/IDE (Institut International des Droits de L'enfant).

Rizzini, Irene, Nisha Thapliyal, and Udi Mandel Butler. 2009. Children and adolescents' perceptions on citizenship. In *Children as citizens? International voices*, eds. Nicola Taylor and Anne Smith. Otago, New Zealand: University of Otago Press.

Sadeck, Francisco. 2005. *De olho no orçamento criança: atuando para priorizar a criança e o adolescente no orçamento público*. São Paulo, Brazil: Inesc and Abrinq.

Sistema de Informações Sobre Mortalidade. Banco de Dados do Sistema Único de Saúde (SIM/DATASUS). 2006. *Ministério da Saúde*. Brasília, Brazil: Sistema de Informações sobre Mortalidade.

Taylor, Nicola, and Anne B. Smith, eds. 2009. *Children as citizens? International voices*. Otago, New Zealand: University of Otago Press.

Ratification by the United States of the Convention on the Rights of the Child: Pros and Cons from a Child's Rights Perspective

By
ELIZABETH BARTHOLET

This article discusses the significance of the United States' ratification of the CRC, concluding that even if the treaty is not self-executing, ratification would make a major difference. It would enable the United States to better promote children's rights abroad, and it would push the United States to develop its domestic law in dramatically new directions that empower children. The CRC provides children with powerful affirmative rights and imposes reciprocal duties on nation-states. It provides rights to participate, including rights to be heard and to make decisions on personal and political matters; rights to receive important benefits, including health, support, and education; rights to protection against maltreatment; and rights to nurturing parental care. All this contrasts with U.S. law's negative rights tradition, its emphasis on parental rights, limited recognition of children's rights, and related restriction of state power to protect children. U.S. ratification could have a positive impact, particularly in connection with parental relationship rights and related maltreatment issues. However, there is also a risk of negative impact, given the problematic CRC provisions on international and transracial adoption. The solution is ratification with a reservation regarding Articles 20 and 21.

Keywords: Convention on the Rights of the Child (CRC); ratification; international; transracial; intercountry; adoption

United States ratification of the Convention on the Rights of the Child (CRC) holds both positive and negative potential for children. On the positive side, the CRC represents one of the strongest legal statements to date that children have full human rights entitlements, comparable with adults, and that their interests should be valued at least equally with adults' interests. As the only country other than Somalia not to have ratified the CRC,[1] the United States would make a major statement both externally and internally by finally ratifying the treaty.

The United States is now limited in its ability to promote children's rights in other countries by its failure to ratify. Ratification would enable us to work more effectively with the

DOI: 10.1177/0002716210382389

United Nations (UN) Committee on the Rights of the Child and others to press for important reforms for children abroad, such as the elimination of child soldiering and child slavery and the promotion of better health and education opportunities.

Ratification would also mean that the United States would accept the CRC as international law for internal purposes. Even assuming that the CRC is not self-executing and thus not automatically legally effective, it would likely have a powerful influence on the future development of U.S. law in a way that would generally advance children's rights.

On the negative side, the CRC presents real risks to unparented children because key provisions limit adoption and thus limit children's prospects for finding the nurturing homes central to their human needs. International and transracial adoption represent important options for unparented children, given the limited likelihood that they will find parents in their national or racial groups of origin and the advantages for children of adoption over foster and institutional care. However, the CRC provides strong preferences for keeping children within their national and racial groups of origin. It requires that in-country options, including foster care and other "suitable" care, be preferred over out-of-country adoption, and leaves countries free to ban international adoption altogether. It also requires that in placing children, "due regard" be paid to ethnic, religious, and cultural backgrounds.

CRC ratification would encourage U.S. action to further restrict international adoption, both of children born abroad and of children born in the United States. It would risk relegating more unparented children abroad to the harmful conditions that characterize life in institutions and on the streets and preventing children in foster care here from finding adoptive homes abroad. It would support reinstitution of the racial-matching policies in the United States that limited black children's opportunities to move from foster care to adoption and were accordingly outlawed by Congress in the mid-1990s in the Multiethnic Placement Act of 1994 (MEPA; amended 1996).

I believe that the United States should ratify the CRC, given its radical vision of children as full rights-bearing individuals. But a reservation should be attached to the ratification rejecting the CRC provisions that limit international and transracial adoption. This would protect against the major harm that CRC ratification

---

Elizabeth Bartholet is the Morris Wasserstein Professor of Law and faculty director of the Child Advocacy Program (CAP) at Harvard University. She teaches civil rights and family law, specializing in child welfare. Her publications include Nobody's Children: Abuse and Neglect, Foster Drift, and the Adoption Alternative *(Beacon 1999);* Family Bonds: Adoption, Infertility, and the New World of Child Protection *(Beacon 1999); "International Adoption: The Human Rights Position" in* Global Policy *(2010); "The Racial Disproportionality Movement in Child Welfare" in* Arizona Law Review *(2009); "International Adoption: The Child's Story" in* Georgia State University Law Review *(2007); "International Adoption: Thoughts on the Human Rights Issues" in* Buffalo Human Rights Law Review *(2007); and "Where Do Black Children Belong? The Politics of Race Matching in Adoption" in* University of Pennsylvania Law Review *(1991).*

might otherwise cause children and send a powerful signal both externally and internally that the United States truly values children's rights.

Below I discuss both the positive and negative potential of CRC ratification, focusing primarily on issues having to do with children's interests in being raised by nurturing parents and protected against maltreatment. There are conflicting views on whether granting children more legal rights is helpful in furthering their interests and whether it is otherwise justified. I have addressed these issues in prior publications referenced here. This article focuses on the *significance* of CRC ratification, and my related recommendations regarding ratification, based on my view regarding the importance of expanding protection of children's rights and interests, particularly in connection with nurturing care.

The Impact of U.S. Ratification of the CRC

An important initial question is whether U.S. ratification would make much difference. Skeptics can point to the fact that in many of the countries that have ratified, children continue to be victimized as soldiers and slaves, continue to suffer and die from diseases that could be prevented or cured, and are condemned by the millions to live in institutions and on the streets, all in violation of the CRC. But while CRC ratification is no magic pill guaranteeing transformative change, it would very likely make a profound difference abroad and in the United States.

Impact in other countries

CRC ratification would enable the United States to work more effectively to influence other countries to comply with CRC mandates. While there is little clear proof that the CRC has had a major impact on child-related policies in other countries, there is good reason to think that it has had at least some impact. Many countries have already adopted all or parts of the CRC in their national legislation or their constitutions (UNICEF Innocenti Research Centre 2004, 3–8). Many have formed new child law reform commissions, government offices, ombudsmen, and coalitions of private and public organizations to promote children's rights (Blanchfield 2009, 16–17; UN Committee on the Rights of the Child 2003b). New legal mandates and agencies generally have some influence in changing policy and practice. And while it is hard to document the discrete influence of the CRC as compared to other factors generating change, a recent study, using statistical analysis to rigorously examine the CRC's impact, concludes that it has produced significant changes with respect to child labor and child health (Simmons 2009, 20).[2]

CRC ratification would enable the United States to make the CRC a more powerful force for change. Failure to ratify means that we are silenced, at least relatively. If we do speak up for children, it is easy to question our credibility and ignore our voice (Todres, Wojcik, and Revaz 2006, 7).

Impact in the United States

CRC ratification would likely have an impact on the United States just as it apparently has had elsewhere. This is true despite the fact that the CRC would not be self-executing. Under recent U.S. Supreme Court law, ratified treaties are presumptively not self-executing, unless the language demonstrates clearly that they are intended to be (*Medellin v. Texas* 2008). The CRC demonstrates instead that ratifying countries are to take action to implement it. It has no enforcement system, save for the creation of the UN Committee on the Rights of the Child and the requirement that States Parties submit reports to this committee, which can comment and make recommendations but take no more forceful action. Accordingly, CRC implementation depends on the passage of enabling legislation by federal or state governments. Given that various CRC principles differ powerfully from current law, the United States might attach a "reservation" or "understanding" to its ratification, clarifying that the CRC would not be self-executing. Also, given U.S. federalism, and traditional state responsibility for family matters, the United States might attach an understanding indicating that any implementation would be the responsibility of either the states or the federal government consistent with their traditional division of responsibilities.

Even if not self-executing, the CRC would be international law binding upon the United States, requiring implementing action.[3] The UN Committee on the Rights of the Child has issued guidance requiring "a comprehensive review of all domestic legislation and related administrative guidance to ensure full compliance with the Convention" (2003b, para. 18). The United States takes such international law obligations more seriously than many nations, which no doubt is one reason for its reluctance to ratify.

The CRC (Article 44)[4] would require the United States to submit extensive, detailed reports to the CRC committee, one within two years after ratification, and one every five years thereafter (UN Committee on the Rights of the Child 2005). The committee can comment on these reports, provide suggestions and general recommendations (Article 45), and otherwise apply various kinds of public shaming pressure. Again, the United States might take these reporting obligations and the related potential for embarrassment more seriously than many nations. The reporting process would, for example, highlight the country's high rates of infant mortality, child poverty, and child deaths due to abuse and neglect (Todres 2006, 31). It would highlight the country's outlier status with respect to juvenile life without parole sentences, given Article 37's express prohibition of such sentences. It would provide children's rights organizations information that they could use to push for child-oriented reforms, including an opportunity for input to the UN committee. In many countries, nongovernmental organizations (NGOs) have submitted alternative reports in connection with the official reports.

CRC ratification together with the reporting process would provide ongoing pressure for the United States to take a range of steps toward CRC implementation, including passing federal and state legislation implementing aspects of the CRC, creating or strengthening the kinds of child ombudsmen that already exist in a number of states, and adopting CRC principles through judicial interpretation of federal and state constitutional and legislative provisions and through the development of common law.[5] The CRC would operate as a constant presence in the law, available to child rights proponents and influential on policy-makers in all these contexts.

International law has often been an important influence on lawmakers even when not part of a ratified treaty. For example, the Supreme Court relied on the CRC in finding the juvenile death penalty unconstitutional, citing the worldwide acceptance of CRC Article 37's ban on such sentences (*Roper v. Simmons* 2005). If the United States were to ratify it, the CRC should have significantly more influence than a treaty that only other countries have ratified.

Federal and state legislatures in the United States regularly consider legislative changes with powerful impacts on children. The CRC would, upon ratification, be available to child rights advocates and policy-makers in considering new social welfare legislation or new child protective legislation.

Much federal and state constitutional doctrine related to child rights and interests and state power to protect children is extremely malleable. Parents' constitutional rights were created by the courts in the absence of any clear constitutional provisions, relying on vague "due process" language. The CRC could lead courts to develop similar constitutional protection for children's rights to be parented. Justice Stevens on the U.S. Supreme Court and some adventurous state court judges are already moving in this direction, concluding that children have some constitutional rights to nurturing parental relationships (*Troxel v. Granville* 2000, 80–102; *In re Gill* 2008).

State legislative law protecting children against parental abuse and neglect is similarly malleable. It is now interpreted in ways that powerfully protect parents' rights to raise children free from state intervention, limiting state ability to protect children's interests. CRC ratification might well lead state courts to give higher value to children's interests and to accord government agencies greater scope to protect them.

Finally, ratification would demonstrate greater willingness to value children's rights and interests highly and on a level equivalent to adults' rights. This in turn would influence the readiness with which U.S. decision-makers would look to the CRC for wisdom.

The Positive Potential for Children in the United States

Children as equal rights-bearing persons

The CRC gives children equal status with adults as rights-bearing persons.[6] The Preamble speaks of "recognition of the inherent dignity and of the equal and inalienable rights of all members of the human family." This does not mean that children must always be treated identically to adults, with, for example, the same right to vote or the same right to individual autonomy. That would be absurd, given that the group protected by the CRC includes young children and infants.

But it does mean that children have equal rights to have their interests taken into consideration.

Giving children equal rights is still a radical idea, despite the widespread ratification of the CRC. As Philip Alston, a leading expert on human rights, has written,

> We should not under-estimate the extent of the changes in attitude and practice that still remain to be achieved. Just as the principle that all individuals are entitled to full and equal respect for their human rights continues to threaten deeply entrenched vested interests in many societies, so too does the very idea of children's rights threaten some long-cherished notions of unfettered parental dominance and of governmental and community abstention in matters arising within the "private" domain of the family. (Alston 1991, 1)

Current U.S. law provides children little in the way of rights. Instead, the emphasis is on parents' rights to make decisions related to their children and on states' rights to protect children's best interests, with states limited in their ability to do so by parents' rights. These limits on state power are justified based on assumptions that parents will be likely to protect children's best interests, beliefs that parental autonomy will promote healthy diversity, and concerns about the dangers of undue state intervention. Many believe strongly in the current U.S. emphasis on adults' rights, arguing that it serves children's interests better than would a new emphasis on valuing children's rights equally. They think that greater emphasis on children's rights would mean more state intervention in the family and that the state would not in the normal course do as good a job protecting children's interests as parents (Guggenheim 2005). I have addressed the debate in prior publications and conclude that it would be better for children and the larger society to recognize children as having greater rights, particularly in connection with protection against maltreatment and related rights to nurturing parenting relationships (Bartholet 1999; 2008, 336–37).

Among the specific rights granted children by the CRC are freedom of expression (Article 13); freedom of religion (Article 14); freedom of association (Article 15); and freedom from interference with their "privacy, family, home" (Article 16). The right to privacy, read into "due process," has been the source in U.S. law of important family rights for adults, rights to make procreation choices and to keep and raise their children free from undue state intervention. This CRC privacy provision could serve as the source of important new family rights for children, such as rights to maintain nurturing relationships with foster parents, prospective adoptive parents, de facto parents, and others. In addition, the CRC makes children's best interests "primary" in all matters concerning children (Article 3), and it talks in the Preamble of children as entitled to particular care. This is very important since, given children's relative powerlessness compared to adults, there is always the risk that adults' interests will trump those of children.

The CRC makes it clear that children have *affirmative* rights, not just negative rights to keep the state from interfering in their autonomy. Rights are written in language implying or specifying state duties to ensure their protection. Article 2 reads, "States Parties shall respect and ensure the rights set forth." Article 6 reads, "States Parties shall ensure to the maximum extent possible the survival and development of the child." Article 16 gives the child "the right to the protection of the law against" interference with privacy, family, and home rights.

By contrast, current law in the United States gives children very little in the way of rights and places overwhelming emphasis on parents' rights, justifying this often as consistent with children's best interests. United States law *allows* the state to protect children but does not impose on states a constitutional *duty* to protect children. Under U.S. law, the state's power to protect children is limited by parents' constitutional rights to be free from undue state intervention. Often U.S. law forbids any consideration of children's interests until adults' interests have been addressed and given priority. Thus, when child protective agencies seek termination of parental rights, freeing children up for adoption, children's best interests can generally not be considered until after a finding that parental unfitness justifies termination. The fact that children may have bonded to foster care parents, and have a strong interest in being adopted by those parents rather than returned home, or kept in foster limbo, is generally not allowed to be considered.

U.S. law has recognized that in a few discrete areas children have constitutional rights, but such law is the product of a period in history when the U.S. Supreme Court was unusually enthusiastic about creating new constitutional rights, and it is limited to very few areas, namely, speech, juvenile justice, the Fourth Amendment protection against search and seizure, and abortion (Abrams and Ramsey 2007, 25–86). The Court has cut back on these rights in recent decades, ruling that even in these areas, children's rights are weaker than adults' rights and are subject to control both by parents and the state (Shepherd 1990).[7] Moreover, the Court has never expanded such rights concepts to areas where arguably children's needs for rights is greatest, failing, for example, to recognize any right to life or to nurturing parenting. CRC ratification has enormous potential to push U.S. law in the direction of strengthening children's rights where such rights are already recognized. The CRC would push back against the move in juvenile justice to treat children more punitively, shifting many of them to adult criminal courts, adult sentencing schemes, and adult correctional institutions. It would provide powerful support for those trying to outlaw the practice of sentencing children to life without parole (LWOP), since this is specifically prohibited by Article 37(a). The United States is the only country in the world that now has a substantial number of children serving LWOP sentences. The Supreme Court ruled in spring 2010 that such sentences were unconstitutional for juveniles who were not guilty of homicide (*Graham v. Florida* 2010), but LWOP sentences survive for homicide. This blatant inconsistency with such a specific CRC provision would put the United States in an embarrassing position. The United States could attach a related reservation, but even then ratification would impose pressure to eliminate LWOP, as the reservation itself, together with the reporting process, would focus attention on our unique insistence on subjecting juveniles to this extraordinarily harsh sentence.

The CRC would push to strengthen children's rights to speech and religion, in the context of efforts by state actors, such as schools, to restrict such rights. It would push in the direction of giving children greater power to stand up to their parents and assert their independent views in these areas. Policy-makers might be compelled to pay more attention to children's levels of maturity and their abilities to make rational decisions on their own behalves and to their best interests when decisions must be made for them.

A case such as *Wisconsin v. Yoder* (1972) indicates the positive potential. In *Yoder*, the Supreme Court upheld Amish parents' rights to keep their children out of high school, despite contrary compulsory education laws. There was a dissenting opinion, arguing that some effort should have been made to hear the affected children's views. The majority thought any such effort might conflict with parents' rights to control the religious upbringing of their children. The CRC would push for greater recognition both of state legislators' rights to protect children's best interests by giving them the high school education that they would need to pursue employment outside the Amish community and of children's rights to make their own religious and related educational choices.

The CRC would also push U.S. law in the direction of according children new rights in areas where they most need rights recognition, such as the provision of nurturing parenting and related protection against abuse and neglect. The problems with current law are exemplified in a number of leading Supreme Court cases, as is the potential for positive change with CRC ratification.

In *DeShaney v. Winnebago County* (1989), a father had beaten his child so badly that the child ended up in a coma, which left him with serious permanent disabilities. The mother sued on the child's behalf, alleging that the state failed in its duty to protect the child. The Court held there was no constitutional violation because the child had no right to protection, while the father had a right to be free from undue intervention. CRC ratification would push to equate the child's right to protection with the father's right to be free from intervention and to recognize some duty on the state's part to provide that protection.

In *Santosky v. Kramer* (1982), the Court ruled that a state law that allowed for termination of parental rights based on showing parental unfitness by only a "preponderance of the evidence" violated parents' constitutional rights. The Court required proof of unfitness by at least "clear and convincing evidence," focusing on parental rights and arguing that given the importance of these rights, the higher burden of proof was appropriate. The Court gave children's interests limited consideration. It failed to recognize that its standard of proof put the children at risk of being returned to unfit parents or continuing in foster limbo in cases where proof demonstrated the probability of unfitness. CRC ratification would push to weigh the risk to the child of wrongfully failing to find parental unfitness at least equally with the risk to the parent of wrongfully finding unfitness. It would push to free more children from unfit parents, enabling them to move more easily and promptly into nurturing adoptive homes. For related reasons, the CRC might also lead to questions about the legitimacy of the Indian Child Welfare Act (ICWA) provisions on removing children and terminating parental rights, as ICWA requires clear and convincing evidence for the former, and evidence beyond a reasonable doubt for the latter.

In *Smith v. Organization of Foster Families* (1977), the Court considered how to balance foster parents' rights to a continued relationship with their foster children against birth parents' rights to be reunited with their child, finding that the birth parents' rights trumped those of foster parents. It concluded that foster parents were accordingly entitled to limited process rights before foster children could be removed from their homes. The Court found it unnecessary to weigh in the balance any child rights to a continued relationship with foster parents. The CRC would push for the recognition of children's rights to such ongoing parental relationships and related rights to hearings that would illuminate whether removal from the foster home would serve the child's interests.

In *Troxel v. Granville* (2000), the Court found a state statute, designed to provide for visitation based on children's best interests, unconstitutional. The state trial court interpreted the law to give grandparents a right to visitation. The Supreme Court found that this violated parents' rights to decide all parenting matters, including visitation with nonparents, free from undue state intervention. CRC ratification would push in the direction of giving states more leeway to make such decisions based on best interests of the child considerations. This would not necessarily mean more state intervention. A court taking the CRC into account might still decide in a case similar to *Troxel* that visitation should be denied, based on the costs of court intervention in the family for children as well as parents. But the CRC would push in the direction of actually weighing children's rights and interests, and not simply focusing on parent rights and relying on the assumption that parents protect children's interests. Child *rights* would mean that children's *actual best interests* would be taken more seriously.

Specific rights in the CRC: Participation, provision, and protection

The CRC has three concepts of rights that have radical potential for the United States, sometimes referred to as the three Ps: Participation, Provision, and Protection. The participation rights give children the right to participate in various kinds of decision-making. The provision rights give children the right to affirmative assistance in terms of welfare, health, education, and other social services. The protection rights give children the right to protection against maltreatment and nation-states a corresponding duty to provide such protection.

Participation

Article 12 of the CRC provides that "States Parties shall assure to the child who is capable of forming his or her own views the right to express those views freely in all matters affecting the child, the views of the child being given due weight in accordance with the age and maturity of the child. . . . [T]he child shall in particular be provided the opportunity to be heard in any judicial and administrative proceedings affecting the child."

Some sense of the potential significance of these provisions is conveyed by a CRC *Implementation Handbook* prepared for UNICEF.

> The committee [on the Rights of the Child] reminds States Parties of the need to give adequate consideration to
>
> — taking appropriate measures to support the right of children to express their views;
>
> — ensuring that schools, as well as other bodies providing services for children, establish permanent ways of consulting with children in all decisions concerning their functioning, the content of the curriculum or other activities;
>
> — increased consideration to the creation of space, channels, structures and/or mechanisms to facilitate the expression by children of their views, in particular with regard to the formulation of public policies from local up to national level. (Hodgkin and Newell 2002, 6)

U.S. law currently provides children little in the way of participation rights, either in the public arena or in their private lives. The law gives parents the right to make almost all decisions for their children. There are exceptions, but these exceptions prove the strength of the general rule, demonstrating how powerful the presumption is that parents are entitled to decide for their children, even when this raises enormous questions as to whether the child's best interests are served.

Parents have the power to make almost all medical decisions for their children, regardless of the age or maturity of the child or the child's apparent best interests. Exceptions are made only where the child's interests are seen as overwhelmingly important, as in the abortion decision, or when the parental decision puts the child's life at risk. The *In re Guardianship of Phillip Becker* (1981) case illustrates the limited power courts have to recognize children's interests when they conflict with parental choice. Phillip had Down syndrome, and his parents had relegated him to institutions throughout his childhood. He had a heart condition, which the medical experts felt required an operation to enable him to live for any significant period and to live in any comfort. The parents refused their consent, and for years no operation was performed despite the efforts of child welfare authorities and others who found it clearly in Phillip's interests. Finally, a couple who had befriended Phillip, taking him home for regular visits, persuaded a judge to appoint them guardians so they could consent to the operation and take Phillip home permanently. This decision was made only after a long and expensive legal battle, and only because a courageous and imaginative judge made the decision that Phillip should be deemed to have the right to decide and that, given his disability, the judge should make a "substituted judgment" for him. The judge then chose what would clearly have been Phillip's decision had he been competent—he chose life for Phillip, rather than an early and painful death, and growing up with loving substitute parents, rather than life in a loveless institution. Ordinarily, however, children have no right to participate in medical decisions, even when the children are relatively mature, the decisions are very important, and parents' choices are in apparent conflict with children's interests.

The only generally recognized child participation right under U.S. law is the right to be represented in court proceedings that others have brought and that are central to the child's welfare. Thus, many state laws provide that children have some right to representation when child custody is at issue in a divorce proceeding or in a care and protection proceeding brought by the state. But generally children have no standing rights to appear as a full party in court proceedings or to initiate such proceedings, even when enormously important interests are at stake. For example, children have no right to challenge state decisions to keep them in foster care, rather than terminating parental rights so that they can be adopted. A leading case involved a child who had languished for many years in foster care and sought adoption by his foster parents. He was denied standing to bring a proceeding, consistent with the general rule (*Kingsley v. Kingsley* 1993). The CRC would push for recognizing children as having rights to go to court to demand enforcement of the laws related to terminating parental rights and adoption.

Participation rights do have some problems and limitations. Many forms of child participation seem relatively meaningless in terms of real power or real ability to push policy in a more child-oriented direction. Efforts to give children a "voice" or a seat at the table where policy is being developed may simply be for show and not translate into any meaningful benefits for children. Also, participation rights are generally interpreted in ways that would be meaningful only for older, relatively mature children and not for the most vulnerable part of the child population—infants and very young children. Even older children will often not be in as good a position as their parents or the state to decide what actually serves their best interests. Moreover, the costs of deciding on an individual basis which children are mature enough to make which decisions justify limiting child decision-making to only certain contexts. Finally, broad participation rights are so contrary to current U.S. law that they might for that reason have less influence than CRC provisions that relate more closely to existing legal concepts.

But participation rights have some interesting upside potential. They might make a positive difference for older, relatively mature children, in many important contexts such as medical treatment. Some states might be willing to experiment with giving older children some political voting power, possibly a fractional vote for each advance in age beyond a certain minimum.[8] Some might include children in the selection process for a child ombudsman, as has occurred elsewhere. Legislatures and courts might expand children's standing rights to initiate court proceedings demanding enforcement of laws designed to serve their interests.

Participation rights could also be interpreted in ways designed to address the concerns that many children most in need of empowerment cannot meaningfully speak for themselves and that even older children might not make the best decisions. If children should not be given actual decision-making power, then decision-makers might have an obligation to engage in what the *Phillip Becker* court called "substituted judgment," putting themselves in the place of the child to make the decision that a rational child would make. This might push courts and others to take more seriously children's actual best interests, as compared to current law, which allows courts to assume too easily that parents will promote their child's best interests and thus deference should be given to whatever parents decide.

Political participation rights could also be defined in ways designed to protect the interests of the most vulnerable children. Rather than simply giving votes, whether full or fractional, to a limited class of older children, legislative slots could be reserved for people elected specifically to represent and promote children's interests.

Provision

The CRC mandates that States Parties affirmatively provide important assistance to children in the areas of social welfare, health, and education. Article 24 provides that "States Parties recognize the right of the child to the enjoyment of the highest attainable standard of health" and requires appropriate measures to diminish infant and child mortality, ensure primary health care, and ensure prenatal and postnatal health care for mothers. Article 27 recognizes the child's right to an adequate standard of living, and Article 28 recognizes the child's right to education. Because of its wealth, the United States generally provides better for children in these respects than do many of the poor countries of the world. But the United States generally does not recognize the idea that children or adults have any affirmative *right* to assistance. Certainly in terms of federal and state constitutional rights, the United States is famous for its negative rights tradition, emphasizing the individual autonomy right to be free from undue intervention by the state.[9] While this tradition would make the United States resistant to the most radical implications of the CRC provision mandates, these mandates would nonetheless likely have interesting positive potential.

The CRC reporting system would require the United States to report its successes or failures in affirmatively providing for children under the CRC provision mandates. This obligation to report, and the ability of the UN Committee on the Rights of the Child to question and comment on these reports, would highlight, for the world, U.S. failures in areas such as high child mortality rates, high child poverty rates, and related limits in health care for children and mothers. Such failures are especially embarrassing in light of the country's relative wealth. Fear of this kind of public shaming might trigger more significant efforts to address these problems.

The CRC provision mandates might also push U.S. law in the direction of developing more in the way of children's affirmative rights to nurturing care and to parenting and other family-like relationships. The Preamble talks of children as "entitled to special care and assistance" and to "special safeguards and care, including appropriate legal protection." Article 3 requires that States Parties "ensure the child such protection and care as is necessary for his or her well-being . . . and, to this end, take all appropriate legislative and administrative measures." Article 6 recognizes the child's inherent right to life and requires that States Parties "ensure to the maximum extent possible the survival and development of the child." Article 16 protects children against interference with "privacy, family, home." Article 19 requires States Parties to take measures to protect children against maltreatment by parents or others. Article 20 requires that children, whose best interests require that they be removed from their parents, are "entitled to special protection and assistance" and "alternative care" that can include adoption.

These provision mandates would push U.S. law in directions that are hugely important for children. The current negative rights tradition is stunningly inappropriate for children. While it may make at least some sense to think of adults as protected by individual autonomy rights that prevent the state from undue intervention in their lives, it makes no sense to think of helpless infants and young children as protected by such rights. For related reasons, the kinds of child rights currently recognized under U.S. constitutional law are of no use to the most needy and vulnerable children. These rights protect older children against undue state intervention with their autonomy—against, for example, state limits on their speech or free association, against unreasonable searches for drugs by public school authorities, against unfair punishment for criminal activities, and against undue barriers preventing them from making the abortion choice. The most vulnerable children—infants and young children—have no need for these rights. What they most need is affirmative help in the form of nurturing parenting so that they can survive and thrive and grow up to actually enjoy autonomy rights and function without too much affirmative help.

CRC ratification could have a significant influence on U.S. law in these areas that are so central to children. It would not be a huge stretch from current law to develop legal concepts that give children more rights to affirmative nurturing. Existing state legislation already gives children the right to protection against abuse and neglect and gives state care and protection agencies duties to remove children at risk of maltreatment from their original parents, to free them for adoption based on findings of parental unfitness, and to place those freed with adoptive parents screened for parental fitness. The CRC would push in the direction of interpreting such law in ways that give less deference to parent rights to control their children free from state intervention and more deference to children's rights to grow up with nurturing parents, whether biological or adoptive.

The CRC would also push in the direction of interpreting federal and state constitutions in ways that recognize children's constitutional rights to nurturing relationships. This would contrast with the current federal and state rule that recognizes parents as having a constitutional right to create or retain relationships with children but gives children no comparable right to create or retain relationships with adults. As noted above, constitutional law is malleable, given that parental rights have been created out of vague due process language in federal and state constitutions, language that could equally be interpreted to provide children with comparable rights. Justice Stevens argued in the Troxel case discussed above that existing federal constitutional doctrine supported recognition of children's rights to maintain ongoing nurturing relationships. One state court judge has already found that children have constitutional rights to nurturing parental relationships, in a case ruling unconstitutional Florida's ban on adoption by homosexuals, which prevented foster children from being adopted by their gay foster parents (*In re Gill* 2008).

Protection

The CRC creates powerful rights for children to be protected against abuse and neglect by parents and reciprocal duties on the state to protect children against such harm. (See discussion of Articles 6 and 19 above.) This stands in significant, but not total, contrast to current U.S. law. The legislative law of all fifty states makes the state responsible for protecting children against abuse and neglect. But children have no generally recognized constitutional right to such protection, in contrast to the generally recognized constitutional right parents have to raise their children free from undue state intervention, as the U.S. Supreme Court famously ruled in *DeShaney*, discussed above. And states have no constitutionally mandated duty to protect children against maltreatment. This imbalance in constitutional rights affects the entire structure of child protective systems, significantly limiting state power to protect children against abuse and neglect, and state power to move children from unfit parents into nurturing adoptive homes. In *DeShaney*, the Court made clear that child protective workers should feel more at risk for removing children from arguably dangerous homes than they should for keeping children in such homes. In *Santosky*, also discussed above, the Court made it hard for the state to prove parental unfitness justifying termination of parental rights, based on its felt need to protect parents' constitutional rights, in part because the child was seen as having no comparable constitutional right to be free from abuse and neglect or to be entitled to move on to a nurturing adoptive home.

More generally, the imbalance in constitutional rights helps to shape the entire child protective system, while simultaneously reflecting the values of that system. State and federal laws make family preservation the powerful priority, often at the cost of children's interests in moving out of the original family to a substitute family that is safer and more nurturing. State legislation creates numerous protections for birth parents charged with child maltreatment, limiting the ability of state protective agencies to remove children at risk. State judges interpret child protective legislation in light of the generally understood powerful protection parents have against state intervention. Typically, state law makes it impossible even to consider the child's best interests in child protective proceedings until after a determination has been made—by the constitutionally required clear and convincing evidence standard—that parents are unfit.

The CRC would push toward a radical change in this area. Congress and state legislatures would be obligated to consider the CRC as they engage in the process of revising legislation governing child protection. Courts would have to think about the implications of the CRC as they interpret legislative and constitutional provisions that are malleable and capable of different interpretations. Existing understandings about legislative and constitutional rights of parents to hold onto their children would have to be weighed against the new rights children are given by the CRC to be protected against abuse and neglect.

In my view, this new pressure to develop law that more powerfully protects children's rights to be free from maltreatment, and their affirmative rights to nurturing parenting, would have a profound positive effect for U.S. children. As I have written elsewhere, the current system values parents' rights and family preservation in ways that put children at undue risk (Bartholet 1999).

The Negative Potential for Children in and outside of the United States: International and Transracial Adoption

CRC ratification poses grave risks to children because of its restrictions on international and transracial adoption. Many millions of children worldwide are growing up in institutions and many more millions on the streets. In the United States, roughly half a million children are in foster care. Adoption provides for many of these children the best opportunity for the nurturing parenting that they need to thrive. And international and transracial adoption have been proven to work extraordinarily well for children. Children placed in homes during early infancy do essentially as well as children growing up in nonproblematic biological families. Children placed at older ages succeed as a group in overcoming, to a significant degree, the damage suffered from maltreatment in their original homes and from foster and institutional care. There is no evidence that placement across national, racial, or ethnic lines has any negative impact on adopted children in terms of well-being. Since there are not nearly enough homes for unparented children available in their countries and their racial groups of origin, restrictions on international and transracial adoption limit children's opportunities to escape the harmful conditions characterizing foster and institutional care and to find the nurturing parenting that they need.

These claims are subject to debate. Both international and transracial adoption are controversial, with many arguing that children are best off in their national and racial groups of origin or that racial minority groups and nations are entitled to hold onto their children. Many argue also that international adoption is subject to abuses, such as child trafficking, which require restrictive regulation. In prior publications, I have addressed the contending claims at length and concluded that international and transracial adoption serve the interests both of children and of the larger society and that adoption abuses can best be dealt with by penalizing those who violate the law, not by locking children into state care as we do when we restrict adoption opportunities (Bartholet 2010, 2008, 2007, 2006, 1991).

International adoption

The CRC provisions related to international adoption limit it to very last resort status as an option for children. The CRC mandates preferences for in-country foster care and other "suitable" in-country care, which some interpret to include institutional care, over out-of-country adoption. It allows countries to forbid international adoption altogether. Article 21's "subsidiarity" section provides that

States Parties that recognize the system of adoption may consider international adoption only "if the child cannot be placed in a foster or an adoptive family or cannot in any suitable manner be cared for in the child's country of origin." Article 20 further denigrates the international adoption choice, providing that in considering placement options, "due regard shall be paid to the desirability of continuity in a child's upbringing and to the child's ethnic, religious, cultural and linguistic background."

These subsidiarity provisions demonstrate deference by those drafting the CRC to the perceived rights of nation-states to hold onto what are seen as "their" children, without regard to children's best interests. This is understandable given the history of the CRC and the major role played by nation-states in negotiating its terms. Many point to the role children played in the development of the CRC, but obviously this was minor as is true for all legal instruments. And it is doubtful that the unparented children most affected by shutting down adoption opportunities—those living in institutions and on the streets—played any role.

These CRC provisions are profoundly antichild. International adoption generally serves the interests of the unparented children of the world. There are not enough domestic nurturing homes available through adoption or otherwise in the poor countries of the world to provide good parental care to all the unparented children in need. Many countries also have cultural biases against adoption, or policies such as China's one-child policy, which severely limit in-country adoptive homes. The social science evidence, combined with developmental psychology and common sense, makes clear that adoption, whether domestic or international, serves children's interests better than foster care and much better than the real-world alternatives for most of the world's unparented children, living in institutions or on the streets. A recent book describes in powerful, graphic detail "the abuse and neglect experienced by some ten million children presently confined . . . in residential institutions. . . . The practices in many thousands of these amount to 'cruel, inhuman and degrading treatment' defined by international law as equivalent to torture" (Helander 2008, 3–4).

It seems clear that the CRC subsidiarity provisions arose not out of any genuine attempt to promote children's interests but rather in deference to nation-states' demands. Notably, while some proposed that the CRC require States Parties "to facilitate adoption of children," this was rejected (Vite and Boechat 2008, 23). International adoption was seen as controversial, with some countries viewing it as related to prior colonialist domination and others finding it inconsistent with Islamic beliefs. Provisions promoting in-country options and giving States Parties freedom to ban international adoption altogether were seen as important to getting broad agreement on the treaty and broad ratification.

Courts in some countries have recognized that the subsidiarity provisions are inconsistent with the CRC's core principles, including principles that make central children's rights to a nurturing family; protect children against the harms characteristic of institutional care; and make children's best interests primary, and indeed "paramount" in the language of Article 21 itself. These courts have found children entitled under the CRC and related human rights documents to be placed in international adoption if the alternative is institutionalization in the country of origin (Bartholet 2010, 94, 98). But these decisions had to struggle to overcome the Article 21 subsidiarity language.

The CRC has generally been interpreted by the UN Committee on the Rights of the Child, UNICEF, and others in ways that severely limit international adoption, often even more than the language demands (Bartholet 2008, 378–79; Dillon 2009, 479). The committee's reporting guidelines require countries to indicate the measures taken to ensure that international adoption "is only considered as an alternative means of care for the child if he or she cannot be placed in a foster or an adoptive family or cannot in any suitable manner be cared for in the child's country of origin" (Hodgkin and Newell 2002, 295). The CRC *Implementation Handbook* prepared for UNICEF notes that "countries considered to have too many adoptions have been the subject of Committee concern" (Hodgkin and Newell 2002, 296). It goes on to make clear that international adoption "must only be undertaken as a last resort" and that "the rising number of intercountry adoptions has been the cause of much concern" (Hodgkin and Newell 2002, 298). It states that the UN Committee on the Rights of the Child has frequently expressed concern about child trafficking in the context of such adoption, and then states that even when such adoption is regulated to address such problems, "the Committee has remained concerned . . . about the number of international adoptions" (Hodgkin and Newell 2002).

Those who led the charge to force Romania to close down its international adoption program as a condition of joining the European Union cited the CRC as giving the child a right to grow up in the country of origin, arguing that international adoption was accordingly an inherent violation of children's rights (Bartholet 2007, 178–81). UNICEF and others have cited the CRC when arguing that countries must impose extensive restrictions on international adoption, including moratoria in response to any adoption abuses; extensive waiting periods for children before international adoption can be considered so as to explore in-country options, which generally do not exist; and the banning of private intermediaries that often function as the lifeblood of such adoptions (Bartholet 2010).

UNICEF and the UN Committee on the Rights of the Child have published reports indicating that international adoption should not function even as a last resort. For example, various reports addressing the desperate crisis faced by unparented children in different parts of the world often list a range of options that should be developed for such children, including improved institutional care, "residential" care, foster care, "family-like" care, and sibling-headed households, without even mentioning international adoption (UN Committee on the Rights of the Child 2003a; UNICEF 2005). Similarly, the UN Guidelines for the Alternative Care of Children cite a range of such alternatives with no indication that international adoption should be considered (UN General Assembly 2009).

The UNICEF Innocenti Research Centre (2004) credits the CRC with having had significant impact in encouraging countries to further restrict international adoption or to shut it down entirely. As an example, it cites Paraguay's 1995 moratorium, which shut down its once extensive international adoption program, and its new 1997 legislation, which gave priority to domestic adoption. The latter has allegedly succeeded in eliminating any international adoption since (UNICEF Innocenti Research Centre 2004, 111). It describes Sri Lanka and Vietnam as having implemented CRC Article 21 with legislation, making international adoption a last resort, and many other countries as adopting legislation implementing the CRC subsidiarity provisions to prioritize in-country options. Additionally, comments by the UN committee on various country reports demonstrate regular concerns with countries that have not done enough to implement the subsidiarity provisions to sufficiently limit international adoption and prioritize in-country options (Holmstrom 2000).

The CRC has also been used to undermine the advance made by the later Hague Convention on Protection of Children and Cooperation in Respect of Intercountry Adoption (1993), which contained subsidiarity language more favorable toward international adoption than the CRC's Article 21 (Bartholet, 2007, 171–73). The Hague requires "due consideration" of in-country placement before out-of-country (Article 4(b)) but makes international adoption preferable to any in-country placement except adoption and other family care, such as care in the family of origin. There is no mention of in-country foster care as preferable and no vague language preferring other "suitable care" in-country that could be interpreted to include institutional care. Since the Hague Convention is subsequent in time to the CRC, and far more specific to international adoption, it should, under standard rules of treaty interpretation, be accepted as the guiding law to the degree that there is a conflict between the two conventions.

However, the UN Committee on the Rights of the Child, UNICEF, and many other important organizations operate as if The Hague made no change to CRC law on subsidiarity and treat the CRC provisions as the governing law. Thus, for example, the CRC *Implementation Handbook* states that intercountry adoption's alleged last-resort status under the CRC "is confirmed in the 1993 Hague Convention, which establishes the 'subsidiarity principle' that an intercountry adoption should only take place 'after possibilities for placement of the child within the State of origin have been given due consideration'" (Hodgkin and Newell 2002, 299).

U.S. ratification of the CRC without any reservation specific to international adoption would likely have a powerful negative impact on U.S. policy related to such adoption and thus on children. The United States plays an important role in terms of other countries' policies related to international adoption. Over the decades, the United States has regularly received by far the largest number of children adopted internationally, roughly half the world's total. The United States has always demonstrated concern with its reputation as a receiving country; it does not want to get into trouble because it is perceived to be complicit in wrongfully taking children. Accordingly, the United States has always been ready to close down programs where there is evidence that adoption law has been violated and to demand more restrictive policies. CRC ratification without any reservation would put pressure on the United States to act even more restrictively.

CRC ratification would also risk negatively affecting U.S. policy governing children in this country who are placed in adoption abroad. In recent years, two hundred or more children in our foster care system have been placed annually with adoptive parents in other countries. The recent U.S. ratification of the Hague Convention has already resulted in restricting this placement process in ways that are likely harmful for children. New regulations inspired by The Hague subsidiarity provisions now require that children be held in the United States for two months prior to adoptive placement abroad, so that in-country placement options can be explored (Bartholet 2008, 362). CRC ratification might mean that the United States would close down its international adoption program altogether, since the vast majority of children in state care here are in foster care. And U.S. authorities might well conclude that the minority in small group, or even in large institutional, care are in "suitable care," and thus under the CRC all should be kept in-country. This would clearly be harmful for the children affected.

Transracial adoption

The CRC would promote damaging restrictions on transracial adoption within the United States because of the Article 20 requirements to give "due regard . . . to the desirability of continuity in a child's upbringing and to the child's ethnic, religious, cultural and linguistic background." This is in conflict with current federal law, since MEPA, as amended in 1996, forbids federally funded agencies from exercising any preference in making foster or adoptive placement based on race, ethnic, or cultural factors. The CRC would support those groups that have been pushing for amendments to MEPA to permit such preferences (Grosz 2006, 218–19). Allowing such preferences would be predictably harmful to black children. As I have discussed extensively elsewhere, such adoption placement preferences delay and deny the adoptive placement that generally best serves children's interests in permanent, nurturing homes. Even so-called mild preferences, officially making race only one factor in the decision-making process, translate on the ground into powerful preferences that delay and deny placement, which is why MEPA was amended in 1996 to forbid any use of race (Bartholet 2006; 1999, 123–40, 192–93; 1991).

The solution: A reservation regarding international and transracial adoption

The problematic CRC provisions related to international and transracial adoption could and should be addressed with a reservation, making clear that the United States would not be bound by Articles 20 and 21. Reservations are commonly attached to treaties, both by other countries and the United States. They are acceptable under the CRC specifically and international law generally, so long as they are not inconsistent with the overall purposes of the treaty.[10]

Such a reservation would be entirely consistent with the overall purposes of the CRC, since the goal would be to enable the United States and other countries to further children's fundamental interests in growing up in nurturing families, free from the constraints imposed by CRC Articles 20 and 21. As noted above, a number of court decisions have found that if the CRC subsidiarity provisions prevent institutionalized children from being placed in international adoption, when this is the only available parenting option, they should be found subsidiary to children's fundamental right to family.

Attaching such a reservation would not only solve the major problem with CRC ratification but would also send an important signal to the world that international and transracial adoption serve children's most basic rights and must, therefore, be protected.

However, precisely because it is so important that the United States send this message, it would be seen as politically problematic for it to do so, at least in connection with international adoption. The United States has, as discussed, been reluctant to be perceived as unduly supportive of international adoption. Bringing children from abroad into this country for adoption represents no clear political gain for the United States but instead obvious political risk.

Conclusion

U.S. ratification of the CRC holds enormous potential for children. It would enable the United States to speak more powerfully abroad on behalf of children. It would push the United States to promote children's interests more vigorously within the United States. But one of the ways in which the CRC has, to date, had a major impact on children is in connection with its Article 21 subsidiarity provisions related to international adoption, and that impact has been profoundly negative, denying children the nurturing homes that they will often find only by crossing international lines. Article 20's provisions threaten additional harm by questioning the legitimacy of MEPA's ban on the use of race and ethnicity in foster and adoptive placement within the United States. MEPA should instead provide an example for the world as how best to reshape policy on international adoption, recognizing the fundamental importance of children's rights to be raised in permanent, nurturing homes, regardless of race and ethnicity. Accordingly, any CRC ratification should be accompanied by a reservation providing that Articles 20 and 21 would not be applicable to the United States.

Notes

1. The United States has ratified the two optional protocols to the CRC on children in armed conflict and on the sale of children, child prostitution, and child pornography.

2. The study found strong evidence of an impact on reducing child labor and weaker evidence of increasing childhood immunization for measles, an important indicator of basic health care for children (Simmons 2009, 322–38).

3. CRC Article 4 imposes a duty to implement domestic laws giving effect to the CRC. See UN General Assembly (1989). Article 26 of the Vienna Convention provides that "every treaty in force is binding upon the parties to it and must be performed by them in good faith" (UN 2005).

4. For all references to articles within the CRC, see UN General Assembly (1989).

5. For examples of how the CRC has operated as a powerful influence on judicial interpretation, see UNICEF Innocenti Research Centre (2004, 7, 15) and Bastarache (2000, 144).

6. The UN Committee on the Rights of the Child describes "the key message of the Convention" as being "that children alongside adults are holders of human rights" (UN Committee on the Rights of the Child 2003b, § 21).

7. See, for example, cases such as *Morse v. Frederick* (2009), *Board of Education v. Earls* (2002), *Bellotti v. Baird* (1979), and *Wisconsin v. Yoder* (1972).

8. Suggestion given by Andrew Rehfeld, The Child as a Citizen Authors' Workshop, American Academy of Arts and Sciences, Cambridge, Massachusetts, November 10, 2009.

9. This tradition has often been cited as a reason that the United States should not ratify the CRC (Nauck 1994).

10. CRC Article 51, § 2 provides that "a reservation incompatible with the object and purpose of the present Convention shall not be permitted." See also UN (2005), Article 19 (a), (c) (reservations not permitted if prohibited by the treaty or "incompatible with the object and purpose of the treaty").

References

Abrams, Douglas E., and Sarah H. Ramsey. 2007. *Children and the law: Doctrine, policy, and practice*. St. Paul, MN: West.

Alston, Philip. 1991. Australia and the convention. In *The UN children's convention and Australia*, eds. Philip Alston and Glen Brennan, 1–5. Canberra, Australia: Human Rights and Equal Opportunity Commission.

Bartholet, Elizabeth. 1991. Where do black children belong? The politics of race matching in adoption. *University of Pennsylvania Law Review* 139:1163–1256.

Bartholet, Elizabeth. 1999. *Nobody's children: Abuse and neglect, foster drift, and the adoption alternative*. Boston, MA: Beacon.

Bartholet, Elizabeth. 2006. Commentary: Cultural stereotypes can and do die: It's time to move on with transracial adoption. *Journal of the American Academy of Psychiatry and the Law* 34:315–20.

Bartholet, Elizabeth. 2007. International adoption: Thoughts on the human rights issues. *Buffalo Human Rights Law Review* 13:151–98.

Bartholet, Elizabeth. 2008. International adoption: The child's story. *Georgia State University Law Review* 24:333–79.

Bartholet, Elizabeth. 2010. International adoption: The human rights position. *Global Policy* 1:91–100.

Bastarache, Michel. 2000. Children's rights in the framework of the Canadian Charter of Rights and Freedoms with reference to section 15. In *Bringing international human rights law home: Judicial colloquium on the domestic application of the Convention on the Elimination of All Forms of Discrimination against Women and the Convention on the Rights of the Child*, 144–59. New York, NY: United Nations.

Bellotti v. Baird, 1979. 433 U.S. 622.

Blanchfield, Luisa. 2009. *The United Nations Convention on the Rights of the Child: Background and policy issues*. Congressional Research Service Report for Congress. Washington, DC: Congressional Research Service.

Board of Education v. Earls. 2002. 536 U.S. 822.

DeShaney v. Winnebago County. 1989. 489 U.S. 189.

Dillon, Sara. 2009. *International children's rights*. Durham, NC: Carolina Academic Press.

Graham v. Florida. 2010. 130 S. Ct. 2011.

Grosz, Maya. 2006. Provisions for alternative care for children deprived of their family environment. In *The U.N. Convention on the Rights of the Child: An analysis of treaty provisions and implications of U.S. ratification*, eds. Jonathan Todres, Mark E. Wojcik, and Cris R. Revaz, 207–44. Ardsley, NY: Transnational Publishers.

Guggenheim, Martin. 2005. *What's wrong with children's rights*. Cambridge, MA: Harvard University Press.

Hague Convention on Protection of Children and Cooperation in Respect of Intercountry Adoption. 1993. Available from http://hcch.e-vision.nl/upload/conventions/txt33en.pdf.

Helander, Einar A. 2008. *Children and violence: The world of the defenceless*. New York, NY: Palgrave Macmillan.

Hodgkin, Rachel, and Peter Newell. 2002. *Implementation handbook for the Convention on the Rights of the Child*. Geneva, Switzerland: UNICEF.

Holmstrom, Leif, ed. 2000. *Concluding observations of the UN Committee on the Rights of the Child: Seventeenth Session, 1993–1998*. Leiden, the Netherlands: Martinus Nijhoff.

In re Gill. 2008. 11th Cir. Available from www.aclu.org/images/asset_upload_file16_37906.pdf.

In re Guardianship of Phillip Becker. 1981. No. 101981. Cal. Super. Ct. Affirmed by *Guardianship of Phillip Becker. 1983. 139 Cal. App. 3d407*.

Kingsley v. Kingsley. 1993. 623 So. 2d 780.

Medellin v. Texas. 2008. 552 U.S. 491.

Multiethnic Placement Act of 1994. 1996 (amended). Pub. L. No. 103-382, §§ 551–55, 108 Stat. 4056. As amended by Interethnic Adoptions Provisions of 1996, Pub. L. No. 104-188, § 1808, 110 Stat. 1755.

Morse v. Frederick. 2009. 551 U.S. 393.

Nauck, Barbara J. 1994. Implications of the United States ratification of the United Nations Convention on the Rights of the Child. *Cleveland State Law Review* 42:675–703.

Roper v. Simmons. 2005. 543 U.S. 551.

Santosky v. Kramer. 1982. 455 U.S. 745.

Shepherd, Robert E., Jr. 1990. Civil rights of the child. In *Children's rights in America*, eds. Cynthia Price Cohen and Howard A. Davidson, 135–47. Chicago, IL: American Bar Association.

Simmons, Beth. 2009. *Mobilizing for human rights: International law in domestic politics*. Cambridge, UK: Cambridge University Press.

Smith v. Organization of Foster Families. 1977. 431 U.S. 816.

Todres, Jonathan. 2006. Analyzing opposition to U.S. ratification of the U.N. Convention on the Rights of the Child. In *The U.N. Convention on the Rights of the Child: An analysis of treaty provisions and implications of U.S. ratification*, eds. Jonathan Todres, Mark E. Wojcik, and Cris R. Revaz, 19–31. Ardsley, NY: Transnational Publishers.

Todres, Jonathan, Mark E. Wojcik, and Cris R. Revaz. 2006. Overview. In *The U.N. Convention on the Rights of the Child: An analysis of treaty provisions and implications of U.S. ratification*, eds. Jonathan Todres, Mark E. Wojcik, and Cris R. Revaz, 3–7. Ardsley, NY: Transnational Publishers.

Troxel v. Granville. 2000. 530 U.S. 57.

United Nations (UN). 2005. Vienna Convention on the Law of Treaties, 1969. Treaty Series 1155. New York, NY: United Nations. Available from http://untreaty.un.org/ilc/texts/instruments/english/conventions/1_1_1969.pdf.

UN Committee on the Rights of the Child. 2003a. General Comment no. 3. HIV/AIDS and the rights of the child. Geneva, Switzerland: UN Committee on the Rights of the Child.

UN Committee on the Rights of the Child. 2003b. General Comment no. 5. General measures of implementation of the Convention on the Rights of the Child. Geneva, Switzerland: UN Committee on the Rights of the Child.

UN Committee on the Rights of the Child. 2005. General guidelines regarding the form and content of periodic reports to be submitted by States Parties under Article 44, Paragraph 1 (b), of the convention. Geneva, Switzerland: UN Committee on the Rights of the Child.

UN General Assembly. 1989. Convention on the Rights of the Child. Res 44/25. New York: NY: United Nations. Available from www.un.org/documents/instruments/docs_en.asp.

UN General Assembly. 2009. Guidelines for the alternative care of children. A/HRC/11/L.13. New York, NY: United Nations. Available from www.unicef.org/aids/files/UN_Guidelines_for_alternative_care_of_children.pdf.

UNICEF. 2005. Children orphaned or made vulnerable by Aids. Available from www.unicef.org/voy/explore/sowc/explore_1652.html.

UNICEF Innocenti Research Centre. 2004. Summary report of the study on the impact of the implementation of the Convention on the Rights of the Child. New York, NY: UNICEF. Available from www.unicef-irc.org/publications/pdf/CRC_Impact_summaryreport.pdf.

Vite, Sylvain, and Herve Boechat. 2008. *Commentary on the United Nations Convention on the Rights of the Child: Article 21: Adoption*. Boston, MA: Martinus Nijhoff.

Wisconsin v. Yoder. 1972. 406 U.S. 205.

Children in the United States of America: A Statistical Portrait by Race-Ethnicity, Immigrant Origins, and Language

By
DONALD J. HERNANDEZ,
NANCY A. DENTON,
and
VICTORIA L. BLANCHARD

The rights that the Convention on the Rights of the Child (CRC) enumerates include the rights to (1) an adequate standard of living, (2) an education directed toward the development of the child's fullest potential, (3) the highest attainable standard of health, and (4) the child's own cultural identity and use of his or her own language. The CRC states that these rights shall be ensured regardless of various statuses of children, including race, ethnic origin, national origin, and language. This article presents a statistical baseline for assessing the diversity of children in the United States with regard to these statuses, presents results for statistical indicators of well-being for children distinguished by these statuses, and discusses public policies to reduce inequalities relevant to these rights.

Keywords: Convention on the Rights of the Child (CRC); immigrants; race; language; poverty; education; health; culture

In Article 2, the Convention on the Rights of the Child (CRC) states that the rights set forth in the CRC shall be respected and ensured "irrespective of the child's or his or her parent's . . . race, colour, sex, language, religion, political or other opinion, national, ethnic, or social origin, property, disability, birth or other status" (United Nations [UN] General Assembly 1989). Yet there is a long history in the United States of disadvantage and discrimination based on many of these statuses. The rights that the CRC enumerates include broad ones, such as "the survival and development of the child" (Article 6), but also more specific ones, including the right to an "adequate standard of living" (Article 27), the right to an education directed toward developing the child's "fullest potential" (Article 28), the right to the "highest attainable standard of health" (Article 24), and the right "to enjoy his or her own cultural identity . . . or to use his or her own language" (Article 30).

The study discussed herein addresses these rights first by presenting a statistical baseline for assessing the diversity of children in the United States with regard to race-ethnicity, immigrant

DOI: 10.1177/0002716210383205

origins, and parental language. Next, it presents results reflecting the extent to which children in diverse groups experience a low standard of living involving material poverty, a lack of access to early education and educational success at the secondary level, and a lack of health insurance coverage. Finally, this article discusses public policy interventions that might reduce inequalities in access to economic, educational, health, and language appropriate resources that are critical for the survival and development of diverse children.

The authors calculated most results presented below from the U.S. Census Bureau's American Community Survey (ACS) for 2005, 2006, and 2007, using the Integrated Public Use Microdata Series (IPUMS), prepared by Ruggles et al. (2010). Results concerning high school graduation and health insurance coverage are from the Current Population Survey for 2001 to 2005.[1]

The Race-Ethnic Transformation of the United States: Immigration, National Origin, and Language

Article 2 of the CRC is especially relevant in the United States with its enormous diversity. For years 2005 to 2007, for example, only 54 percent of children were whites in native-born families, that is, white children born to parents who also were born in this country. (The terms white, black, Asian, Native American, and Hawaiian and other Pacific Islander refer in this article to persons who are non-Hispanic.) Thus, nearly half of children belong to Hispanic or nonwhite race-ethnic groups, or they live in immigrant families with at least one foreign-born parent, or both.

Charting the race-ethnic transformation

The trend is toward still greater diversity. U.S. Census Bureau population projections indicate that the percentage of white children fell sharply from 75 percent

---

Donald J. Hernandez is a professor in the Department of Sociology at Hunter College and the Graduate Center at City University of New York. He recently completed a UNICEF project developing indicators for immigrant children for eight wealthy countries. Currently, he is studying race-ethnic, immigrant, and socioeconomic disparities in child well-being using the Foundation for Child Development's Child Well-Being Index (CWI).

Nancy A. Denton is a professor in the Department of Sociology at the University at Albany, State University of New York (SUNY), where she is also the director of the Lewis Mumford Center and associate director of the Center for Social and Demographic Analysis. She is currently working on a National Institute of Child Health and Human Development (NICHD)–funded project about the neighborhood locations of children in immigrant families.

Victoria L. Blanchard is a PhD student in the Department of Sociology at the University at Albany, SUNY. She has recently published research that examines the effectiveness of marriage education. Her research interests include fertility trends and predictors.

of the total in 1980 to 61 percent in 2000 and that by 2030, only 20 years from this writing, the proportion will fall to only 46 percent, while 54 percent will be members of other race-ethnic groups. By 2030, Hispanics are projected to account for 31 percent of all children, while 13 percent will be black and 9 percent Asian or Hawaiian or other Pacific Islander. In fact, the Census Bureau projects that by 2023, only 13 years from this writing, whites will be a numerical minority.

Immigration is driving this race-ethnic transformation. Twenty-three percent of U.S. children have at least one immigrant parent, and nearly all of these children, 93 percent, have origins in Latin America, the Caribbean, Asia, or Africa. Even among the remaining 7 percent, many are distinguished from most whites in native-born families by the fact that English is not their immigrant parents' first language, especially children from Central and Eastern Europe and the former Soviet Union. In fact, most recent projected population growth is accounted for by immigration and births to immigrants and their descendants. Between 2005 and 2007, children of immigrants accounted for one in eight black children (12 percent), and this increased to more than six in ten for Hispanics (63 percent) and more than eight in ten for Asians (85 percent).

The emergence of race-ethnic minorities as the majority population is occurring most rapidly among children. In 2030, the baby boom generation born between 1946 and 1964 will be in the retirement ages of 66 to 84 years old. The Census Bureau projects for 2030 that 71 percent of the elderly will be white, compared with only 54 percent for working-age adults and 46 percent for children. As a result, when the predominantly white baby boomers reach retirement, they will depend increasingly for their economic support on the productive activities and civic participation, including voting, of working-age adults belonging to a wide range of race-ethnic minorities. Many of these workers will have grown up in immigrant families.

Diversity in race-ethnicity, national origin, and language

Children in the United States in 2005 to 2007 were extremely diverse regarding statuses for which the CRC urges specific rights to be respected and ensured, including race, ethnicity, national origin, and language. Fifty-four percent—a slight majority—of children in the United States are whites in native-born families, while 46 percent live in race-ethnic minority families, immigrant families, or families that are both minority and immigrant.

Among the nearly one-fourth (23 percent) of children who are race-ethnic minorities in native-born families, more than one-half are black (13 percent), followed by Hispanic (7 percent), Native American (1 percent), and Asian or Hawaiian and other Pacific Islander (1 percent). Among the equally large 23 percent of children in immigrant families, those with origins in Mexico form the largest group (9 percent), and the remaining 14 percent, one of every seven children, have origins widely scattered across the globe (see Figure 1). All together, sample data from the 2005 to 2007 ACSs identify 128 distinct countries of origin for children of immigrants.

FIGURE 1
Percentage of Children in Families with Specific Regional Origins

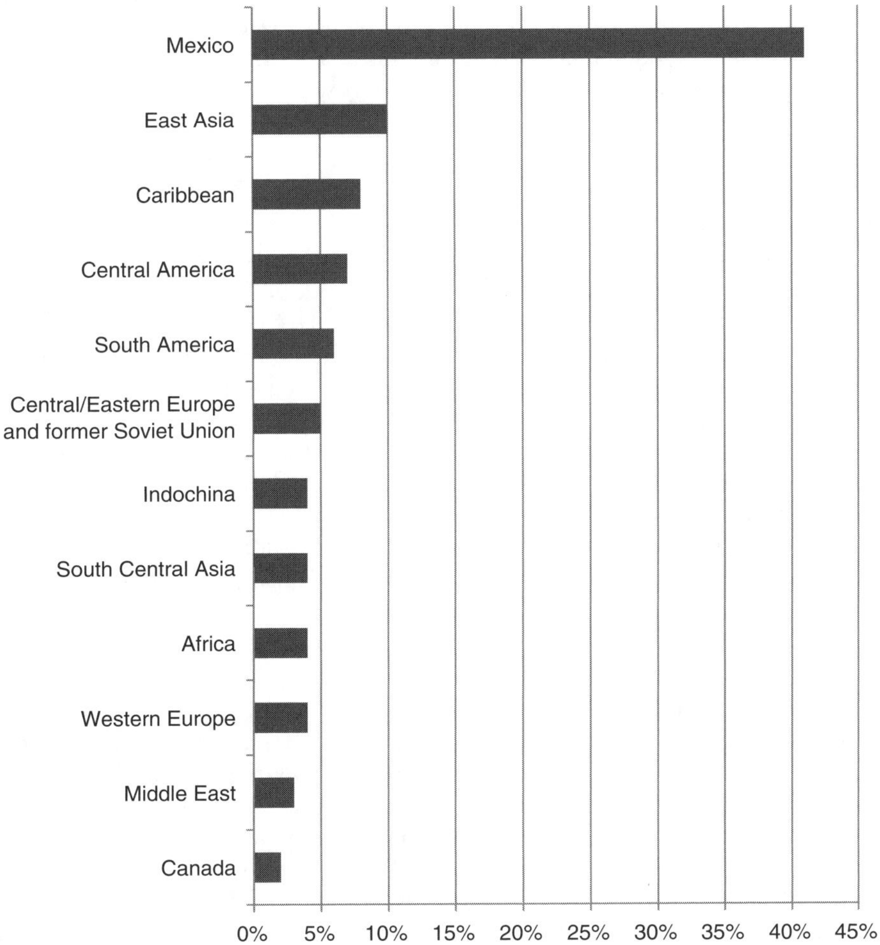

In view of the diversity of immigrant origins, children are also quite varied in their English language skills, since children first learn to speak from their parents or others in the family. Nearly one in six children of immigrants (16 percent) live with both an English-fluent parent and an English language learner parent, while more than two in five (41 percent) live with only English-fluent parents, and a similar proportion (44 percent) live with only English language learner parents. Proportions in these three parental language groups vary widely, however, depending on national origin of the family.

Taken together, these results document enormous diversity among children in the United States along dimensions relevant to the CRC. We discuss, here, results for children in nine race-ethnic groups in native-born families and for an array of immigrant national origins for children with only English-fluent parents, with only English language learner parents, or with one English-fluent parent and one English language learner parent. This article focuses on groups particularly likely to experience shortfalls in access to resources relevant to the CRC.

The Standard of Living Experienced by Diverse Children

Article 27, paragraph 1, of the CRC states that "States Parties recognize the right of every child to a standard of living adequate for the child's physical, mental, spiritual, moral and social development" (UN General Assembly 1989). Article 27, paragraph 3, states further that "States Parties, in accordance with national conditions and within their means, shall take appropriate measures to assist parents and others responsible for the child to implement this right and shall in case of need provide material assistance and support programs, particularly with regard to nutrition, clothing and housing" (UN General Assembly 1989).

In this section, we discuss three sets of indicators reflecting the standard of living of children: measures of poverty, overcrowded housing, and homeownership.

Poverty rates

Children in families with poverty-level incomes often lack resources for decent housing, food, clothing, books, other educational resources, child care/early education, and health care. Children from low-income families also are more likely than others to experience a variety of negative developmental outcomes, including less school success, lower educational attainments, and lower incomes during adulthood (Duncan and Brooks-Gunn 1997; McLoyd 1998; Sewell and Hauser 1975). Poverty rates also merit attention because extensive research documents that poverty has greater negative consequences than either limited mother's education or living in a one-parent family (Duncan and Brooks-Gunn 1997; McLoyd 1998).

Poverty rates among children in native-born families are substantial but are lowest for whites and Asians in native-born families (8 to 9 percent), while the rates are two to three times higher for other race-ethnic groups (see Figure 2). Official poverty among children in immigrant families is 20 percent, but rates vary enormously, from 9 percent for those with only English-fluent parents to 15 percent for mixed-fluency parents to 31 percent for only English language learner parents. Within English-fluency groups, the poverty rates for specific national origins among children with only English-fluent parents and with mixed-fluency parents generally range between 5 and 20 percent. Among children with

FIGURE 2
Percentage in Official Poverty for Children in Native-Born Families by Race-Ethnicity and in Immigrant Families with Only English Language Learner Parents and Origins with Official Poverty Rates of 24 Percent or More

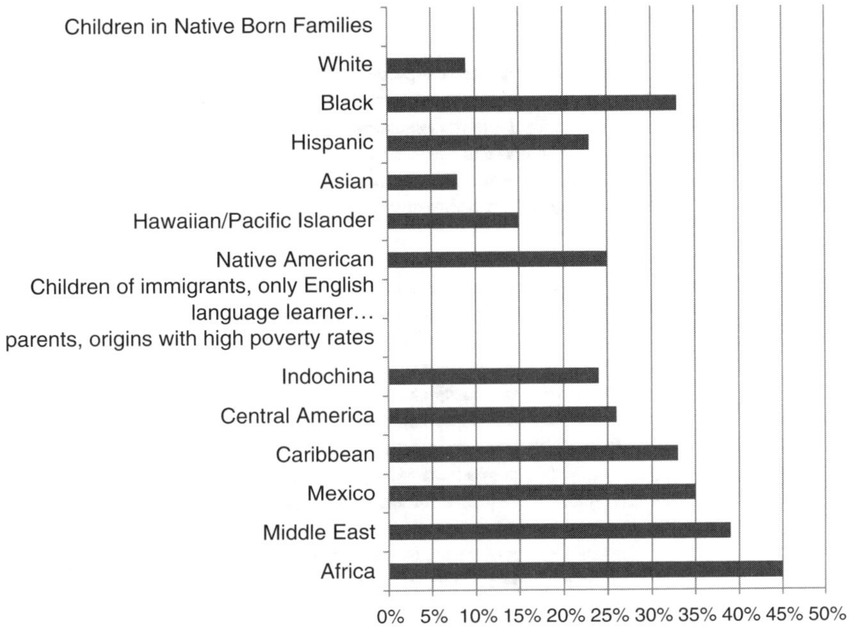

only English language learner parents, however, official poverty rates rise to about one in four or more for children with a variety of origins around the world (see Figure 2).

Although the official poverty rate is most commonly used to assess economic need, it has come under increasing criticism because it has not been updated since 1965 for increases in the real standard of living (Citro and Michael 1995; Hernandez, Denton, and Macartney 2007). The National Research Council report by the Panel on Poverty and Family Assistance, in particular, recommended that the official measure be revised because "it no longer provides an accurate picture of the differences in the extent of economic poverty among population groups or geographic areas of the country, nor an accurate picture of trends over time" (Citro and Michael 1995, 1). Drawing on these recommendations, the U.S. Census Bureau is preparing for the release in fall 2011 of a "Supplementary Poverty Measure" that will complement but not replace the existing statistic (U.S. Department of Commerce 2010).

Recognizing limitations of the current official approach to measuring poverty, public programs increasingly set eligibility criteria at higher levels. For example,

FIGURE 3
Percentage with Family Incomes below 200 Percent of the Official Poverty Threshold: Children in Native-Born Families by Race-Ethnicity and Children in Immigrant Families with Only English-Fluent Parents, for Immigrant Origins Experiencing Rates Greater than 30 Percent

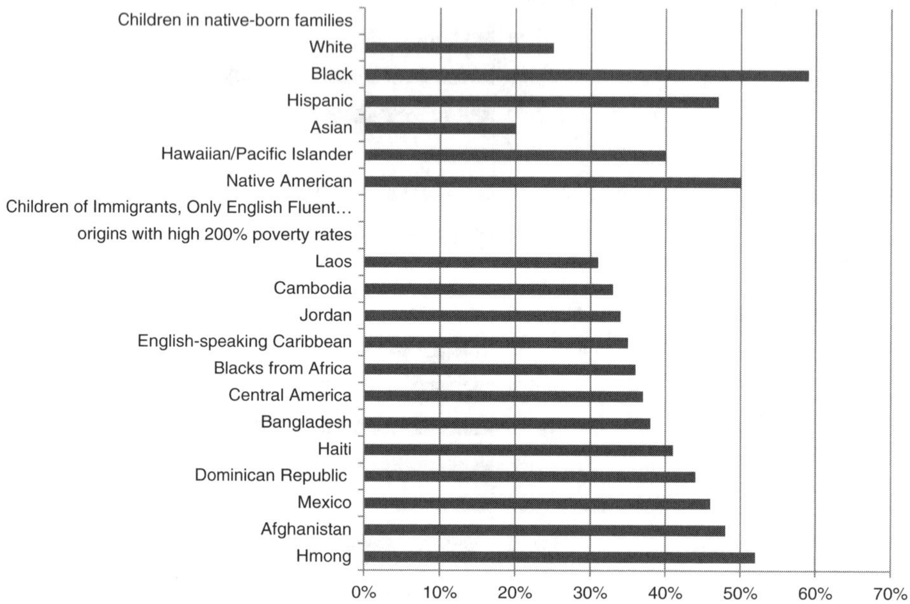

most households eligible for food stamps have a gross monthly income as high as 130 percent of the federal poverty threshold (U.S. Department of Agriculture 2007). Also, eligibility thresholds for the State Children's Health Insurance Program (SCHIP) in 2006 were set substantially above the official poverty threshold in every state. In particular, 26 states use 200 percent of the official poverty threshold as the upper income eligibility standard; 9 states set the standard in the lower range of 140 to 185 percent; however, 6 states set the standard in the higher range of 235 to 280 percent, and 9 states set the standard in the much higher range of 300 to 350 percent (Herz, Peterson, and Baumrucker 2007). The proportion below 200 percent poverty is also often used in policy discussions (Annie E. Casey Foundation 2006).

To provide a more accurate portrayal of economic need, results are presented here for an alternative poverty indicator calculated as the proportion with family incomes below 200 percent of the official poverty line. By this measure, 20 to 25 percent of whites and Asians are designated as poor, and this rises to 40 to 59 percent for other native-born groups (see Figure 3). Among children in many immigrant groups, the proportion with incomes below 200 percent of the official threshold is comparatively low at less than 20 percent, but for those with only English-fluent parents, the proportions are between about one-third and one-half for a wide range of origins (see Figure 3) and higher still for children in immigrant families as a whole from the Sudan (71 percent) and Somalia (88 percent). The rates of 200 percent poverty are even higher for children with mixed-fluency parents and higher still among children whose parents are more limited in English fluency. For example, among children with only English language learner parents, the proportion below the 200 percent threshold is 58 to 78 percent for most of the high-poverty groups in Figure 3 and for some other origins, including Iraq; this rises to 97 percent for Somalia.

In short, poverty rates vary enormously across race-ethnic, immigrant origin, and English-fluency groups from 10 percent or less to 25 percent or more based on the official rate, with even wider dispersion from 20 percent or less to 50 percent or more for the 200 percent poverty rate. These poverty measures do not take into account the value of taxes paid or the benefits received through the federal Earned Income Tax Credit (EITC) and from programs such as food stamps, federal housing assistance, energy assistance, and free/reduced-price school meals. But additional studies using poverty measures indicate that, taken together, taxes and social transfer programs reduce real poverty rates among children in native-born and immigrant families by no more than a few percentage points (Hernandez, Denton, and Macartney 2007; Hernandez, Macartney, and Blanchard 2009; Smeeding, Wing, and Robson 2010).

Thus, results presented here provide a broadly accurate picture documenting enormous differences in poverty levels among diverse groups in native-born and immigrant families. At the end of this article, we discuss policies that could be expanded to reduce economic inequality and help to ensure that all children in the United States experience an adequate standard of living, regardless of race-ethnicity, immigrant origins, or language.

Overcrowded housing

Overcrowding is one key measure of access to appropriate housing, because children living in overcrowded housing may have difficulty finding a quiet place to do homework and may experience negative consequences in behavioral adjustment and psychological health (Evans, Saegert, and Harris 2001; Saegert 1982). Overcrowded housing is defined as more than one person per room (U.S. Census Bureau 1994).

Because housing is a large component of a family's budget (Bernstein, Brocht, and Spade-Aguilar 2000; Boushey et al. 2001), groups with higher poverty rates tend to experience overcrowding. Children in native-born families are least likely to live in overcrowded housing if they are white (5 percent), Asian (11 percent), or black (12 percent), with much higher rates for Hispanics (18 percent), Native Americans (20 percent), and Hawaiian and other Pacific Islanders (34 percent). While overcrowded conditions are more common among children of immigrants (28 percent) than most native-born groups, they vary greatly from 14 percent for

FIGURE 4
Percentage of Children in Overcrowded Housing: Children in Native-Born Families by Race-Ethnicity and Children in Immigrant Families by Region of Origin

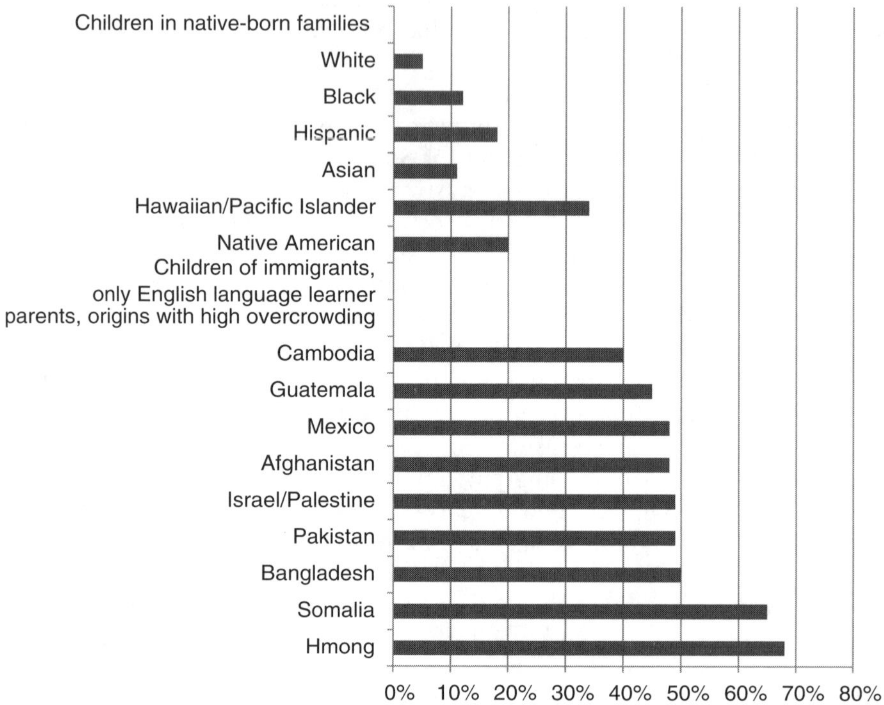

those with only English-fluent parents, to 29 percent for children with one English-fluent parent and one English language learner parent, to 41 percent for English language learner parents only. The highest overcrowding rates, at 40 percent or more, are among children in immigrant families with only English language learner parents with a range of national origins, spanning Africa, Asia, and Latin America (see Figure 4).

Homeownership

Homeownership rates do not necessarily reflect housing quality, but they do reflect access to housing and the investment in and commitment to neighborhoods and communities by families. Living in homes that their parents own has been shown to positively affect children's outcomes because of a higher-quality home environment, which, in turn, leads to higher scores on cognitive and math tests and fewer behavioral problems (Haurin, Parcel, and Haurin 2002; Denton 2001).

FIGURE 5
Percentage of Children in Home Owned by Family: Children in Native-Born Families by Race-Ethnicity and Children in Immigrant Families by Region of Origin

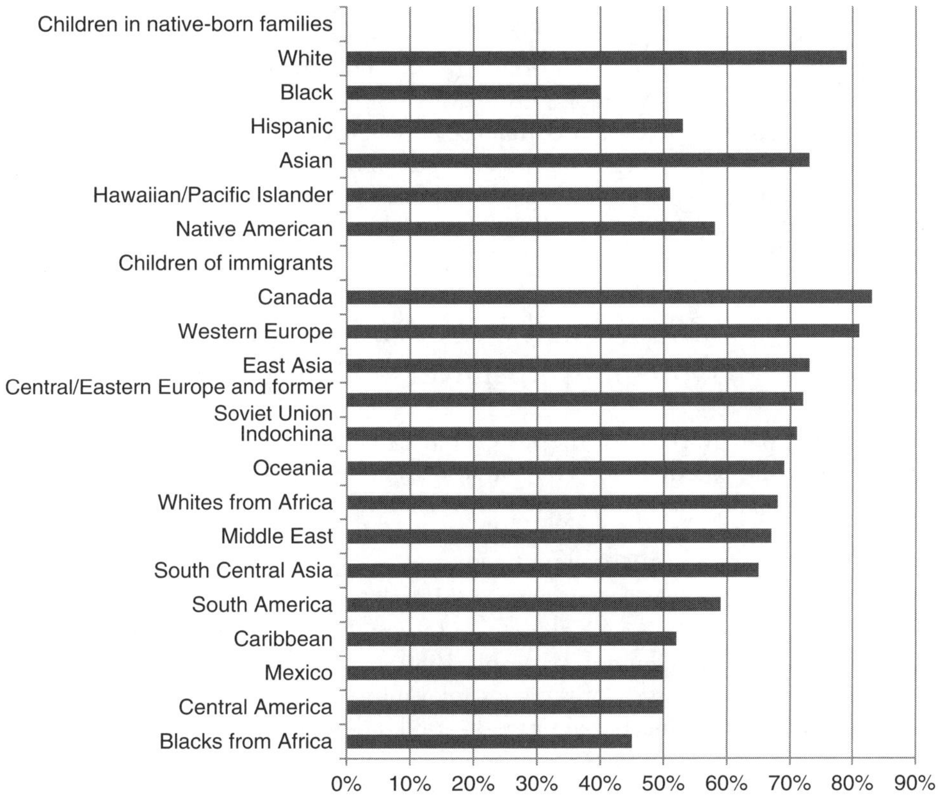

Among children in native-born families, the proportion living in a family-owned home varies from 73 to 79 percent for whites and Asians; to 51 to 57 percent for Hispanics, Native Americans, and Hawaiians and other Pacific Islanders; to 40 percent for blacks. By global region of origin for children of immigrants, homeownership rates range from 81 to 83 percent for Canada and Western Europe to 50 to 52 percent for Mexico and Central America, the Caribbean, and Africa (see Figure 5).

The range of homeownership rates is much wider for more narrowly defined national-origin groups, with particularly low rates for children of immigrants from the Dominican Republic and the Sudan (32 percent), which may be accounted for by factors including the high cost of housing in the New York metropolitan region where many from the Dominican Republic live, the very low income and recent arrival of many immigrants from the Sudan, and the discrimination that these and other race-ethnic groups experienced in the lending and housing markets (Engel and McCoy 2008; Massey and Denton 1993; Squires and Kubrin 2006; Turner et al. 2002, 2003).

Despite large differences in homeownership across groups, and low rates for some groups, it is striking that for specific native-born race-ethnic groups and for most specific immigrant national origin groups, homeownership rates are about 40 percent or more, even among groups with very high poverty rates and even among immigrant groups who, by definition, have at least one parent born in another country. These results indicate that many native-born and immigrant families are tangibly investing in their communities by purchasing homes and thereby showing a strong and lasting commitment to their local neighborhoods, towns, and cities.

Educational Opportunities and Outcomes for Diverse Children

Article 28, paragraph 1, of the CRC states that "States Parties recognize the right of the child to education, with a view to achieving this right progressively and on the basis of equal opportunity, they shall in particular. . . . Take measures to encourage regular attendance at schools and the reduction of drop-out rates" (UN General Assembly 1989). Article 29, paragraph 1, states further that "States Parties agree that the education of the child shall be directed to: (a) The development of the child's personality, talents and mental and physical abilities to their fullest potential" (UN General Assembly 1989).

Here, we discuss two sets of statistics relevant to these rights. First, we explore the beginning of the educational process—prekindergarten/nursery school enrollment rates. Second, we discuss the proportion of young adults, ages 20 to 24, who have not completed high school. This measure reflects high school dropouts that occur at somewhat younger ages. High-quality early education programs have been found to promote school readiness and educational success in elementary school and beyond, with especially large returns for race-ethnic minority children growing up in low-income families (Gormley 2007; Haskins and Rouse 2005; Lynch 2004; Heckman and Masterov 2007). Moreover, children's language development begins early, and participation in high-quality early care and education can contribute and may be particularly valuable for the cognitive and language development of children in immigrant families with limited English proficiency (Gormley et al. 2005). Formal education clearly must begin early in the lives of children in families with limited resources if they are to achieve their fullest potential.

Enrollment in early education

Among twenty-four OECD countries, the United States ranks near the bottom at twentieth in early education enrollment for children age four, and twenty-first in

FIGURE 6
Percentage of Children Enrolled in Pre-K/Nursery School at Age Three: Children in Native-Born Families by Race-Ethnicity and Children in Immigrant Families by Origins with Highest and Lowest Enrollment Rates

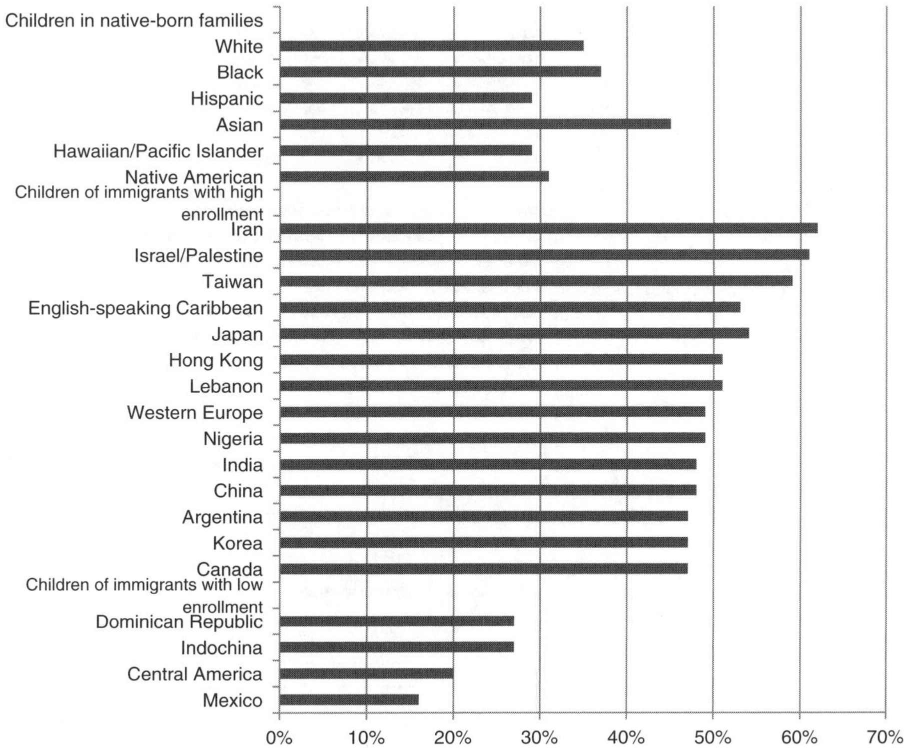

enrollment for the broad age group of three- to six-years-old (UNICEF 2008). Our results from the ACSs for 2005 to 2007 show that the rates are much lower for some groups. For many native-born and immigrant groups, 35 percent or more of children age three are enrolled in prekindergarten/nursery school, and enrollments are especially high among particular immigrant groups (see Figure 6).

But enrollment rates for children age three fall to 29 to 31 percent for children in native-born families who are Hispanic, Hawaiian or other Pacific Islander, or Native American; and lower still to 27 percent for children of immigrants from the Dominican Republic and Indochina, 20 percent for those with Central American origins, and 16 percent for those with Mexican origins. Enrollment rates increase substantially by age four, but the patterns across groups are largely unchanged (see Figures 6 and 7).

FIGURE 7
Percentage of Children Enrolled in Pre-K/Nursery School at Age Four: Children in Native-Born Families by Race-Ethnicity and Children in Immigrant Families by Origins with Highest and Lowest Enrollment Rates

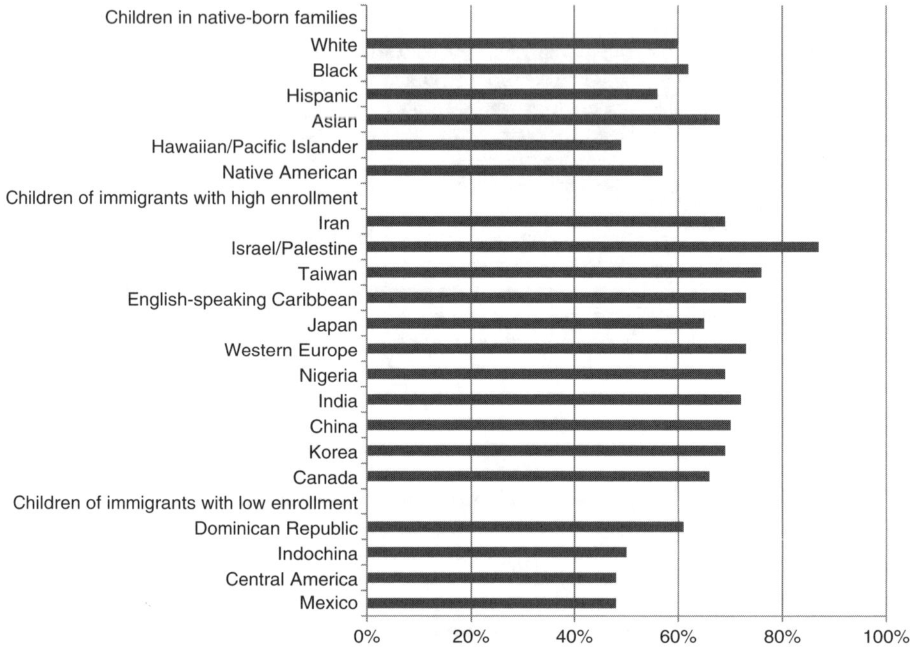

What accounts for the low enrollment rates of some groups? One possible reason, sometimes cited, particularly for Hispanic immigrants, is more familistic cultural values leading parents to prefer their children to be cared for at home, rather than in formal educational settings by nonrelatives (Liang, Fuller, and Singer 2000; Uttal 1999). Alternative explanations include socioeconomic or structural factors (Takanishi 2004; Hernandez, Denton, and Macartney forthcoming).

First, cost can be an insurmountable barrier for poor families. Because of limited funding, most low-income families eligible for child care assistance do not receive such assistance (Mezey, Greenberg, and Schumacher 2002). Second, parents with limited educational attainments may not be aware that early education programs are important and are used by the most highly educated parents to foster their children's educational success. Third, in immigrant neighborhoods with many non-English speakers, there may be too few openings in early education programs to accommodate demand (Hill-Scott 2005). Fourth, even if spaces are available, access may be limited for parents who are not proficient in English, because programs may not reach out to parents in their home language (Matthews and Ewen 2006). Fifth, parents may hesitate to enroll children in programs that are not designed and implemented in a culturally competent manner, especially if teachers lack a minimal capacity to communicate with children in the child's home language (Holloway and Fuller 1999; Shonkoff and Phillips 2000).

Recent research indicates that socioeconomic or structural influences, especially poverty, mother's education, and parental occupation, account for most or all of the enrollment gaps separating white children in native-born families from children in immigrant and native-born Mexican families and children in immigrant families from Central America and Indochina (Hernandez, Denton, and Macartney forthcoming). Depending on the age and the group, socioeconomic and structural factors account for at least half and perhaps all of the enrollment gap, while cultural influences account for no more than 14 percent of the gap for the Mexican groups, no more than 39 percent of the gap for Central Americans, and no more than 17 percent for the Indochinese.

While these results may be surprising, especially for the Hispanics, they are consistent with the strong commitment to early education in contemporary Mexico, where universal enrollment at age three became obligatory (though not fully implemented) in 2008–2009 (OECD Directorate of Education 2006). In fact, in Mexico, where preschool is free, 81 percent of children age four were enrolled in 2005, compared to only 61 percent among whites in U.S. native-born families in 2005 to 2007 and 48 percent for children in the United States in 2005 to 2007 who lived in immigrant families from Mexico (Yoshikawa et al. 2006).

In sum, familistic cultural values are sometimes cited as a plausible explanation for lower early education enrollment rates among children in immigrant families than among white children in native-born families, but recent research indicates that socioeconomic and structural influences can account for at least 50 percent of the gap and, for some groups, essentially all the gap. Insofar as socioeconomic and structural barriers can account for much or all the lower enrollment in early education programs for these groups, public policies could be developed and implemented to ensure access to early education for these children.

High school dropouts among diverse groups

High school graduation is widely recognized as the minimum level of education needed in the United States for many jobs. Since our focus here is on both race-ethnic groups and immigrant groups, and because young adults are especially likely to be recent immigrants who may never have entered the U.S. educational system, it is important to calculate proportions of young adults who do not complete high school to distinguish between first-generation immigrants born outside the United States and the second generation born in the United States.

For children who live with their parents, the ACS can be used to ascertain whether they are children of immigrants by looking at the parents' country of birth. But after age 17, an increasingly large number of youths do not live with parents, and there is no separate question in the ACS about parents' place of birth for parents who do not live in the household. Therefore, it is not possible to accurately distinguish second-generation immigrants from those who are third generation or more. Fortunately, the Census Bureau's Current Population Survey asks each person, including children, where both he or she and his or her parents were born, allowing persons in the survey to be classified as first generation, second generation, or third and later generation.

For this reason, Current Population Survey data rather than ACS data are presented here to compare first- and second-generation to third- and later-generation youth at ages 20 to 24. Because the Current Population Survey sample size is much smaller than the ACS, Current Population Survey data for 2001 to 2005 are combined to increase overall sample size but, nevertheless, provide information for a smaller number of race-ethnic and immigrant origin groups than are reported for most indicators in this article.

Fewer than one in ten third- and later-generation whites (9 percent) ages 20 to 24 have not graduated from high school, but the proportion is twice this level for blacks (19 percent) and for Mexican-origin third- and later-generation youth (20 percent), with a still higher rate for Native Americans (23 percent) (see Figure 8). The proportion not graduating from high school among first-generation youth is comparatively low, between 1 and 11 percent, for first- and/or second-generation youth with many origins (see Figure 8), with somewhat higher ranges for the English-speaking Caribbean (9 to 15 percent) and South America (5 to 16 percent).

The proportions not graduating from high school are much higher for first-generation youth from the low- and middle-income countries of the Dominican Republic (23 percent), Haiti (26 percent), Central America (53 percent), and Mexico (56 percent). These very high proportions for first-generation immigrant youth from low- and middle-income countries can be accounted for in large part by the fact that the typical amount of education completed by children and youth in these countries is much lower than in the United States. Many of these young adults should not be considered dropouts from the U.S. educational system, because many probably arrived in late adolescence or early adulthood and never entered the U.S. system. Education policies for first-generation immigrants with little or no experience in U.S. schools must address a very different set of issues than policies for immigrants who arrive at younger ages and obtain most or all their education in the United States.

Educational attainments among the second generation present a mixed picture for youth with these origins. The sample size for Haiti does not provide an adequate basis for a corresponding estimate for the second generation. But results for other countries show a remarkable drop for youth from Central America in the proportion not graduating from high school from 53 percent in the first generation to 12 percent in the second generation, smaller declines from 31 to 19 percent for youth from the Dominican Republic, and 56 to 22 percent for youth from Mexico. However, it is a concern that the high school dropout rates for the second generation from the Dominican Republic and for the second generation and the third and later generations from Mexico and Central America are a high 18 to 22 percent, a level more than twice the 9 percent dropout rate for third- and later-generation

FIGURE 8

Percentage Not Graduating from High School at Ages 20 to 24 for the Third and Later Generation by Race-Ethnicity and for Immigrant Origins with Low Percentage Not Graduating

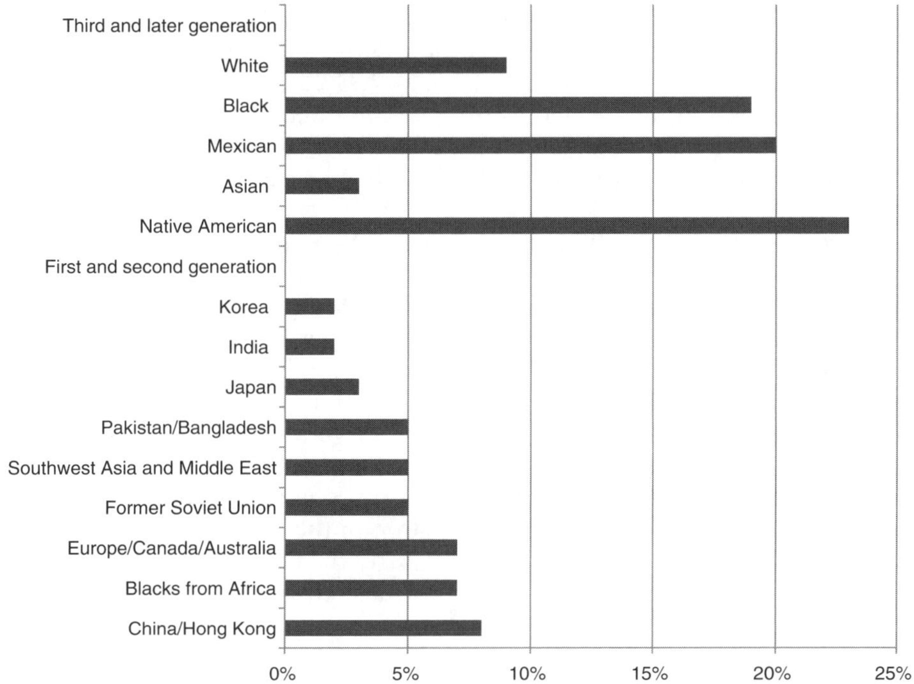

whites and similar to the high level experienced by Native Americans (23 percent) and native-born blacks (19 percent). The comparatively high dropout rates for these groups indicate a need for more effective or new education policies to foster school success, reduce dropout rates, and ensure that children in these groups have the opportunity to develop to their fullest potential.

Health Insurance Coverage for Diverse Children

Article 24, paragraph 1, of the CRC states that "States Parties recognize the right of the child to the enjoyment of the highest attainable standard of health and to facilities for the treatment of illness and rehabilitation of health. States Parties shall strive to ensure that no child is deprived of his or her right to access such health care services" (UN General Assembly 1989). Article 24, paragraph 2, states further that "States Parties shall pursue full implementation of this right and, in particular, shall take appropriate measures. . . . To ensure the provision of necessary medical assistance and health care to all children with emphasis on the development of primary health care" (UN General Assembly 1989).

All nations in Europe, and many in other regions, have either national health services or national health systems that governments fund, which serve to ensure that children have access to medical services and health care (Kamerman and Kahn 1995). Decades later than most affluent—and many other—nations created national health care systems, on March 23, 2010, President Obama signed the Patient Protection and Affordable Care Act. Upon signing the health care reform legislation, President Obama stated "that everybody should have some basic security when it comes to their health care" (Stolberg and Pear 2010).

Key components of the bill are scheduled to be implemented in a staggered fashion across several years, beginning in 2010; it may be many years before available statistics indicate the extent to which the legislation leads to health insurance coverage for all children, which it is intended to cover. In this context, results are presented here from the 2001 to 2005 Current Population Survey to serve as a baseline highlighting differences in access to health insurance across race-ethnic and immigrant national origins prior to the passage of the legislation (the ACS began collecting information about health insurance coverage only in 2008). The elimination of these differences can be viewed as a major goal of the recent legislation that would ensure the right of children in the United States to medical assistance and health care. The small sample size of the Current Population Survey, compared to the ACS, limits the number of race-ethnic groups and immigrant national origins for which data are available.

At the beginning of the twenty-first century, among most native-born and immigrant groups, about one in ten children were not covered by health insurance, and this rises to much higher levels for children in immigrant families from Central America (28 percent), Haiti (31 percent), and Mexico (31 percent) (see Figure 9). Many children in immigrant families, as well as fewer but substantial numbers of children in native-born race-ethnic groups, particularly minorities, were not covered prior to the recent health care reform.

In addition, and important, while health insurance coverage is a key determinant of access to medical services and health care, other circumstances, such as language, can impede access for children in immigrant families. This and related issues are discussed in the next section of this article, which focuses on public policy.

Policies and Programs to Ensure the Rights of Children

What policies and programs would help to ensure that all children, regardless of their race-ethnicity, national origins, or language, enjoy the rights designated in the CRC: namely, the right to an "adequate standard of living"; the right to an

FIGURE 9

Percentage Not Covered by Health Insurance: Children in Native-Born Families by Race-Ethnicity and Children in Immigrant Families by Country of Origin

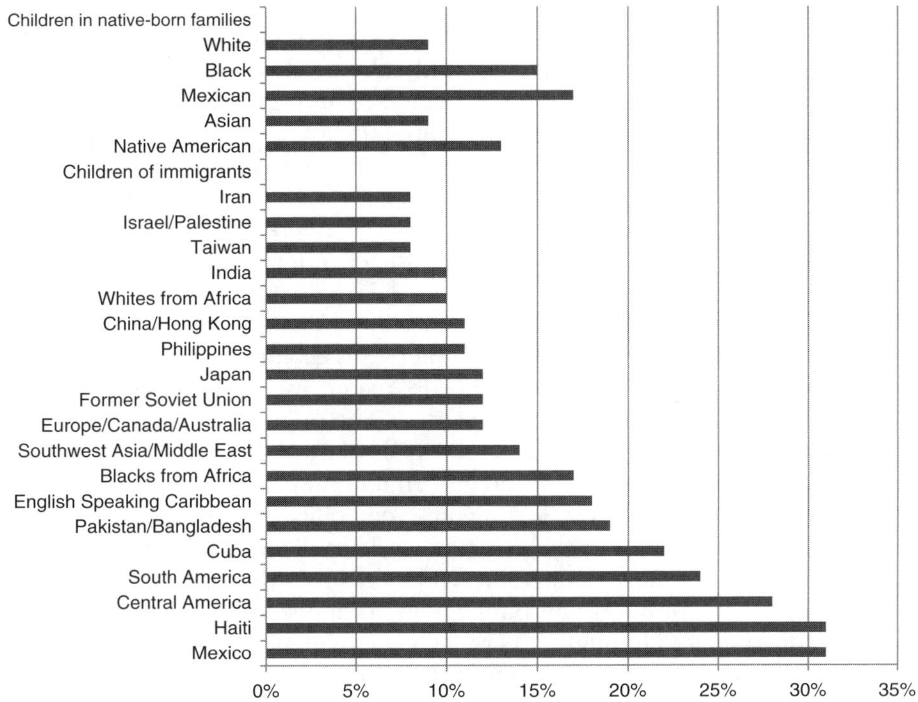

education directed toward the development of the child's "fullest potential"; the right to the "highest attainable standard of health"; and the right to "his or her own cultural identify, language, and values"? This section discusses strategies that federal, state, and local governments (including school districts) could pursue to foster the well-being of children along dimensions inherent in these rights.

The right to an adequate standard of living

Two major policies are presented here to help to ensure that children and their families have the economic resources needed to sustain an adequate standard of living. First, the EITC should be expanded and increased. This is a policy embedded in the tax code that acts to increase the economic resources available to children and families with working parents whose earnings are low. The 1996 federal welfare reform brought increased funding for the EITC, which was intended to encourage work among low-income persons. With this change, the EITC acted as of 2004 to reduce the child poverty rate by about 2.3 percent, that is, lifting out of poverty about one in eight children who would otherwise be classified as poor.

If eligibility for the EITC were extended to include more families with lower and higher income levels, and if the monetary value were increased for all eligible families, but especially lower-income families, the EITC would become even more effective in increasing the standard of living among children in low-income working families, including those in immigrant families and with English language learner parents. Despite parents' strong work ethics, many children in native-born and immigrant families live with fathers or mothers who cannot find full-time, year-round work or who can find only low-paying work. The expansion of the EITC proposed here would help to improve the economic situation and standard of living for all these children.

The Temporary Assistance for Needy Families (TANF) program also should be revised. It is a second major policy that increases economic resources available to children and families with limited income, mainly among families whose parents earn extremely low incomes from work or who do not or cannot work. With changes brought by the 1996 welfare reform, as of 2004, TANF acted to reduce children in poverty by less than 1 percent. In addition, although TANF is available to some families with very low income, eligibility requirements under the 1996 welfare reform drew, for the first time, a sharp distinction between citizens and noncitizen documented immigrants, with noncitizen documented immigrants becoming ineligible for important public benefits and services. As a result, many noncitizen documented immigrant parents who are ineligible for TANF or other specific public benefits may not be aware that their citizen children are eligible, or they may hesitate to contact government authorities on behalf of their children for fear of jeopardizing their own future opportunities to become citizens (Capps, Kenney, and Fix 2003; Fix and Passel 1999; Fix and Zimmermann 1995; Hernandez and Charney 1998; Zimmermann and Tumlin 1999).

Insofar as some immigrant parents are excluded from welfare programs, which then deprives their U.S. citizen children of important public benefits and services, and insofar as most of the children and parents are or will become American citizens, the elimination of these eligibility exclusion rules is in the interest not only of immigrant children and families; it is in the interest of all Americans, including the baby boom generation, who will benefit from having a healthy and productive labor force to support it during retirement.

The right to education directed toward developing the child's fullest potential and the right to enjoy his or her own culture and language

The education system is an institutional locus with especially great potential to affect both the right to the development of the child's fullest potential and the right to enjoy his or her own culture and language. All children should have access to high-quality early education programs, including children in immigrant families. Seven states are either currently providing (Florida, Georgia, Oklahoma), or phasing in (Illinois, Iowa, New York, West Virginia) voluntary universal pre-kindergarten programs in which parents can enroll their four-year-old children (Pre-K Now 2007).

Because the United States has low enrollment rates compared with many other OECD countries, additional resources should be devoted to ensuring that all children have access to high-quality early education, but especially children with immigrant origins who experience very low enrollment rates. Early education programs should be welcoming and effective for children and parents in immigrant families. This approach may require active outreach in the home languages of families within some communities to foster the inclusion of children whose parents are English language learners, as well as a culturally competent early education workforce.

It is important that children learn English, because this is the primary language used in schools, as well as in the health system, labor market, judicial system, and most other organizations and institutions in the United States. At the same time, speaking the language of the country of origin may be critical in maintaining elements of the parents' cultural or religious heritage that are embedded in this language (Alba and Nee 2003) as well as to communicate with parents whose first language is not English.

In addition, a recent longitudinal study in the United States and a recent cross-national study of thirteen countries, including the United States, suggest that adolescents who have fluency in both their parents' home language and the language of the settlement society and who identify with and participate in both the culture of the society of origin and the society of settlement adjust more successfully than do those with other acculturation profiles (Portes and Rumbaut 2001; Sam et al. 2006). Measures of adjustment in these two studies include higher self-esteem, higher education and occupation expectations, higher academic achievement, lower levels of mental health problems (e.g., anxiety, depression, and psychosomatic symptoms), as well as higher satisfaction with life and lower levels of antisocial behavior.

There is, therefore, a need for education policies, programs, and curricula at all levels that encourage fluency not only in English but also in the home languages of children and that foster bilingual spoken fluency and literacy (reading and writing).

There also is a need for English language training for immigrant parents. Two-generation family literacy programs should be examined as a strategy for providing the opportunity for both children and parents who are English language learners to learn together how to build literacy into their homes and daily lives. While the most recent national evaluation of the Even Start Family Literacy Program did point to gains in literacy outcomes for participants, it did not provide evidence that gains were greater for those assigned to the program than for those in the control group (St. Pierre et al. 2003). The researchers note the need for better understanding of the bases for variation in the effectiveness of the Even Start program as implemented in various localities. Work is needed to understand the specific features of family literacy programs that can help parents in immigrant families to improve their capacity to provide economic support for their families while also fostering the children's development.

Children in immigrant families are well positioned to become fluent bilingual speakers, writers, and readers—if they receive formal training in both English and the heritage language of their parent(s). Dual-language programs for all children would also increase economic opportunities for the United States in the increasingly competitive global economy.

Results presented in this article further suggest the need for two sets of policies for adolescents and youth. Education policies, programs, and curricula for recent first-generation, adolescent immigrants with little or no experience in U.S. schools must address a very different set of issues than policies for first-generation immigrants who arrive at younger ages and who obtain most or all their education in the United States prior to reaching high school. In addition, because many immigrant adolescents and youth with limited education who are also English language learners have bypassed the U.S. education system to directly enter the workforce, immigrant adolescents and youth need special outreach activities to draw them into the schools and specially designed programs to help to ensure their educational success.

The right to the highest attainable standard of health

The Patient Protection and Affordable Care Act of 2010 mandates that all persons lawfully present in the United States, including lawfully present children, be covered by health insurance beginning within a few years (see U.S. Congress 2010, 160). Thus, one group not included in this coverage is unauthorized immigrant children, who accounted for 11 percent of children in immigrant families or about 3 percent of all children in 2005 (Passel 2006). An additional 18 percent of children in immigrant families (4 percent of all children) were born in the United States but have an unauthorized parent who will not under this law be covered by insurance. A variety of mechanisms are mandated to ensure coverage under this law, including the requirement that insurance be bought, with fines to be paid by persons not purchasing health insurance coverage.

As results presented here indicate, many children experience low rates of health insurance coverage, including many race-ethnic minority children in native-born families and many children in immigrant families with origins in Mexico, the Caribbean, Central and South America, Africa, South West Asia, and the Middle East. Therefore, it is important during the coming decade to monitor the extent to which children in these groups actually do become covered by health insurance.

Of particular concern is the possibility that children in immigrant families with an undocumented parent may not have access to health insurance, because their parents are not included under the provisions of the Patient Protection and

Affordable Care Act, and the parent(s) may not have the economic resources to pay for health insurance for themselves or their children. In addition, home language outreach and interpretive services, as well as the culturally competent provision of health care, are essential, because many children and parents are English language learners, and many come from cultures with different traditions of health care provision. Without such services, many children may not have access to health insurance or, if covered by health insurance, access to health care that they require to survive and develop fully.

Language outreach

Children and parents who are English language learners may have great difficulty communicating not only with insurance and health care providers but also with educators and officials in social service, justice, and other institutions. In families where only the adolescents or young children are fluent in English, the parents are not in a position to communicate with professionals on their behalf or that of their children. In fact, it may be the children who must act as the primary intermediary between family members and professionals in various institutional settings.

It is, therefore, critical that health, educational, and other organizations provide outreach and interpretive services in the home languages of children and their parents. Without these efforts, these organizations may be cutting themselves off from the rapidly growing client population of immigrant children and families.

Enforcement of immigration laws

One additional set of issues arises for children with undocumented parents. During recent years, worksite raids have been used increasingly by U.S. Immigration and Customs Enforcement (ICE) as a means of enforcing immigration laws. A recent study of three sites found that on average, for every two adults affected, there was a child whose parent was arrested (Capps et al. 2007). Two-thirds (66 percent) of these children were American citizens. At the sites collecting information about age, the vast majority of affected children were ages ten or younger (79 to 88 percent), and in one site, 71 percent were under age six. This study, as well as two additional, recent studies, document negative consequences for children and offer important recommendations for reforming the nation's immigration laws to take the best interests of U.S. citizen children into account (Chaudry et al. 2010; International Human Rights Law Clinic, Chief Justice Earl Warren Institute, and Immigration Law Clinic 2010). There is wide agreement that immigration laws are necessary and should be enforced, but there are many possible approaches, and the manner in which enforcement occurs should not bring harm to children, including those who are American citizens.

Conclusion

The rights enumerated by the CRC include the right to an adequate standard of living, the right to an education directed toward the development of the child's fullest potential, the right to the highest attainable standard of health, and the right to the child's own cultural identity and the use of his or her own language. The CRC states that these rights shall be ensured irrespective of various statuses of children, including their race, ethnic origin, national origin, and language.

This study documents the enormous diversity among children regarding these statuses. It also documents that children who are members of various race-ethnic, immigrant national origin, and language groups differ greatly in their rates of poverty, overcrowded housing, family homeownership, enrollment in early education, high school dropout, and health insurance coverage. Thus, the results presented here point to the need for policies that more effectively ensure that all children have access to critical resources reflected in the associated rights. With better public policies, the United States could move closer to the ideals for child well-being that have inspired the CRC.

Note

1. Additional indicators for specific ages, for states and metropolitan areas, and for additional native and immigrant groups are available at www.albany.edu/csda/children. Hernandez, Macartney, and Blanchard (2009) also discuss results comparing children in the United States and seven other affluent countries. See also www.unicef-irc.org/cgi-bin/unicef/Lunga.sql?ProductID=570. Finally, for research using an overall index of child well-being to assess changing race-ethnic disparities from 1985 to 2004, see Hernandez and Macartney (2008) at www.fcd-us.org/resources/resources_show.htm?doc_id=648676.

References

Alba, Richard, and Victor Nee. 2003. *Remaking the American mainstream: Assimilation and contemporary immigration*. Cambridge, MA: Harvard University Press.

Annie E. Casey Foundation. 2006. *2006 Kids Count data book*. Baltimore, MD: Annie E. Casey Foundation.

Bernstein, Jared, Chauna Brocht, and Maggie Spade-Aguilar. 2000. *How much is enough? Basic family budgets for working families*. Washington, DC: Economic Policy Institute.

Boushey, Heather, Chauna Brocht, Bethney Gundersen, and Jared Bernstein. 2001. *Hardships in America: The real story of working families*. Washington, DC: Economic Policy Institute.

Capps, Randy, Rosa Maria Castañeda, Ajay Chaudry, and Robert Santos. 2007. *Paying the price: The impact of immigration raids on America's children*. Washington, DC: National Council of La Raza.

Capps, Randy, Genevieve Kenney, and Michael Fix. 2003. *Health insurance coverage of children in mixed-status immigrant families*. Snapshots of America's Children no. 12. Washington, DC: Urban Institute.

Chaudry, Ajay, Randy Capps, Juan Manuel Pedroza, Rosa Maria Castañeda, Robert Santos, and Molly M. Scott. 2010. *Facing our future: Children in the aftermath of immigration enforcement*. Washington, DC: Urban Institute.

Citro, Constance F., and Robert T. Michael, eds. 1995. *Measuring poverty: A new approach*. Washington, DC: National Academy Press.

Denton, Nancy A. 2001. Housing as a means of asset accumulation: A good strategy for the poor? In *Assets for the poor*, eds. Thomas M. Shapiro and Edward M. Wolff, 232–66. New York, NY: Russell Sage Foundation.

Duncan, Greg J., and Jeanne Brooks-Gunn, eds. 1997. *Consequences of growing up poor*. New York, NY: Russell Sage Foundation.

Engel, Kathleen C., and Patricia A. McCoy. 2008. From credit denial to predatory lending: The challenge of sustaining minority homeownership. In *Segregation: The rising costs for America*, eds. James H. Carr and Nandinee K. Kutty, 81–123. New York, NY: Routledge.

Evans, Gary W., Susan Saegert, and Rebecca Harris. 2001. Residential density and psychological health among children in low-income families. *Environment and Behavior* 33 (2): 165–80.

Fix, Michael, and Jeffrey Passel. 1999. *Trends in noncitizens' and citizens' use of public benefits following welfare reform: 1994–97*. Washington, DC: Urban Institute.

Fix, Michael, and Wendy Zimmerman. 1995. When should immigrants receive public benefits? In *Welfare reform: An analysis of the issues*, ed. Isabel V. Sawhill, 69–72. Washington, DC: Urban Institute.

Gormley, William T. 2007. Early childhood care and education: Lessons and puzzles. *Journal of Policy Analysis and Management* 26 (3): 633–71.

Gormley, William T., Ted Gayer, Deborah A. Phillips, and Brittan Dawson. 2005. The effects of universal pre-K on cognitive development. *Developmental Psychology* 41 (6): 872–84.

Haskins, Ron, and Cecilia Rouse. 2005. *Closing achievement gaps*. The Future of Children, Policy Brief. Princeton, NJ: Princeton-Brookings.

Haurin, Donald R., Toby L. Parcel, and R. Jean Haurin. 2002. Impact of homeownership on child outcomes. In *Low-income homeownership: Examining the unexamined goal*, eds. Nicolas P. Retsinas and Eric S. Belsky, 427–46. Washington, DC: Brookings Institution Press.

Heckman, James J., and Dimitriy V. Masterov. 2007. The productivity argument for investing in young children. T.W. Schultz Award Lecture given at the Allied Social Sciences Association annual meeting, 5–7 January. Chicago, IL. Available from http://jenni.uchicago.edu/human-inequality/papers/Heckman_final_all_wp_2007-03-22c_jsb.pdf (accessed 23 January 2009).

Hernandez, Donald J., and Evan Charney, eds. 1998. *From generation to generation: The health and wellbeing of children in immigrant families*. Washington, DC: National Academy Press.

Hernandez, Donald J., Nancy A. Denton, and Suzanne E. Macartney. 2007. Child poverty in the U.S.: A new family budget approach with comparison to European countries. In *Childhood, generational order and the welfare state: Exploring children's social and economic welfare*. Vol. 1 of *COST A19: Children's welfare*, eds. Helmut Wintersberger, Leena Alanen, Thomas Olk, and Jens Qvortrup, 109–40. Odense: University Press of Southern Denmark.

Hernandez, Donald J., Nancy A. Denton, and Suzanne Macartney. Forthcoming. Early childhood education programs: Accounting for low enrollment in newcomer and native families. In *The new dimensions of diversity: The children of immigrants in North America and Western Europe*, eds. Richard Alba and Mary A. Waters. New York, NY: New York University Press.

Hernandez, Donald J., and Suzanne E. Macartney. 2008. *Racial-ethnic inequality in child well-being from 1985–2004: Gaps narrowing, but persist*. New York, NY: Foundation for Child Development. Available from www.fcd-us.org/resources/recources_show.htm?doc_id=648676 (accessed 7 July 2010).

Hernandez, Donald J., Suzanne Macartney, and Victoria L. Blanchard. 2009. *Children in immigrant families in eight affluent countries: Their family, national, and international context*. Florence, Italy: UNICEF Innocenti Research Centre.

Herz, Elicia J., Chris L. Peterson, and Evelyne P. Baumrucker. 2007. *State Children's Health Insurance Program (SCHIP): A brief overview*. Congressional Research Service Report for Congress. Washington, DC: Congressional Research Service.

Hill-Scott, Karen. 2005. *Facilities technical report*. Los Angeles, CA: First 5 LA.

Holloway, Susan, and Bruce Fuller. 1999. *Through my own eyes: Single mothers and the cultures of poverty*. Cambridge, MA: Harvard University Press.

International Human Rights Law Clinic, Chief Justice Earl Warren Institute on Race, Ethnicity and Diversity, and Immigration Law Clinic. 2010. *In the child's best interest? The consequences of losing a lawful immigrant parent to deportation*. Berkeley, CA: University of California School of Law and University of California Davis School of Law. Available from www.law.berkeley.edu/files/IHRLC/In_the_Childs_Best_Interest.pdf (accessed 5 April 2010).

Kamerman, Sheila B., and Alfred J. Kahn. 1995. *Starting right: How America neglects its youngest children and what we can do about it*. Oxford: Oxford University Press.

Liang, Xiaoyan, Bruce Fuller, and Judith D. Singer. 2000. Ethnic differences in child care selection: The influence of family structure, parental practices, and home language. *Early Childhood Research Quarterly* 15 (3): 357–84.

Lynch, Robert G. 2004. Exceptional returns: *Economic, fiscal and social benefits of investment in early childhood development*. Washington, DC: Economic Policy Institute.

Massey, Douglas S., and Nancy A. Denton. 1993. *American apartheid: Segregation and the making of the underclass*. Cambridge, MA: Harvard University Press.

Matthews, Hannah, and Danielle Ewen. 2006. *Reaching all children? Understanding early care and education participation among immigrant families*. Washington, DC: Center for Law and Social Policy.

McLoyd, Vonnie. 1998. Socioeconomic disadvantage and child development. *American Psychologist* 53 (2): 185–204.

Mezey, Jennifer, Mark Greenberg, and Rachel Schumacher. 2002. *The vast majority of federally eligible children did not receive child care assistance in FY2000*. Washington, DC: Center for Law and Social Policy. Available from www.clasp.org/publications/1in7full.pdf (accessed 16 March 2005).

OECD Directorate of Education. 2006. *Early childhood education and care policy: Country note for Mexico*. Paris: OECD Directorate of Education. Available from www.oecd.org/dataoecd/11/39/34429196.pdf (accessed 4 March 2006).

Passel, Jeffery S. 2006. *The size and characteristics of the unauthorized migrant population in the U.S.* Washington, DC: Pew Hispanic Center. Available from http://pewhispanic.org/files/reports/61.pdf (accessed 4 August 2010).

Portes, Alejandro, and Ruben Rumbaut. 2001. *Legacies: The story of the immigrant generation*. Berkeley and Los Angeles, CA: University of California Press.

Pre-K Now. 2007. *Votes count: Legislative action on pre-K fiscal year 2008*. Washington, DC: Pre-K Now. Available from www.preknow.com//documents/LegislativeReport_Sept2007.pdf (accessed 19 May 2008).

Ruggles, Steven J., Trent Alexander, Katie Genadek, Ronald Goeken, Matthew B. Schroeder, and Matthew Sobek. 2010. Integrated Public Use Microdata Series: Version 5.0 [Machine-readable database]. Minneapolis, MN: University of Minnesota.

Saegert, Susan. 1982. Environment and children's mental health: Residential density and low income children. In *Handbook of psychology and health*, vol. II, *Issues in child health and adolescent health*, eds. Andrew f. Baum and Jerome E. Singer, 247–71. Hillsdale, NJ: Lawrence Erlbaum.

Sam, David L., Paul Vedder, Coleen Ward, and Gabriel Horenczyk. 2006. Psychological and sociocultural adaptation of immigrant youth. In *Immigrant youth in cultural transition: Acculturation, identify, and adaptation across national contexts*, eds. John W. Berry, Jean S. Phinney, David L. Sam, Paul Vedder, 117–42. Mahwah, NJ: Lawrence Erlbaum.

Sewell, William H., and Robert M. Hauser. 1975. *Education, occupation and earnings*. New York, NY: Academic Press.

Shonkoff, Jack P., and Deborah A. Phillips. 2000. *From neurons to neighborhoods: The science of early child development*. Washington, DC: National Academy Press.

Smeeding, Timothy, Coady Wing, and Karen Robson. 2010. Differences in social transfer support and poverty for immigrant families with children: Lessons from the LIS. In *Immigration, diversity, and education*, eds. Elena L. Grigorenko and Ruby Takanishi, 26–47. London: Routledge/Taylor and Francis Group.

Squires, Gregory D., and Charis E. Kubrin. 2006. *Privileged places: Race, residence and the structure of opportunity*. Boulder, CO: Lynne Rienner.

Stolberg, Sheryl Gay, and Robert Pear. 23 March 2010. Obama signs health care overhaul bill, with a flourish. *New York Times*. Available from www.nytimes.com.

St. Pierre, Robert, Anne Ricciuti, Fumiyo Tao, Cindy Creps, Janet Swartz, Wang Lee, and Amanda Parsad. 2003. *Third national Even Start evaluation: Program impacts and implications for improvement*. Washington, DC: U.S. Department of Education, Planning and Evaluation Service, Elementary and Secondary Education Division.

Takanishi, Ruby. 2004. Leveling the playing field: Supporting immigrant children from birth to eight. *The Future of Children* 14 (2): 61–79.

Turner, Margery Austin, Beata A. Bednarz, Carla Herbig, and Seon Joo Lee. 2003. *Discrimination in metropolitan housing markets phase II: Asian and Pacific Islanders*. Washington, DC: Urban Institute. Available from www.urban.org/url.cfm?ID=1000502 (accessed 7 July 2010).

Turner, Margery Austin, Stephen L. Ross, George Galster, and John Yinger. 2002. *Discrimination in metropolitan housing markets*. Washington, DC: Urban Institute. Available from www.urban.org/url.cfm?ID=410821 (accessed 7 July 2010).

UNICEF. 2008. *The childcare transition*. Report no. 8. Florence, Italy: UNICEF Innocenti Research Centre.

United Nations General Assembly. 1989. Convention on the Rights of the Child. Res. 44/25. New York: NY: United Nations. Available from www.un.org/documents/instruments/docs_en.asp.

U.S. Census Bureau. 1994. *Housing of lower-income households*. Statistical Brief SB/94/18. Washington, DC: U.S. Census Bureau. Available from www.census.gov/aspd/www/statbrief/sb94_18.pdf (accessed 9 January 2006).

U.S. Congress. Senate. 2010. Patient Protection and Affordable Care Act of 2010. HR 3590. 111th Cong., 1st sess. Available from http://democrats.senate.gov/reform/patient-protection-affordable-care-act.pdf.

U.S. Department of Agriculture (USDA). 2007. *USDA food stamp program: Food stamps make America stronger*. Washington, DC: USDA. Available from www.fns.usda.gov/cga/FactSheets/food_stamps.htm (accessed 13 July 2007).

U.S. Department of Commerce. 2 March 2010. Press release: Census Bureau to develop supplemental poverty measure. Washington, DC: U.S. Department of Commerce. Available from www.commerce.gov/news/ (accessed 4 August 2010).

Uttal, Lynet. 1999. Using kin for child care: Embedment in the socioeconomic networks of extended families. *Journal of Marriage and the Family* 61 (4): 845–57.

Yoshikawa, Hirokazu, Kathleen McCartney, Robert G. Myers, Kristen L. Bub, Julieta Lugo-Gil, Maria A. Ramos, and Felicia Knau. 2006. Educacion preescolar en Mexico. In *Aprender más y mejor: Politicas, programas y oportunidades de aprendizaje en educacion basica en Mexico*, ed. Fernando Reimers. Mexico City: Fonda Cultura y Economica.

Zimmermann, Wendy, and Karen C. Tumlin. 1999. *Patchwork policies: State assistance for immigrants under welfare reform*. Occasional Paper no. 24. Washington, DC: Urban Institute.

Children and the Rights of Citizens: Nondomination and Intergenerational Justice

By
JAMES BOHMAN

The Convention on the Rights of the Child (CRC) emphasizes the importance of the temporal dimension of childhood and children's need for special protection. Such protection is necessary because of their susceptibility to domination, especially intergenerational domination. The same is true for past and future generations, where such domination includes the domination of and by the current generation of children, especially around intergenerational, public goods important for a good human life. Such an account of intergenerational justice captures the focus of the CRC's Preamble on improving the quality of the lives of children.

Keywords: human rights; child rights; intergenerational justice; global warming; nondomination

The Convention on the Rights of the Child (CRC) formulates a diverse set of rights oriented toward the situation of the child. Children are the bearers of robust rights, even if they cannot lay claim to the entire complement of rights and statuses found in documents concerned with fully developed adult citizens. The CRC gives moral and legal statuses to children, giving them special protections and entitlements, many of which protect their particular vulnerabilities. While children have some moral and legal statuses that are different from those of adult citizens, the CRC recognizes that they will become independent adults, giving some of the rights of the child an obvious temporal dimension. This temporal dimension of human maturation is expressed in the Declaration on the Rights of the Child and forms part the Preamble to the

James Bohman is Danforth Professor of Philosophy and professor of international studies at Saint Louis University. He is author of Democracy across Borders *(MIT Press 2007),* Public Deliberation: Pluralism, Complexity and Democracy *(MIT Press 1996), and* New Philosophy of Social Science: Problems of Indeterminacy *(MIT Press 1991).*

DOI: 10.1177/0002716210383114

CRC, where children are recognized as needing "special safeguards and care, including appropriate legal protection" (United Nations [UN] General Assembly 1989). Indeed, many of the distinctive claims that children can make, such as rights to education, nutrition, and other requirements for development, are put in the context of the child's becoming an adult and a full citizen. Children, even if owed important legal protections, are clearly not yet the authors and subjects of the laws in the ways that their parents may be (at least in democratic political communities).

These same circumstances of development and maturation make it such that children may be dominated in various ways because of their lack of full legal and moral statuses. Thus, children are subject to what Michael Walzer calls "the oldest form of domination," the domination of noncitizens by citizens or, in this case, of those who are not yet citizens by those who already are (Walzer 1983, 62). This problem of the lack of status extends beyond children alone and includes many who lack rights and political statuses, including, most important, the rights of others who are not yet citizens: future generations. Similar to children, future generations seem to have at least prospective rights as members of an intergenerational and intertemporal polity. Understanding the temporal dimension of various political statuses will help us to understand the type of obligations that are owed to incomplete, partial citizens such as children and perhaps even to those who may in the future be citizens.

Most citizens in existing democracies assume that their polity will remain democratic, if not for centuries, at least for the foreseeable future. Likewise, most framers of constitutions assume that the framework that they formulate will be inherited by future generations, even as they often make it possible for future generations of citizens to respond to any imperfections and to change the constitution through the amendment process. Except in these moments of revision, the workings of democracy are often thought of in ways that leave out temporality. We the "People," or more often our representatives, are able to decide authoritatively for the present and the future. So conceived, the democratic political community is doubly bound: spatially by the borders of the demos and temporally by those who are assembled. Such a narrow temporal interpretation implies that democracies are a succession of independent generations. While any generation may know some of their predecessors and their successors, more distant past and future generations are often thought to lie outside of the political community. While we have concerns for the lives of our children and their children, the temporally narrow scope of the political community makes it possible and, under certain circumstances (such as global warming), very likely that the current generation will dominate future generations. Such domination may even make it difficult for future generations not only to live well but also to inherit the democratic constitution.

Given changes in the nature of modern polities, many people may lack political and legal statuses even if they have for some time lived within an already constituted political community. Rawls (1996, 68), for example, thought that we could model persons on the assumption that they will live a complete life within a single polity, "entering at birth and exiting only at death." Such an assumption makes it difficult to deal with a pervasive fact of modern polities: citizens live out their lives in many different locations, sometimes as noncitizens and sometimes as citizens. For this reason, it seems implausible to say of most democracies that subjects of the law are also its authors. This makes it even more important to conceive of a variety of rights and statuses in the present that can enable people to avoid various harms and evils in the future in the absence of some overarching status such as citizenship. Until recently, citizenship served to bundle together various kinds of rights and moral and political statuses. This lack of political and legal statuses hinders a vulnerable segment of the present political community and potentially leads to the domination of some citizens over others; but it may also undermine the achievement of well-being for many people in the future political community. If they are dominated, then their overall prospects of fulfilling the democratic ideal are greatly diminished. Rawls, for example, argued that any democratic conception of justice must include "a provision for the just claims of future generations," precisely because of the peculiar features of democracy and majority rule (Rawls 1971, 296). Such future generations include not only hypothetical persons but also the next generation of children already living in the present.

The CRC reflects the fact that children live under many different circumstances, with and without basic rights and statuses that might permit them to avoid evils and achieve various goods. Rights, in this view, are primarily to be thought of in terms of statuses and not simply based on basic interests or autonomous choices. The CRC develops those statuses that are necessary for the nondomination of children, regardless of their other statuses or rights. They are distinctly human rights because they are not derived from some other status, such as being a citizen of a particular state. I argue for this interpretation of the CRC in three steps. First, I turn to the capabilities approach to human rights to criticize certain restrictive notions of children's rights, in which full rights require already achieved functionings. The lack of important functionings is ubiquitous in all phases of human life, especially for those who live in poverty. Second, I argue that certain important statuses that enable agents not to be dominated are developed in the CRC, starting with a communicative status or rights of communication. Other crucial statuses, such as political status and the right to education and other goods can best be understood in terms of the availability of substantial freedom for development.

Finally, I turn to the overall justification of such rights and statuses for children and for noncitizens. In light of the possibility that democracies can dominate future generations as they do noncitizens, some version of Edmund Burke's view of a political community as a partnership across generations should be extended across many democratic concepts; for example, popular sovereignty can only be made intergenerational if each generation regards itself as the "temporary possessor" of democratic power and thus will not act "as its entire master" (Burke 1890, 106). While this idea seems to be directed to the future, Burke clearly thinks that the present generation can exercise mastery over the past by erasing historical obligations to previous generations, which are built into political and democratic relationships. In each case, concepts of nondomination, capabilities, and intergenerational justice help to specify some of the important interests of the child and the obligations of the political community toward the child as a developing human being.

Children and Capabilities

The rights listed in the CRC are quite diverse in their aims. While some are concerned with protective rights, others focus on various kinds of statuses and identities, and still others are directed to other aspects of the achievement of a full human life. The philosophical debate about the rights of children has tended to only really consider two justifications for rights: (1) autonomous choices, which children do not have; and (2) basic interests, which all human beings have. These include interests related to living a worthwhile human life, and these rights are often thought of as positive rights to various goods, such as the right to education, health care, nutrition, and those related to disabilities. Rawls's (1971) idea of primary goods does not really capture the distinctive character of these rights as related to children. This conceptualization tends to see rights as having an instrumental value in attaining various kinds of goods or fulfilling various interests. Feinberg and others have come closer to the rights of the child by talking about opportunities expressed in the idea of having "an open future" (Feinberg 2007). Feinberg's (2007) conception not only introduces a temporal dimension; it also attempts to delineate what is distinctive about the temporally mediated rights of children. The standard debate falsely states that adults can exercise their rights as long as their choices are not interfered with. But for many of the goods that are necessary for a worthwhile life, neither children nor adults can achieve these ends on their own, including such important goods as an epidemiologically secure environment. This good is not only related to basic interests; it is also related to freedoms that one would enjoy with such security. Indeed, anyone who has such a public good also has a greater extent of freedom than someone who lacks this good. This freedom exists because having such a good not only affects peoples' choices or interests but also peoples' "beings and doings," what they can do and become, to use Amartya Sen's (1992) terms. As in the case of children, human beings in general often lack various capabilities and must develop them. Rights can thus be seen as entitlements to the opportunities to achieve certain capabilities for important human functionings, both in general and through maturation.

Sen's (1992) conception of capabilities provides a more apt and general normative basis than does a general interests approach, with the added advantage that the conception of capabilities also appeals to a broad conception of equality of opportunity. But these opportunities must be substantial and provide the basis for the achievement of valuable functioning, where the resources needed to achieve such functioning are quite variable across persons. Poverty is the failure to achieve minimally adequate functioning, so that poverty (or any capability failure) is measured in terms of the scope of the person's overall freedom, his or her "achievings and doings." Thus, freedom consists of one's "capability set," those real options from which an agent is able to choose (Sen 1992, 111). This sort of freedom takes two forms: the first is "agency freedom," by which people are able to attain their various goals, including justice. The second is "well-being freedom," a freedom that may not be an "achieving or doing" at all, such as the freedom to an epidemiologically safe environment or the freedom from starvation and the endless search for food that takes up the lives of the malnourished. While a person on a hunger strike may sacrifice his or her well-being for his or her agency goals, a starving person lacks the opportunity to achieve well-being and, thus, well-being freedom.

The resource approach cannot easily be used to understand the consequences of capability failures both for adults and for children. As Ronald Dworkin (2000, 167) admits, a resourcist approach has "no basis for interpersonal comparisons of liberty deficits," since resources require liberties that can be used for their own ends. In the case of children, such liberty deficits would surely lead to a more restrictive capability set than would be necessary for a good human life. Using the idea of capabilities with respect to the rights of the child has the advantage of seeing the diversity of requirements needed for achieving basic functioning, but the idea also can conceptualize a variety of rights in terms of the scope of the freedom to live a worthwhile human life. Following Sen (1992), we can also employ a conception of freedom, with regard to these rights, that is essential to the development of the child, not freedom from domination but capability freedom, understood as the greatest extent of freedom necessary for good human functioning. As in the case of nondomination, such an account of substantial opportunities and access to functionings help to define fundamental interests of the child.

But not all rights of the child reflect inner requirements of the development of the person, such as the development of various capacities of powers that are internal properties of the person. The capabilities approach goes beyond such a limited conception of development and well-being, a bias that is pervasive in economics, particularly when it is concerned with issues and policies related to well-being. The problem is not simply that measures of wealth focus on production and consumption indices but that even the broader measures of well-being, such as the UN Human Development Index, focus entirely on current well-being. However, many such indices represent improvements over previous measures, such as GDP (gross domestic product). Nevertheless, their emphasis on present capabilities leaves out the important contributions of the natural environment to human well-being. The environment contributes most directly to long-term processes of change and development, so that its degradation directly affects the security of democratic institutions and individual well-being. There is a high correlation between poverty and environmental degradation, particularly in areas where people depend on the natural provision of many valuable goods, such as fertile soil, drinkable water, and other basic necessities, which Partha Dasgupta (2001) aptly calls "ecological services." Indeed, large migrations from the country to urban areas most often occur "when local common-property resources degrade to the point where life at home is impossible" (Dasgupta 2001, 192). According to Dasgupta, when forests and watersheds suffer degradation and the environment loses biodiversity and resilience, the poorest in a society suffer the most due to their more direct dependence on such environmental services.

Because of these blind spots concerning environmental and other intergenerational public goods, we tend to discount future well-being on the assumption that economic growth always increases rather than decreases well-being. But the effects of environmental insecurity may not be manifest within any single generation. Indeed, the lack of environmental security is often signaled by the fate of the worst off, who are most likely to be affected more quickly by the loss of environmental goods. It may also be that they are the products of a generation that did not have to bear the brunt of their own indifference. With respect to the environment, children are also vulnerable to domination, even within a democratic polity. Children may inherit a lack of such a capability, the consequences of which may mean that they lack the means to lead a life in an open future. The single clearest contemporary example of harming future generations and doing irreversible damage is global warming, the consequences of which are likely to be extremely bad and very difficult to reverse given how long such gases remain in the atmosphere.

Environmental security is now a global and intergenerational public good, so that conceptualizing security in terms of sovereign states no longer illuminates the scope of the issue. Environmental security with regard to global warming is shared, in the sense that it is achievable only if all possess it. Thus, from the perspective of shared freedom, the natural environment contributes to well-being in the same way that a safe epidemiological environment contributes to health. In the case of global warming, environmental security applies across political communities and, thus, is worsened because these communities lack the means to effective collective action. Issues of environmental security are truly global problems that cannot be easily solved by the current state system that seeks to protect the sovereignty of its members. It is not clear that the exercise of authority by a global sovereign would be any more effective than the current system of sovereign nations—neither system has the capacity to solve global problems.

It is easy to see the effects of the absence of such security: there is a strong negative correlation at work between environmental degradation on one hand and poverty on the other. One explanation that economists offer for this is that the poor degrade their resource base, because they discount the future at high rates for the sake of current income. But an alternative explanation is based on the failure of current institutions to supply the needed security of the rights and entitlements for poor citizens to secure their commonly held natural resources, such as water and grazing land, that they have often managed sustainably for centuries. As Dasgupta argued, the loss of such entitlements and rights is most often due to "political instability," a direct cause of environmental degradation (Dasgupta 2001, 113). The entitlements here are not rights to ownership but of access to environmental resources and to their intergenerational management. In the absence of this, there is no assurance that more powerful actors will not expropriate the commons and deny the use of existing rights to their local communities. With the degradation of the local resource base, local people then lack the well-being freedom that enables them to use these resources sustainably and preserve them for future generations.

Most of all, many of the problems of environmental security as an intergenerational public good follow upon processes of global warming, the effects of which will surely produce more domination, even as the states and the current state system are unable to control them. It is also true that the greatest insecurity will be felt several generations in the future as the environmental insecurity will worsen and become irreversible because the atmosphere will no longer be able to regenerate itself. As Barry Holden correctly argued, global warming requires extending democracy and popular control both spatially and temporally, since it "affects all the people of the world" (Holden 2004, 117). Here, we must remember that popular control can be dominating, and, hence, its expansion must be aimed at making well-being freedom more robust not merely in the present but also across future generations and at the institutional level. Robustness here is a measure of the security of rights and entitlements and their multiple realizations across various levels makes them more secure; in the example of resource degradation discussed above, rights and entitlements at the state and the local levels often work against each other. Rather than positively making each more secure, rights of use are undermined by legal rights of ownership. Environmental security is an intergenerational and global public good—none have the freedom to live in a secure environment unless all have it. The global people, then, are a community of those who share the same fate and atmosphere.

Using an intergenerational understanding of the rights of children, neglecting to address global warming is a potentially massive failure to extend the protective reach of democracy to children as representatives of future generations. They will be environmentally less secure than we are today. The CRC declares in its Preamble that one of the main tasks is to "improve the living conditions of all children," and Article 6 states that the States Parties must "ensure to the maximum extent possible the survival and development of the children" (UN General Assembly 1989). I have argued in this section that intergenerational issues bring out the fact that children can be dominated through the policies of present governments that could impose on children exceptionally difficult living conditions; by doing so, governments deprive them of basic liberties, including the freedom to achieve a decent human life.

Nondomination, Rights, and Statuses

According to Philip Pettit (1997), domination is defined as the dominator's "capacity to interfere" on an arbitrary basis in the choices of another. Pettit includes among these capacities "financial clout, political authority, social connections, communal standing, informational access, ideological positions, cultural legitimation and the like" (1997, 52). But the capacity to interfere is a necessary, but not sufficient, condition for domination, precisely because such a capacity can be exercised by a "nonmastering interferer" (1997, 55), such as a government that acts in accordance with the rule of law and also "tracks" the opinions and interests of those with whom it interferes. Such tracking is entirely consistent with Article 12 of the CRC, in which children have a right to say what they think their interests are, even if they do not have final authority over those interests. To avoid domination, I must enjoy a "secure and resilient form of noninterference" and, thus, must "be in a position where no one has that power of arbitrary interference and I am correspondingly powerful" (Pettit 1997, 69). These powers derive from the status of being a citizen, the great benefit of which is the possession of "the power to prevent certain ills from happening" (Pettit 1997, 69). Given the myriad sources of domination, agents must be powerful indeed. The ability to plan one's life and to live it is impossible when one is dominated; not to be free in this way is to live without the security that we associate with a worthwhile human life. Nondomination is a condition for such security. Children who are subject to long hours of debilitating labor in many parts of the world lack even the most basic kind of statuses and are often dominated by the will of adults.

One weakness of Pettit's account is that the linkage between domination and arbitrary interference is difficult to specify, since any exercise of public power, such as legal coercion, is potentially dominating. In the context of democracy, I propose that domination is the use of authoritative normative powers to impose obligations and change entitlements without recourse or remedy. In light of this requirement, Pettit argues that "a suitable legal regime" is necessary for nondomination in the sense that this normative status and its powers do not depend on the good will of others (1997, 35). Democracy itself is, then, the joint exercise of these powers and capacities, so that the demos are not under the control of any given individual or group of citizens. Such powers must be redefined jointly and creatively when the circumstances of domination change.

The fundamental reason for achieving nondomination is for individuals to have control over their own obligations and over the scope of these normative statuses, which are central to achieving democratic self-rule. In the absence of such security, the CRC argues, the child is subject to domination by others who have more power and full statuses. Accordingly, one functional role of the rights of the child is to make children legally secure from domination even without having attained full legal or political status. Such rights, however, are not simply legal protections. Rather, they are statuses—indeed, just those statuses that make it possible for children to mature and develop from partial to full members of society. As a form of freedom, nondomination does not specify how children are to develop but makes it possible to do so in the context of relationships that, as Pettit (1997) puts it, do not arbitrarily interfere to the extent that they track the child's opinions and interests. Today, falling under the control of another is, more often than not, due to the difficult circumstances under which many people who lack legal and civil statuses live in the world. To have a status, as Hegel (1991) remarks, is to be someone; to lack it is to be nobody. Children are certainly among the many human beings, including stateless persons and refugees, who lack important statuses usually bundled in the achievement of full citizenship: communicative status to express oneself in public and be recognized and heard by others; and decisional status, the capacity to make important decisions over one's life as a whole and over the common life that one lives with others.

What statuses make such tracking possible? For Pettit (1997, 31–32), this status is "the civil condition," which could apply to full and partial citizens. One way that the civil condition could create conditions for tracking interests and opinions for children is to see them as having a full legal status of persons as well some of the statuses of citizens (such as the right to nationality, documentation, and so on). The moral harm of domination is not just the psychological and other costs of arbitrary interference in the life of another but, rather, that when one is so dependent and subordinated, "one ceases to be a person" (see Kant 1996, 104).[1] The injustice of domination is to have no status at all. The turn to such a universal status is an answer to the question of *whose* freedom is important in assessing a just legal order. The only possible answer consistent with nondomination is "*all* persons." This is not the only important status implied in the CRC. Many articles develop various rights of communication, including freedom of expression and the right to be heard. Lacking the effective capacity to address institutions and officials directly, dominated persons could nonetheless address each other and other citizens as members of a public, whose response entails their recognition of a shared communicative freedom. This communicative status provides a standing on which a child or others without status become a "self-originating source of claims" (Rawls 1996, 509) and may also be recognized by social movements that aim to achieve the protections of legal status for migrants and others who lack citizenship. Similar to the status of person, such recognition of a shared communicative status in the public sphere is cosmopolitan in the sense that it is not derived from some other membership but rather from a mutually granted, and thus a shared, communicative freedom of addressing others and being addressed by them.

These examples serve to show ways in which some of the rights developed in the CRC clearly have the role of establishing various statuses and capabilities for children. Article 7—the right of a child to preserve his or her identity—is certainly among the core rights of status. Article 12 establishes a communicative status and a general tracking of opinions and interests. These statuses are important for children's capacity for nondominated development with an open future and for freedom from arbitrary power. Rather than merely enumerating legal practices that might lead to deprivation of liberty (as in Article 37), many of these rights instead consist of freedoms and statuses that make it possible for children to have sufficient agency over their lives to contest the loss of liberties by having their opinions heard and their interests considered. If that were not the case, the political community would fail to exercise nondomination across generations. This is part of the concern for intergenerational justice, and in this respect, our treatment of children is part of a wider obligation to future generations.

Intergenerational Justice and the Rights of the Child

I have thus far argued that the rights owed to children express not only their statuses as human beings, communication partners, and so on, but that children are also owed these rights because of their duties to the future of an intergenerational community. As Roger Paden (1997, 47) has argued, saving for the future is on a par with foreign aid. "Since it is impossible to tell if future generations will accept the principles of justice, they would count as outsiders" (see also Schelling 1995).[2] Rawls (1971) also thought for this reason that any obligations that come from sharing a political community extend only to the near future (no further than our children's children), much in the way that many think that our obligations of justice in general give priority to those nearest to us spatially. His idea of a just savings rate—the amount of savings that we owe future generations—might even be considered as one of the duties a political community owes to outsiders rather than to its own future members. To avoid the potential for domination, it is better in both cases to treat these others as potential members of the same political community, who are able to make public claims of justice across space and time. Certainly, the next generation of our children can make direct claims on us, and their children upon them, and so on. In light of the possibility that democracies can dominate future generations as they do noncitizens, some version of Burke's view of a political community as a partnership across generations should be extended in a variety of ways; for example, popular sovereignty can only be made intergenerational if each generation regards itself, in Burke's terms, as a "temporary possessor" of democratic power rather than "as its entire master" (Burke 1890, 106).

In the present, things can be organized so that it is more likely that the concerns of future generations will be considered as guiding the present generation. Dennis Thompson (2005) proposed that citizens see themselves as part of a temporal series of sovereigns, in which the form of future democracy is left open. Nonetheless, given the ways that the present generation can still affect future democratic sovereigns, each generation should institutionally "represent future sovereigns by acting as trustees of the democratic process" (Thompson 2005, 248). Each generation is thus entrusted to hand democracy on to the future sovereign people, in such a way as to allow them at the very least to exercise competent control over their lives. The notion that the present generation is a trustee holding past, present, and future sovereignty is an appropriate development of the idea of an intergenerational polity. Thus, if democracies are to avoid intergenerational domination, pooling sovereignty requires sharing statuses and freedoms across time. The insecurity of intergenerational democratic domination can be avoided only if each generation has both forward- and backward-looking rights and obligations to other *generations* (and not simply to past and future *individuals*). Environmental security—a shared form of freedom across borders and generations—is achieved only when no spatial or temporal demos can assert final authority over the past, the present, and the future.

It is instructive to turn first to the intergenerational significance of the past, perhaps because interaction between past and future generations seems unavoidably mediated by the present. In fact, the past often has political claims upon the present, usually related to past injustices and harms. But such claims are always intergenerational, in the sense that they are as much about the future as about the past. Intergenerational democracy requires that the past is not closed, at least in the sense that those living in the present can make legitimate claims based on ongoing domination in the present. This means that dealing with claims of past generations can change the polity in the present. Indeed, the very attempt to close the past inevitably democratically reopens it and potentially creates a novel past from which new claims of justice may emerge. This has been the case in New Zealand, where treaty violations are not merely matters of the past but are now seen as ongoing into the future. Intergenerational democracy thus resists closure and finality within the democratic community, leaving it open to change in both temporal directions as deliberators construct the ongoing relations between past, present, and future. The atemporal character of current democracy is actually a form of temporal bias that entrenches enormous asymmetries of power among generations. If the past of a democracy is closed in cases of intergenerational domination, then so too is its future. As Thompson put it, "Even if no values except popular sovereignty were at stake, the principle cannot give any particular majority final authority" (2005, 246). Since the claims of future sovereigns are undervalued in the present, it is not surprising that they are left to fend for themselves, despite the fact that many decisions not only pose significant constraints on the future but may last for many generations or even be irreversible.

Even if it is clear that sovereignty must be pooled and that security is a public good held across generations, it is not clear how to institutionalize these relationships temporally. It seems clear that some form of trusteeship in both temporal directions is necessary; at the same time, the presentist bias of current democracy seems to undermine such a possibility. The issue is as much structural as it is epistemic. Thompson (2005) argues that what is needed is a form of representation, in which officials participate in parliamentary debate, as a way to represent the interests of future generations in the present. However important it is to give voice to the interests of children and future generations in some way, this solution does not fundamentally address the structural causes for the presentist bias of democracy that undermine trusteeship. Nor does it make much sense to have biased institutions and expect some representative of the past or future to be able to effectively make claims on the institutions' behalves or even to know what their interests are. Here the focus should be on making domination structurally impossible; we can assume that domination will be a cause of great ills experienced by future generations. Thus, we might think of transnational institutions as providing a certain analogy. The European Union (EU) established a transnational polity, rather than a system of representation; and thus a transgenerational democracy cannot simply establish an embassy for future generations. The EU offers a political order that allows for a positive feedback relationship of pooled sovereignty that enables democratization to occur, in which it is precisely the transnational-level institutions that enhance democracy at the lower levels. With such mutual interaction across levels and locations, a highly differentiated polity works not merely in policy areas but also in creating a regime of human rights that can realize the powers of citizenship and make them more, rather than less, robust.

The founding moment of the EU, as articulated by Spinelli and others (see Menendez 2007), was explicitly intergenerational—multiple generations experienced the war and demanded the transformation of democracy beyond individual states. Thus, the present can be a trustee for democracy, ensuring not merely that democracy is possible in the future but that it rules itself in such a way that the past does not dominate the present, nor the present dominate the future. The transnational public must see itself as communicating across time with the future, among all those who form part of the indefinite audience to whom the present owes justifications and with whom it shares basic liberties. Thus, we can see security as a kind of primary good, as that public good that any generation at any temporal location would seek if it attempts to realize self rule. Or, to use Rawls's (1971) first principle, each generation must see to it that the just claim of a future is possible and, thus, that each generation is able to make use of the fair value of the liberty that it shares with all others. For democracies, the consideration of the freedom of future generations is a constitutive requirement of intergenerational justice.

Conclusion

One of the main motivations for the rights of the child is to provide protection and security for children as bearers of a partial and developing status as a person and a citizen. Many of the CRC's its rights are aimed at the structural possibility of domination inherent in the dependence of children. I have extended this analysis to future generations, of which our children are only the temporarily closest. Instead of seeing these rights only in terms of individuals, however, we can extend this reasoning to regard each generation as a trustee for future generations that takes those future generations' legitimate claims as an important part of present deliberations. Rather than some proxy, the future is part of the indefinite audience to which the public addresses its justifications, giving it a similar political status in present deliberation. Here we should not consider just the interests of individuals—important as they are in articulating basic rights claims—but instead future generations' interests as well. The present generation can dominate future generations, as is the case now with the imposition of opportunity costs on the future in global warming. The rights framework of the CRC frames the discussion in terms of children living in the present. If we accept that nondomination is the goal of many of the provisions of the CRC, we must include the imposition of enormous costs on future generations as a temporal form of domination and as the failure of the present generation to act as temporary possessor of the power it shares with future generations.

Notes

1. For this reason, the voluntary surrender of one's freedom entirely to another was impossible for Kant. Thus, the right to freedom is imprescriptible and unalienable. Hegel similarly argued that "my right to my distinct personality in general and to my universal freedom of the will" are also inalienable. See Hegel (1991, 92).

2. Schelling (1995) considers money used to abate global warming to be a form of "foreign aid."

References

Burke, Edmund. 1890. *Reflections on the revolution in France*. ed. F. G. Selby. London: MacMillan.

Dasgupta, Partha. 2001. *Human well being and the natural environment*. Oxford: Oxford University Press.

Dworkin, Ronald. 2000. *Sovereign virtue*. Cambridge, MA: Harvard University Press.

Feinberg, Joel. 2007. The child's right to an open future. In *Philosophy of education*, ed. Randall Curren. London: Blackwell.

Hegel, George Wilhelm Friedrich. 1991. *Philosophy of right*. Cambridge: Cambridge University Press.

Holden, Barry. 2004. *Democracy and global warming*. London: Continuum.

Kant, Immanuel. 1996. *Metaphysics of morals*. Trans. and ed. Mary Gregor. Cambridge: Cambridge University Press.

Mendenez, Jose, ed. 2007. *Alterio Spinelli: From Ventotene to the European Constitution*. Oslo, Norway: Recon Report 1/7.

Paden, Roger. 1997. Rawls' just savings principle and the sense of justice. *Social Theory and Practice* 23:39–54.

Pettit, Philip. 1997. *Republicanism*. Oxford: Oxford University Press.

Rawls, John. 1971. *A theory of justice*. Cambridge, MA: Harvard University Press.

Rawls, John. 1996. *Political liberalism*. New York, NY: Columbia University Press.

Schelling, Thomas. 1995. Intergenerational discounting. *Energy Policy* 23:395–401.

Sen, Amartya. 1992. *Inequality reexamined*. Oxford: Oxford University Press.

Thompson, Dennis. 2005. Democracy in time: Popular sovereignty and temporal representation. *Constellations* 12:241–58.

United Nations General Assembly. 1989. Convention on the Rights of the Child. New York, NY: United Nations. Available from www.un.org/documents/instruments/docs_en.asp.

Walzer, Michael. 1983. *Spheres of justice*. New York, NY: Basic Books.

The Child as Democratic Citizen

By
ANDREW REHFELD

The United Nations Convention on the Rights of the Child (CRC) justifiably emphasizes welfare over participation rights of children for two reasons. First, children are by nature an at-risk population. Second, democratic citizenship rights require a minimal bundle of cognitive and emotional capacity—which may be called "political maturity"—that children, again by nature, lack. However, the CRC goes too far in prioritizing welfare over participation, again for two reasons. First, millions of children have their basic welfare needs met, and second, participation would be useful in cultivating the very political maturity that citizens need. In this article, the author argues that participatory institutions should be designed to further the interests of children, cultivate their political maturity, and mitigate the harm that giving power to the politically immature might cause. The author discusses three institutional designs that might achieve this result (fractional voting, national electoral constituencies, and political spending accounts) and discusses how federalism might also help to implement these designs.

Keywords: voting rights; representation; proxy voting; children; voting age; citizenship; institutional design

> Children are a nuisance to most adults; they are a particular nuisance to the democratic theorist who wishes to exclude them from having a voice in the direction of the policy with as much vehemence as he wishes to include every adult (except, of course, felons, the insane, the mentally retarded, and aliens).
>
> —Schrag (1975, 443)

NOTE: Preliminary versions of this article were presented at the Child as Citizen Conference, which the Harvard University Committee on Human Rights Studies and the Harvard School of Public Health hosted in Cambridge, Massachusetts, November 9–10, 2009; at the annual meeting of the Canadian Political Science Association, in Montreal, June 1–3, 2010; at the Faculty Workshop of Washington University Law School, St. Louis, July 7, 2010; and at the Political Theory Workshop at Washington University in St. Louis, September 17, 2010. Thanks to Felton Earls, Samantha Brennan, Anna Stilz, and Laura Rosenbury, and participants in those fora for their input and feedback. Additional thanks to Annette Appell, Jenny Diamond Cheng, Claudio López-Guerra, David Koenig, Ron Levin, Frank Lovett, Ian MacMullen, Neil Richards, and Daniel Weinstock for their additional feedback. This article does not fully take into account their responses. I intend to expand on the discussion in this article in later publications.

DOI: 10.1177/0002716210383656

Statement of the Problem

The United Nations Convention on the Rights of the Child (CRC) reflects the widely held view that children are in need of protection and should not be treated as full citizens of a democratic polity. Thirty-five of its forty-one substantive Articles (listed in Part I of that document) protect, secure, and guarantee welfare rights for children. The six articles that specify some legal and political rights of children—including provisions for very limited freedoms of expression, thought, conscience, religion, association, privacy, and access to information (Articles 13–17)—treat children more as a protected class than as active agents, subordinate to their parents' views, particularly in the areas of religion and privacy. Providing that "States Parties shall assure to the child who is capable of forming his or her own views the right to express those views freely in matters affecting the child," Article 12 exemplifies in three ways this prioritization of welfare over citizenship. First, it limits the expression of children's voices to cases in which they have a direct personal interest. Second, they only have the "opportunity to be heard in any judicial and administrative proceedings affecting the child"—not, that is, in legislatures. And third, these purported rights are fully executable by an "appropriate body" who may execute this function without oversight or post hoc accountability by the child on whose behalf the body acts. In contrast, democratic citizens justifiably (1) are involved in decisions that affect their interests much more broadly and indirectly than the narrowness implied in Article 12;[1] (2) are entitled to participate across judicial, administrative/executive, *and* legislative venues; and (3) have the power to hold a representative to account for her or his actions even when acting on the citizen's behalf. According to widely endorsed principles of representative government, these are necessary elements for a polity to be reasonably democratic.

The emphasis on children's welfare is, however, understandable. Children are, by nature, an at-risk population, and their inclusion, as political citizens, must rank behind their basic security. Even where their welfare is for the moment secured, the exclusion of children from politics may be reasonable because children,

---

Andrew Rehfeld is an associate professor of political science at Washington University in St. Louis. He received his MPP and PhD in political science from the University of Chicago, where he has taught as a lecturer and visiting assistant professor. His main area of research is in the theory and practice of political representation, with ancillary interests in the philosophy of social science and the politics of the Hebrew Bible. His book The Concept of Constituency *(Cambridge University Press 2005) explored the negative consequences of representing citizens by where they live and proposed national, permanent, randomized constituencies as a preferable alternative. He is completing a second book with Cambridge University Press about the relationship between representation and democracy. His other articles have appeared in the* American Political Science Review, *the* Journal of Politics, *and* Studies in American Political Development, *along with other journals. He serves as the secretary and treasurer of the American Society for Political and Legal Philosophy and is on the governance committee of the Association for Political Theory.*

again by nature, appear to lack the minimal bundle of cognitive, emotional, and moral capacity necessary for justifiable participation in a democratic polity. The prospect of two-year-olds voting is absurd because they presumably lack these features.

Nevertheless, this bundle of capabilities—what I call "political maturity"—is continuous and developmental, not something a person or group suddenly comes to possess. By contrast, we tend to think of benefits of citizenship as discontinuous—one has the right to vote, for example, or one does not. The failure to think more creatively about institutions that might respond to the continuity of development has exacerbated the exclusion of children from politics, particularly where their welfare is reasonably secure. For this viewpoint makes it appear that there is no way to partially include them in the polity without giving them full rights and power of citizenship that, owing to their political immaturity, they admittedly do not deserve or ought not to have.

The argument proceeds in five sections. In the first section of this article, I speak to the importance of addressing children's welfare prior to the development of their citizenship capabilities. Children pose a specific problem for democratic institutional design: they are a population that is incrementally developing among institutions that are usually all-inclusive or all-exclusive. In the second section, I take up the topic of political maturity and argue for a developmental approach to institutional design that reflects the fact that children's political maturity develops incrementally.

In the third section, I argue that political institutions should be designed to represent the interests of children, while developing their citizenship capability and mitigating the harm that they, as politically immature citizens, might do to the polity. By way of illustration, I suggest four examples: increasing fractional votes for children beginning at age 12, forming national children's electoral constituencies to promote their voice and interest in the legislature, creating children's political spending allowances of $10 each that children could allocate to political campaigns and interest groups as they saw fit, and using federalism to limit the reach of children's involvement in politics. By using the incentive structure at the heart of representative government, each of these institutional designs would provide mitigated voice and representation to children. Children, in turn, would use political institutions to cultivate their citizenship capacity, rather than leave that to the politically impotent realm of the schools.

In the fourth section, I take up various approaches to political representation that can provide children with opportunities to be *democratically* represented (rather than virtually or by proxy). Finally, in the fifth section, I develop the four institutional designs mentioned above to flesh out how these approaches might look in practice.

Three important presumptions precede the following argument. First, in what follows, I do not define "childhood" in any precise way. Instead, I presume that all humans are "children" when born, and the vast majority of them stop being children sometime before the age of 25. Zero to 25 years old is admittedly an overly inclusive span to treat as "childhood." But I leave the developmental milestones to developmental psychologists. What I mean to ask is how should we treat humans who at some point have enough developmental capacity to engage appropriately in political citizenship prior to the point at which they have fully matured.

Second, I do not take up the prior question of what principles more generally should govern the granting of political rights. Instead, in what follows, I presume that whatever those standards are, they will also exclude the politically immature. Thus, the arguments concern the extension of rights in a preexisting political community and are thus consistent with a broad range of citizenship principles. The arguments here thus apply whether one would limit voting rights to certain groups, or to those living within a territorial space, or, in its broadest conception, to those whose interests are plausibly affected by the decisions of a government (Goodin 2007).

Third, in what follows, I make two assumptions about the kinds of errors that political immaturity is likely to cause. First, I presume that these errors will be systematic but hard to correct,[2] but not random. If political immaturity simply made people random decision-makers, then in the aggregate, the effect of giving the politically immature voting and other power would cancel itself out. Second, I also presume that political maturity develops positively, if not linearly, so that with each year of age, a person is more politically mature (to a certain limit of human ability). However, it is entirely possible that the tumultuousness of adolescence makes teenagers regress in political maturity from where they had been prior to the onset of puberty.[3] These issues—along with the establishment of precise age proxies for the stages of political maturity—would all have to be tied to an empirical account of developmental psychology, as would the institutional recommendations that would follow. But these presumptions affect only the particular institutions that map onto this development and not the form of the argument itself.

Welfare before Politics

There are good reasons that the CRC and democratic governments generally emphasize welfare and protection rights over political rights for children. First, childhood is a naturally precarious time; human beings are born at risk of death and are easily abused and neglected if not attended to for many years after they are born. Furthermore, millions of children currently live under conditions of material, political, and psychological instability. The primacy of welfare and protection rights over political rights is thus appropriate and justifiable. Claims to and protections of political rights of any kind are justified only where these basic protections are first secured or justified as a means to securing these protections if they are close enough at hand.[4]

However, children are not always in diapers, nor do all or most of them live in conditions of material, psychological, and educational deprivation. Even as many children remain at risk from external threats, tens if not hundreds of millions of children have their basic welfare needs met; are protected and living in conditions of relative stability and affluence; and receive a minimal, if still not necessarily adequate, education. So while the primacy of welfare over political rights is understandable and appropriate, it leaves the political questions open for a large proportion of the population who is not facing these extreme conditions. We can thus move to ask whether, in situations where reasonable protections have been secured, the exclusion of children from politics is in fact justifiable and, if not, what institutions might be endorsed to promote their involvement and why.

As David Archard and Colin Macleod (2002, 4) have noted, most political philosophers ignore the moral and political status of children.[5] Where they do take up children, their focus is on children's education, welfare, and development, reflecting the relative importance and insecurity of these kinds of goods to swaths of the globe. Within democratic theory, children feature largely in debates about public education and indirectly through the treatment of justice in the family and gender roles (Gutmann 1987; Okin 1989; Reich 2002; MacMullen 2007). Within the law, children have been more extensively treated, but here mostly in terms of the protections of their interest from abuse and defenses of paternalism (Buss 2003, 2004). We need not deny the primary importance of the developmental issues to children's welfare or the very real fact that even in the most prosperous nations there may be groups in which poverty or minority status renders children's security particularly insecure or uncertain. It is simply to say that basic welfare and developmental needs have been reasonably secured for a significant number of children, and it is time then to ask what benefits might be gained from having these children participate as emerging political citizens.

Political Maturity, Political Citizenship, and Political Rights

The academic literature reflects the emphasis of the CRC on child welfare and protection rather than active engagement, which appears justifiable for two primary reasons. First, as I mentioned above, claims to political rights are justifiably secured and protected only under conditions of stability and relative prosperity. Securing children's welfare and development must be a priority before considering whether or how they should participate as members of the political community. Instrumental considerations are the exception that proves the point: we might give votes to children, for example, if it made it more likely that their security and interests would be protected and advanced (Schrag 1975; Peterson 1992).

Even in nations where much of the population live in relative peace and stability, children by nature remain at risk because children—however one reasonably defines the bounds of childhood by age—lack the physical, emotional, and cognitive capacity that adults have to protect and advance their own interests as they develop. This natural state of childhood, into which all humans are born, creates a substantive political justification to exclude them from political citizenship: children, certainly at birth and for some time after, lack the skills that are reasonably required for a claim to political participation in a democratic polity. These qualities include a minimal level of cognitive capacity (what has historically been called "reason"), moral and emotional development to understand arguments about the good and empathize with others, the ability to communicate with others, and the capacity for independent action. When first born, children lack these four features, even if it is reasonable to expect that almost all humans are capable of developing them by the age of 25.[6] Even when they have access to some feature(s) of this set, it is partial and incomplete. Children of a young enough age do not have full command of reason; they lack the ability to think complexly about moral problem solving; and they have an extremely limited ability to communicate, let alone the ability to act independently. In short, we can say that children lack "political maturity," that bundle of cognitive, emotional, communicative, and agency capability that justifies a claim to citizenship rights within any democratic society.

Although the actual development of these capability will depend on the security, nurturing, and education that a child actually receives, I presume that all human offspring are developmentally the same in regard to the lower limits of when political maturity can set in; a newborn, for example, is not and will not be politically mature in any culture or society. Thus, the argument here is universal in its most general form.[7] However, since culture, nutrition, education, and material conditions affect the rate at which a child becomes politically mature, we should expect that the particular age of political maturity varies by culture or historical time frame. So while the argument that follows is universal in its categorical descriptions, the precise ages that children mature politically will depend on the interaction between developmental psychology and culture broadly conceived.

Why is political maturity a justifiable prerequisite for democratic citizenship? First and at the very least, rights claims usually entail the ability to make choices about the exercise of those rights. Goodin and Gibson (1997) have put it this way:

> What makes the rights of the immature young problematic . . . is the inability of such people to articulate a "choice" in any meaningful sense at all. They lack the requisite autonomy, in the moral much more importantly than in the merely physical sense of the term. Their will is unformed or deformed, their judgment deficient or impaired. (P. 187)[8]

Even where choice seems to be unnecessary, a purportedly "interests-based" account—in which rights are said to adhere to those who have interests—cannot help us here for reasons that Goodin and Gibson also persuasively articulate. "We can know what children's interests are without their making any choices because they will be making lots of choices in the future, and anything that preserves that future choice for them is in their (choice-maximizing) interests" (1997, 195). I do not want to take up the ontological question about whether children have rights, what rights they have, and how they may be protected or expressed.[9] We can still ask whether children ought to have the right to participate for other reasons, and it is on this point as well as the questions of rights that political maturity appears just as necessary for their inclusion.

A second reason that political maturity is a justifiable prerequisite for democratic citizenship has to do with the justification for democracy in particular, whether epistemic (Estlund 2007) or equality-based (Christiano 1996; Beitz 1990). On a strong epistemic account, democracy is endorsable because leaving decisions to the people is the most reliable way to arrive at the right answers to questions such as "Who should write our laws?" if not to questions about what the right policies and laws should be. Such an approach would require that citizens have at least a better than random chance of choosing correctly, and this grounds the need for political maturity (along with education). Even on a modified epistemic account, in which we endorse democracy as a good enough means of realizing the right answers, political maturity is necessary to ensure that decisions are not terrible. Similarly, on a political equality account, each citizen's interest is owed equal treatment, and that, as Goodin and Gibson (1997) describe above, presumes that each has the kind of competency to know his or her own preferences and determine his or her own interests, which requires political maturity.

More broadly, Schrag (1975) argues that participation rights should follow one's ability to deliberate in a way that approximates ideal considerations. The key capability that deliberators must have is offering reasons that would appeal to other reasonable persons. If we think that the role of the voter is simply to articulate her or his interests and vote for what she or he believes is in the public good, then a higher level of mental competence is necessary for voting than we usually think. But if not, voters younger than 18 would certainly be able to identify their preferences and quite possibly their narrow interests vis-à-vis political matters (Schrag 1975, 445–46). Such a view would exclude only "very young children," as older kids (Schrag suggests as young as 10) would be able to deliberate appropriately. Schrag, for example, imagines two kinds of arguments offered by children against closing a public music program. "A child who simply says she wants the chance to learn to play the violin will not have met the requisite standard. But a child who says that it is not fair that some children have their parents to pay for violin lessons at home while other children whose parents are poor never have a chance to find out if they have musical talent would, I take it, be offering an 'independent justification.'" We might accept with Schrag that "most 10 year olds would be able to offer such justifications," although this is a matter of empirical debate about child development (Schrag 2004, 367).

The necessity of political maturity to ground citizenship claims, at whatever age it arrives, can be seen best in the breach by considering arguments that would deny its necessity to democratic participation.

Some might reject the necessity of political maturity to claim a right of political participation for one of two reasons. First, democratic citizenship might seem to be simply a right owed on account of being "human" (where one's status as "human" is not in any way linked to the very possession of "political maturity").[10] Proceeding this way is difficult and likely impossible. Yet if the possession of political maturity matters *not at all* to the granting of political rights, then we might ask why we do not give citizenship to baboons or other life forms (see López-Guerra 2010). That humans develop into politically mature beings distinguishes us from other mammals who at birth appear to be more politically mature than we are. But the fact that we do not have political maturity until later in life, justifies the current exclusion of the very young from political rights. It is thus their *future* status as politically mature adults who have opportunities to participate in the democratic polity that make a child's status as "currently immature" worth thinking more carefully about.[11] If we deny the necessity of these goods to the claim on political rights, we are in a very difficult position to explain why only humans should claim them and then why newborns should not.

A second reason one might deny that political maturity is necessary for political rights is simply practical: in most democracies, any human over the age of 18 is given the right to vote, and some of them, if not many, lack political maturity. This practical fact may seem to demonstrate that this capacity is not, in fact, a necessary requirement for allocating participation rights. Since these immature adults over 18 are permitted to vote without regard to their *actual* political maturity, we should be consistent and allow children to have political rights (or at least the vote) as well. Indeed, as Schrag has argued (2004, 367–69), the exclusion of children on the basis of *their* political immaturity cannot be maintained on the basis of any number of standard arguments in favor of democracy (equitable treatment, interests protection, and other beneficial consequences to citizens) without running into a problem of consistency. "None of the standard theoretical defenses of democracy, then, provides a reason for excluding children that would not at the same time be applicable to some proportion of adults" (Schrag 2004, 369).

Yet such a view confuses arguments we make concerning the *principles* upon which we design institutions. Most laws and rules that we write employ proxies that roughly approximate the results at which we aim, rather than directly achieving the aim itself (Rehfeld 2005, 2010). As such, most rules will, in practice, overinclude or underinclude those who ideally qualify. In this case, if we had a reliable and fair way of distinguishing the politically mature from the politically immature of any age, we would have a strong reason to employ it.

This is not to say that if we had such a test we should use it; in fact, there are compelling reasons to reject such tests. We might reject a perfect test of political maturity that is impervious to manipulation on purely consequentialist views: if the benefits of allowing the politically immature to participate as democratic citizens outweigh the costs. First, following López-Guerra (2010), publicly identifying some people as politically immature might cause considerable harm either directly to those who are excluded or indirectly by making the rest of us more callous toward those without this competency. Second, the effect of treating the politically immature as full citizens might be small either because there simply are not that many who are politically immature or because, contrary to the third assumption I made at the start of this article, their immaturity leads not to systematic errors of a particular kind but to random decision-making and actions.[12]

These two sides of the consequentialist coin provide possible reasons to *override* the otherwise justifiable exclusion of those who are politically immature even in the case where we have reliable and fair tests. But in any real-world context, most proposed tests of political maturity would likely be objectionable because they would not be reliable or fair. We should not employ tests because they are likely to introduce far more error and to be prone to devious manipulation than following a general, if imperfect, rule. Literacy tests that excluded African Americans in the South are only one tragic example of such misuse. Still, the fact that tests can be manipulated does not mean that the underlying principle—minimal capacity—is a bad principle upon which to include people in citizenship.

By contrast to tests, a general age requirement corresponds reasonably well to the fact that the cognitive and moral prerequisites to democratic citizenship closely correspond to age; moreover, it is hard to manipulate, and it applies to all. We simply cannot sustain the view that minimal cognitive and moral capability should not be one *principle* guiding institutional design, even if we disagree about what age is best to secure minimal competency and even if these rules wind up overincluding or underincluding those who, on that basis, deserve to have them.

If the possession of political maturity justifiably guides claims to participate in a polity, then any argument for including children among rights-holders must be advanced by reference to these capacity, not by denying their necessity or using the fact that some adults who now have them do not deserve them. In this case, political rights—first among them, the right to vote—are granted to 18-year-old citizens. But as many have argued, 16- and 17-year-olds are not *that* different on these dimensions from 18-year-olds; and this has grounded a small movement among some American states, as well as other nations, to lower the voting age to 16.[13] Such a view, though, will run into a regress problem: 15-year-olds are not that much different from 16-year-olds, 14-year-olds not much different from 15-year-olds, and so on. In other words, using any set age as a proxy for capability will be arbitrary in some sense.

However, age distinctions are not arbitrary in every sense. The fact is that as a group, 15-year-olds are more politically mature than 4-year-olds, and 25-year-olds have greater political maturity than their younger cohorts.[14] Additionally, the development that this age-related tendency reflects is a continuous phenomenon, varying by individual, and not something that someone "suddenly" has. So one way to nonarbitrarily set the age for inclusion in the polity would be to survey children in a particular society and see when, generally speaking, some proportion of them have the minimal capability to participate in the polity. Of course, doing so will open up two subjects of intense debate: What proportion of a particular age is "enough" to treat all of that age as having political maturity? and What means do we have of testing our sample such that it is not prone to the kind of error or manipulation already described? But these problems are generally true of every general rule that we establish (Schauer 2003) and should not be seen as a reason to end the inquiry.

To set the proxy, we need to know whether we care to avoid Type 1 or Type 2 errors: excluding those who have the capacity or including those who do not, respectively. Setting the age requirements at a high level in an attempt to include only the politically mature will exclude those who mature earlier and have the capacity to participate; requirements that include young age groups will include more of those who lack the capacity to participate but also include more who do. To determine which groups to include, we would rely first on developmental psychologists and second on some process to select which of these errors we feel justified in making.[15] Most democracies have set the age to something that approximates when perhaps "most" or "almost all" have the capacity required: 16 to 21 years old.[16]

If political maturity is necessary for inclusion in citizenship rights, it nevertheless develops incrementally. It is easy to say when someone is politically mature and when he or she is not, but it is less clear where that line should be drawn. Political maturity similarly develops continuously, and although we could, following Brighouse (2002, 45), treat it as a threshold capacity, the only reason we might do so is if the good to be allocated—political rights—were a discontinuous good itself. But political rights need not be, despite their usual treatment as such. While a child over time becomes an adult, citizenship rights are treated as discontinuous: one either has them or one does not. These two conflicting facts—the continuousness of development versus the seeming discontinuity of rights—pose the central challenge to giving children full citizenship rights.[17]

Principles of Institution Design

So far, I have only argued that political maturity ought to be included in any principle that guides the distribution of political rights. As I said above, this minimum may be only imperfectly achieved because we cannot always perfectly translate the principles upon which we design institutions to the institutions. Reviewing further, we may choose not to institutionalize those principles when doing so would violate other, perhaps more important, principles. In this case, even if we had a perfect competency test that was administered fairly, we might find that the marginal gain of excluding the politically immature was not worth the stigma that it caused them in society. But these two facts—that institutions only imperfectly instantiate principles and that the principle of minimal competence might in practice be trumped by the effects of institutionalizing it—do not affect the view that competency ought to be a central principle in designing institutions.

I do not propose to speak any more about what other conditions we might add to the allocation of political rights, nor about the relationship of political rights to human or welfare rights more generally. In this section, I argue that children—the politically maturing—ought to be given participatory opportunities first to cultivate their ability to exercise political judgment and second in a manner that mitigates the harm that their politically immaturity might do to the polity as a whole.

First, if competency forms a minimal requirement for political rights, it might also be reasonable to limit political rights to individuals who have not been properly trained and educated—a related but different dimension from the emotional and cognitive *capacity* so far discussed. I think that minimal levels of education—to read, communicate, and understand the issues of the day—should be part of any principle that guides institutional design in much the same way as basic capacity does. But to avoid manipulation and discrimination, we do not test or require one kind of education but use age again as a proxy.

However, while we can leave the question of how much education and nurturing is required for the full development of political maturity, we can, with Brighouse (2002), recognize the value of having political rights in the first place to the competency of their exercise (see López-Guerra 2010).

> Children cannot come to be competent agents without some experience of agency. They must have the experience of choice before it makes sense for them to be seen as having the right to choice. I do not think this justifies children's agency *rights*: instead what it justifies is an obligation on parents (and the agencies of the state) regularly to introduce children, as they age, to situations in which they can make choices, and in which they are not fully protected from the consequences of their decisions. As they get older they should be protected ever less from the consequences of their choices, until, on the cusp of being rights-holders, they should be protected from consequences no more than adults are. . . . The child can be said to have a right to an upbringing that prepares her for competent agency (which will include many opportunities for agency) but not to have agency rights. (Brighouse 2002, 46)

That children are not permanently politically immature but developing toward maturity is—from a democratic polity's point of view—the decisive feature of their status. Any democratic nation has an interest in cultivating the citizenship capacity of those who will be its members; as Nussbaum (2007) argues, a nation may also have a general reason to promote the capacity of future citizens as well. Thus, governments have a good reason to give their citizens the kind of training that they need to participate well in politics when they come of age. Since having power is an extremely good way to train one for its use, this becomes a reason to provide children with political power as a way to cultivate their political maturity.

Giving children some political power from a very early age would also allow them to habituate the practices of citizenship at a younger age and may make it more likely that they engage in and with the polity as adults. To use the United States today as an example, despite having a voting age of 18, most citizens do not vote until much later in life. There are many reasons for this, but one may be the lack of familiarity and comfort with the process of registration and voting. If voting rights were given in some form at a much earlier age, and if the exercise of those rights were to be instructed and executed in schools, citizens would become accustomed and habituated to the practice of voting. These political rights might be received while still in middle or secondary school, where children would get into the habit of internalizing civic engagement at a time critical to their development. Having even a small set of political rights would encourage children to think strategically about the issues most important to them as active participants, including how best to frame their arguments to influence others. In short, such a practice would cultivate a habit of citizenship that would more likely produce lifelong habits of engagement than the current practice of waiting until the age of 18 to cast a vote. So, in addition to the cultivation of political maturity, early political engagement would more likely produce more engaged citizens when they are mature.

Yet granting political power to the politically immature may entail harm to others. This is no more so the case than with participatory rights, where the good to be used is designed to affect public outcomes. Even if an individual's vote has virtually no chance of affecting the outcome of an election, the effect of granting a new group a vote, of which that individual is part, can have the decided effect of altering the incentives of representatives to work toward that group's interest and, thus, policies and laws. In short, any institutional power that is granted to a group that is sufficient enough to provide some educational value to its use will have the potential of causing harm to others, along with whatever benefits it brings. This is no more or less true of children than it is or was for any subgroup in the polity or for the polity as a whole more generally.

This leads us to endorse a limitation on how we allocate citizenship opportunities to children (or again, any group): we should limit political rights to individuals if the allocation itself violates justice or if it were to cause harm to the individual or the polity as a whole. In some sense, this is a corollary of the very necessity of minimal capacity that I have discussed above. As Schrag has put it, "There *is* something amiss in the idea that our children might be considered competent to make decisions affecting millions of fellow citizens" (2004, 373).

Now it may seem to be a violation of political, if not human, rights to try to limit membership in a polity based on a principle of mitigating harm to others. But what I mean to do is to think about the grant of membership itself as limited in the same way that substance of legislation is itself limited by unjust harms to others. In most modern democracies, for example, the substance of permissible law is limited by substantive protections of fundamental rights even to minorities or individuals. The acceptance or rejection of a group of people—children in the present case—may be seen in the same way: we should not grant a group of people the right to vote if we know in advance that they are likely to use that vote to cause the polity unjust harm. The usual "Who's to say what groups constitute harm?" applies here and may, in practice, mean that we cannot exclude most people. But that again is a different question from the principle of excluding from membership those who will cause harm.

The account here, then, proceeds provisionally on the basis of what would be good for a polity over the long term rather than thinking about what justice or deontic considerations require us to give to children or, with O'Neill (1988), what obligations—perfect, imperfect, fundamental, or universal—we may otherwise have to children. By this view, and respecting the minimal competency argument, we should encourage the distribution of opportunities to participate if, all things considered, it contributes to the public good and discourage it if not. This is not to deny that children might actually have fundamental rights that need to be respected; nor is it to deny that children might have a claim of justice to participate in the politics as full citizens. Nor does this weak consequentialist principle commit us to consequentialism or utilitarianism per se: if children do have such rights or if justice or obligation requires that we give them these opportunities, the argument here will only be stronger. In this way I differ from Schrag (1975, 2004), whose argument was based on the injustice done *to children* by excluding them from the vote.

The one problem with this provisional approach arises only if justice were to require that children be *denied* the right to participate or if our moral obligations to children require such a denial, perhaps, on the basis of keeping children from harming themselves, as it were. (No such corresponding problem arises if children do not have a deontic *right* to these goods, since lacking a right to *X* does not mean one must be denied *X*, only that one is not entitled to *X*.) We might be worried that the opportunity to participate *politically* constitutes an expression of power over other people as well as over the voter himself or herself and, thus, that justice would require us restraining children because they are likely to do unjustifiable harm to others. Similarly, if our obligation to children is to keep them from harming themselves, and giving them positive rights of political inclusion would cause them to harm themselves, this provisional account may lead to problems. That the good being distributed here is political power means that we have to be sensitive not only to the rights of those exercising it but to the consequences of its exercise over other people.

A more serious objection to any proposal to expand political rights to children is the potential harm it would cause children to engage in adult political discourse.[18] The concern is that adults have an interest in promoting a healthy childhood that in some ways is protected from the concerns of adults, even if children are cognitively able to consider political concerns. Do we want, for example, a 12-year-old to deliberate about how best to deal with female circumcision in Africa or debate whether waterboarding is a good or bad policy of interrogation? Since "political maturity" as defined here encompasses both cognitive and emotional capabilities, I take it that the latter would be reflected as well. To deal with this serious concern, adults might limit the scope of issues that candidates could raise with younger citizens.

More generally, it is hard to see any in-principle violation of justice that a granting of participatory opportunities causes others, apart from the material gains to the public good that the expansion brings about. Put differently, the injustice to others involved in granting children the opportunity to have political rights should be conceived by reference to the material harm to others that their involvement brings about. It will be difficult, if not impossible, to claim that having children vote, for example, is an injustice to others if it turns out that extending the franchise benefits the nation as a whole.

With this discussion, we arrive at the two primary principles guiding the allocation of political rights to children. First, reflecting their developing political maturity, children should be given opportunities to participate with an eye toward cultivating their own capacity as citizens. Second, again owing to their political immaturity, children should be given rights in such a manner that mitigates the harm likely to arise as a result of their exercise of such rights.

Political Representation: Passive and Active

Given the aims of promoting interests, cultivating capacities, and mitigating harm, how should we think about institutional design from the perspective of the representation of children? The question presumes that we have something in mind when we say "the representation of children," and so I want to begin with that view before moving in the next section to think more concretely about what institutions can achieve those aims.

Representative government has long been defended as a democratic form to the extent that it allows individuals to participate in the protection and promotion of their own interests *and* to the extent that it provides a mechanism for individuals to participate in the articulation and determination of the public good. Whether the distance that representation creates between citizens and the laws that govern makes representative government an elective aristocracy (Manin 1997) or whether it instead promotes the very essence and value of democracy (Urbinati 2006) need not concern us here. Following Hannah Pitkin's (1972) account, the critical feature of representative government is that it empowers citizens to rule over their rulers by

1. authorizing their representatives to act,
2. holding their representatives to account for their actions after they have acted, and
3. using their roles in 1 and 2 to incentivize their representatives to pursue the substantive interests of their constituents (or the polity more generally).[19]

As a starting point, we can distinguish between active forms of political representation and passive forms on the basis of the represented's involvement in the process of representation. Active forms are ones in which citizens actually authorize their representatives and later hold them to account. As described above, representation within representative government is an active affair—all three parts involve the activity of citizens to authorize and hold accountable their representatives and use that power to incentivize their representative's activity while in office. By contrast to active forms of representation, "passive" forms of representation are ones in which a citizen's (or someone else's) interests are pursued by a representative over whom that citizen (or person) has no electoral (or other) control.

Most democratic nations treat the political representation of children in passive ways, in an indirect "virtual" fashion, much as they did the representation of women before the early twentieth century. Although such nations view children as having a special interest worth deliberating about and protecting through law, children, as illustrated in the CRC, have no direct "voice" or participation in government but rely on others to pursue their interests. Although other groups—African Americans in the United States and non–property holders more generally—have historically been excluded from representative institutions, women are the best historical analogue to the treatment of children for three reasons. First, like children today (but unlike other excluded groups), women were seen as a special class, needing their interests protected and advanced in the legislature. Second, the perception that women lacked capabilities very similar to what I have called "political maturity" justified their exclusion; other groups were denied on the basis that they were not deserving of representation at all. Indeed, it was in large part by persuading men that women were not politically immature, that they were not "like children," that helped suffragists to win them their political rights (Keysaar 2000).

Third, and most important, women were seen as already being represented through the process of "virtual representation" and thus not in need of any further rights to participate. Virtual representation, also known as "surrogate representation" or "proxy representation," is the process by which a representative pursues a person's or group's substantive interests but where the represented has no formal (electoral or otherwise) connection to the representative. Edmund Burke made virtual representation famous in his defense of the American cause: the Americans did not necessarily need to vote for representatives as long as there were English members of Parliament who would take it up for them. In contemporary democracies, elected representatives can serve as virtual representatives for groups and causes in other constituencies. When the late Ted Kennedy, the former U.S. senator from Massachusetts, proposed raising the minimum wage, he was in large part virtually representing the poor everywhere and not just in Massachusetts.[20]

One recent extension of passive representation for children is the promotion of proxy voting for children. Various proposals support giving parents additional votes based on the number of children that they have, justified by the view that they would more likely use that power to incentivize representatives to pursue the interests of children. Other proposals in the United States advocate counting children in the apportionment calculus, something not universally done. This would effectively reduce the number of *voters* within each child-rich constituency (relative to child-poor constituencies) and, thus, give added voting weight to voters in these districts relative to voters in other districts.

Proxy voting is often framed as a way to enhance the political rights of children, but it does no such thing (Minow 1986; Rutherford 1998). All it does is shift where the passivity of representation "happens," if you will. This would be seen clear enough if instead of providing women the right to vote, we allowed husbands to have proxy votes to cast on women's behalves. Similarly, we might suggest that animals and perhaps the environment get special protection by giving additional decisional weight to voters in animal-rich or environmentally protected areas. The structural identity between these proposals and proxy voting for children should illustrate that in no way is a proxy vote a right for the person being represented. It is rather a granting of a right (or additional power) to some people to look out for those things that they, or we as a society, wish to protect. The conceptual error of treating "proxy voting" as an actual political right of those for whom the proxy is cast is regularly made in the literature on children's voting.

This is not meant to deny that proxy votes might promote children's interests well; this is an empirical question. Indeed, it would be worth quantifying in greater detail whether and to what extent children's interests are underrepresented in legislatures on account of the virtual representation they now receive or might receive under such a plan. There is some evidence to support that: Paul Peterson (1992) notes that spending on the elderly in the United States between 1975 and 1990 was 7.5 percent of GDP compared to 2 percent for children (see also Schrag 2004, 375). Relative spending is hardly a proof—in this case, it seems we would want the government to spend more, much more, on seniors who do not usually have parents providing for them and whose care is likely to be far more costly than for the healthier population of children. But it would be a good place to start, particularly given that children in some advanced democracies, such as in the United States, experience far higher rates of poverty than do the elderly.

Still, there is reason to think that proxy voting on this score would do an imperfect job of protecting children's interests and perhaps come at too high a cost to the polity because it relies too much on the altruism of parents. Following Becker (1981), most parents have only imperfectly overlapping interests with their children—a parent's desire for his or her child's success is often satisfied only at a direct material and temporal cost to the parent, so parents should be expected to systematically underprovide for their kids (and support provisions that therefore underprovide for their children as well). Giving parents additional votes because they have children may promote more funding for playgrounds and schools but at the cost of providing even greater targeted benefits for 30- to 50-year-olds (roughly the age of parents) that have nothing to do with children. We should also expect on the margins that proxy voting would motivate bad reproductive decisions as well.

Treating proxy votes as a way of giving children political rights is thus a spurious argument. It may or may not promote their interests. But as a means of political representation, proxy voting simply shifts the representation of children from their surrogates who serve in government to their parents (or neighbors) closer to home. In no case does the move promote or even speak to the political participation and engagement of children in political citizenship.

A second form of passive representation comes in the form of descriptive representation. Descriptive representation happens whenever there is a correspondence between some feature of two individuals or one individual and a group. By this standard, any woman in office is a descriptive representative of women. And by this standard, African Americans are equally represented as blacks (as a descriptive matter) by J. C. Watts (a black Republican and former U.S. representative from Oklahoma) as they are by John Lewis (a black Democratic U.S. representative from Georgia). Descriptive representation is sometimes appealed to for instrumental reasons—we want more people who look like "us" because we believe that they will pursue our interests. But as with the case of Watts, and more generally individuals who do not share the views of most of the members of their descriptive groups, this is an imperfect standard. It is important conceptually to distinguish descriptive representation from interest or "substantive" representation because, with Anne Philips (1995), there may well be something normatively wrong with a legislature that does not look like the rest of us, no matter what interests they are pursuing.

Descriptive representation is a passive form because it is achieved merely by the existence of someone descriptively similar to the relevant group and requires nothing on the part of the group itself. In this case, the descriptive representation of children would be achieved just in case a child were elected to the legislature. Current age restrictions notwithstanding, such a move is ill advised for two reasons. First, descriptive representation of children does not in fact encourage the development of children's political maturity because it is a passive form. This is not to deny that having "one of our own" elected to government can be tremendously inspiring and indirectly encourage people to get involved. The 2008 election of Barack Obama as the first African American U.S. president is a case in point. Nor does it deny that the experience of the child elected might be tremendously helpful in cultivating her or his particular political maturity. But she or he is simply a single person. The inspiration that such an election might occasion among members of the described group to be involved in politics presumes first that there are ways to be involved in politics. It seems, on this score, that the inspirational value of a child serving as an elected representative would have little developmental effects on children generally.

Added to the diminished value of descriptive representation to cultivate political maturity among children, the mitigation of harm in this case would cut decisively against such a proposal. Although one might create a seat in Congress held by a child (or a number of children), their political immaturity would necessitate restricting the voting power of that child perhaps to simply a symbolic role.[21] In a passive role, children holding office might thus be neutralized by having honorary seats that enable them to add their voice to the debate but without the corresponding power to influence the legislature.

Instituting Active Representation of Children

Along with the promotion of their interests, we return to the two guiding principles of institutional design for children that I articulated at the end of the third section: the promotion of children's capacity as politically maturing citizens and the mitigation of harms that their political immaturity would cause them and the polity. Institutionalizing virtual representation of children through proxy votes may or may not advance their substantive interests; in any case, it fails to engage children in any direct way in the process of politics. In these terms, virtual representation is all mitigation with no eye to the promotion of children's capacity.

Active institutions by contrast must give children a direct role in representative government by giving them real power with which to shape representative deliberation, incentivize and hold accountable those who represent them, and have their voices heard within a legislative body. At the same time, they must do so in a manner that reflects children's developmental capacity by minimizing the harm that they can do to others (and themselves) with such power.

In this section, I consider four institutions that illustrate the dual aims of promoting capacity and mitigating harm: fractional votes for children; defining national electoral constituencies to enable group representation for children; providing small ($10) political spending accounts to children, who could allocate them to candidates and interest groups of their choosing; and using federalism to grant and limit the power of children as political actors. Although these institutional designs are conceptually distinct, they might nevertheless be combined or used in tandem.

Fractional votes for children

The most direct way to promote the political power of children is to give them the vote. In all but a few nations, citizens have the right to vote at the age of 18. In a few places, that age has been lowered to 16. Few serious proposals have been made to give children of much younger ages the vote. In large part, this reflects the broadly held view that children are politically immature. But it also reflects the fact that voting rights are seen as discontinuous rather than partial. This discontinuous treatment of voting—either one has the right to vote or one does not—makes lowering the age of voting more problematic. In the terms that I have developed here, as long as the vote is something one either has or does not have, we have to agree that below some age near 16, the harms that the vote will cause are likely to be too great to be worth the grant.

As we saw above, Brighouse (2002) and others have termed the problem of political maturity to be a threshold problem. Still, the nature of the good to be distributed—the vote—exacerbates the "thresholdness" of the problem. The problem is compounded by the fact that we are applying a discontinuous good—the vote—on the basis of a continuous variable—maturity. I think a better solution is a variation of a solution that John Vasconcellos has proposed: to create a continuous voting right by the allocation of fractional shares to children as they grow into their political maturity. Imagine that upon turning 12, a child received 1/7 of a vote, with an additional 1/7 added for every year after (at 18 they have a full vote).[22]

Fractional voting would immediately answer the concern that we are giving power to a group that does not know how to use it: we are giving a fraction of power to those who are coming to know what to do with it; it is the voting equivalent of a learner's permit. But as Brighouse (2002) suggests, it would also likely have a powerful citizenship effect on those who received it. Instead of the vote being something that adults have but do not use, children would be encouraged to be active members of the polity at a very early age and try on real power as they entered adolescence. Like a learner's permit that comes with limitations built in, these votes are self-limiting. Fractional shares would allow adolescents to internalize civic engagement at a time that their habits are forming and developing. They would also be the target of ads and other influence that would heighten their interest, though others have argued that this would introduce new problems and concerns as well.

It is in the aggregate that children's fractional voting power stands also to promote and protect their substantive interests by providing representatives incentives to propose and follow through on issues of concern to children.[23] Middle schools and high schools would become environments in which representatives could campaign directly for votes, engaging students directly in the political process. This again raises the specter of improper influence, a harm that would need to be mitigated, but given the constraints of a school environment, these influences might be more easily controlled and justified by the citizenship effects that would result from representatives truly campaigning for the student vote. And compared to universities, where college students are transient members of the community, 12- to 17-year-olds are, and would have been, longer-standing members of the communities in which they vote.

Of course, college-age students have had the right to vote for almost 40 years, with limited effects, so perhaps we should be skeptical about the effects of political rights for even younger children. But the analogy from college-age students may not be the right one to use. College-age students are in the middle of a great transformation, forging their own identity as adults. Whether the minority of Americans who go to college or those who take on employment just out of high school, this age is often a time of great exploration and experimentation, one in which young adults rely on the habits and practices cultivated in their youth. By contrast, the middle and high school years are precisely the time during which we should work to cultivate civic virtues and habits—such as voting and political participation—so that when students enter adulthood, they more reliably vote and take part, having habituated the participation as part of what it means to be politically active and engaged. We have a cycle of nonvoting by parents who do not instruct and cultivate this civic virtue in their children at home. This is one way to address that problem. In any case, there is no reason to think that the lessons of college-age nonvoting will readily apply to younger voters, whose lives are more structured in the institutions of family and schools.

Finally, fractional vote shares may appear to raise a problem of political equality. Indeed, they are an inversion of John Stuart Mill's suggestion that we give double votes to those with higher education and explicitly treat some people as fractional citizens (Mill 1998). However, fractional vote shares for children do not violate any underlying principle of equality in force today, since there is no presumption that children are politically equal to adults. Indeed, compared to having no votes, fractional shares represent a step toward equality at an earlier age for children.[24]

National constituencies for children

Although voting has been the primary way that political rights for children have been promoted (and "proxy voting" only erroneously described as enhancing children's political rights), we can think more creatively and flexibly about institutional design beyond the right to vote. Along with a vote—fractional or otherwise—a second way that children may be brought into the political sphere to enhance their citizenship capacity, protect and promote their interests, and mitigate the harms that their immaturity might cause is by giving them group representation through the creation of electoral constituencies defined around age.

Defining electoral constituencies by age would have tremendous incentive effects over representatives elected from them. In virtually all democracies, constituencies are defined territorially by where a citizen lives, although, as I have argued at length (Rehfeld 2005), this is not at all necessary and leads to lots of perversions of the system ("politics is local" only because we represent ourselves that way; it need not be). But democratic governments could define electoral constituencies instead by votes cast (in the case of proportional representation) or a host of other ways, including by self-definition (Pogge 2002) or by random assignment (Rehfeld 2005, 209–39).

As I have argued, by concentrating one kind of interest into a constituency, a representative to a national legislature is less able to deviate from the pursuit of that narrow interest when the public good demands it. For this reason, I have argued that group representation, as a principle of democratic institutional design, is ill advised, even if on occasion it is necessary for reasons of justice or the promotion of a deliberation.[25] In the case of children, such an exception may be warranted for those who are not likely to fare well under territorial systems because their distribution in these constituencies is not likely to be random but rather systematically biased. Because of the tendencies for individuals to follow public service provisions based on their needs (Tiebout 1956), we should suspect there are more children living in a suburban or urban congressional district in, say, Michigan, than there are in Broward County, Florida, or, prior to the 1990s, most of Nevada. The same is true in systems of proportional representation: if party support varies by age, then younger voters with children will tend to group together, and children will be nonrandomly distributed.

Reflecting the need to mitigate the harms of the politically immature, we might define national, age-based electoral constituencies that would elect a certain number of representatives to the legislature based on age. Using the United States again as an example, we might create a "12-year-old" constituency in which all 12-year-olds nationally would elect a single representative to Congress with the full rights and privileges of office. Thirteen-year-olds might send two representatives to serve, 14-year-olds three, and so on until the age of 17 or 18, at which children would be assimilated and integrated into the body politic. This method would leave the current system of territorial districting in place but provide some corrective for children.

As I said, creating group representation often renders a representative less able to deviate from the narrow interests of the group that he or she represents even when the public good requires it. In this case, that the electoral constituency is temporary (each changes every year) mitigates that harm. Furthermore, the fact that children would receive far less representation than their numbers would normally allow would further mitigate the harm that this level of participation could cause the polity. Having their own constituencies would encourage kids to develop citizenship capacity in a slightly better way than by simply including them in regular electoral constituencies, because it would more completely shield children from the influence and intimidation of their parents, whose interests in the outcome of the election would overlap less perfectly with their own.

Political spending accounts for children

In addition to voting power, children might also be encouraged to engage politically by being given small political spending accounts to allocate to any certified nonprofit or political organization, including campaigns. Again, a small amount of money would go a long way, and the amount, like the fractional vote and the number of representatives, might also incrementally advance by year. In the United States, for example, if there are between 3 and 4 million children in each of the age cohorts from 13 to 17, a grant of $10 to each cohort creates a pool of $30 to $40 million of possible revenue for campaigns and interest groups. Even a tenth of that would produce significant contributory power. With that level of spending available to them, interest groups and campaigns would have a substantive interest in pitching themselves to children, a prospect that poses its own risks to be sure but has the benefit of again fostering the engagement of children as active members of the polity.[26]

Using federalism to promote and limit influence

Finally, children's participation may be promoted and mitigated by encouraging it in, and limiting it to, the exercise of political power within local jurisdictions. Again, reflecting the developmental stages of political maturity, children might be allowed to participate with fractional (or whole) votes first in local, then state, and finally national elections.[27] By doing so, children might learn about the issues they were closest to, if not cared most about (Cohen 1975), in preparation for acting as full citizens and voters (partial or otherwise) in national elections.

Conclusion

The CRC prioritizes the welfare of children, treating them as a protected, at-risk class and marginalizing them from active engagement as political citizens. I argue that such treatment is not only justifiable but also reflects the nature of childhood and the specific harms that children face throughout the globe, even in situations of relative peace, material security, and stability. Welfare ought to be a priority before political participation. And, further, participation rights are, and rightly should be, linked to the possession of political maturity: a collection of cognitive, emotional, and moral capacity that develop with age and that children, by definition, lack. Thus, the priority of welfare over citizenship appears entirely justified.

However, the complete exclusion of children as political agents ignores the relative prosperity in which millions of them live and is a result of a failing to consider creative institutions to respond to the developmental fact of political maturity. Political maturity is a developmental, continuous bundle that does not suddenly emerge fully in a person but rather does so gradually and often in a manner that is positively influenced by engagement in politics. By contrast, institutions that permit citizens' political engagement tend to be discontinuous: either one has a vote or does not. Thus, children—defined here as the politically immature—have rightly, but detrimentally, been excluded from political citizenship on account of their political immaturity. By tailoring institutions to provide more continuous, gradual power to children as they mature, I suggest that they would be better citizens for that early engagement. But such institutions must also mitigate the harm that their political immaturity might cause to the polity as a whole. I reject passive forms of representation—proxy voting and descriptive representation—as not cultivating the capacity of children and propose involving children in active forms instead.

Much of the practical recommendations of this analysis will depend on the academic literature that can specify the trajectory of political maturity in human beings as well as more precisely indicate the specific ages at which it incrementally advances. Whether humans begin to mature at age 8 or 12, we ought to think more creatively about institutional design to respond to that developmental pattern.

Notes

1. For a general defense of this view, see Goodin (2007).

2. It may be surprising that systematic errors would be difficult to correct. Consider that at an individual level, systematic errors of judgment are in principle easier to correct than random errors, since the systematic nature of the error can lend itself to correction. By contrast, random errors—at the individual level—are impossible to correct, since we cannot know in advance in what manner the person erred. The difficulty of correction is entirely normative: we do not want the state "correcting" errors that citizens make for fear that such corrections will unmake democracy. This is a much larger point that I have explored elsewhere. See Rehfeld (2010).

3. I thank Emma and Hoben Greenberg Rehfeld for helping me entertain this possibility.

4. It is the justifications of *claims to* and *protections of* these rights that require stability, not necessarily the rights themselves. I, thus, leave aside here questions of the ontological nature of rights, whether they are naturally occurring or politically and socially constructed. Both Schrag (1975, 2004) and Peterson (1992) argue for the rights of children in part on this instrumentalist framing. See also Van Parijs (1998) on this point.

5. Schrag (2004), Archard (2007), and López-Guerra (2010) similarly make this point. See as well Schrag (1975), Pantell and Shannon (2009), O'Neill (1988), Lecce (2009), and Minow (1986).

6. Goodnough (2010) describes research that may indicate that humans develop a moral sensibility well before they can fully reason or otherwise communicate about the principles that motivate them. Even if moral sentiments emerge much earlier than thought, they are not present or not accessible at birth, and thus the central questions of this article remain.

7. That children separated at birth from the culture in which they were born conform to the culturally and socially influenced (not "determined") standards of political maturity should be evidence enough for this claim.

8. Goodin and Gibson (1997) here are arguing about a choice-based conception of rights. They argue, at greater length, that an interest-based conception of rights runs into the same problems. They also extend their point logically to the mentally infirmed.

9. On this point I follow López-Guerra (2010), whose paper and subsequent correspondence on this point were influential.

10. If we simply defined "human" as a creature that has "political maturity," the argument that all humans deserve citizenship rights would not be an objection to the present argument.

11. This is a fact that some who have advocated for giving children a vote have not noticed. For one example, see Lecce (2009). While Lecce acknowledges that "equality under the laws" might justify participation by children in a polity, equality alone does not explain why those with a similar bundle of emotional and cognitive goods would be denied. See also López-Guerra (2010).

12. This is a prime motivation of López-Guerra (2010), who sees granting the vote to children and the mentally impaired worthwhile because the harm done to the polity is marginal if it exists at all. I agree with Martha Nussbaum's claim that disenfranchising the politically mature (as I would describe it) is "disrespectful and wrong," based on the view that such a denial is tantamount to their being treated as inhuman, rather than the view that mental competence or political maturity is irrelevant to citizenship claims (see Nussbaum 2007, 248, as discussed in López-Guerra 2010, 20).

13. See Daniel Hart, "American Sixteen- and Seventeen-Year-Olds Are Ready to Vote," in this volume. Hart cites evidence that cognitive development escalates from 11 to 16 years of age. The evidence that he cites to support lowering the voting age to 16, however, is based on survey data among U.S. teens who are allowed to vote at age 18. That means that it would be difficult to detect whether the results that Hart documents are due to individuals being 16 or, alternatively, because they are close to voting age (whatever it is). If it is their proximity to the legal voting age that explains why 16- and 17-year-olds are more politically aware, then Hart's conclusion that voting should be extended no lower than 16 is unwarranted.

14. I remind the reader that though the general developmental trend is critical to the argument, the particular ages that I discuss are merely illustrative. In practice, they would have to be determined relative to any particular culture and society.

15. I do not address how to determine this, as it raises a separate set of issues. I do presume, however, that the selection of a voting age would be done in a deliberative fashion, though of course the inclusion problem asserts itself: one would not permit those currently excluded from voting based on whether they would later be included. But deliberative models would allow for their voices, nevertheless, to be heard. See Gutmann and Thompson (1996) and Cohen (1997).

16. Historically, in the United States, the argument to lower the voting age to 18 from 21 was not based on this "capabilities" view but simply on the argument of affected interests: since 18-year-olds were being drafted, they should have the right to vote. I do not find this argument philosophically persuasive—having an interest in policy may be a necessary but not a sufficient condition for justifiably being granted voting rights in a polity—even if it does causally explain why the vote was changed (Keysaar 2001). For a counterargument, see Goodin (2007).

17. Brighouse and Fleurbaey (2010) have argued more generally for a principle of proportionality that is more sensitive to the partial political rights that might leave room for a progressive allocation of political rights to children as they develop.

18. David Estlund raised this objection to me in a personal communication.

19. Pitkin's (1972) account conflated the "concept" of representation with these three features that plausibly render any case of it democratic. For more on that critique, see Rehfeld (2006).

20. For the best statement of virtual representation, see the discussion in Pitkin (1972, 171–80). For a contemporary discussion and defense of "surrogate representation" as an alternative, see Mansbridge (2003) and also Rehfeld (2009).

21. It is possible that if adults elected the child-representative, these adults would be more likely to elevate the politically mature child to office. But if only the political mature child were elected to the "child's seat," it would beg the question as to whether that child was properly descriptive of children as *politically immature citizens* at all.

22. This proposal is a variation of one that California State Senator John Vasconcellos proposed in 2004 that would have given 14- and 15-year-olds 1/4 of a vote and 16- and 17-year-olds 1/2 of a vote. See

California State Senate (2004). It was defeated for being hard to administer and generally "crazy." I thank Jenny Diamond Cheng for directing me to the proposal.

23. I think López-Guerra (2010) underplays the influence that children as a collective could have on electoral politics, even taking into account that individually their votes would not matter most. In competitive districts, or among competitive parties, the marginal effect of adding their votes to the mix could be significant. This effect will be even greater if children were to form their own electoral constituencies.

24. In the American context, fractional vote shares will face the superficial objection that they are offensive, given the purported history of treating African Americans as three-fifths human. African Americans were considered to be property and subhuman, if human at all. This view translated into a three-fifths representation, providing more power to white property owners in the South. Indeed, were African Americans treated as even three-fifths human and given a corresponding vote (and the protection to use it), they would have fared much better. It is no coincidence that proponents of slavery advocated for *not counting* slaves *at all*. The prospect of giving anyone three-fifths of a vote will likely seem offensive to many for historically inaccurate reasons that will limit the kinds of institutional reform possible in the United States.

25. For defenses of group representation to pursue justice, see Williams (1998), James (2004), and Young (1990). For the argument in favor of heterogeneous constituencies, see Rehfeld (2005, 177–208). For a general discussion of many of these issues, see Stone et al. (2008).

26. Public grants—whether of $0.10 or $10—would equalize children's giving, which would be a necessary component of the system. In the United States, for example, children's right to give their own money was recently protected by the Supreme Court. But that decision does not speak to the general issue that most children do not have money to give and are thus unable to take advantage of its participatory effect.

27. A similar discussion on using tiered structures appeared in the earlier colloquy between Schrag and Cohen. Schrag completes his earlier article by suggesting that children be given the vote at age 15 and then only over local issues (Schrag 1975, 456). In his response, Cohen rejects this idea because local issues seem no less complicated yet at the same time are less apparent to children, who have a greater sense of national and international issues (Cohen 1975, 462). I take no stand on which of these positions is correct; I only suggest that one might use the tiered nature of federalist governments to mitigate the harms of political immaturity.

References

Archard, David. 2007. *Children: Rights and childhood*. Oxford: Taylor & Francis.

Archard, David, and Colin Macleod. 2002. *The moral and political status of children*. Oxford: Oxford University Press.

Becker, Gary. 1981. *A treatise on the family*. Cambridge, MA: Harvard University Press.

Beitz, Charles R. 1990. *Political equality: An essay in democratic theory*. Princeton, NJ: Princeton University Press.

Brighouse, Harry. 2002. What rights (if any) do children have? In *The moral and political status of children*, ed. David Archard and Colin Macleod. Oxford: Oxford University Press.

Brighouse, Harry, and Marc Fleurbaey. 2010. Democracy and proportionality. *Journal of Political Philosophy* 18 (2): 137–55.

Buss, Emily. 2003. Children's associational rights? Why less is more. University of Chicago Public Law Working Paper 41, Chicago, IL.

Buss, Emily. 2004. Constitutional fidelity through children's rights. *Supreme Court Review* 2004:355–407.

California State Senate. 2004. Voting age. SB 1693. Sacramento, CA: California State Senate.

Christiano, Thomas. 1996. *The rule of the many: Fundamental issues in democratic theory*. Boulder, CO: Westview.

Cohen, Carl. 1975. On the child's status in the democratic state: A response to Mr. Schrag. *Political Theory* 3 (4): 458–63.

Cohen, Joshua. 1997. Deliberation and democratic legitimacy. In *Deliberative democracy: Essays on reason and politics*, eds. James Bohman and William Rehg, 67–92. Cambridge, MA: MIT Press.

Estlund, David. 2007. *Democratic authority: A philosophical framework*. Princeton, NJ: Princeton University Press.

Goodin, Robert E. 2007. Enfranchising all affected interests, and its alternatives. *Philosophy and Public Affairs* 35 (1): 40–68.

Goodin, Robert E., and Diane Gibson. 1997. Rights, young and old. *Oxford Journal of Legal Studies* 17 (2): 185–203.

Goodnough, Abby. 8 April 2010. The examined life, age 8. *New York Times*. Available from www.nytimes.com (accessed 15 May 2010).

Gutmann, Amy. 1987. *Democratic education*. Princeton, NJ: Princeton University Press.

Gutmann, Amy, and Dennis Thompson. 1996. *Democracy and disagreement*. Cambridge, MA: Belknap Press.

James, Michael Rabinder. 2004. *Deliberative democracy and the plural polity*. Lawrence: University Press of Kansas.

Keysaar, Alexander. 2000. *The right to vote: The contested history of democracy in the United States*. New York, NY: Basic Books.

Lecce, Steven. 2009. Should democracy grow up? Children and voting rights. *Intergenerational Justice Review* 9 (4): 133–39.

López-Guerra, Claudio. 2010. Enfranchising minors and the mentally impaired. Paper presented at the Symposium in Honor of Brian Barry, Columbia University, 19 May. New York, NY.

MacMullen, Ian. 2007. *Faith in schools? Autonomy, citizenship, and religious education in the liberal state*. Princeton, NJ: Princeton University Press.

Manin, Bernard. 1997. *The principles of representative government*. New York, NY: Cambridge University Press.

Mansbridge, Jane. 2003. Rethinking representation. *American Political Science Review* 97 (4): 515–28.

Mill, John Stuart. 1998. Considerations on representative government. In *On liberty and other essays*. New York, NY: Oxford University Press.

Minow, Martha. 1986. Rights for the next generation: A feminist approach to children's rights. *Harvard Women's Law Journal* 9:1–24.

Nussbaum, Martha. 2007. *Frontiers of justice*. Cambridge, MA: Harvard University Press.

Okin, Susan Moller. 1989. *Justice gender and the family*. New York, NY: Basic Books.

O'Neill, Onora. 1988. Children's rights and children's lives. *Ethics* 98 (3): 445–63.

Pantell, Robert H., and Maureen T. Shannon. 2009. Improving public policy for children: A vote for each child. *Intergenerational Justice Review* 9 (4): 139–43.

Peterson, Paul E. 1992. An immodest proposal. *Daedalus* 121 (4): 151–74.

Philips, Anne. 1995. *The politics of presence*. Oxford: Oxford University Press.

Pitkin, Hanna F. 1972. *The concept of representation*. Berkeley, CA: University of California Press.

Pogge, Thomas. 2002. Self-constituting constituencies to enhance freedom, equality, and participation in democratic procedures. *Theoria* 49:26–54.

Rehfeld, Andrew. 2005. *The concept of constituency: Political representation, democratic legitimacy, and institutional design*. New York, NY: Cambridge University Press.

Rehfeld, Andrew. 2006. Towards a general theory of political representation. *Journal of Politics* 68 (1): 1–21.

Rehfeld, Andrew. 2009. Representation rethought. *American Political Science Review* 103 (2): 214–30.

Rehfeld, Andrew. 2010. On quotas and qualifications for office. In *Political representation*, eds. Ian Shapiro, Susan Stokes, Elisabeth Woods, and Alexander Kirschner. New York, NY: Cambridge University Press.

Reich, Rob. 2002. *Bridging liberalism and multiculturalism in education*. Chicago, IL: University of Chicago Press.

Rutherford, Jane. 1998. One child, one vote: Proxies for parents. *Minnesota Law Review* 82:1463–1525.

Schauer, Fredrick. 2003. *Profiles, probabilities and stereotypes*. Cambridge, MA: Belknap Press.

Schrag, Francis. 1975. The child's status in the democratic state. *Political Theory* 3 (4): 441–57.

Schrag, Francis. 2004. Children and democracy: Theory and policy. *Politics, Philosophy & Economics* 3 (3): 365–79.

Stone, Peter, David T. Canon, Michael Rabinder James, Melissa S. Williams, and Andrew Rehfeld. 2008. Polity forum: Reflections on Andrew Rehfeld's *The concept of constituency*. *Polity* 40 (2): 216–71.

Tiebout, Charles. 1956. A pure theory of local expenditures. *Journal of Political Economy* 64 (5): 416–24.
Urbinati, Nadia. 2006. *Representative democracy: Principles and genealogy*. Chicago, IL: University of Chicago Press.
Van Parijs, Philippe. 1998. The disfranchisement of the elderly, and other attempts to secure intergenerational justice. *Philosophy and Public Affairs* 27 (4): 292–333.
Williams, Melissa. 1998. *Voice, trust and memory: Marginalized groups and the failure of liberal representation*. Princeton, NJ: Princeton University Press.
Young, Iris Marion. 1990. *Justice and the politics of difference*. Princeton, NJ: Princeton University Press.

To Be (Come) or Not to Be (Come): Understanding Children's Citizenship

This article explores notions of the "child as citizen" and "children's citizenship" in the context of possibilities and promises for the rights of children that are laid out in the United Nations Convention on the Rights of the Child. It poses the question, Can "children's citizenship" ever be fully accomplished for and/or by children? The article begins with an examination of contemporary theories of citizenship and considers the grounds for children's citizenship in the light of the ways in which "childhood" is culturally, socially, economically, and politically constructed in different societies. It suggests that in social investment states, such as the United Kingdom, the contemporary cultural politics of childhood mean that children's citizenship remains ambiguous. What is needed, the article suggests, is a greater understanding at the local level of how children's experiences as members of society unfold. Thus, taking England as a case study, and drawing on some empirical research with children's experiences in children's hospitals, the article illustrates the ways in which adults' ideas about childhood limit children's agency and actions, thereby denying them status as citizens.

Keywords: childhood; citizenship; politics; agency; rights; hospitals; social construction

By
ALLISON JAMES

This article sets out to examine some of the theoretical conundrums that the notions of the "child as citizen" and "children's citizenship" raise. The aim is to explore the extent to which the possibilities and promises for the rights of children to participate in society, as laid out in the United Nations Convention on the Rights of the Child (CRC) in 1989, can ever be fully accomplished for and/or by children.[1] I begin by examining the ways in which these concepts are being articulated for children themselves, as ways of being and acting, through the cultural

Allison James is a professor of sociology at the University of Sheffield and a professor at the Norwegian Centre for Child Research, Trondheim. She has worked in the sociology and anthropology of childhood since the 1970s, pioneering theoretical and methodological approaches to research with children that are central to childhood studies.

DOI: 10.1177/0002716210383642

politics of childhood currently shaping children's everyday experiences in England (see James and James 2004). Using as a case study data from empirical research carried out in children's hospitals,[2] the article suggests the need for changes in adults' ideas about childhood, including ideas about what children are, what they can do, and how their relationships with adults take place.

As this article argues, exploring the ways that the identity of "child" is practiced is core to understanding the cultural politics of children's citizenship. It is out of the conceptual differences in identity, between children and adults (Jenks 1996), that the very problem of children's status as citizens arises. Thus, as James and James (2004, 37) note for the English context, despite the government's recent emphasis on the importance of citizenship education for children and its introduction into the country's curriculum, in practice, in their everyday lives, children and young people "remain marginalised and treated as non-citizens by the systems of surveillance and control through which 'childhood' is protected as a social space in the life course."

To understand, therefore, how children's citizenship might be enacted and made a real possibility for children, it is important to move beyond abstract discussions of legislative and policy frameworks. What is critical to changing children's experiences is unpacking the cultural discourses through which children's everyday lives, *as children*, are constructed on an ongoing and mundane basis.

I begin by exploring the concept of the cultural politics of childhood, demonstrating the insights that the sociology of childhood can bring to theories of citizenship. Next, I provide empirical illustrations of the obstacles that can arise for children's citizenship when attempts are made to put such ideas into practice. The article concludes with some suggestions for the future directions that children's citizenship might take.

The Cultural Politics of Children's Citizenship

Since the early 1990s, one of the most significant contributions to understanding children's lives has been made by the sociology of childhood through its identification of the socially constructed character of childhood. It was an insight that prompted a sea change in understandings of childhood through the recognition that children's own experiences of childhood, though in part shaped by the biological facts of infancy, nonetheless vary historically and culturally (James and Prout 1997). These notions raised the question of the extent to which childhood could be regarded as a singular and universal concept, applicable to all children everywhere. The sociology of childhood also questioned the part that Western developmental psychology played in shaping understandings of childhood, arguing that it promoted a particularized construction of childhood within the life course that might not be of universal significance. Early social constructionist accounts questioned, for example, the cultural inevitability of seeing children, simply by virtue of their age and stage of physical and cognitive development, as necessarily dependent and in need of protection (Burman 1994; Woodhead 1997).

As Wyness (2006) suggests, what sociologists of childhood (and others) argue is that

> children's biological differences from adults need to be separated from the cultural components of childhood. The idea that children are commonly believed to be morally and culturally weaker or less significant than adults does not necessarily indicate that this incapacity or subordination is based on their physiological or biological weakness. . . . Children in different historical and cultural contexts are quite capable of actions that belie their physiological immaturity. (P. 23)

It is clear that in every society some concept of childhood does help to distinguish children from adults—concepts that may indeed reflect children's physiological and psychological differences from adults. However, it is the cultural evaluations about what those differences amount to, on what basis such distinctions are to be made and what social consequences they might have for children, that vary (Archard 1993; Qvortrup 1994).

These different social and cultural conceptions of what childhood is and should be are made manifest in laws, policies, and a range of age-based social divisions and institutions that contextualize the everyday lives of children in any society. It is the dynamic between the structuring effects of these social institutions and children's experiences of and reactions to them that composes what James and James (2004) have termed the ongoing cultural politics of childhood. As they suggest,

> Within any particular cultural context, therefore, policy works to delimit conditions of possibility and the arenas of restraint through which meanings are given to social practice and, ultimately, to ideas of the person. Thus one of the ways in which people come to know not only their own social place and selves but also those of others is, in effect, through experiencing the process and outcomes of policy as it shapes and reshapes the humdrum pattern of their everyday lives. (P. 45)

The cultural politics of childhood must be core, therefore, to understanding the ways in which children's citizenship unfolds for children in any setting.

Some social theorists of children's citizenship have embraced such understandings. Cockburn (1998), for example, has unpacked the historical discourses of childhood that underpinned T. H. Marshall's (1950) argument that children should be seen as citizens *in potentia* only. In Marshall's view, children could not be regarded as full members of a community since, although they had some social and civil rights, they had no political rights that might facilitate their full participation as citizens of society. Marshall envisaged children only as "becomings," rather than "beings"; this view is consistent with the idea that it is children's lack of social competence that separates their citizenship status from that of adults. Cockburn claims that this understanding of children's supposed inability to participate as citizens in society is not fixed or invariable. Rather, he shows that it reflects a specific historical process. Examining the case of the United Kingdom over the nineteenth century, he traces the gradual exclusion of children from full community membership and participation through their confinement, under the guise of protection and welfare, into age-segregated, child institutions (Hendrick 1997). Cockburn claims that Marshall's view of children's social citizenship was necessarily conceptualized as partial, since it was based on a particular Western cultural understanding that lacked trust in children's competence. It embraced a vision of children as incomplete in comparison to the adults that they would become. Indeed, Lee (2001, 9–10) has argued that one of "our convenient fictions about adulthood" in contemporary Western societies is that the status of "adult" represents "journey's end," a function of our "wish to preserve the existing age-based distributions of authority in society."

Lister (2007) has further explored the outcomes of such ideas of "the child" for conceptions of children's citizenship and participation in society. She shows that in social investment states, such as England, Canada, and those in the European Union, children's citizenship is problematic, since a number of the basic building blocks of citizenship are ambiguous when they are applied to children. Thus, although children *are* seen as members of these societies—and therefore are regarded as citizens by virtue of their belonging—she argues that their membership is skewed. As a consequence of adults' particular ideas about what children can and cannot do, young people take little active part in shaping the societies to which they belong. For children to become active members of these societies, adults would have to "facilitat[e] their participation as political and social actors" and "[equip] them with skills and capacities for effective citizenship" (p. 701). However, as long as conceptions of childhood rely, largely, on a deficit model of children's developmental needs and their limited competences, such progress, Lister argues, is unlikely. Thus, although there are some examples of good practice, inclusive opportunities for children to participate fully in a society, such as in England, remain patchy (Hart 2009). On the whole, social investment societies have "future-oriented constructions of children and young people's citizenship," in which "children are typically constructed in instrumentalist terms" through reference to their adult futures as workers, rather than their present contribution to society as children (Lister 2007, 697).

Such views can be contrasted with Kjørholt's (2002) analysis of the Norwegian cultural context. Through the introduction of a variety of projects and policies since the 1980s, she argues that this social democratic society has offered "new visions of childhood, intending to empower a disenfranchised group in society, replacing the notion of 'the vulnerable and dependent child' with 'the competent child' who is given the right to participate in society to a certain degree" (p. 64).

In Norway, Kjørholt suggests, children are seen as vital to the resurgence of communities and to the "continuity and renewal of discourses about Norway as a democratic nation" (2002, 75). Children's participation in their local communities is considered key, signaling, in this cultural context, that there has been a shift from seeing children as "human becomings" to "human beings" (Qvortrup 1994). Indeed, in Norway, where the CRC has become incorporated into domestic legislation, children age seven and older have the right to be heard in divorce proceedings. In contrast, in England, children have no such right; their ability to speak remains a matter of adult discretion (James, Haugen, and Raintalaiho 2010). Thus, the cultural politics of childhood in a social democratic state, such as Norway, encourage children's active citizenship as a present, rather than just a future, possibility, as a result of the different social constructions of childhood and the child that are central to Norwegian discourses of egalitarian individualism.[3]

These contrasting examples show how different conceptions of children's citizenship are a reflection of, and a response to, different cultural politics of childhood in which cultural ideas about children's "being" and "becoming" play a central role. In societies where children are largely judged in terms of the future adults they will become, their citizenship status as full participants in society is often heavily circumscribed. This is because, as Uprichard (2007) has noted, such understandings assume that "competency" is something that is acquired the closer one is to becoming "adult." This means, in effect, that "competency is necessarily (and only) an adult characteristic, i.e. one that children cannot possess" (p. 305). Elsewhere, as in Norway and other Scandinavian countries, children are seen much more as competent people and are encouraged and enabled to participate in society, to act as citizens in the here and now.

Fundamental questions are how far, in what ways, and under what circumstances are the status of children as citizens to be understood in terms of their difference from or their similarity to adults—those who are currently regarded as citizens? In trying to solve the problem of the lack of children's citizenship in social investment states such as England, Lister (2007) draws on a feminist model to argue for an approach that might embrace an idea of children's "differentiated citizenship." If, by virtue of their age and stage of physical and congitive development, children are positioned as dependent and in need of protection, then a different model of citizenship might be applied. This could acknowledge children's different, but equal, entitlement to citizenship rights and the recognition that although children might need special protection, they can nonetheless still participate in their own ways in society. As Lister argues, "The autonomy associated with citizenship does not require an illusory self-sufficiency" (p. 713). Cockburn (1998), meanwhile, suggests another model, one that is incremental: children's citizenship could be based on children's changing needs and experiences as they grow older and could also acknowledge that social interdependency is as necessary for adults as it is for children. Alternatively, according to Roche (1999), children's citizenship should not be viewed as precisely the same as that of adults: while children should be regarded as having human rights, they can also be seen to have special rights, *as children*.

However, notwithstanding the significance of these three proposals for identifying a number of practical ways that children's citizenship might be developed in those states that are so apparently averse to it, they remain underpinned by the familiar social construction of the importance of children's "natural" differences from adults. Citizenship on this basis can still, therefore, only ever be child-sized (Jans 2004).

Lived Citizenship

While it is possible, as suggested above, to envisage new models of children's legal rights that might confer a kind of citizenship status on children, in practice, these may turn out to be problematic. As Lister (2007) argues, for such models to work, there needs to be "a conversation between citizenship as a legal status and citizenship as a socio-political practice" (p. 695). What is needed, she argues, is an understanding of "lived citizenship," of how, *in particular contexts*, agency is attributed by adults to children in and across different spheres of life so that their participation in society is facilitated—or not. In particular, given the notion that childhood is socially constructed, this would involve exploring, in any cultural context, how adults are actively interpreting the competences and capacities that children have. And what is more, it would also involve discovering how children themselves are experiencing and responding to these adult conceptualizations of childhood since this, too, is a key aspect of the cultural politics of childhood (James and James 2004). The idea of lived citizenship draws attention, therefore, to the significance of children's own agency with respect to their citizenship status since, while children may have theoretical rights in law, whether or not, and how, they come to exercise these rights in their everyday lives will provide an important gauge of their status as citizens, in practice.

Focusing on children's lived citizenship also draws attention to the possibility of social change and helps to identify shifts in the ways in which ideas about children's competences, and hence their citizenship status, might alter over time. Indeed, such changes are often in response to children's own actions in society. The emergence of children's social movements bears witness to this kind of possibility. Liebel (2008), for example, has suggested that, despite the apparent powerlessness of children vis-à-vis adults, in some contexts, children have begun, nonetheless, to assert their rights. Through mobilizing themselves, they have found ways to exercise their rights in society and to be, as a consequence, recognized as competent, participating citizens. Thus, for example,

> The movement of the working children of Bolivia concluded an agreement with the mayor of La Paz that guarantees the children the free use of public spaces in the city for their work, instead of being as hitherto, repeatedly dispersed by the police or private security guards. In the Peruvian capital, Lima, the children's movement agreed with the city administration on a working and training project for children who had previously been obliged to survive by begging, stealing or prostitution in the streets. (P. 41)

However, important, this kind of citizenship from below "is significantly different to the kinds of participation approaches in which children are offered participation in adult-decision-making," which are so common in northern social investment states (p. 42). In the latter context,

> even if such offers go beyond mere non-binding consultations or symbolic forms of participation, children's possibilities for action stay limited within a space predefined by adults. . . . In contrast, citizenship from below is expressed by children themselves setting goals they want to reach and choosing the way they want to act. (P. 42)

Similarly, Spyrou (2008), in his ethnographic study of educational policy and practice in Cyprus, shows that

> ideas of Cypriot childhood are . . . being reconstituted through changes in educational policy and practice, changes to which children have also contributed, not through any formal consultation or right to participation but through the exercise of their own agency. (P. 168)

He cites the small acts of resistance and direct action taken by children that provoke reflection by adults on the nature and purpose of the curriculum. Such examples demonstrate that to understand fully the nature of children's citizenship, we need to explore, in any context, not only how "citizenship" is made legally available to children but also how children experience that framing—and respond to it—through their everyday lives.

To demonstrate the usefulness of such an approach for understanding children's citizenship, the next section turns to the example of England, where, as a social investment state, children are ambiguously regarded. First, they are seen very much as "becomings," with their futures, as adults, being held to constitute the nation's wealth. Such a view underpins the strong emphasis currently being placed on education and, through the Every Child Matters (Department of Education and Skills 2004) agenda, on the idea that children need protection against risks of different kinds. Against this, however, children are constructed simultaneously as also being a risk to society and in need of stringent social control. Thus, as James and James have observed, in their analysis of recent policy changes in England, what once were arguments used to "support a rationale for intervention in the name of the prevention of risk, developed in the very particular context of child abuse and protection" are now used to "justify a much broader agenda for the social control of children and young people" (2008, 124). The outcome of this, they suggest, has been to

> usher in an era in which childhood and children are ever more closely regulated, and in which the exercise of choice by children is likely to bring them increasingly into conflict with those who would deny their individuality in the name of protecting and defending the child's best interests. (2008, 126)

Such is the current ambiguity with which English children are regarded that, as Such and Walker (2005) have shown, children are seen as competent and hence responsible for the crimes they commit at the age of 10 within the criminal justice arena; however, within family law, they are assumed to lack such abilities and competences to participate responsibly in cases such as articulating their own wishes and feelings in parental divorce proceedings (see also James 2008).

Children's Lived Citizenship: The Example of Children's Hospitals in England

Apt illustration of the deep-seated ambivalence in English attitudes toward children's status as citizens can be found in our recent research into children's experience of hospitals in England. While a new framework has been developed for children's services, drawing on the aspirations of the CRC with a purportedly child-centered focus (Department of Health 2003), children's lived experiences of being in the hospital left them with relatively few opportunities to exercise competence and responsibility, even in relation to the most mundane aspects of their health care (see Alderson 1993).[4]

The research took place over 27 months (2005–2007) in three different hospital settings and sought to examine children's perspectives on hospital space. The research question asked how children understood and used the spaces in hospitals and what, from a child's perspective, it felt like to be a patient. Our child informants were either outpatients or were in the hospital for short overnight stays, although some children had conditions that meant that they were frequently in the hospital for short visits. Children who were terminally ill or who had life-threatening illnesses were excluded from the study, since we wanted to capture the most common experiences that children have as patients. Two hundred and fifty-five one-on-one interviews were carried out with children and young people, and a range of participatory research tools were used to enable children to express their views about different spaces within the interior of the hospitals.

The first setting was a well-known and established children's hospital, dating from the Victorian era, the second was a relatively new and dedicated children's facility located in a larger general hospital, while the third field site comprised a children's outpatient department and a ward located in a district general hospital that had been built in the 1970s. While these settings presented many differences in their physical environments, there was also much in common in the ways in which they were used.

As we have discussed in detail elsewhere (Birch, Curtis, and James 2007), one key commonality was the particular construction of childhood that permeated the temporal and spatial order of all the hospital settings. Despite the fact that they cater to children and young people from birth to 16 years old, the predominant image of the sick child that permeated the hospitals was that of the "child-as-infant": walls and floors were painted bright colors and decorated with cartoon pictures; mobiles dangled from the ceilings; and the soft, cuddly toys and books to be found in the hospitals were most suitable for their youngest patients. This left the older children feeling that their needs were not really being met. Even children as young as seven told us that they felt that the hospital's décor and the facilities that it provided were too childish. While the older children appreciated that babies and young children might like this environment, they felt marginalized by it. A 13-year-old girl responded that "it's colorful . . . [but] it's more for children," while a 14-year-old boy replied, "Sponge Bob Square Pants. I hate him.

They are good for children though." Another boy, 13 years old, stated that he did not "like those things hanging from the ceiling. They are just drawn and they don't brighten up the room . . . it's a bit kiddy"; while his 6-year-old counterpart complained, "I don't like the baby toys in the place where I first came in."

However, more insidious, and perhaps in part as a consequence of this childish framing, another construction of childhood could also be found. The idea of children's potential irresponsibility was apparent in the ways in which space within the hospitals was demarcated and used, and the view that irresponsible children are deemed to be in need of protection or control also permeated aspects of hospital space.

For example, there was an adolescent room in one hospital, designed as a space where young people could go to watch TV or play computer games, away from the more childish atmosphere of the main wards. This room was, however, kept locked, and patients always had to ask the nursing staff for the key before they could use it, resulting in the room rarely being used. In another hospital, use of the adolescent room required signing a formal contract, which also discouraged use. The language of this contract highlighted the potential irresponsibility, rather than responsibility, of any young person who might wish to use this room and suggested why it might have acted as a deterrent for young people.

The contract set out to position young people as having "needs [that] are different from those of a child" and the hospital as being able to provide for these. It stated, "We are proud to have a designated room allocated to young people." Indeed, it should be. As long ago as 1959, it was argued in the Platt report that, since adolescents have their own special interests, these should be catered to while they are in the hospital, a suggestion that underscores well the link between social status and rights that is core to questions of citizenship (Ministry of Health 1959). However, any hope that the contract for the adolescent room in this contemporary hospital reflected adult acknowledgement of young people's special citizenship status was dashed in the very next sentence of the contract, which repositioned young people as being in need of both protection and control.

First, the contract drew on the familiar discourse of protection: "we feel it is necessary to produce a contract for your own safety and comfort"; but this was quickly followed by a discourse of control: "we hope that you can help us by complying with the following." The "following" was a set of rules of behavior, the majority of which did little to enable young people's agency to participate or to recognize their competences. For example, the first two rules are (1) "You must inform a member of staff when you are using the room. Time spent is to be on trust therefore no rude or disruptive behaviour is permitted"; and (2) "Books, games and equipment are to be treated with respect. Loss or damage to them means loss of your right to use the room."

And although young people's responsibility was referred to in two other clauses, this was framed by a set of conditions that indicated young people's primary potential for being irresponsible: (1) "The room must be kept tidy at all times or this will result in closing of the room. So this is YOUR responsibility"; and (2) "It is your responsibility to report any damage or incidents that occur."

The discourse of protection surfaced in the remaining clauses of the contract, only the first of which was underpinned by any medical concern; the rest reflected broader cultural concerns about the risks that young people face from each other and from strangers: (1) "It will be stated within your care plan the reason why you are not allowed in this room i.e., if your condition is unstable or requires you to be isolated due to infection"; (2) "Staff will use discretion regarding closing the room when the safety of an individual is thought to be at risk"; (3) "No visitors or adults other than nursing staff are allowed in"; and (4) "Whilst not being supervised, this room will have a member of staff who will from time to time be checking on the room's users."

Out of the nine rules/clauses in the contract, only one permitted young people any sense of agency in relation to their use of the room: "It closes at 10pm on weekdays and at 11pm at weekends. This may be negotiated with staff on duty."

The contract had to be signed at the bottom, not only by the young person but also by his or her parent or guardian. Such a requirement immediately dispels the feelings of empowerment that a young person might gain from deciding to sign up to use the room. Is it any wonder that the room was so often empty? Just as Such and Walker remark in relation to general social policy for children and young people in England, so too in the day-to-day world of a children's hospital, "children appear only to be granted agency and autonomy in the context of wrongdoing; children are able to be willfully irresponsible but not willfully responsible" (2005, 46).

While the contract had been originally drawn up as a consequence of the misuse of the room on one occasion by one group of young people, such is the cultural politics of childhood in England: often it is the exception that proves the rule.[5] For example, the recent introduction of night curfews for young people in certain cities in England, in an effort to curb the unruly behavior of the few, has meant that the lives of all children and young people who live in that area are also affected. More important, however, the drawing up of such a contract—for the use of one room within the confines of a hospital—opens up what Lister calls the tension between citizenship as an "expression of human agency" and citizenship as the set of "rights that enable people to act as agents" (2007, 695). The introduction of the contract was a response to the former kind of lived citizenship that impacted negatively upon the latter. As one 15-year-old girl observed,

> You need to like have a key to get in and I think that's quite awkward because you have to ask the nurses every time and like it's good if you can just go in by yourself. If everyone like keeps it tidy then there should be no problem and since the little babies don't go in there I don't like see why older people can't keep it tidy.

Ironically, therefore, to gain some peace or privacy, some of the young people had to resort to rule-breaking; they used the parents' kitchen area to make private phone calls or to chat with their family and friends—a space that, theoretically, was out of bounds to them.

These discourses about children's lack of competence and responsibility are fundamental to the contemporary cultural politics of childhood in England and are grounds for the denial of citizenship status to children and young people. As described in detail elsewhere (James, Curtis, and Birch 2008), when asked about their access to particular spaces within the hospital and whether they would be allowed to go into them on their own, the children's responses were twofold. On one hand, they told us that certain spaces would be dangerous and risky for children while, on the other, they said that children—in general—would act irresponsibly and that, therefore, their access to certain spaces should be restricted. As we suggest,

> That children can so readily articulate a version of childhood as a social space that is hedged around with danger and risk . . . should . . . give pause for thought about . . . the import that this has for children's citizenship. It suggests that the greatest danger in the risk society is not that we fail to protect our children sufficiently but, rather, that, in caring too much, the controls that are put in place work to limit not only children's participation—in terms of the kinds of things they might do—but also their imagination about the kinds of people they are or might be. (James, Curtis, and Birch 2008, 95)

Conclusion

The cultural politics of childhood are central to understanding the ways in which concepts of citizenship unfold for children and young people in any society; their citizenship status will reflect the particular constructions of childhood through which laws and policies for children and young people are brought into being. In the English hospital case, it becomes clear that not until children can be regarded as willfully responsible, rather than incompetent and irresponsible, will their status as citizens be ameliorated. Irrespective of their rights, as enshrined in the CRC, a continued reliance on the determinism of the developmental paradigm will work to legitimize adults' power over children. It is this that enables adults to ignore the interdependency that necessarily characterizes all social relations and, instead, to underscore children's dependency on them as both "natural" and "inherent." And it is precisely this construction of childhood that enables children in England to largely still be seen as "becomings," rather than "beings" and for their status as citizens to be denied.

As a global policy instrument, potentially one of the most significant impacts of the CRC *could* have been to question the linking of citizenship solely with children's futures as is common in many societies. Through its promise to bestow rights of participation on children as social beings in the here-and-now, a new vision of children's citizenship might have become possible. That it has largely failed to generate this vision is revealing of the cultural politics of its original inception as a charter of children's rights: "the child" whose rights the CRC wishes to promote is in many ways a generalized abstraction that draws, as Boyden notes, "primarily on northern, and especially Christian, thinking" by positioning children as dependent and in need of protection (1997, 219). This positioning means that the image of the rights-bearing, "globalized child" enshrined within the CRC often fails to correspond with the everyday realities of children in different parts of the world since, as outlined above, the experience of "being a child" has always been understood in relation to the particularities of local contexts.

Notes

1. The CRC does not specify any specific rights of participation. However, in discussions of children's participation, it is usually Articles 3 and 12 that are referred to as indicating rights to participate.

2. The study "Space to Care: Children's Perceptions of Spatial Aspects of Hospitals" was funded by the Economic and Social Science Research Council (RES-00-23-0765) between 2005 and 2007. Dr. Joanna Birch carried out the fieldwork, with Dr. Penny Curtis as principal investigator for the project. See Birch, Curtis, and James (2007) and James, Curtis, and Birch (2008).

3. Interestingly, as these authors note, however, the actual impact of this on mediation practices in relation to divorce has been limited. Children are still not routinely involved in such proceedings, suggesting that cultural attitudes and practices often lag behind changes in the legal framework.

4. Alderson (1993) explores the ways in which ideas about children's competence to make decisions about their treatment is mediated by adults' conceptions of childhood.

5. When the toddler James Bulger was murdered in 1993 by two 10-year-old boys, the public outcry that followed their trial led to the age of criminal responsibility being lowered to 10. There was no court ruling as such, but the government abolished the presumption of *doli incapax*, which had required the prosecution to prove that a child between the ages of 10 and 14 was aware of wrongdoing in relation to an alleged offense.

References

Alderson, Priscilla. 1993. *Children's consent to surgery*. Buckingham, UK: Open University Press.

Archard, David. 1993. *Children: Rights and childhood*. London: Routledge.

Birch, Joanna, Penny Curtis, and Allison James. 2007. In search of the child-friendly hospital. *Built Environment* 33 (4): 405–16.

Boyden, Jo. 1997. Childhood and the policy makers: A comparative perspective on the globalization of childhood. In *Constructing and reconstructing childhood: Contemporary issues in the sociological study of childhood*, 2nd ed., eds. Allison James and Alan Prout. London: Falmer.

Burman, Erica. 1994. *Deconstructing developmental psychology*. London: Routledge.

Cockburn, Tom. 1998. Children and citizenship in Britain. *Childhood* 5 (1): 99–117.

Department for Education and Skills. 2004. *Every child matters: Change for children*. London: Department for Education and Skills.

Department of Health. 2003. *Getting the right start: National service framework for children*. London: Department of Health.

Hart, Roger. 2009. Charting change in the participatory settings of childhood. In *Children, politics and communication*, ed. Nigel Thomas. Bristol, UK: Policy Press.

Hendrick, Harry. 1997. Constructions and reconstructions of British childhood: An interpretive survey, 1800 to the present. In *Constructing and reconstructing childhood: Contemporary issues in the sociological study of childhood*, 2nd ed., eds. Allison James and Alan Prout. London: Falmer.

James, Adrian L. 2008. Responsibility, children and childhood. In *Responsibility, law and the family*, eds. Jo Bridgeman, Heather Keating, and Craig Lind. Aldershot, UK: Ashgate.

James, Adrian L., Gry Mette D. Haugen, and Minna Raintalaiho. 2010. The voice of the child in family mediation: Norway and England. With Rebecca Marples. *International Journal of Children's Rights* 18 (3): 313–33.

James, Allison, Penny Curtis, and Joanna Birch. 2008. Care and control in the construction of children's citizenship. In *Children and citizenship*, eds. Jane Williams and Anatola Invernizzi. London: Sage.

James, Allison, and Adrian L. James. 2004. *Constructing childhood: Theory, policy and social practice*. Basingstoke, UK: Palgrave Macmillan.

James, Allison, and Adrian L. James. 2008. Changing childhood in the UK: Reconstructing discourses of "risk" and "protection." In *European childhoods: Cultures, politics and childhoods in Europe*, eds. Allison James and Adrian L. James. Basingstoke, UK: Palgrave.

James, Allison, and Alan Prout, eds. 1997. *Constructing and reconstructing childhood: Contemporary issues in the sociological study of childhood*. 2nd ed. London: Falmer.

Jans, Marc. 2004. Children as citizens: Towards a contemporary notion of child participation. *Childhood* 11 (1): 27–44.

Jenks, Chris. 1996. *Childhood*. London: Routledge.

Kjørholt, Anne Trine. 2002. Small is powerful: Discourses on "children and participation" in Norway. *Childhood* 9 (1): 63–82.

Lee, Nick. 2001. *Childhood and society: Growing up in an age of uncertainty*. Buckingham, UK: Open University Press.

Liebel, Manfred. 2008. Citizenship from below: Children's rights and social movements. In *Children and citizenship*, eds. Jane Williams and Antonella Invernizzi. London: Sage.

Lister, Ruth. 2007. Why citizenship: Where, when and how children? *Theoretical Inquiries in Law* 8 (2): 693–718.

Marshall, T. H. 1950. *Citizenship and social change*. London: Pluto.

Ministry of Health. 1959. *The welfare of children in hospital. Report of the committee chaired by Sir Henry Platt*. London: HMSO.

Qvortrup, Jens. 1994. Childhood matters: An introduction. In *Childhood matters*, eds. Jens Qvortrup, Marjatta Bardy, Giovanni Sgritta, and Helmut Wintersberger. Aldershot, UK: Avebury.

Roche, Jeremy. 1999. Children: Rights, participation and citizenship. *Childhood* 6 (4): 475–93.

Spyrou, Spyros. 2008. Education and the cultural politics of childhood in Cyprus. In *European childhoods: Culture, politics and childhoods in Europe*, eds. Allison James and Adrian L. James. Basingstoke, UK: Palgrave.

Such, Elizabeth, and Robert Walker. 2005. Young citizens or policy objects. *Journal of Social Policy* 34 (1): 39–57.

Uprichard, Emma. 2007. Children as "being and becomings": Children, childhood and temporality. *Children and Society* 22:303–13.

Woodhead, Martin. 1997. Psychology and the cultural construction of children's needs. In *Constructing and reconstructing childhood: Contemporary issues in the sociological study of childhood*, 2nd ed., eds. Allison James and Alan Prout. London: Falmer.

Wyness, Michael. 2006. *Childhood and society: An introduction to the sociology of childhood*. Basingstoke, UK: Palgrave Macmillan.

Participatory Niches for Emergent Citizenship in Early Adolescence: An International Perspective

By
JUDITH TORNEY-PURTA
and
JO-ANN AMADEO

This article is based on the assumption that the right to vote in national elections is not an essential dimension of citizenship for early adolescents as long as adolescents' other competencies and attitudes are nurtured in their everyday settings. The article addresses the issue of children or early adolescents and their political and civic participation from three perspectives. First, it examines how human rights and action in community settings have been viewed across the several decades in which political socialization research has been conducted. The idea of emergent participatory citizenship for young adolescents is introduced. Second, the authors examine findings from survey research to determine whether the socialization and developmental experiences of the majority of early adolescents entering the twenty-first century have resulted in attitudes and skills appropriate to being full citizens. The third section examines studies using qualitative methodologies—observations and interviews—to show how the spaces for adolescents to exercise participatory and deliberative capabilities can be enhanced.

Keywords: developmental niche; participatory rights; adolescents; deliberative capacity; Convention on the Rights of the Child; human rights education; political socialization; IEA Civic Education Study

The United Nations (UN), almost since its inception, has had a major role in defining, promoting, and assisting in the implementation of human rights for individuals regardless of age.

Judith Torney-Purta is a professor of human development at the University of Maryland, College Park. The international IEA Civic Education Study, which she led, and her research with young people aged 7 to 21 have covered political socialization and human rights attitudes from the perspective of a developmental social psychologist.

Jo-Ann Amadeo is an educational researcher teaching in the Department of Human Development, University of Maryland. She has conducted research as part of the IEA Civic Education Study since 1994, including responsibility for the study of upper secondary students; she has evaluated experiential civic education programs in Washington, D.C.

DOI: 10.1177/0002716210384220

A recent history emphasizes that the organization operates not only directly through its own officials and agencies but depends on the actions of its member governments, on a broad network of nongovernmental organizations (NGOs), and on the public (and those who inform the public, from traditional journalists to individuals operating in electronic spaces). Three key issues in which the UN has made a difference are human rights implementation, women's empowerment, and an integrated approach to the development of human potential (Jolley, Emmerij, and Weiss 2009).

The UN Convention on the Rights of the Child (CRC) is the key instrument mobilizing support for the idea that children have rights to be protected and nurtured and rights to participate in decisions about their lives. Those who write about the CRC see these rights as existing in a social context and have a realistic view of impediments to their widespread implementation or protection (Ruck and Horn 2008). There is considerable debate about what it means for children to exercise participation rights as citizens and whether this should include the right to vote in elections locally or nationally. To mount a campaign to lower the voting age would require, among other things, making optimistic judgments about the ability of educational systems (or other socializing agents) to prepare young people for electoral participation. Furthermore, a variety of political and bureaucratic obstacles would stand in the way of any plan to lower the age at which individuals acquire the right to vote. Applauding the spirit behind proposals such as this, we nevertheless argue that international institutions, countries, and individuals should instead devote their resources to ensuring that early adolescents across the world are learning daily to express their views and deliberate about courses of action in matters that concern them and acquiring a variety of citizenship skills and dispositions not dependent on the right to vote. In short, we argue for promoting "emergent participatory citizenship" during the adolescent years. Directing serious attention to enhancing the politically and civically relevant niches that those between ages 10 and 18 occupy in their everyday lives, in our view, has greater potential for positive effects than does a campaign to lower the voting age worldwide.

We propose a theoretical framework new to this area, which uses a sociocultural approach to developmental psychology (Gauvain and Parke 2010; Rogoff 1995). For at least 20 years there has been a move toward viewing socialization in all areas as socially constructed (involving an interplay between deep-seated social and cultural practices and institutions), as reciprocal and bidirectional (not flowing only from parent to child or teacher to student), and as dynamic (changeable in response to events in a particular time period). For example, Haste and Torney-Purta (1992) highlighted individual and social construction in the development of political understanding. The sociocultural framework is broad enough to encompass other theoretical concepts such as Bandura's ideas about observational learning or collective efficacy (Bandura 1999).

Recently Gauvain and Parke (2010) dealt in depth with the sociocultural approach to socialization, pointing out that individuals live their everyday lives in

FIGURE 1
Aspects of the Developmental Niche for Emergent Participatory Citizenship

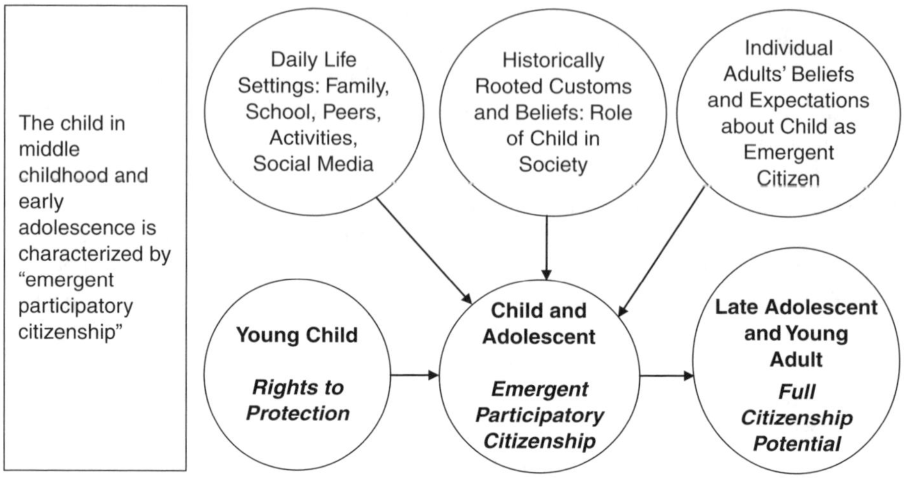

what are defined as developmental niches. These authors credit Beatrice Whiting, an anthropologist deeply involved in the cross-cultural study of children, as one of the first to describe how cultures create different micro and macro settings in which children develop and to describe parents' roles as organizers of these settings (Whiting and Whiting 1975). Super and Harkness (1986, 1999) pointed to three dimensions of the developmental niches in which individual children are embedded (see Figure 1). First is the physical and social setting in which the child lives his or her daily life. Second are the culturally regulated customs of child care and child rearing (many rooted in historical circumstances or ecological demands). Third are the beliefs of caretakers about the nature of children and their developmental processes, called "ethnotheories" (Super and Harkness 1999; Harkness et al. 2007).

Some of the characteristics of the niche are unique to the individual child (shaped by gender, age, or temperament) and to a particular family (an absent parent or kin living nearby); other characteristics may be shared within the local community (limited economic resources or the circumstances of a particular ethnic group); still others are defined by political and social institutions (requirements for compulsory school attendance or limitations on speaking openly about politics). Parents attempt to organize their children's niches in line with the history of the groups with which they identify; their own experiences or inclinations; and the available economic, educational, and social resources. Activities that take place regularly within developmental niches fuel socialization. Socially acceptable practices, rituals, and routines are enmeshed in the process by which young people are socialized in every area of life, including their exercise of participatory rights, also called their political socialization.

The expectations that adults hold for young people are constructed according to what parents or educators believe young people will need to know when they are mature (although parents are never perfect prognosticators of the futures in which their children will be adults). These expectations are also age-graded, typically using common cognitive and social capacities. No one expects a 4-year-old to be a fluent reader, but lack of progress toward literacy a few years later would be of concern. Few would give much credence to a 6-year-old's opinions on a political issue, but the opinions of an 11-year-old might be the topic for conversation within the family. Most psychological research cited about political awareness, for example, finds an increase in the ability to look at several sides of a social problem, to consider others' opinions, and to make an argument sometime between the ages of 10 and 14 for many children (Gallatin and Adelson 1970). This and other evidence has led some to argue for lowering the voting age. We argue that this is not the best action to enhance the maturation of participatory rights.

In summary, young people; adults; other children with whom young people interact on a proximal basis; as well as more distant social, economic, and educational institutions coconstruct the niches in which young people develop. Niches in which children develop may be rich in experiences relevant to the exercise of participatory rights or "voice." Or children may be expected to conform to the beliefs of adults, without much chance to engage in social practices allowing them to explore or deliberate about their opinions (or have an impact on the thinking of others).

This article provides evidence that enhancing opportunities for the exercise of participatory rights within the developmental niches of young people is a worthwhile direction for action. Our arguments regarding children and participatory rights have three parts. First, we look at how political action apart from elections and in everyday community settings has been viewed across the several decades in which political socialization research has been conducted. We introduce the concept of emergent participatory citizenship for adolescents. We bring together research about political socialization and civic engagement and landmarks in the understanding of human rights, especially children's participatory rights. Table 1 lists some of these landmarks over the past 40 years to illustrate several relevant themes (the actions of UN bodies as well as empirical, interdisciplinary research). Although collaborative approaches to these activities could have been helpful, in most cases no connections were made between these themes. The second section introduces research that uses a quantitative methodology to examine these issues—responses to survey questions. We examine whether the socialization and developmental experiences of the majority of early adolescents entering the twenty-first century have resulted in attitudes and skills appropriate to being full citizens with the vote. Of course, many argue that few who are of voting age possess these skills or attitudes. However, if the voting age were to be lowered, the status of young people in this regard would have to be considered. The third section examines studies using qualitative methodologies—observations and

TABLE 1
Time Line Covering 40 Years of Selected Actions and Publications Relating to Young People and Their Emergent Citizenship

Year	Action or Publication	Description
1960s	Early studies of political socialization	Proposed that young people are developing political attitudes and that many actions take place between elections (Hess and Torney 1967/2006; Gallatin and Adelson 1970)
1965	"Political Socialization" (Volume 361), *The Annals of the American Academy of Political and Social Science*	Primarily political scientists' view of the process (Sigel 1965)
1971	First IEA Civic Education Study (ten countries)	Included measures of authoritarianism and support for women's political rights. Found that an open classroom climate for discussion fosters civic knowledge and attitudes (Torney, Oppenheim, and Farnen 1976)
1974	UNESCO Recommendation on Education for International Understanding, Cooperation and Peace and Education Relating to Human Rights and Fundamental Freedoms	Introduced a connection between education for international understanding (global education) and human rights education; provided the basis for countries to justify programs in these areas (Buergenthal and Torney 1976; Savolainen 2010)
1980	UN Convention on the Rights of the Child (CRC)	Formalized the rights to protection and rights to participation (Articles 12, 13, 14, 15, 17)
1990	World Values Survey	Examined attitudes of samples ranging from young adults to seniors on a variety of political topics (see Tilley [2002] for an analysis of young adults)
1999	Second IEA Civic Education Study among 14-year-olds (twenty-eight countries)	Included measures of citizenship obligations of adults, rights of minorities, and women. Again found that open classroom climates for discussion foster civic knowledge and attitudes (see Torney-Purta et al. 2001).
2000	Second IEA Civic Education Study among upper secondary students (sixteen countries)	Findings similar to IEA study of 14-year-olds (see Amadeo et al. 2002)
2001	"Children's Rights" (Volume 575), *The Annals of the American Academy of Political and Social Science*	Covers issues in implementing the CRC, including a sociological view of childhood (James and James 2001).
2008	A special issue of the *Journal of Social Issues* including articles on support for international human rights and children's rights	Showed that governments' participation in the international dialogue about human rights and the human rights records of different countries related to what 14-year-olds knew and believed about human rights, including knowledge of the CRC (Torney-Purta, Wilkenfeld, and Barber 2008)
2008	"Young Citizens: A Case Study of Institutionalizing Children's Participation in Community Decision-Making"	Perspective from a legal scholar on defining children's capacity to participate in deliberation as an alternative to an arbitrary age for participation rights and thus to implement the CRC (Morse 2008)

interviews—showing how the niches or spaces for adolescents to exercise participatory capabilities can be enhanced.

Political and Civic Activity That Is Not Linked to Elections

Activity between elections has been seen as important since early political socialization research. For example, a chapter in R. Hess and Torney (1967/2006) discussed the sense of political efficacy as a quality that develops in children across time and not primarily in response to periodic elections. Beaumont (2010) makes the same point for late adolescents. The emphasis in countries such as England, which has recently mandated the study of citizenship, and other countries in the European Union (as well as the United States) has been on active citizenship taking place in youth organizations, community problem solving or service groups, and teen councils (Torney-Purta, Amadeo, and Richardson 2007).

The emphasis on citizenship skills and attitudes as part of everyday experience is even more explicit when developing countries are discussed. Kassimir and Flanagan (2010) argue that in much of Africa, adolescents take up the slack for inefficient and even corrupt political institutions that adults run. In the process they find niches that allow them to transition more effectively from adolescence to young adulthood. These youth are not focused on being part of an electorate voting from time to time (in elections that may or may not meet international standards of openness and fairness) but on everyday activities that improve their lives along with those of their communities and families. This direction is quite consistent with the CRC and, in fact, moves the action "away from Geneva" (and from UN agencies in general) and into places that are more likely to have positive influences on the everyday lives of children (Veerman and Levine 2000). These authors argue that local ombudsmen, walk-in centers providing advice, and involving children in improving their local physical environments have both short- and long-term positive effects and have appropriately moved the center of gravity for implementing children's rights away from States Parties and diplomatic debate in the UN and its agencies. Compelling examples of such a transition are found in many parts of the world.

How do political scientists view this issue? To take one example, Cohen (2005, 2009) discusses children and adolescents as "semi-citizens," a category that also includes undocumented adult immigrants: "Children hold nationality and have strong social citizenship, but little political standing or status" (Cohen 2009, 73). Furthermore, she notes that "children are individuals with pressing political interests and needs prior to reaching the age of majority" (Cohen 2005, 230). She argues that many school policies, such as the starting hours and what food is served in the lunchrooms, consider the needs of adults (e.g., parents' work schedules and support for farmers selling surplus food) rather than the needs or preferences of children. We prefer a positive view and propose the term *emergent participatory citizenship* rather than "semi-citizenship."

Possessing the right to vote in national elections may not be an essential dimension of citizenship for early adolescents as long as other competencies and attitudes are nurtured in everyday settings. These competencies include awareness of human rights and the capacity to understand and the right to take part in respectful deliberations of potentially controversial issues. They also include willingness to accept the obligation to undertake both conventional and social-movement-related citizenship activities. Furthermore, we argue that emergent participatory citizenship for young adolescents should include respect for ethnic minorities and the political rights of women. Having a voice in matters that concern them and lack of discrimination are among the themes that Peterson-Badali and Ruck (2008) identified when they questioned young people about the meaning of participatory rights. These characteristics associated with emergent participatory citizenship are discussed in the next two sections, where we consider both quantitative and qualitative studies.

International Survey Data as a Basis for Defining Citizenship in Young People

In establishing a research base for defining the parameters of citizenship in light of the CRC, it seems counterintuitive to rely primarily on research conducted in the United States. Explicit implementation of the CRC will not take place in the United States until and unless the U.S. government ratifies the CRC. As a result, this article emphasizes research conducted outside the United States.

Fortunately, there has been a recent increase in this research cross-nationally. The *Sage Handbook on Education for Citizenship and Democracy* (Arthur, Davies, and Hahn 2008), the *Handbook of Research on Civic Engagement in Youth* (Sherrod, Torney-Purta, and Flanagan 2010), and the *Handbook of Cultural Developmental Science* (Bornstein 2010) present international research results throughout. They also suggest the value of using multiple methods and theories to examine issues relating to human development and citizenship for young people (Gauvain and Parke 2010; Torney-Purta, Amadeo, and Andolina 2010). The two handbooks that have a focus on citizenship define effective experiences for young people as those that lead to positive attitudes toward human rights, engagement in society, and a willingness to participate in a range of activities (including some that might be called conventional politics and others related instead to social movements or groups involved in protecting the environment or volunteering in the community). Electoral participation and political parties receive relatively little attention in these volumes.

Our conceptualization of "emergent participatory citizenship" is new, but its roots can be seen in earlier issues of *The Annals of the American Academy of Political and Social Science* (see Table 1). In 1965, Roberta Sigel edited volume 361, entitled "Political Socialization"; and in *The Annals* volume 580, an article by

TABLE 2
Sample Items from IEA Civic Education Study Scales (2001)

Scale	Items
Obligations of conventional citizenship	An adult who is a good citizen . . . • Votes in every election • Knows about the country's history • Follows political issues in the newspaper, radio, or TV
Obligations of social movement citizenship	An adult who is a good citizen . . . • Participates in activities to benefit people in the community • Takes part in activities promoting human rights • Takes part in activities to protect the environment
Positive attitudes toward ethnic minorities	• All ethnic groups should have equal chances to get a good education in this country. • Schools should teach students to respect members of all ethnic groups. • Members of all ethnic groups should be encouraged to run in elections for political office.
Support for political rights for women	• Women should run for public office and take part in the government just as men do. • Women should stay out of politics. (negative) • Men are better qualified to be political leaders than women. (negative)
Open classroom climate for discussion	• Students are encouraged to make up their own minds about issues. • Teachers respect our opinions and encourage us to express them in class. • Students feel free to express opinions in class even when their opinions are different from most of the other students.

James Tilley (2002) appeared entitled "Is Youth a Better Predictor of Sociopolitical Values than Is Nationality?" The article is particularly relevant here. Tilley employed data from adults who participated in the World Values Survey to discuss regional differences in political attitudes and values. The categorization of countries that Tilley used is employed here to frame an analysis of data from the IEA Civic Education Study, which collected data from 140,000 adolescents in twenty-nine countries in 1999 and 2000 (Torney-Purta et al. 2001; Amadeo et al. 2002). The responses of adolescents (who are 14 years old) in seven regions are compared on four IEA scales, all related to emergent participatory citizenship: acceptance of obligation to engage in conventional political activities (such as voting and discussing political issues) and acceptance of the obligation to support social movements (including environmental organizations, human rights organizations, or community service groups). We also look at support for the rights of ethnic/minority groups and women, who often experience denial of their rights, especially rights such as running for office or speaking out on issues. As a fifth scale, we look at the extent to which the respondents reported the opportunity to discuss controversial issues in their classrooms. Sample items are in Table 2.

Tilley (2002) examined differences by gender, age of respondent, and region of the world in responses to attitude scales (collected in 1990), looking for evidence about Ronald Inglehart's theory of value change across generations in about thirty countries. The oldest group of respondents that Tilley analyzed was composed of 65-year-olds. The countries do not completely overlap with IEA countries (nor were the questions asked exactly the same). However, we were able to build on Tilley's designation of regional groups of countries developed from a multidimensional scaling analysis of country clusters. Our analysis of the IEA Civic Education Study uses the following country clusters: Anglo-Saxon, Nordic, Western European, Southern European, post-Communist, and Hispanic/Iberian-heritage. The United States is presented separately. The IEA Study was conducted after the democratic changes in Eastern Europe, and we have a relatively large group of countries from that region (here called "post-Communist" countries). Three attitude scales were similar enough that we could compare IEA findings from 14-year-olds to Tilley's findings from adults.

The two sets of IEA Civic Education items about obligations or norms of citizenship show the following regional patterns (similar for the two types of obligations) (see the first two columns of Table 3). Young people from Southern Europe and Hispanic/Iberian-heritage countries showed the highest sense of obligation to participate in both types of activities. The United States and the post-Communist countries were intermediate on these two scales, while the Anglo Saxon, Nordic, and Western European countries were least likely to feel obligated to undertake conventional political participation. The preference for social movement activities over conventional political activities was especially striking in Denmark, Norway, and Sweden. These results are similar to those of Tilley (2002), with young adults tested about 10 years earlier for attitudes toward social movement activities. However, he found relatively more conventional political activity among the Nordic young adults than we found among Nordic adolescents.

Discussing the activity levels of young people in Scandinavia, Amnå and Zetterberg (2010) introduce the concept of "stand-by citizen" to describe individuals in this region. This is a person who is sufficiently content with current political, economic, and democratic conditions so that he or she feels little obligation to be active in conventional political activities but is ready to be mobilized in case these conditions change. Nordic young people have the highest levels of trust in governmental institutions of any of the countries tested in the IEA Study, and this may partially explain their status as relatively passive observers of politics (Torney-Purta et al. 2001); their governments also receive very high scores on the Freedom House Index (see Torney-Purta, Wilkenfeld, and Barber 2008).

We also have information, which corroborates Tilley's (2002) findings, about the post-Communist countries and the Hispanic/Iberian-heritage countries,

TABLE 3
Regional Differences in 14-Year-Old's Acquisition of the Characteristics Associated with "Emergent Participatory Citizenship"

Mean	Obligations of Conventional Citizenship	Obligations of Social-Movement Citizenship	Support for Rights for Ethnic Minorities	Support for Political Rights for Women	Experience of an Open Classroom Climate
11.0	SoEu				
10.9		SoEu			
10.8		HsIb	U.S.		
10.7	HsIb			AngS/Nrdc	
10.6			HsIb		
10.5				U.S.	U.S.
10.4				WeEu	SoEu
10.3	U.S.	U.S.	SoEu/AngS		
10.2					Nrdc/HsIb
10.1	PCom			SoEu	AngS
10.0		PCom	Nrdc	HsIb	WeEu
9.9					
9.8			PCom		
9.7					PCom
9.6		Nrdc	WeEu		
9.5	WeEu	WeEu		PCom	
9.4					
9.3	AngS	AngS			
9.2	Nrdc				
9.1					

SOURCE: IEA Civic Education Study. IRT Scale means with an international mean of 10 and standard deviation of 2 (for individual scores). Country categories similar to those that Tilley (2001) used based on a multidimensional scaling analysis of World Value Survey data.

NOTE: **Anglo-Saxon (AngS)**: Australia and England; **Hispanic/Iberian (HsIb)**: Chile, Colombia, Portugal; **Nordic (Nrdc):** Denmark, Finland, Norway, Sweden; **Post-Communist (PCom)**: Bulgaria, Czech Republic, Estonia, Hungary, Latvia, Lithuania, Poland, Rumania, Russian Federation, Slovak Republic, Slovenia; **Western Europe (WeEu)**: Belgium (Fr), Germany, Switzerland; **Southern Europe (SoEu)**: Cyprus, Greece, Italy; and **U.S.**: United States

where students have a relatively high sense of obligation toward conventional participation. In other analysis of these data, we have found that 14-year-olds who resided in "countries where the observance of human rights is less consistent (those with low Freedom House scores) were more likely to answer a question about the Universal Declaration of Human Rights correctly . . . after controls for several other relevant factors" (Torney-Purta, Wilkenfeld, and Barber 2008, 876).

We speculated that the memories of abuses of political rights in these countries (such as former dictatorships in Chile and Portugal or in post-Communist countries) have led recently to enhanced teaching about ways to protect human rights. These are also countries whose governments mention the protection of human rights in reports submitted to intergovernmental groups. Students were more likely to correctly answer an IEA Study question about the purpose of the CRC in countries that placed this emphasis on human rights in their international discourse (Torney-Purta, Wilkenfeld, and Barber 2008).

The IRT (item response theory) scales on which Table 3 is based are designed to compare countries, but it is also helpful to examine percentages to give concrete meaning to these findings. Across the twenty-eight countries, less than one-quarter of the adolescent respondents thought it "very important" for adult citizens to follow political issues, and only 10 percent thought it "very important" to engage in political discussions. In contrast, about a third thought it "very important" for adult citizens to participate in environmental organizations or in organizations that benefit the community. About one-sixth of the students across countries were already participating in either environmental or community volunteer organizations, though with wide variability across countries.

Our regional comparisons also deal with support for rights, especially political rights such as running for office or openly discussing issues. The first of these scales is Support for the Rights of Ethnic Minorities (detailed in Husfeldt, Barber, and Torney-Purta 2005). Young people from the United States as well as the Hispanic/Iberian-heritage, Southern European, and Anglo-Saxon regions show the greatest support for the rights of ethnic groups, with the Nordic region at the mean and post-Communist and Western European countries below the mean. Looking across the entire sample, only about 20 percent of adolescents strongly agreed that "members of all ethnic groups should be encouraged to run in elections for political office." A larger percentage of students approved the provision of education for all groups.

Inglehart and Norris (2003) have argued that support for women's political rights is another dimension of attitudes that is important when considering the meaning of citizenship. Table 3 shows data from 14-year-olds in the IEA Civic Education Study. The highest levels of Support for Women's Rights is found in the Nordic, Anglo-Saxon, and Western European countries (and the United States), with moderate support in the Hispanic/Iberian-heritage and the Southern European countries. Post-Communist countries are considerably below the international mean. These results largely confirm Tilley's (2002) analysis of young adults 10 years earlier, which found the strongest support for women's rights among Nordic and Anglo-Saxon countries and the lowest among Eastern and Central Europeans.

Looking at the percentages across the IEA sample, about 40 percent of the 14-year-olds believe that both women and men should run for political office. A different type of analysis has shown, however, that a disturbing 8 to 10 percent of young people across Western and Eastern Europe are deeply alienated. They are opposed to women's rights as well as rights for immigrants and ethnic groups; they have very low trust in institutions and do not believe that it is important to obey the law (Torney-Purta 2009).

We also have data from a population of students about three years older than the 14-year-olds on three of these five scales (the Obligations of Conventional Citizenship; Obligations of Social-Movement Citizenship; and Support for Political Rights for Women) (Amadeo et al. 2002). Two of these three scales show little change across the late adolescent years: the international means for the two citizenship scales were almost the same across the two age groups. Both the younger and older adolescents were supportive of political rights for women. However, in ten of the thirteen countries where comparisons could be made between age groups, the older adolescents were more likely than the 14-year-olds to have supportive attitudes toward political rights for women.

Dalton (2008) used International Social Survey data to contrast what he termed "dutiful citizenship," including voting and obeying the law, with "engaged citizenship," including political tolerance and respect for ethnic minorities and for groups holding nonmainstream views. The dimensions he considers correspond with those that we have chosen, and the differences he reports largely corroborate those above.

We draw several conclusions from these results. First, where it is possible to compare with Tilley's (2002) or Dalton's (2008) young adult respondents, the country differences are similar. Second, there is little support for the belief that young people have new perspectives that could only be elicited by giving them the vote. Many of the activities in which they are interested (environmental groups or community service) do not require membership in the electorate. Third, there are groups in every country that might actively discriminate against disadvantaged groups by voting for parties with exclusionist policies, participating in illegal activities, or denying rights to certain groups. No region stands out as having adolescents who are well prepared for citizenship.

The last column in Table 3 presents regional differences in students' reports that they experience an open classroom climate for the respectful discussion of issues. This opportunity to learn deliberative strategies (such as those that Earls and Carlson [2002] identify) is least characteristic of the newer democracies in Central and Eastern Europe. Looking across the sample, only a quarter (or less) of the students strongly agree that teachers "encourage us to discuss political or social issues about which people have different opinions" or "present several sides of an issue when explaining it in class."

We cannot guarantee that young people in any of these countries will be model citizens once they have reached the age at which they receive the right to vote. However, we believe it is possible to enhance the everyday niches that adolescents occupy with opportunities to explore conventional political activities as well as participation in social movement groups and also to give them opportunities to deliberate with others as part of the exercise of participatory rights.

A Review of International Qualitative Data about Citizenship among Young People

This section reports studies using multiple methods (often qualitative) in countries other than the United States. These studies demonstrate positive ways in which adolescents in their everyday lives and settings are currently reorienting the practice of citizenship. These approaches have potential for countries other than those where they originated.

England implemented new citizenship education programs in the early years of the twenty-first century. This effort was in response to "worrying levels of apathy, ignorance and cynicism about public life" (Qualifications and Curriculum Authority [QCA] 1998, 8, cited in Weller 2007). The Crick Report (QCA 1998) identified three strands upon which these programs were based: social and moral responsibility; community involvement, including service activities; and political literacy, especially about democratic institutions.

Susie Weller (2003, 2007), a geographer, expresses sympathy with the need for school-based citizenship education but has some skepticism as well. She reports the results of a teen-centered, multimethod study (including narrative approaches) conducted on the Isle of Wight in the United Kingdom with 13- to 16-year-olds early in the newly mandated civic education program. She studied the role of spaces and places in young people's citizenship.

Schools are obviously one of those places, and the curriculums and programs provide spaces designated for teaching citizenship topics (Weller 2007). She believes that there is unrealized potential because a classroom subject that could be highly participative, involving and relevant for students, often was not. In some cases, school councils served as regulated spaces, and only sometimes did students believe that their voices were heard. Where area-wide youth parliaments existed, they did provide this opportunity. Many young people were involved outside of school in charity organizations or public campaigns on an issue chosen because of its personal importance to them; only about a third of these students said that something they had learned in the classroom was useful in these activities. Several young people reported that it was discouraging to be asked for an opinion by an adult decision-maker who then disregarded it while complaining about "youth apathy."

Young people, however, developed much of their sense of political agency in what Weller (2007) called the "geographies of micro-politics," in places where they hung out together (sometimes private spaces in their homes; sometimes public spaces such as parks, commercial spaces, or cyberspaces). Often these were what she called "claimed spaces," meaning that the young people had taken a place designed for another purpose, such as an unused bus shelter, and through collective effort had converted it into a place to spend time with each other. This also helped them to negotiate subgroup cultures such as the Goths or the skateboarders. This type of active citizenship within local and individualized developmental niches is quite different from the centralized and nationalized view in most formal civic education programs.

The author concluded that there are many places more conducive to fostering collaborative decision-making and action than those that involve elections or voting. This approach reminds us that theorizing in this field must go beyond individually centered approaches to talk about collective efficacy, not merely personal efficacy (Beaumont 2010), and to deal with situations in which young people can fill different types of participative roles and move over time toward greater involvement and responsibility (Lave and Wenger 1988).

A parallel study was conducted at the same period in a large town in southern England, using semistructured interviews with 8- to 11-year-olds (Chamberlin 2003). These authors arrived at similar conclusions about the lack of understanding of politics among young people and their minimum levels of participation. While school leaders described a wide variety of activities organized by school councils, the pupils in these schools had little memory of these activities.

Smith et al. (2005, 429) examined young people's ideas about themselves as citizens based on the assumption that it is essential to consider "what citizenship means in the context of young people's experiences and relationships." The researchers conducted a study in Leicester, England, where 16-, 19-, and 22-year-old participants were interviewed once a year for three years. The authors concluded that a more inclusive view of citizenship allows young people to identify themselves as citizens and recognize their informal activities as expressions of citizenship. The authors also noted the fluid nature of citizenship identity.

Another study of the meaning of citizenship took place in Vancouver, Canada, with 14- to 16-year-olds living on the fringe of the inner city (Kennelly and Dillabough 2008). Vancouver was of interest because of the intersecting currents of global activity and the ways in which young people saw themselves positioned in relation to hierarchies of class, race, and gender. This study included an inventive methodological approach drawn from visual sociology to study economically marginalized youth. Students produced photo-narratives of everyday experiences and also wrote letters expressing their views of citizenship to an imaginary new immigrant to Canada (some including pictures drawn or taken by the students). Some students were also interviewed. The good citizen, according to these young people, is "the compliant, self regulating individual who participates in the public sphere only through acts of charity, and only if the risks . . . are not great" (Kennelly and Dillabough 2008, 505). These young people regularly attributed poverty, which was associated with bad citizenship, to personal faults and expressed views of foreigners, often Asians, as undeserving. Without interventions that take account of the everyday niches, positions, and experiences of youth in these local cultures, it will be impossible to implement participation rights for all, no matter whether young people have a vote or not.

A fifth qualitative study comes from Africa and brings the legal perspective and the opportunities that the CRC presents into focus, as well as providing a description of the everyday settings and developmental niches of 10- to 12-year-olds. Morse (2008) describes the Child Safety Audit Project, which was modeled on a project that took place in Chicago (Earls and Carlson 2002), in conjunction with the Young Citizens Project in Tanzania; the latter was a community-based cluster randomized control trial of an intervention that included dramatic presentations that 10- to 14-year-olds made about HIV/AIDS. Adults who attended these presentations were more likely to react favorably to young people as health promoters and more likely to discuss HIV/AIDS with their children (Kamo et al. 2008).

The Child Safety Audit Project was based on the idea that the ability to deliberate about a problem is central to children's realization of their rights to protection and safety as well as to participation.

> I challenge the prevailing view in law that children are not ready or able to act as responsible citizens. I do not propose that children should draft legislation or vote, but rather I present convincing evidence that children are capable of participating in some of the most important deliberative functions, enabling them to contribute to solutions for challenging issues facing their communities. (Morse 2008, 24)

The Tanzanian participants, ages 10 to 12, were invited to generate lists of safety problems that they experienced in their homes, neighborhoods, or schools and sometimes mapped the locations where those problems occurred. This was followed by a facilitated discussion, equipping them to see these issues in more generalized or abstract terms; prioritizing of these issues by individuals and then by the group; brainstorming about solutions to these problems; authoring and presenting a participatory drama about some of the issues; making plans to survey the community more broadly; generating detailed action plans; and collaborating with local leaders in a workshop.

A number of scholars have concluded that basic cognitive, linguistic, and emotion-regulation skills can be enhanced by experiences such as these. Appropriate pacing, sufficient time, and adult guidance are among the necessary external conditions. Finally, the deliberative capacities that the children were capable of achieving included the ability to clearly communicate their ideas and arguments along with the ability to think analytically about arguments, issues, and feelings, as they prioritized problems or solutions according to available evidence (see Hess 2009).

Morse's project makes a considerable contribution to our argument here. It gives concrete examples of

1. A collective capacity-set for children's citizenship [nurtured at the local level];
2. Structural conditions necessary to establish their authentic participation; and
3. A possible model for the legal institutionalization of children's participation in community decision-making (Morse 2008, 24).

This is illustrated in a country where threats, such as the HIV/AIDS epidemic and widespread poverty, may seem intractable to the outside observer. The author argues that an informed judgment about children's capacity to deliberate is a better standard across nations than any arbitrary age limit would be for evaluating children's capacity to enact their participatory rights as defined in the CRC. The author makes extensive reference to apprenticeship as a mode of learning and to Rogoff's developmental psychology research, which has contributed greatly to sociocultural approaches and the concept of developmental niches.

This initiative has also described several challenges, for example, the reluctance many adults have about recognizing children's participatory capacities as citizens. Parents often fear that children who have had experiences, such as those in Morse's project, will become too assertive in the home setting. Furthermore, when such projects are either seen by participants as tokenism or are begun but prematurely abandoned, they have a negative impact upon young people's views of themselves as citizens. Morse's (2008) detailed presentation, linking legal concepts of children's rights to activities in the local setting, is a strong contribution to our argument for enhancing participation opportunities in the child's own developmental niche.

A related approach that has been influential is Roger Hart's (1992) ladder describing the evolving participation of children in citizenship. The bottom rungs are identified as inauthentic and not consistent with the CRC's view of participatory rights. These include manipulation of children for adults' political ends, decoration of an event with child participants, and tokenism where children's voices are heard but not valued. The five rungs of the ladder that follow are consistent with the CRC in their authenticity. At the top level, children decide what role adults are to play and invite them for a specific purpose. For a more detailed connection with human rights education, see Howe and Covell (2005).

Conclusion

Several strands have been drawn together, ranging from survey findings to in-depth qualitative studies to ways to look at the everyday experience of young people, especially ways in which they can move from more peripheral to more central engagement in and with society. We argue that efforts should be directed toward approaches other than national campaigns to gain the vote for 16- or 17-year-olds. Even political scientists (who historically have focused on electoral activity) are beginning to recognize that activities within the niches of everyday life are the best culture (in the biological laboratory sense) for growing citizenship among young people. Russell Dalton, well known for his research on Western European political systems, has a recent book titled *The Good Citizen: How a Younger Generation Is Shaping American Politics* (2008). He argues that among younger generations, the concept of citizen duty (e.g., voting and obeying the law) is being replaced with a concept of engaged citizenship that includes political action to benefit others (not just voting) and places emphasis on political tolerance of groups with different viewpoints and ethnic group attitudes.

In a parallel way, a chapter by Bennett, Freelon, and Wells (2010) contrasts dutiful citizenship with actualizing citizenship and moves beyond the usual domains of action to focus on electronic media (especially Web sites that young people constructed). This builds on a broader trend to see the electronic media as mobilizing socially conscious and critically aware citizen-consumers who are concerned with issues rather than broader political ideologies (see Gerodimos 2008; Ward 2008).

The sketch by these political scientists of the qualities of citizenship looks very much like the five aspects of attitudes that we examined in the IEA Study data—obligations that go beyond conventional politics to support for rights and social movements as well as opportunities to develop skills of deliberation. It is also consistent with points made with respect to the moral and citizenship requirements of the CRC (Torney-Purta 1999). It is not accurate to say that political scientists no longer pay attention to the right to vote, but it is certainly modest relative to their attention to a range of other activities in which young people can engage irrespective of their age or immigrant status.

One of the major advantages of trying to enhance developmental niches for emergent participatory citizenship is that it allows young people to construct and choose those aspects of the polity, the economy, or the society in which they want to take action. They are primed to act on issues that make them angry (low-wage labor used in the production of garments) or that they see influencing individuals in their own families (HIV/AIDS or poor schooling available to their siblings or unsafe streets in their neighborhoods). Haste and Hogan (2006) found these motives to be very powerful among adolescents. Young people do not want to be limited to the agendas of political leaders or their parties, which may be constructed mainly with the next election in mind or may be designed not to offend wealthy adults.

Another reason to focus on the child or adolescent's developmental niche is a pragmatic one. To change the voting age in the majority of the countries of the world would take an enormous effort and expenditure of resources, first to build constituencies in the public and then to enact and implement the required legislation. How many more positive uses can we think of for these personal and financial resources? Two such uses include micro-loans to set up youth programs and electronic networks to engage young people in actions to discourage untrustworthy behavior on the part of their governments.

The idea of enhancing developmental niches for emergent participatory citizenship is also consistent with ideas voiced by a specialist in legal and psychological aspects of this issue:

> If children's rights are to have meaning they must be norms for life in the community setting of which children are a part. . . . Whether children's rights to participate are meaningful in practice is much more a function of how they are treated in the everyday settings of life than whether they are heard in judges' chambers. (Melton 2005, 650)

A next step is to theorize and specify the elements of a developmental model that could provide guidance. The concept of a developmental niche, described earlier, was initially proposed as a way to understand young children in relation to their parents. This concept can also play a vital role in understanding "emergent participatory citizenship" during childhood and adolescence.

Our conceptualization of the participatory niche for encouraging emergent citizenship among 10- to 15-year-olds (found in Figure 1) also includes physical and social settings of daily life, as did Super and Harkness's (1999) concept. The settings especially relevant to early adolescents include not only the home, but also the school, the peer group, and both formal and informal organizations to which they belong in their communities. Because institutions of society play such an important role in citizenship (from schools to social media to national governments), culturally regulated social practices (many with strong historical aspects) should be viewed with an explicit institutional dimension. The second dimension of our participatory niche concept also includes societal customs, including an emphasis on formal or informal learning relevant to political socialization. The third dimension is the characteristics and beliefs of those who care for or teach children and adolescents (expanding the list beyond caregivers such as parents to include teachers and informal mentors, as Harkness at al. did in a 2007 study of teachers' ideal students across five countries).

We are also interested in several of the processes of socialization and development implied in this model. Three planes of analysis that Rogoff (1995) discussed can be seen as influencing these processes. The young person may participate in an apprenticeship in a culturally organized activity; the young person may engage in social participation with partners who are either adults or peers; and finally, young people may appropriate the practices honed on the first two planes into their own repertoire of behavior. Sometimes the apprenticeship or social participation takes place in what is called a "community of practice." This provides a sense of meaning, identity, and contextualized practice and encourages the individual to move from more peripheral to more central positions as he or she becomes more skilled in practices such as deliberation and then appropriates them into his or her own repertoires (Lave and Wenger 1988).

No one has fully considered possible approaches to creating niches for fostering emergent citizenship as part of implementing the participatory rights detailed in the CRC, though the work of Weller (2007), Morse (2008), Hart (1992), and Melton (2005) suggest some directions. A next step is to mobilize the energy of psychologists, those who have the opportunity to shape policy, advocates for children's rights, teachers, journalists (in the mainstream media and online), social movement activists, and those who conduct formal and informal education programs to propose ways to enhance the participatory character of the developmental niches of children and adolescents. This effort has the potential to contribute to all three areas in which the UN, its agencies, and associated NGOs have made a difference in the world.

References

Amadeo, Jo-Ann, Judith Torney-Purta, Rainer Lehmann, Vera Husfeldt, and Roumiana Nikolova. 2002. *Civic knowledge and engagement: An IEA study of upper secondary students in sixteen countries*. Amsterdam: IEA.

Amnå, Erik, and Pär Zetterberg. 2010. A political science perspective on socialization research: Young Nordic citizens in a comparative light. In *Handbook of research on civic engagement in youth*, eds. Lonnie Sherrod, Judith Torney-Purta, and Constance Flanagan, 43–66. Hoboken, NJ: John Wiley.

Arthur, James, Ian Davies, and Carole Hahn, eds. 2008. *The Sage handbook of education for citizenship and democracy*. Thousand Oaks, CA: Sage.

Bandura, Albert. 1999. Social cognitive theory: An agentic perspective. *Asian Journal of Social Psychology* 2:21–41.

Beaumont, Elizabeth. 2010. Political agency and empowerment: Pathways for developing a sense of political efficacy in young adults. In *Handbook of research on civic engagement in youth*, eds. Lonnie Sherrod, Judith Torney-Purta, and Constance Flanagan, 525–58. Hoboken, NJ: John Wiley.

Bennett, W. Lance, Deen Freelon, and Chris Wells. 2010. Changing citizen identity and the rise of a participatory media culture. In *Handbook of research on civic engagement in youth*, eds. Lonnie Sherrod, Judith Torney-Purta, and Constance Flanagan, 393–424. Hoboken, NJ: John Wiley.

Bornstein, Marc, ed. 2010. *Handbook of cultural developmental science*. New York, NY: Psychology Press.

Buergenthal, Thomas, and Judith Torney. 1976. *International human rights and international education*. Washington, DC: Government Printing Office.

Chamberlin, Rosemary. 2003. Citizenship? Only if you haven't got a life: Secondary school pupils' views of citizenship education. *Westminster Studies in Education* 26 (2): 87–97.

Cohen, Elizabeth. 2005. Neither seen nor heard: Children's citizenship in contemporary democracies. *Citizenship Studies* 9 (2): 221–40.

Cohen, Elizabeth. 2009. *Semi-citizenship in democratic politics*. Cambridge: Cambridge University Press.

Dalton, Russell J. 2008. *The good citizen: How a younger generation is reshaping American politics*. Washington, DC: CQ Press.

Earls, Felton, and Mary Carlson. 2002. Adolescents as collaborators in search of well-being. In *Youth in cities: A cross-national perspective*, eds. Marta Tienda and William Julius Wilson, 8–83. Cambridge: Cambridge University Press.

Gallatin, Judith, and Joseph Adelson. 1970. Individual rights and the public good: A cross-national study of adolescents. *Comparative Political Studies* 3 (2): 226–42.

Gauvain, Mary, and Ross Parke. 2010. Socialization. In *Handbook of cultural developmental science*, ed. Marc Bornstein, 239–58. New York, NY: Psychology Press.

Gerodimos, Roman. 2008, Mobilising young citizens in the UK: A content analysis of youth and issue websites. *Information, Communication and Society* 11 (7): 964–68.

Harkness, Sara, Marjolijn Blom, Alfredo Olivab, Ughetta Moscardinoc, Piotr Olaf Zyliczd, Moises Rios Bermudez, Xin Fenga, Agnieszka Carrasco-Zyliczd, Giovanna Axiac, and Charles M. Super. 2007. Teachers' ethnotheories of the "ideal student" in five Western cultures. *Comparative Education* 43 (1): 113–35.

Hart, Roger. 1992. *Children's participation: From tokenism to citizenship*. Florence, Italy: Innocenti Research Centre, UNICEF.

Haste, Helen, and Amy Hogan. 2006. Beyond conventional civic participation, beyond the moral-political divide: Young people and contemporary debates about citizenship. *Journal of Moral Education* 35 (4): 473–94.

Haste, Helen, and Judith Torney-Purta. 1992. Social construction and individual construction in the development of political understanding. In *The development of political understanding*, eds. Helen Haste and Judith Torney-Purta, 3–10. San Francisco, CA: Jossey-Bass.

Hess, Diana. 2009. *Controversy in the classroom: The democratic power of discussion*. New York, NY: Routledge.

Hess, Robert, and Judith Torney. 1967/2006. *The development of political attitudes in children*. Chicago, IL: Aldine. (Reissued by Transaction Press.)

Howe, R. Brian, and Katherine Covell. 2005. *Empowering children: Children's rights education as a pathway to citizenship*. Toronto, Canada: University of Toronto Press.

Husfeldt, Vera, Carolyn Barber, and Judith Torney-Purta. 2005. Adolescents' social attitudes and expected political participation: New scales in the enhanced database for the IEA Civic Education Study. Available from www.terpconnect.umd.edu/~iea (accessed 10 August 2010).

Inglehart, Ronald, and Pippa Norris. 2003. *Rising tide: Gender equality and cultural change around the world*. Cambridge: Cambridge University Press.

James, Allison, and Adrian L. James. 2001. Childhood: Toward a theory of continuity and change. *The Annals of the American Academy of Political and Social Science* 575:25–37.

Jolley, Richard, Louis Emmerij, and Thomas G. Weiss. 2009. *UN ideas that changed the world*. Bloomington, IN: Indiana University Press.

Kamo, Namo, Mary Carlson, Robert T. Brennan, and Felton Earls. 2008. Young citizens as health agents: Use of drama in promoting community efficacy for HIV/AIDS. *American Journal of Public Health* 98 (2): 201–4.

Kassimir, Ronald, and Constance Flanagan. 2010. Youth civic engagement in the developing world: Challenges and opportunities. In *Handbook of research on civic engagement in youth*, eds. Lonnie Sherrod, Judith Torney-Purta, and Constance Flanagan, 91–113. Hoboken, NJ: John Wiley.

Kennelly, Jacqueline, and Jo-Anne Dillabough. 2008. Young people mobilizing the language of citizenship: Struggles for classification and new meaning in an uncertain world. *British Journal of the Sociology of Education* 29 (5): 493–508.

Lave, Jean, and Etienne Wenger. 1988. *Situated learning: Legitimate peripheral participation*. New York, NY: Cambridge University Press.

Melton, Gary. 2005. Treating children like people: A framework for research and advocacy. *Journal of Clinical and Adolescent Psychology* 34 (4): 646–57.

Morse, Mika. 2008. Young citizens: A case study of institutionalizing children's participation in community decision-making. *Children's Legal Rights Journal* 24 (3): 23–55.

Peterson-Badali, Michele, and Martin Ruck. 2008. A study of children's perspectives on self-determination and nurturance rights. *Journal of Social Issues* 64 (4): 749–69.

Qualifications and Curriculum Authority (QCA). 1998. *Education for citizenship and the teaching of democracy in schools (The Crick Report)*. London: QCA.

Rogoff, Barbara. 1995. Observing socio-cultural activity on three planes: Participatory appropriation, guided participation, and apprenticeship. In *Sociocultural studies of mind*, eds. James V. Wertsch, Pablo del Rio, and Amelia Alvarez. Cambridge: Cambridge University Press.

Ruck, Martin, and Stacey Horn. 2008. Charting the landscape of children's rights. *Journal of Social Issues* 64 (4): 685–99.

Savolainen, Kaisa. 2010. *Education as a means to world peace: The case of the 1974 Recommendation*. Jyvaskyla, Finland: University of Jyvaskyla.

Sherrod, Lonnie, Judith Torney-Purta, and Constance Flanagan, eds. 2010. *Handbook of research on civic engagement in youth*. Hoboken, NJ: John Wiley.

Sigel, Roberta, ed. 1965. Political socialization: Its role in the political process. *The Annals of the American Academy of Political and Social Science* 361.

Smith, Noel, Ruth Lister, Sue Middleton, and Lynne Cox. 2005. Young people as real citizens: Towards an inclusionary understanding of citizenship. *Journal of Youth Studies* 8 (4): 425–43.

Super, Charles M., and Sarah Harkness. 1986. The developmental niche: A conceptualization of the interface of child and culture. *International Journal of Behavioral Development* 9:545–70.

Super, Charles M., and Sarah Harkness. 1999. The environment as culture in developmental research. In *Measuring environment across the life span*, eds. Sarah Friedman and Theodore Wachs, 279–323. Washington, DC: American Psychological Association.

Tilley, James. 2002. Is youth a better predictor of sociopolitical values than is nationality? *The Annals of the American Academy of Political and Social Science* 580:226–56.

Torney, Judith, Abraham N. Oppenheim, and Russell Farnen. 1976. *Civic education in ten countries: An empirical study*. New York, NY: Halsted.

Torney-Purta, Judith. 1999. The meaning of a standard of living adequate for moral and civic development. In *Implementing the U.N. Convention on the Rights of the Child: A standard of living adequate for development*, eds. Arlene Andrews and Natalie Kaufman, 105–16. Westport, CT: Praeger.

Torney-Purta, Judith. 2009. International psychological research that matters for policy and practice. *American Psychologist* 64 (8): 825–37.

Torney-Purta, Judith, Jo-Ann Amadeo, and Molly Andolina. 2010. A conceptual framework and multi-method approach for research on political socialization and civic engagement. In *Handbook of research on civic engagement in youth*, eds. Lonnie Sherrod, Judith Torney-Purta, and Constance Flanagan, 497–523. Hoboken, NJ: John Wiley.

Torney-Purta, Judith, Jo-Ann Amadeo, and Wendy K. Richardson. 2007. Civic service among youth in Chile, Denmark, England and the Unites States: A psychological perspective. In *Civic service worldwide: Impacts and inquiry*, eds. Amanda McBride and Michael Sherraden, 95–132. Armonk, NY: M. E. Sharpe.

Torney-Purta, Judith, Rainer Lehmann, Hans Oswald, and Wolfram Schulz. 2001. *Citizenship and education in twenty-eight countries: Civic knowledge and engagement at age 14*. Amsterdam: IEA. Available from www.terpconnect.umd.edu/~iea (accessed 20 August 2010).

Torney-Purta, Judith, Britt Wilkenfeld, and Carolyn Barber. 2008. How adolescents in 27 countries understand, support and practice human rights. *Journal of Social Issues* 64 (4): 857–80.

Veerman, Philip, and Hephzibah Levine. 2000. Implementing children's rights on a local level: Narrowing the gap between Geneva and the grassroots. *International Journal of Children's Rights* 8:373–84.

Ward, Janelle. 2008. The on-line citizen-consumer: Addressing young people's political consumption through technology. *Journal of Youth Studies* 11 (5): 513–26.

Weller, Susie. 2003. Teach us something useful: Contested spaces of teenagers' citizenship. *Space and Polity* 7 (2): 153–71.

Weller, Susie. 2007. *Teenagers' citizenship*. London: Routledge.

Whiting, Beatrice, and John W. M. Whiting. 1975. *Children of six cultures: A psycho-cultural analysis*. Cambridge, MA: Harvard University Press.

American Sixteen- and Seventeen-Year-Olds Are Ready to Vote

By
DANIEL HART
and
ROBERT ATKINS

American 16- and 17-year-olds ought to be allowed to vote in state and national elections. This claim rests upon a line of argument that begins with an exegesis of legal and philosophical notions of citizenship that identify core qualities of citizenship: membership, concern for rights, and participation in society. Each of these qualities is present in rudimentary form in childhood and adolescence. Analyses of national survey data demonstrate that by 16 years of age—but not before—American adolescents manifest levels of development in each quality of citizenship that are approximately the same as those apparent in young American adults who are allowed to vote. The lack of relevant differences in capacities for citizenship between 16- and 17-year-olds and those legally enfranchised makes current laws arbitrary, denying those younger than age 18 the right to vote. Awarding voting rights to 16- and 17-year-olds is important, given the changing age demographics in the country, which have resulted in the growing block of older voters displacing the interests of younger Americans in the political arena. Finally, the authors critically examine claims that adolescents are neither neurologically nor socially mature enough to vote responsibly and conclude that empirical evidence and fairness suggest that 16- and 17-year-olds ought to be awarded the vote.

Keywords: civic maturity; voting; adolescence; citizenship; development

Sixteen- and 17-year-olds living in the United States ought to be allowed to vote in local, state, and national elections. This claim rests on a variety of grounds, elaborated in the sections that follow, about the nature of citizenship, the developmental status of 16- and 17-year-olds *as citizens*, and a deepening divide between the political representation of interests of the young and the old. A fair consideration of these issues, we argue, leads to the conclusion that 16- and 17-year-olds meet minimal criteria for full citizenship and can vote responsibly. We also indicate that the developmental evidence suggests that those younger than 16 years of age should be excluded from the electorate.

DOI: 10.1177/0002716210382395

In addition, we consider several lines of evidence that might be marshaled against allowing 16- and 17-year-olds to vote. One of the most popular of these—often prominent in contemporary discussions of adolescents' limitations—is that their brains are too immature to permit responsible, adult-like conduct. There are many problematic elements to such a conclusion, notably that there is virtually no evidence linking neurological maturation in adolescence to the qualities of citizenship (which we outline below). It might also be argued that setting the voting age at 16—while the ages of criminal responsibility, entering into legally binding contracts, and medical-decision making might be set at older ages—contributes to the fragmentation of citizenship. We suggest that not all of these other qualities are actually central to citizenship and that a graduated entry into these responsibilities is consistent with at least some developmental evidence.

What Is Citizenship?

Legal citizenship

In the United States, citizenship is required for a person to vote in state and federal elections. Citizenship in the United States can be obtained through several means. First, the Fourteenth Amendment of the Constitution of the United States provides citizenship to those born within the United States (excluding children of foreign diplomats). Citizenship in the United States can also be obtained through naturalization, a process through which a permanent resident of the United States can become a citizen following a demonstration of competency in English and a demonstration that he or she "is a person of good moral character, attached to the principles of the Constitution of the United States, and well disposed to the good order and happiness of the United States" (U.S. Department of Homeland Security 1952b). The naturalization process also requires a demonstration of civic knowledge concerning the political processes of the United States (questions on the test ask for the branches of government, the names of leaders of different institutions, and so on).

While the details of how citizenship is determined in the United States differ from those that define citizenship in other countries, the thrust of citizenship laws in most countries relates to classical understandings of citizenship.

Daniel Hart is a distinguished professor of psychology in the Departments of Childhood Studies and Psychology at Rutgers University in Camden, New Jersey, and serves as director of Rutgers's Center for Children and Childhood Studies. His research and applied work focuses on child and adolescent civic, social, and moral development in urban contexts.

Robert Atkins is an assistant professor with a joint appointment in childhood studies and nursing at Rutgers University in Camden, New Jersey. He is interested in studying the social and institutional processes that mediate the relationship of high-poverty neighborhoods to the health and well-being of youths living in those neighborhoods.

Citizenship as a political construct

Citizenship is largely defined by three qualities: rights, participation, and membership (Bellamy 2008). *Membership* refers to the sense of belonging to the nation and communities of which one is a citizen. Citizens are entitled to rights by virtue of membership, and as citizens, they shape these rights through participation in the political process. Full citizenship requires participation in the life of a society.

Citizenship demands some degree of solidarity with other citizens. Participation in democratic government often presumes that those who vote and those who govern identify, to some degree, with the people and institutions constituting the state. Indeed, democracy functions best when those individuals holding elected positions are concerned for the well-being of their constituents and of the state. Although citizens recognize that politicians have their own interests that they hope to fulfill while holding public office—whether these be psychological or material in nature—the public ordinarily expects these interests to be subjugated by the public good. The United States and many other countries have laws and regulations intended to diminish government officials' inclinations to pursue private goals at the expense of the public good.

Similarly, some sense of identification with the state is often seen as a prerequisite for citizenship. To the extent that voters and representatives act out of self-interest and an interest in the prosperity of one's community, citizenship guarantees a certain protection for the state—in the form of citizens' investment in their communities and nations. Critics of permissive immigration policies sometimes argue that large immigrant populations create communities in which subjective identification remains with the country of origin rather than the country of residence, resulting in limited motivation to participate civically in the host country (see Huntington 2004). While there are many reasons to doubt that such arguments are correct (see Hart, Richardson, and Wilkenfeld forthcoming), such arguments do serve to highlight the facets of citizenship concerning attachment to the community.

As noted previously, a functioning democracy requires that citizens feel that their lives are joined in important ways with their counterparts. The absence of such a sentiment reduces civic life to the point that it is expressed as instrumental action intended to fulfill purely selfish interests—and such a scenario is incompatible with a healthy democracy. Although it is possible to assign the identity of "citizen" to an individual who feels no identification with fellow citizens—indeed, every democratic society has citizens for whom this is true—this is not the kind of civic identity that can serve as the goal toward which analysis and practice ought to build.

Legal and political citizenship

The criteria for legal citizenship in the United States, and the steps necessary to obtain it for those who do not have it, are intended to ensure the three elements of citizenship discussed above—membership, concern for rights, and participation. Consider again U.S. naturalization law that requires that a candidate be "attached to the principles of the Constitution of the United States, and well disposed to the good order and happiness of the United States" (U.S.

Department of Homeland Security 1952b). The requirement for "attachment" to the principles of the Constitution clearly emphasizes the importance of membership for citizens. To be a citizen is not only to know about the Constitution but also to identify with its underlying principles. Attachment implies a visceral commitment of the individual, the result of which is that the individual is emotionally invested in the principles and, presumably, motivated to enact and defend them.

"Good moral character" as a prerequisite to naturalization is surely intended to provide a rationale for denying citizenship to chronic criminals and others whose behaviors are judged to be destructive. But "good moral character" also refers to the elements of citizenship concerned with participation in civil society and the formulation and legislation of rights. There is a broad consensus that citizens in the United States must be committed to some moral virtues for a liberal democracy to function. One of these is tolerance. *Tolerance* refers to a willingness to allow others to speak about and to participate in society, even when their views and actions are unlike those of the majority. In the United States, groups of all sorts seek to advance political agendas quite at odds with those of most Americans (for example, the legalization of marijuana) and are accorded legal protection to do so. Sullivan and Transue (1999) have argued that tolerance is a cardinal virtue of successful liberal democracies. It is likely because of the recognition of the centrality of tolerance to democracy that the United States judges that those who are members of groups and organizations that promulgate decidedly intolerant, totalitarian political views are ineligible for citizenship (U.S. Department of Homeland Security 1952a).

The processes by which citizenship can be obtained in the United States seem less directly oriented toward participation, perhaps because some forms of civic participation may be required by laws (jury duty, for example), while others are generally viewed as strictly voluntary. Nonetheless, the requirement that potential citizens demonstrate a minimal level of civic knowledge seems intended to ensure that the foundation for informed civic action is present. Civic knowledge is one of a set of dispositions that seem to motivate and inform civic action. There is solid evidence that adults with civic knowledge are more likely to participate in various ways in the political system (Galston 2001). Political scientists (see Craig, Niemi, and Silver 1990; Niemi, Craig, and Mattei 1991) have identified other dispositions related to civic knowledge that are important for motivating civic and political participation. For example, *political skills* facilitate participation; knowing how to participate effectively in the political system may be just as important in energizing voting, lobbying, and so on as possession of the facts about the political system. *Political efficacy*, reflected in the beliefs that one is an effective political actor, is one of the most widely studied characteristics of voters and citizens and is related to participation. *Political and civic interest* is also crucially important; those who are interested in community and national news possess more civic knowledge and are more likely to participate in civic life. That an ideal citizen is knowledgeable about the political system, possesses the skills to engage with the system effectively, feels a sense that his or her efforts are effective, and shows an interest in the functioning of the community seems consistent with, if not specified by, legal and philosophical connotations of citizenship.

Moreover, these qualities appear to be psychologically interconnected; they are not simply qualities that legislators and theorists admire. Civic knowledge, political efficacy, and political action are mutually reinforcing; knowledge contributes to the sense of oneself as an individual who can contribute to the political process, which in turn motivates civic action; civic action, in turn, contributes to political efficacy and efforts to acquire political knowledge (see Finkel 1985).

Legal and political notions of citizenship overlap in their emphases on the importance of membership, concern for rights and values, and participation. While legal constructions of citizenship surely have arbitrary elements, this brief exposition illustrates how facets of requirements for citizenship in the United States reflect broad, widely shared, historically meaningful notions of citizenship. Furthermore, that legal definitions of citizenship rest upon a foundation of shared understandings that derive from thoughtful considerations of individuals in their relations to political institutions suggests that the qualities of citizenship are important—for citizens and democratic institutions. It follows, therefore, that according citizenship has implications for the individual and the political institutions to which he or she belongs. Citizenship is important; it ought to be accorded to all who are deserving (for example, the Athenians' exclusion of slaves, women, and many others from citizenship was illegitimate, as was the exclusion of blacks and women in the United States) but should not be granted to those who are unable to fulfill the responsibilities of citizenship.

In the next section, the question of when children are capable of citizenship in its full sense is addressed. Though not the focus here, some of the elements discussed in the next section are also relevant when considering whether adults with cognitive and psychiatric impairments ought to be allowed to vote (Appelbaum 2000) and whether convicted felons should be enfranchised (Manza and Uggen 2004).

Children and Citizenship

Citizenship includes experiences, beliefs, and emotions concerning membership, rights, and participation (Bellamy 2008). Although these three qualities are conceptually related and necessary for citizenship, psychologically they are likely to be partially independent. It is conceptually possible, for example, for one to identify with one's fellow citizens yet not be highly involved in civic life; similarly, an individual might be concerned about the rights of citizens without identification with others in the community and absent political participation.

Development in childhood

The sense of membership in a nation and of civil rights both emerge at very young ages. For example, Barrett, Wilson, and Lyons (2003) demonstrated that English schoolchildren as young as five years of age were able to distinguish between British citizens and those from America and Germany. Moreover, even young children preferred citizens of their own nations to those of others. Barrett, Wilson, and Lyons (2003) found that the importance of national identity increased over the course of childhood, with older children judging nationality to be more important to them than gender- and age-based identities.

Young children are also able to infer that citizens have rights. In a series of studies, Helwig and colleagues (Helwig 1998, 2006; Helwig et al. 2003) found that children and adolescents believe that citizens have rights that should not be abrogated by the government. In Canada, the United States, and China, six-year-old children used the principle of fairness to judge that citizens should not be prevented by legislation or authority from criticizing the government (Helwig 1998). Although older children's judgments on the principle of fairness are more differentiated and more pragmatic about the consequences of such actions (for example, it might be dangerous to voice opposition to governmental policies if the country officially opposes free speech) than are those of six-year-olds, Helwig's findings demonstrate that a sensitivity to citizens' rights emerges early in life. Moreover, the sensitivity to rights appears even in countries that are traditionally viewed as less rights-oriented than Western democracies, such as China (Helwig et al. 2003).

Less is known about children's sense of themselves as civic actors. However, children do volunteer, which is a precursor to adult forms of civic participation (Hart et al. 2007), and by adolescence, volunteering can be consolidated into adolescents' identities (Hart and Yates 1997).

It is clear from these studies that the capacities necessary for citizenship are present in children, in at least rudimentary forms. Children identify with their countries and perceive themselves to be members of their societies; children are concerned with the rights and obligations of citizens; and in some respects, children participate in and contribute to civic welfare.

Yet rudimentary capacities for citizenship may not warrant full participation in political life. It is probable that children lack some of the qualities necessary to participate effectively as voters. While these necessary qualities flower in adolescence, the precise timing during adolescence is uncertain. In the next section, we present findings suggesting that sometime in midadolescence, adolescents likely have the necessary capacities to vote.

The Developmental Readiness of Adolescents for Voting

One approach to determining the age threshold for voting is to compare age groups on each side of the threshold to determine whether there are differences relevant to citizenship and voting between the two groups. For example, a proposal to move the age threshold for voting from 18 to 25 could be defended by demonstrating that 27-year-olds have more qualities, or better-developed qualities, necessary for effective voting than do 23-year-olds. We use this approach in this section to compare the qualities associated with citizenship and voting in midadolescence to those in late adolescence and adulthood. In the analyses that follow, we examine the developmental trajectories for *tolerance*, *civic knowledge*, *political skills*, *political efficacy*, *political interest*, and *volunteering*. Each of these qualities, except for volunteering, are, as discussed above, reflections or facets of citizenship. Volunteering is considered here as one form of civic participation. For each of these qualities, we use data from a national survey to trace the developmental course from early adolescence into adulthood. This analysis suggests that there are few indications that 16-year-olds are sufficiently distinct from adults to warrant exclusion from voting.

Methods

Participants. We used two samples in the analyses that follow. The first is the adult sample of the National Household Educational Survey of 1996 (NHES:96), which was intended to allow estimates "representative of all civilian U.S. adults" (Collins et al. 1997, 1). Random digit dialing was used to contact representative households throughout the United States (Collins et al. 1997), with oversampling of neighborhoods with high concentrations of blacks and Hispanics. There were 2,250 participants in this sample.

The second sample is the youth sample of NHES:96; it included 4,217 participants between 14 and 18 years old. Households with one child or adolescent were telephoned, with children serving as the participants (see Nolin et al. 2000).

Survey questions. In both samples, two parallel sets of five questions were used to assess *civic knowledge* (e.g., "Which of the two major political parties is most conservative at the national level?"). The number of correct responses for each set was used as the summary measure of civic knowledge. The two sets of questions differed slightly in average difficulty; we added the difference in means to the sum of correct answers to the more difficult set to equalize the scores across question sets.

Participants in both samples were asked whether in their communities a person ought to be permitted to make a speech opposing religion and whether books with unpopular messages should be banned from public libraries. Those who advocated tolerance in both instances were judged to be *tolerant*.

Political skill was determined using the sum of affirmative answers to two items concerning political participation ("Could you write a letter to a public official?" and "Could you make a statement at a public meeting?"), with high scores indicating greater political skill than those with low scores.

Political efficacy was assessed by asking whether participants agreed with two statements tapping political understanding ("I can't understand politics and the government") and efficacy ("My family has no say in what the government does"). Responses indicating disagreement with these two responses were totaled and used as an index of political efficacy.

Political interest was measured with two items that assessed the frequency (from infrequent to daily) with which participants followed national news in print

("How often do you read about national news?") and on television or the radio ("How often do you watch or listen to national news on the TV or radio?"). We used the average as the index of political interest.

Unfortunately, *community service* was not assessed in exactly parallel fashions in the youth and adult samples. In the youth sample, participants were asked if they had done voluntary community service or volunteer work at school or in the community in the previous year. Those who responded affirmatively to this question, and who also reported that the community service was neither required by school nor contributed to a grade, were judged to be involved in voluntary community service. Adults were asked whether in the past year they had performed any community service.

Analyses

Mean scores for participants at each year of age were calculated for each of the variables described above (we used the survey weights provided with the NHES:96 data to ensure that the mean scores were characteristic of the population in the United States). These scores were then plotted against age in separate graphs, with separate lines for the youth and adult samples. The goal was to determine for each construct at what age participants in the youth sample first resembled adults.

Consider Figure 1, which depicts the association between civic knowledge and age. The small circles in the graph correspond to average scores for civic knowledge for adults at each age, and the triangles provide the same information for participants in the youth sample. The lines in the graph represent interpolated points (spline) joined to yield an estimate of the actual developmental trajectory. The line estimate is helpful because it makes clear that the average scores for civic knowledge vary from one year to the next; this is especially true for the adult sample. The wider variation in estimates from year to year for adults is a consequence of the relatively small number of adults in the total sample (~2,200) and the wide age range, with the consequence that on average there were only thirty-eight scores to average for each age in years. That is, there is more error in the estimation of what American adults know about civics at each age (because the sample for each age is small) than in the estimation of what American adolescents know about civics (for which on average there are more than nine hundred participants per each age group).

Despite the error in the estimates, several trends are evident. The first of these is that civic knowledge increases between ages 14 and 16 and then changes relatively little thereafter, although, 18-year-olds might be slightly higher in civic knowledge than are 16-year-olds. Most important for the argument in this article, 16-year-olds apparently know as much about the American political system as do many young adults; indeed, the average score for 16-year-olds is higher than the averages for civic knowledge for 19-, 21-, and 23-year-olds, all of whom are entitled to vote.

Figure 2 depicts the association of tolerance with age. Tolerance increases sharply in adolescence. While less than 30 percent of 14-year-olds express a willingness to endorse the right to unpopular speech and controversial books in their

FIGURE 1
The Relation of Civic Knowledge with Age

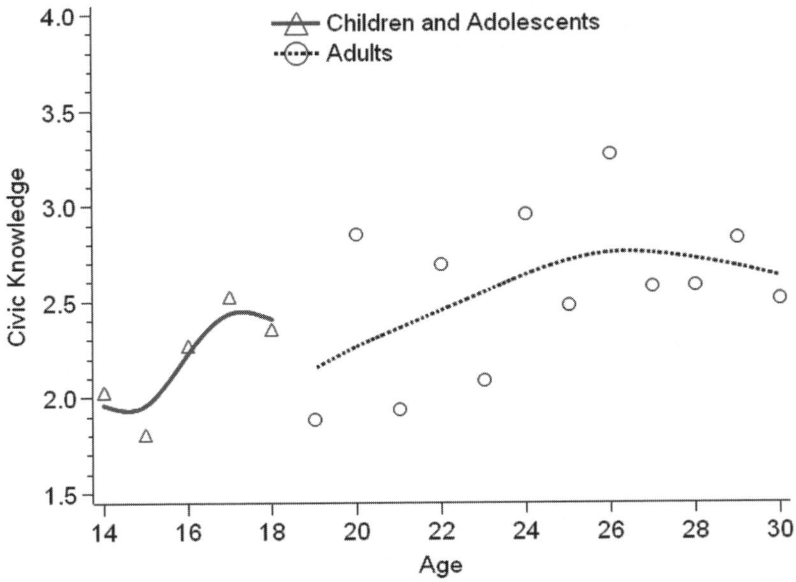

FIGURE 2
The Relation of Tolerance with Age

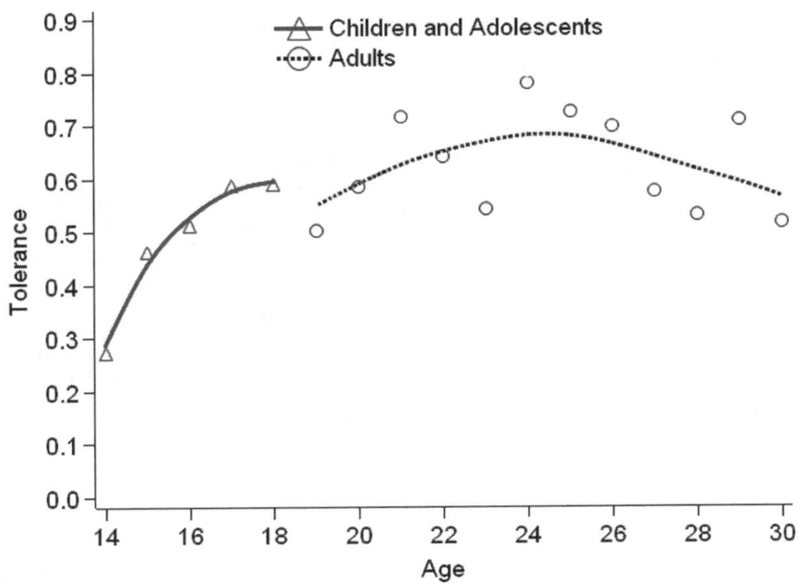

FIGURE 3
The Relation of Political Skill with Age

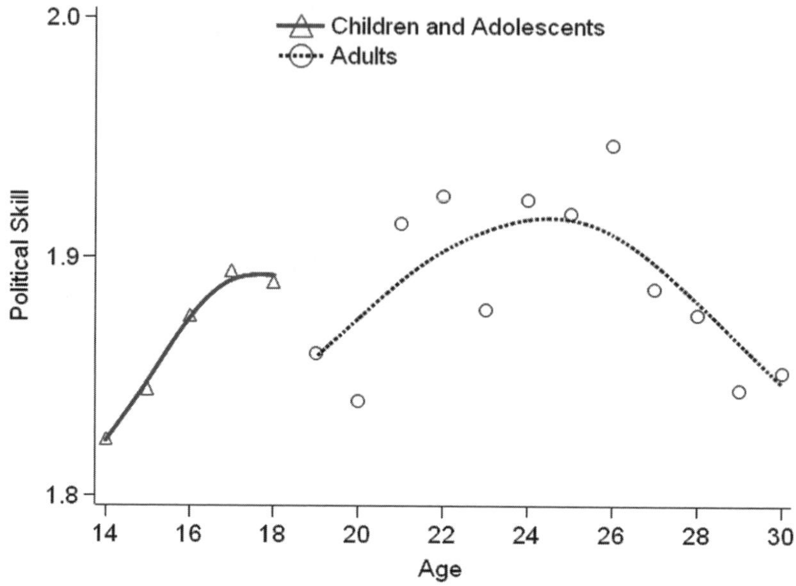

libraries, more than 50 percent of 16-year-olds do so. Tolerance continues to increase, although more slowly, in late adolescence, with 59 percent of 18-year-olds rejecting intolerant stances about unpopular speech and controversial books.

The percentage of tolerant 16-year-olds is higher than that found for 19-year-olds and only slightly lower than that found for several other ages in adulthood (ages 23, 28, and 30). In contrast, tolerance among 14-year-olds is much less likely than in every age range in adulthood.

Political skill—the perceived ability to participate effectively in civic life by writing to political leaders and by speaking publicly at meetings—grows steadily between ages 14 and 16 and then more slowly through age 18, as Figure 3 illustrates. Fourteen-year-olds receive lower scores for political skill than every age between ages 19 and 30; in contrast, the average for 16-year-olds is the same as, or higher than, that of six ages between ages 19 and 30.

Figure 4 suggests that even 14-year-olds feel as politically efficacious as do many adults. Political efficacy increases slightly between ages 14 and 18, but the average level of political efficacy at 14 is already equivalent to that observed in many adults.

Civic interest increases over the course of adolescence, as illustrated in Figure 5, but is generally lower than that observed among adults. One possible interpretation for this trend is that the trends depicted in Figure 5 reflect changes in media consumption rather than interest in political affairs. Reading newspapers and listening to news programs has fallen among all age groups but particularly sharply among younger cohorts of Americans (Pew Research Center

FIGURE 4
The Relation of Political Efficacy with Age

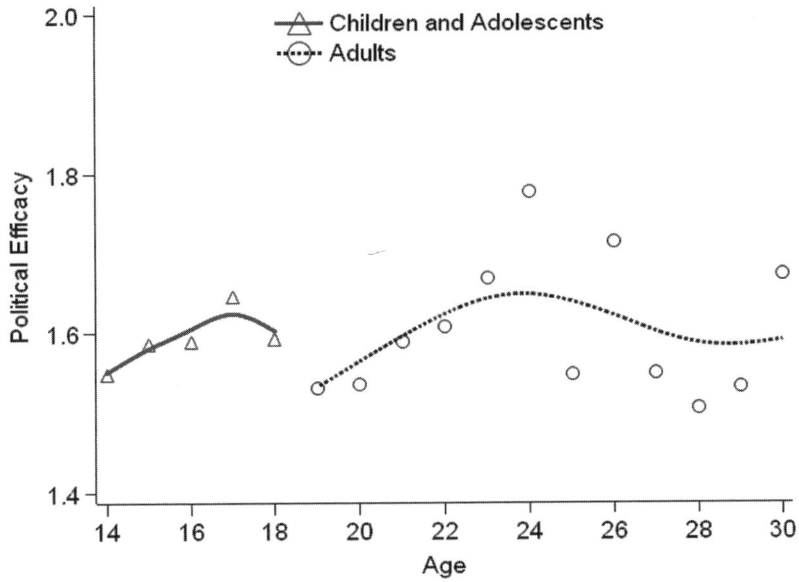

FIGURE 5
The Relation of Civic Interest with Age

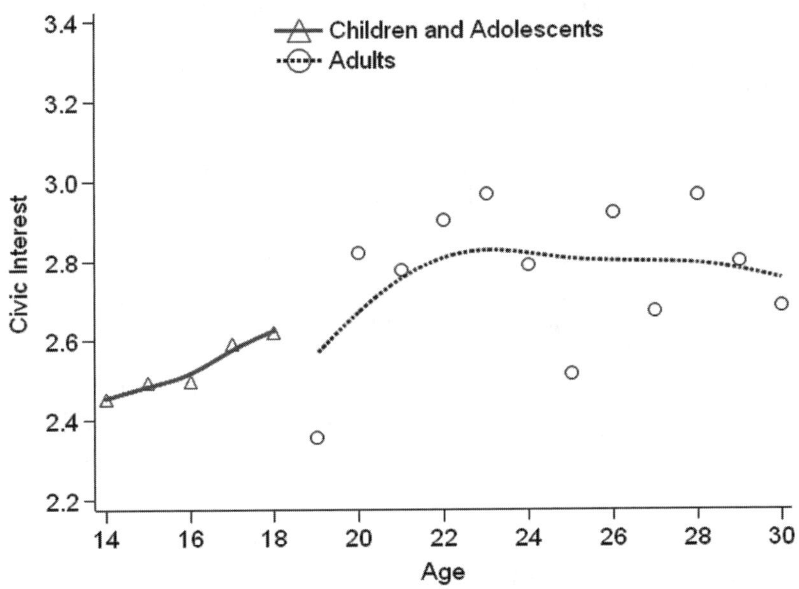

FIGURE 6
The Relation of Community Service Participation with Age

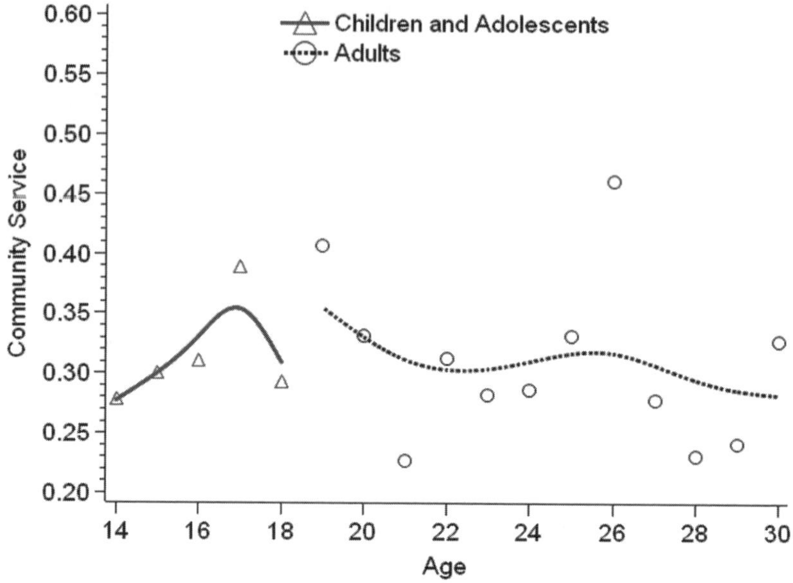

2009). This finding means that the adolescents assessed in the survey are simply less likely to be reading newspapers and listening to news stories on the radio than are adults, and as a consequence of this broad trend, they are less likely than adults to be exposed to political stories in these media, rather than disinterested in political matters specifically.

Figure 6 presents trends for voluntary community service in the youth and adult samples. Because the questions used to assess voluntary service in the two samples differed, it is difficult to make precise comparisons. Nonetheless, it is apparent that adolescents are volunteering at a rate that seems not much different from that observed among adults.

Finally, Figure 7 depicts the ratio of an age group's mean score in adolescence to the mean for adults between the ages of 19 and 30. For example, the average score for 16-year-olds for political efficacy is .99 of the average political efficacy score of adults between the ages of 19 and 30. In contrast, the average for tolerance for 14-year-olds is only .44 of the mean for adults ages 19 to 30. The benefit of Figure 7 is that it indicates that for most of the indices of citizenship discussed in the preceding pages, 16-year-olds are at or near adult levels. There is little development after age 16 on these variables and considerable development before that age.

Interpretations

The evidence from the NHES:96 suggests that 16-year-olds are prepared to vote responsibly. On measures of civic knowledge, political skills, political efficacy,

FIGURE 7
Ratio of Adolescent Age Groups' Mean Scores to Mean Scores for Adults, Ages 19 to 30

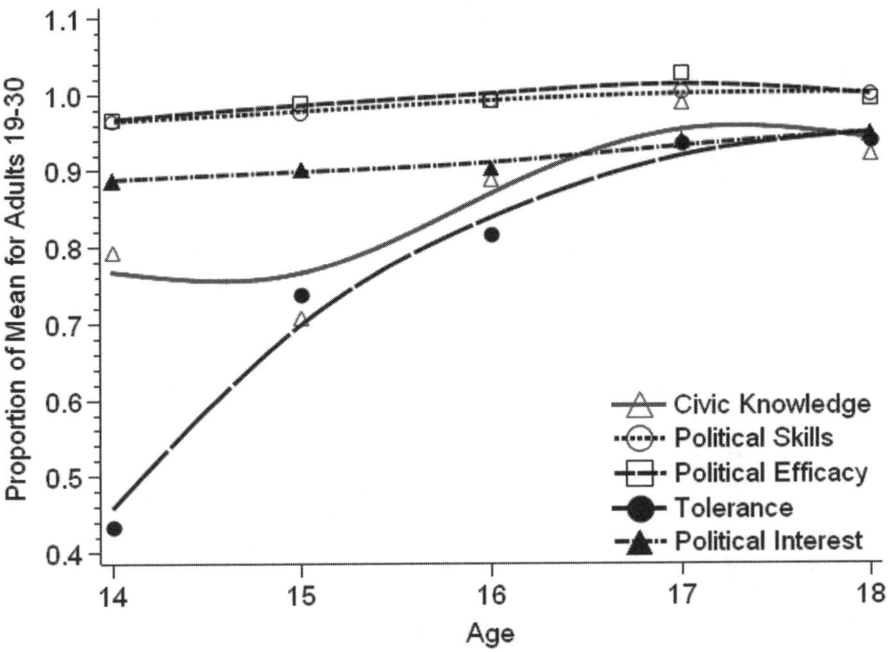

and tolerance, the 16-year-olds, on average, are obtaining scores similar to those of adults. Moreover, while there appears to be substantial evidence for rapid development in some of these constructs through age 16, development after it seems relatively slow. Based on the developmental trajectories traced in Figures 1 through 7, there is little empirical reason to award the vote to 18-year-olds but to deny it to 16-year-olds.

It might be argued that the trends depicted in Figures 1 through 7 are somewhat dated and are not representative of adolescents assessed 15 years later. There is little evidence on national exams testing civic knowledge that there are any differences between historical cohorts of adolescents (Lutkus and Weiss 2007) of the past 15 years. It seems unlikely that historical forces would leave civic knowledge unchanged but transform the other indicators. Moreover, it might be argued that if 16-year-olds in 1996 were basically as civically mature as 18-year-olds and achieved this level of competence without special programs, then 16-year-olds clearly have the capacity to acquire these abilities in the context of typical institutional experiences in schools, families, communities, and so on.

Dejaeghere and Hooghe (2009) have reported similar findings. These authors found that Belgian 16-year-olds had differentiated conceptions of citizenship that reflected, in many respects, the distinctions that adults made. However, Chan and

Clayton (2006) reviewed survey findings concerning civic knowledge among youths and adults in the United Kingdom and found that adolescents knew less than did adults. They used this finding to argue against extending the vote to 16-year-olds. These findings and the conclusion are complicated by the measures and age trends. First, the questions tapping into civic knowledge were presented to adolescents in the context of a survey that was very different from the survey used to measure civic knowledge in adults. Second, the age trends within adolescence for correct responses for four questions assessing civic knowledge suggest that 15- and 16-year-olds knew more than did 19- and 20-year-olds for three of the questions. While 15- and 16-year-olds in the United Kingdom may have less civic knowledge than do adults in their thirties and forties (a conclusion complicated by the measurement of civic knowledge in two different surveys), they apparently have *more* civic knowledge than 19- and 20-year-olds who are allowed to vote.

Why Should 16-Year-Olds Be Allowed to Vote?

Representation of the interests of young people

The changing demographics of American society are central in the argument for extending the vote to 16- and 17-year-olds. Over the past 50 years, the age structure of the United States has changed dramatically (Shrestha 2006). For example, the proportion of the population composed of children (those younger than 18) was nearly 50 percent higher in 1960 (approximately 36 percent of the population was 17 years old or younger then) than it is in 2010 (the estimate is that 24 percent of the American population is under the age of 18) (see Federal Interagency Forum on Child and Family Statistics 2009). As the percentage of children has declined, the percentage of older adults has increased. These demographic changes in the structure of American society set up the possibility for diverging political interests between young and old.

The American National Election Studies (ANES) have data against which the possibility of diverging political interests between young and old can be judged (ANES n.d.). The ANES have data concerning voting and political attitudes dating back to the 1940s. We have used the cumulative data file, augmented with the 2008 postelection data, to examine the association of age to political attitudes concerning federal funding for social security, public schools, and financial aid for colleges. We selected these three topics because of their manifest interest to citizens of different ages. Participants in the ANES were asked whether federal spending in each of these areas ought to be increased (coded 1), decreased (coded –1), or kept about the same (coded 0). We assume in these analyses that 16- and 17-year-olds would resemble 18- to 24-year-olds in their interests. We graphed the average score for 18- to 24-year-olds who voted (because only those who vote have their interests directly represented) for each attitude as well as the average for voters between the ages of 65 and 74—an age bracket that is expanding rapidly.

FIGURE 8
Support for Federal Expenditures for Social Security as a Function of Age Group and Year

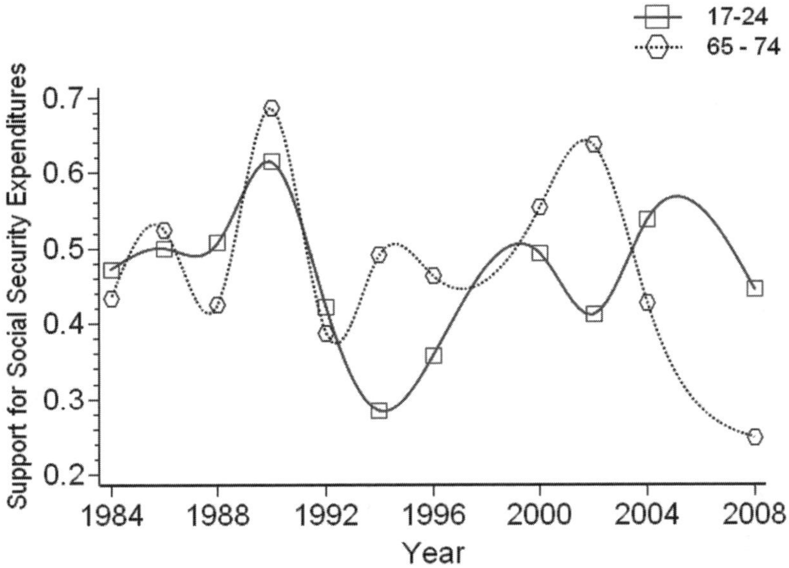

Figure 8 depicts historical trends in support of federal spending in social security by age group. Perhaps contrary to what might be predicted (Bergstrom and Hartman 2005), for much of the past 30 years, the young and old have been similar in their advocacy for federal support for social security. However, in 2008, the age groups diverged; the older voters have apparently become disenchanted with social security, while the younger voters seem to have maintained faith in the system. Surprisingly, then, there is little historical evidence that younger voters differ from older voters in the level of support for social security—a major federal program that benefits, primarily, older Americans.

However, younger and older voters differ substantially in attitudes concerning support for education. Figure 9 illustrates average support for federal funding of public schools for the two age groups of voters over the past 30 years. At each measurement point, younger voters view federal funding of public schools more favorably than do older voters. A similar picture, with more exaggerated differences between young and old, emerges in historical trends for support of federal funding for financial aid for college students (see Figure 10; data for this question were available only for a few measurement points).

These differences likely have real implications for public policy. Poterba (1998) reviewed research suggesting that school districts with large fractions of older voters are less likely to approve increases in school budgets than are districts with small fractions of older voters—a finding consistent with the trends

FIGURE 9
Support for Federal Expenditures for Public Schools as a Function of Age Group and Year

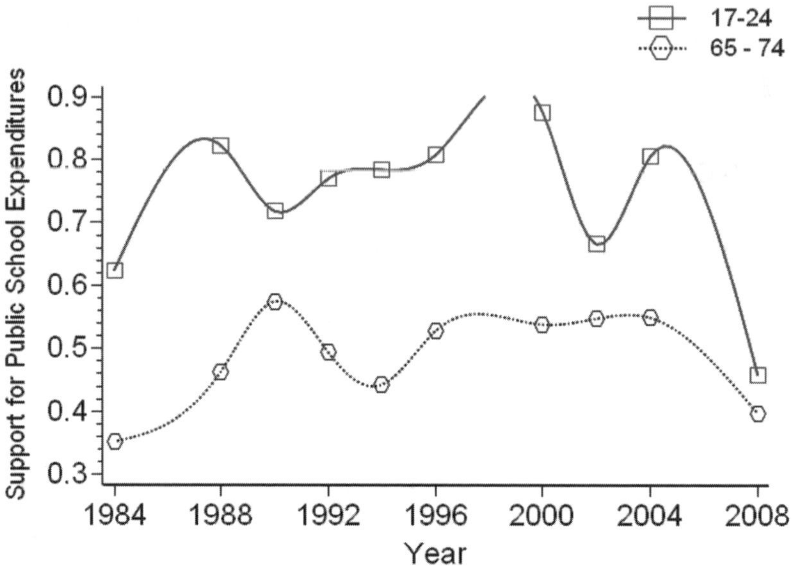

FIGURE 10
Support for Federal Expenditures for Financial Aid for Colleges as a Function of Age Group and Year

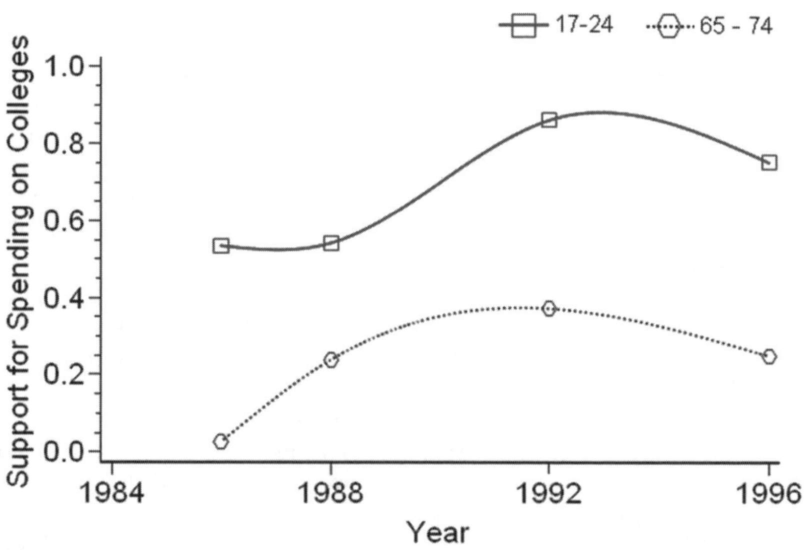

illustrated in Figure 9. Moreover, Poterba described reports indicating that older voters were particularly unlikely to support increases in school budgets when the ethnic makeup of the school-aged population was substantially different than that of the older voters. The demographic trends in the United States suggest that the ethnic composition of children and youths will be increasingly diverse (Johnson and Lichter 2010); if the observations reported by Poterba are correct—that is, that aging white voters are not inclined to support public schools serving ethnically diverse populations—then enfranchising 16- and 17-year-olds may be particularly important as a means of representing the interests of those enrolled in schools.

What these graphs suggest is that if the attitudes of 16- and 17-year-olds are similar to those 18- to 24-year-olds who vote and the former were also enfranchised, then there would be more public support among voters for federal spending on public schools and colleges. Undoubtedly, there are other issues that divide the electorate by age. Given that the relative size of the young age group has declined sharply over the past 40 years, and the relative size of the older age groups is increasing substantially, it may be more important now than ever before to extend the vote to 16- and 17-year-olds in the United States. As Johnson and Lichter (2010, 169) note, over the past 40 years "the social and economic realities of children [have] deteriorated while the circumstances of the elderly [have] improved." This has happened, we suggest, because the fraction of voters who are elderly has increased, and this group has used its right to vote to advance its interests. One way to improve the circumstances of children and adolescents is to allow their members who are capable of voting responsibly—16- and 17-year-olds—the opportunity to use the electoral process to improve the lots of youths.

Participation deepens civic commitment

Because 16- and 17-year-olds have not been allowed to vote in the United States, we know little about the long-term consequences for their own political development if they were permitted to do so. However, there is converging evidence of a variety of sorts to indicate that there likely would be considerable benefits to allowing 16- and 17-year-olds to vote. Most of this evidence points to the importance of participation in deepening commitment to civic life. For example, Hart et al. (2007) used longitudinal data gathered from adolescents who were followed from high school into early adulthood. They found that those who were involved in community service in high school—even those who participated as a result of a school requirement—were more likely than those with no volunteer experience to vote and to volunteer in early adulthood. The implication of this finding is that providing opportunities for adolescents to participate civically deepens the civic propensities in adulthood.

Discussions about voting and elections also seem to promote the development of civic knowledge and civic commitment. Syvertsen et al. (2009) found that adolescents in classrooms randomly selected to deliver an election-oriented curriculum were more advanced in their civic knowledge, civic interest, and self-reported civic disposition than adolescents in classrooms in the control condition. It seems likely that the impact of such a curriculum would be deepened by the opportunity to cast votes. Evidence from similar civics interventions that feature the opportunity to cast mock votes also indicates that emphasis on voting, and the opportunity to cast mock votes, increases civic knowledge and the propensity for political participation (Meirick and Wackman 2004). Together, then, these studies suggest that participation—volunteering, mock voting—and discussion of voting and elections create a foundation for civic participation. If voting is in part a habit (Plutzer 2004) acquired in late adolescence and early adulthood, then this habit will likely be strengthened by allowing 16- and 17-year-olds to vote. The value of the opportunity to vote would be increased by building civics curricula and experience around it.

Sixteen- and 17-year-olds vote in other countries

In recent years, other countries have enfranchised 16- and 17-year-olds, and many others are considering doing so. Austria permitted 16- and 17-year-olds to vote (Associated Press 2008), and preliminary analyses of the consequences of this decision are positive. Austrian researchers polled a representative sample of Austrian teenagers between the ages of 16 and 18, following the first national election for which 16- and 17-year-olds were eligible to vote, and found that the newly enfranchised voters reported voting at approximately the rate of the general population (Institute for Social Research and Analysis 2008). Moreover, the researchers found little evidence to indicate that 16- and 17-year-olds made voting decisions that reflected immaturity. England (Electoral Commission 2003) and Australia (Berkovic 2009) are considering enfranchising 16- and 17-year-olds; the Isle of Man has recently done so (Tonge 2009). There are no reports, thus far, indicating that mistakes were made by awarding the vote to 16- and 17-year-olds in countries that have done so.

Little cognitive development after age 16

Analyses presented earlier indicated that 16-year-olds had acquired, or nearly acquired, the competencies and qualities of citizenship. Although these findings in respect to citizenship are new, findings from other studies generally indicate that 16-year-olds are as cognitively sophisticated as young adults. For example, Steinberg et al. (2009) tested nearly one thousand adolescents and young adults, using simple measures of cognitive ability as reflected in vocabulary and memory as part of a project to estimate the capacities of adolescents in respect to decisions important for legal considerations. They reported that "scores increased between ages 11 and 16 and then leveled off, with no improvement after this age. This gives us greater confidence that the absence of age differences in cognitive capacity after age 16" (Steinberg et al. 2009, 592). Steinberg and his colleagues use this finding to argue for the propriety of 16-year-olds to make important health care decisions on their own.

Arguments against Extending the Vote to 16- and 17-Year-Olds

A variety of reasons have been offered in opposition to the proposal for allowing 16- and 17-year-olds to vote.

Public opinion

Chan and Clayton (2006) have suggested that one important issue is whether the general public supports an extension of voting privileges to this new group. There are no survey data on this issue in the United States (to the best of our knowledge), so it is difficult to judge with any precision the degree to which such a proposal would be supported by the American electorate. Extending the vote to 16- and 17-year-olds does not seem to attract much discussion in the media, so it seems safe to conclude that it is not an idea that is of widespread appeal. Certainly there would need to be some public support for enfranchising 16- and 17-year-olds for the idea to be discussed seriously and to mobilize political action.

Yet the extent of prevailing public support for the idea cannot stand by itself as the criterion for deciding whether to enfranchise younger voters. Once a public discussion concerning the idea is under way, public support might very well shift. Moreover, public opinion on a matter such as extending the vote to 16- and 17-year-olds also reflects self-interests. To the extent that American adults prefer not to enfranchise younger Americans, because such a step might increase public funding toward public schools and college (for example) and consequently raise taxes, public support for allowing 16- and 17-year-olds to vote seems an inappropriate criterion. Denying women the right to vote—people who met the criteria for citizenship and who were capable of voting responsibly—was wrong even when the enfranchised males opposed it.

Deficits in neurological maturity

In recent years, much research has examined neurological maturation, occurring over the course of adolescence, in the frontal lobes of the brain. The thrust of this research is that young adolescents' brains differ from those of young adults in ways significant for decision-making (Reyna and Farley 2006; Ernst and Paulus 2005). For example, young adolescents' brains seem particularly sensitive to reward and novelty and lack full maturation in areas responsible for the modulation of emotion and impulse control (Reyna and Farley 2006). The consequences for decision-making are likely to be that under conditions of emotional arousal. Young adolescents are more likely than young adults to act impulsively, seeking to gain immediate reward, and without weighing long-term consequences of such behavior.[1]

No doubt, 16- and 17-year-olds are not fully mature. They are more susceptible than are adults to peer pressure and risk-taking behavior (Steinberg and Scott

2003) and know little about work, stable romantic relationships, or the responsibilities in raising families. While it is likely true that adolescents' capacities to restrain impulsive, emotional behavior may be reduced relative to that of adults, and their life experiences are relatively circumscribed, these capacities do not figure prominently in citizenship and particularly in voting. Neither the sense of membership, the concern with rights, nor the ability to participate in the community rests heavily upon the ability to resist emotional, impulsive actions. Citizenship and voting in the electoral process require, for the most part, decisions made over long periods of time, which allows for deliberation and discussion with others. To date, there is no neurological evidence that indicates that 16- and 17-year-olds lack the requisite neurological maturation necessary for citizenship or for responsible voting; nor is there evidence to indicate that a breadth of life experience is necessary for effective citizenship.

Conclusion

Sixteen- and 17-year-olds in the United States ought to be permitted to vote in local and national elections. This claim rests upon the exploration of the notion of citizenship, in some of its legal meanings in the United States, as well as its connotations in political philosophy. Citizens should be entitled to vote, unless there is good reason to imagine that they cannot fulfill their responsibilities as citizens or as voters. The research reviewed in this article, as well as the new analyses that were presented, demonstrates that 16- and 17-year-olds are generally indistinguishable in their capacities to function as citizens and to vote responsibly from the youngest adults (18-year-olds) who are entitled to vote. The implication is that to deny 16- and 17-year-olds the right to vote is arbitrary.

Extending the right to vote to 16- and 17-year-olds is particularly important at this point in American history. The proportion of the American population composed of children has declined dramatically in the past 40 years, while the fraction of older voters, who are less inclined to support policies beneficial to the interests of children and youth, is increasing rapidly. By enfranchising 16- and 17-year-olds, the political power of children and adolescents would be increased and perhaps necessarily so to balance the growing population of older voters.

The evidence presented here suggests that the voting threshold ought to be set at age 16. There is rapid development in many qualities related to citizenship and voting in early adolescence up to age 16 and then slow development thereafter. Adolescents in this age range are developmentally ready to vote. This pattern is in accord with research on adolescents' reasoning and cognitive abilities, which suggests that development in these areas plateaus at age 16. Finally, providing 16- and 17-year-olds with the right to vote will likely deepen their civic knowledge and strengthen their civic habits. By removing an arbitrary barrier to their full participation in society, enfranchising 16- and 17-year-olds adds to the moral legitimacy of our democracy.

Note

1. This body of research has led theorists to conclude that adolescents may lack the legal culpability of adults for some forms of criminal behavior (see Steinberg and Scott 2003).

References

American National Elections Studies. n.d. Time Series Cumulative Data File. In American National Election Studies Data Center [database online]. Available from www.electionstudies.org (accessed 13 April 2010).

Appelbaum, Paul S. 2000. Law & psychiatry: "I vote. I count": Mental disability and the right to vote. *Psychiatric Services* 51 (7): 849–63.

Associated Press. 25 September 2008. Austria first to lower voting age to 16. *USA Today*. Available from www.usatoday.com/news/world/2008-09-25-austria-voting-age_N.htm (accessed 12 July 2010).

Barrett, Martyn, Hannah Wilson, and Evanthia Lyons. 2003. The development of national in-group bias: English children's attributions of characteristics to English, American and German people. *British Journal of Developmental Psychology* 21 (2): 193–220.

Bellamy, Richard. 2008. *Citizenship: A very short introduction*. New York, NY: Oxford University Press.

Bergstrom, Theodore C., and John L. Hartman. 2005. Demographics and the political sustainability of pay-as-you-go Social Security. CESifo Working Paper no. 1378, Munich, Germany.

Berkovic, Nicola. 2009. 28 February 2010. Push to give 16-year-olds the vote in federal elections. *The Australian*. Available from www.theaustralian.com.au (accessed 12 July 2010).

Chan, Tak Wing, and Matthew Clayton. 2006. Should the voting age be lowered to sixteen? Normative and empirical considerations. *Political Studies* 54 (3): 533–58.

Collins, Mary A., Michael J. Brick, Mary Jo Nolin, Nancy Vaden-Kiernan, Susan Gilmore, Kathryn Chandler, and Chris Chapman. 1997. *National Household Education Survey of 1996: Data file user's manual*, vol. I, 97–425. Washington, DC: Government Printing Office.

Craig, Stephen C., Richard G. Niemi, and Glenn E. Silver. 1990. Political efficacy and trust: A report on the NES pilot study items. *Political Behavior* 12 (3): 289–314.

Dejaeghere, Yves, and Marc Hooghe. 2009. Brief report: Citizenship concepts among adolescents. Evidence from a survey among Belgian 16-year olds. *Journal of Adolescence* 32 (3): 723–32.

Electoral Commission. 2003. *How old is old enough? The minimum age of voting and candidacy in UK elections*. London: Electoral Commission. Available from www.electoralcommission.org.uk/files/dms/AEM_10002-8073_E_N_S_W_.pdf.

Ernst, Monique, and Martin P. Paulus. 2005. Neurobiology of decision making: A selective review from a neurocognitive and clinical perspective. *Biological Psychiatry* 58 (8): 597–604.

Federal Interagency Forum on Child and Family Statistics. 2009. America's children: Key national indicators of well-being, 2009. Available from www.childstats.gov/pubs/pubs.asp?PlacementID=2&SlpgID=20 (accessed 23 July 2010).

Finkel, Steven E. 1985. Reciprocal effects of participation and political efficacy: A panel analysis. *American Journal of Political Science* 29 (4): 891–913.

Galston, William A. 2001. Political knowledge, political engagement, and civic education. *Annual Review of Political Science* 4:217–34.

Hart, Daniel, Thomas M. Donnelly, James Youniss, and Robert Atkins. 2007. High school community service as a predictor of adult voting and volunteering. *American Educational Research Journal* 44 (1): 197–219.

Hart, Daniel, Cameron Richardson, and Britt Wilkenfeld. Forthcoming. Citizenship and civic identity. In *Handbook of identity theory and research*, eds. Seth Schwartz, Koen Luyckx, and Vivian Vignoles. New York, NY: Springer.

Hart, Daniel, and Miranda Yates. 1997. Identity and self in adolescence. In *Annals of Child Development, 1996*, ed. Ross Vasta, 207–42. London: Jessica Kingsley.

Helwig, Charles C. 1998. Children's conceptions of fair government and freedom of speech. *Child Development* 69 (2): 518–31.

Helwig, Charles C. 2006. The development of personal autonomy throughout cultures. *Cognitive Development* 21 (4): 458–73.

Helwig, Charles C., Mary Louise Arnold, Dingliang Tan, and Dwight Boyd. 2003. Chinese adolescents' reasoning about democratic and authority-based decision making in peer, family, and school contexts. *Child Development* 74 (3): 783–800.

Huntington, Samuel P. 2004. The Hispanic challenge. *Foreign Policy* 141 (2): 30–45.

Institute for Social Research and Analysis. 2008. Post election study—Voting with 16. Available from www.sora.at/fileadmin/downloads/wahlen/2009_waehlen-mit-16_summary-english.pdf.

Johnson, Kenneth M., and Daniel T. Lichter. 2010. Growing diversity among America's children and youth: Spatial and temporal dimensions. *Population and Development Review* 36 (1): 151–76.

Lutkus, Anthony D., and Andrew R. Weiss. 2007. *The nation's report card: Civics 2006*. Washington, DC: National Center for Education Statistics.

Manza, Jeff, and Christopher Uggen. 2004. Punishment and democracy: Disenfranchisement of nonincarcerated felons in the United States. *Perspectives on Politics* 2 (3): 491–505.

Meirick, Patrick C., and Daniel B. Wackman. 2004. Kids voting and political knowledge: Narrowing gaps, informing votes. *Social Science Quarterly* 85 (5): 1161–77.

Niemi, Richard G., Stephen C. Craig, and Franco Mattei. 1991. Measuring internal political efficacy in the 1988 National Election Study. *American Political Science Review* 85 (4): 1407–13.

Nolin, Mary Jo, Jill Montaquila, Jean Lennon, Brian Kleiner, Kwang Kim, Christopher Chapman, Kathryn Chandler, Sean Creighton, and Stacey Bielick. 2000. *National Household Education Survey of 1999: Data file user's manual*, vol. I. Washington, DC: National Center for Education Statistics.

Pew Research Center. 2009. Newspapers face a challenging calculus. Available from http://pewresearch.org/pubs/1133/decline-print-newspapers-increased-online-news (accessed 23 July 2010).

Poterba, James M. 1998. Demographic change, intergenerational linkages, and public education. *American Economic Review* 88 (2): 315–20.

Plutzer, Eric. 2004. Becoming a habitual voter: Inertia, resources, and growth in young adulthood. *American Political Science Review* 96 (1): 41–56.

Reyna, Valerie F., and Frank Farley. 2006. Risk and rationality in adolescent decision making: Implications for theory, practice, and public policy. *Psychological Science in the Public Interest* 7 (1): 1–44.

Shrestha, Laura B. 2006. *The changing demographic profile of the United States*. Congressional Research Service Report. Washington, DC: Congressional Research Service.

Steinberg, Laurence, Elizabeth Cauffman, Jennifer Woolard, Sandra Graham, and Marie Banich. 2009. Are adolescents less mature than adults? Minors' access to abortion, the juvenile death penalty, and the alleged APA "flip-flop." *American Psychologist* 64 (7): 583–94.

Steinberg, Laurence, and Elizabeth S. Scott. 2003. Less guilty by reason of adolescence: Developmental immaturity, diminished responsibility, and the juvenile death penalty. *American Psychologist* 58 (12): 1009–18.

Sullivan, John L., and John E. Transue. 1999. The psychological underpinnings of democracy: A selective review of research on political tolerance, interpersonal trust, and social capital. *Annual Review of Psychology* 50 (1): 625–50.

Syvertsen, Amy K., Michael D. Stout, Constance A. Flanagan, Dana L. Mitra, Mary Beth Oliver, and S. Shyam Sundar. 2009. Using elections as teachable moments: A randomized evaluation of the student voices civic education program. *American Journal of Education* 116 (1): 33–67.

Tonge, Jon. 2009. Revitalising politics: Engaging young people. *Representation* 45 (3): 237–46.

U.S. Department of Homeland Security. 1952a. Immigration and Nationality Act. Title 3, Sec. 313. Prohibition upon the naturalization of persons opposed to government or law, or who favor totalitarian forms of government. Available from www.uscis.gov/ilink/docView/SLB/HTML/SLB/0-0-0-1/0-0-0-29/0-0-0-9771.html (accessed 30 March 2010).

U.S. Department of Homeland Security. 1952b. Immigration and Nationality Act. Title 3, Sec 316. Requirements as to residence, good moral character, attachment to the principles of the Constitution, and favorable disposition to the United States. Available from www.uscis.gov/ilink/docView/SLB/HTML/SLB/0-0-0-1/0-0-0-29/0-0-0-9822.html (accessed 12 July 2010).

Adolescents as Deliberative Citizens: Building Health Competence in Local Communities

By
MARY CARLSON
and
FELTON EARLS

Given the host of tragic events that children experience, it is often compelling for well-intended adults to respond in a protective and charitable fashion. The child rights approach asks for more. Building on their collective experiences in the developmental and social sciences, the authors present in roughly chronological fashion a synopsis of the theoretical explorations and scientific evaluation that completes a framework to advance the status of children as citizens. The recognition of the agency and capability of a child and the dynamic and enduring source of socialization from and social integration within the community are fundamental to this project. The participatory rights enshrined in the Convention on the Rights of the Child serve as an impetus and inspiration to this project, the Young Citizens Program. What began with small-scale deliberative groups in Chicago matured into a cluster randomized controlled trial in northern Tanzania.

Keywords: deliberative citizenship; communicative action; child rights; collective efficacy; health promotion

While Africa is rife with examples of the tragic condition of children, there are many reasons for optimism. The current HIV/AIDS epidemic, disproportionately affecting

Mary Carlson is an associate professor of psychiatry at Harvard Medical School and Children's Hospital, Boston. Her major career transition in 1991 from developmental neurobiology to social policy was facilitated by study at Harvard Kennedy School and with Amartya Sen, centered on his capability approach. Her new research focuses on early child deprivation (and enrichment) and the development of methods to enable deliberative citizenship in adolescents to promote the health and well-being of their communities.

Felton Earls is a professor of human behavior and development at Harvard School of Public Health and professor of social medicine at Harvard Medical School. From 1990 to 2005, he was the principal investigator of the Project on Human Development in Chicago Neighborhoods. His current project, Ecology of HIV/AIDS and Child Mental Health in Tanzania, is a cluster randomized control trial that aims to strengthen adolescents' capacities to promote community health through the Young Citizens Program.

DOI: 10.1177/0002716210383648

sub-Saharan Africa, has led to the popular characterization of children in this region as "orphans and vulnerable." Labeling children by their circumstances rather than their capacities is unfortunate and stigmatizing (Earls, Raviola, and Carlson 2008). It is an orientation that invites charity rather than respect. Every energetic, knowledgeable, and joyful child represents the hope of a more positive future—an Africa that is socially and politically vibrant, economically developed, and equitable. Children cannot thrive if their communities are not capable of providing consistent, responsive, and competent care, along with good governance and human services. Nor can communities prosper if their youngest members are not recognized as respected and active participants. Such a hopeful attitude for Africa and its children applies to all children and in all settings, as envisioned by the United Nations (UN) Convention on the Rights of the Child (CRC). This remarkable document inspires our view that children be recognized as "young citizens" (YCs).

The first half of this article characterizes the theoretical formulation and research that establishes our perspective on children as citizens. From a theoretical foundation that Amartya Sen, Jürgen Habermas, and others inform, we developed the Young Citizens Program (YC Program). The second half of the article presents the evolution of the YC Program from a small-scale series of deliberative groups in Chicago and Cambridge to its rigorous evaluation in a community-based randomized control trial in Tanzania. The objectives of the Tanzanian study are to measure the consequences of children's participation in promoting community competence. The adequacy of our evolving theory is judged by how well it addresses children of different ages and across a range of advantaged to disadvantaged environments. The legitimacy of this approach requires the perspectives of children and must be judged by the ethical and practical implications such formulations have for children's current well-being and extended life course.

Children and Deliberative Citizenship: A Theoretical and Pragmatic Framework

The status of children as citizens who genuinely participate in the community requires the recognition and guidance of adult citizens. In a thought-provoking essay, *Children: Noble Causes or Worthy Citizens* (1997), Swedish social scientist Karl-Eric Knutsson argues that we must move beyond the charitable approaches of "noble causes" to the post-CRC vision of "worthy citizens." In his concluding chapter, "Recognizing the Child Citizen," he states,

> To lay a basis for finally recognizing the child as citizen we must consider the larger contexts of globalization and intergenerational perspectives as well as more immediate political environments on the national and local levels. We must also consider the need for new partnerships for children and with children based on the conviction that the best interest of the child is in most cases also the best interest of the larger society. (Knutsson 1997, 123)

His reflective and critical thesis builds on a practical understanding gained through several significant positions held with UNICEF. His experiences provide the ideal blending of scholarship and practice and a source of confirmation that academics can contribute to the behavioral and social foundations necessary to give direction and validity to the many CRC articles. He brings the clarity, skepticism, and depth of a veteran social scientist to this controversial and demanding tension between participation and protection rights.

Considering the multiple contexts that frame both the protection and participation domains requires looking beyond conventional medical, public health, and neurobehavioral disciplines for new theoretical constructs to guide measurement and analysis. The synthesis, application, and evaluation required of biological, behavioral, and social factors and their interactions with political and material resources for children at different ages across their life course is daunting. Our project to determine the interests and competencies of children, along with the required support and guidance of adults, is framed in a public health schema. The intent is to evaluate this program with a rigorous experimental design. The revolutionary new status of children as "rights holders" endows them with respect, equality, legal guarantees of protection by state and nonstate actors, as well as their recognition as social agents. The bold and expansive CRC document transforms the basis of policy analysis and formulation from simply the "developmental sciences" to include political philosophy and social science to address issues such as identity and membership, equity, authority, legitimacy, obligations, and social justice.

In the search for social theories that bolster the conceptual framework for our project, five major features are required to meet the high standards of the CRC. First, the presumption of *universality* is a distinguishing feature of the CRC. Second, the theory must incorporate *agency* as a fundamental characteristic of the child as a rights holder. Third, the theory must be *equity*-sensitive to compare individuals and groups with regard to resources and opportunity disparities. Fourth, it is important to address *governance* as an integral aspect of its scope since it is governments that ratify the CRC, enact legislation, and enforce the rule of law. Finally, it must be emphasized that the CRC is concerned with adverse issues such as abuse, exploitation, deprivation, and conflict yet routinely addresses children in a positive *framework* of rights promotion, disease prevention, conflict resolution, and social progress.

Public and social choice theories have a long political history through the analysis of voting and other forms of social preference. Kenneth Arrow's (1963) penetrating analysis of the "impossibility of rationally deriving social choice from individual preferences" has led to major rethinking of social preferences in the political realm (Sen 1999). Amartya Sen, an economist and social philosopher, responds to the challenges that the impossibility theorem poses by exploring new informational spaces where coherent interpersonal assessment of valued outcomes is possible. Sen's pioneering work on the capability approach provides an alternative model for situating social agents and evaluating distributional properties of their well-being. Rather than a model in which well-being equity is based on mental states (such as preferences or utilities) or on resources (such as commodities or primary goods), he proposes one that measures human "functionings"—defined as the various things a person may value doing or being (Sen 1985, 1993). A second parameter is "capability sets," defined as a space in which a person is free to choose among alternative bundles of functionings. In more common parlance, sets are valued lifestyles from which individuals can choose, based on their personal characteristics and the availability of opportunities and resources (Sen 1992). A third important distinction is between functionings (valued by a person) and capability sets (bundles of available alternative functionings) and "achieved functionings"—characterized by what a person actually chooses, does, or becomes. Achieved functionings can be observed, measured, and assessed as constituent features of a person. Finally, "capability" can be understood as a substantive freedom to achieve alternative sets of functionings and does not require a choice to actually be exercised (Sen 1992, 1993). Capability and its components operate in a distinct, multidimensional informational space, less restricted than the social choice/voting space that Arrow's theorem addressed. Capability, as freedom, is seen as having both an intrinsic, as well as instrumental, value (Sen 1992, 1999).

Sen's remarkable theory, with its origins in welfare economics and social philosophy, meets all the criteria by which we frame our research on child citizenship. Sen aims for his capability theory to have a universal application, as he intentionally underspecifies functionings, except to say that they range from simple to complex and vital to trivial. Human agency is foundational to capability, and equity issues are crucial to interpersonal comparisons. Capabilities are envisioned as positive and optimistic states of being, without ignoring the causes and consequences of capability deprivations. In discussing possible functionings, Sen often refers to the political freedom to participate in public life. The applications of Sen's theories to children are summarized in his *Development as Freedom* (1999). In his most recent and ambitious work, *The Idea of Justice* (2009), he begins with a quote from Dickens's *Great Expectations*: "In the little world in which children have their existence, there is nothing so finely perceived and finely felt, as injustice" (Dickens 2003, 63, quoted in Sen 2009, vii). Through this quote, Sen acknowledges that capability and well-being begin in childhood and that justice is a remedial concept.

Our first application of the capability theory was in an alternative approach to inform programs on early crime prevention (Earls and Carlson 1995). Building on our research on early brain and behavioral development, we proposed that capability added an important new perspective of children as agents. It allowed one to measure their socioeconomic contexts as either constraining or expanding their capability sets at different ages. "Choice" is not a sufficient parameter by which to measure a child's engagement with his or her available capability sets, because many of children's key functionings are social, such as intimacy, language, and play. A parameter that captures the shared exchange between a child and caregiver is needed to explain the reciprocal interaction necessary to achieve functionings, and such a parameter is critical in early development.

Our growing interest in deliberative democracy as a context for children's competencies as citizens led us to look for complementary models that could adequately incorporate reciprocity. Unlike electoral citizenship, deliberative citizens can be recognized at any age at which they are ready to engage in rational discourse. Whereas electoral citizenship simply aggregates preferences, deliberative democracy provides for a public exchange of information, perspectives, and reasons. It is a process designed to achieve consensus among all individuals affected by an explicit, publicly generated decision. In exploring the types of functionings required for children's participation in deliberative activities, we are influenced by the extensive writings of Jürgen Habermas.

Habermas's *The Structural Transformation of the Public Sphere* (1991) presents a two-level concept of society. The public sphere is where people assemble and are free to engage in discourse about common societal problems. Along with the private sphere, it represents networks of communication and sources of socialization and social integration and together they are what he refers to as the "lifeworld." He distinguishes the lifeworld from the media-steered system composed of the corporate/economic and state/administrative subsystems that operate through purposive-rational action in pursuit of money and power. His view that the media has transformed citizens into spectators, rather than individuals actively engaged in public discourse, is a major concern. He concludes this treatise by suggesting that one study the extent and manner by which the pubic sphere can be rehabilitated.

In his major, two-volume work, *The Theory of Communicative Action* (1984, 1987), Habermas fully develops his optimistic claim that this function can be restored and posits language (defined as speech acts) as both "a medium for reaching understanding and . . . as a medium for coordinating action and socializing individuals" (1987, 23). His scholarship expands notions of citizenship by placing emphasis on democratic procedures that value reason and an open exchange of ideas as a basis for legitimate governance. He asserts that consensus achieved in the lifeworld through communicative practices must be based on reasons and intersubjective recognition of validity claims. In taking a discursive and rational approach to justification, he distinguishes three dimensions of validity claims and associated modes of communication: (1) truth, as the objective world of existing affairs; (2) rightness, as the normative context that provides legitimacy; and (3) truthfulness, as subjective intent of expression and privileged access to lived experience. Yet he cautions that "communicative action relies on the cooperative process of interpretation in which participants relate simultaneously to something in the objective, the social, and the subjective worlds, even when they thematically stress only one of the three components in their utterances" (Habermas 1987, 20). He distinguishes between the social and objective domains of the external world and describes how individuals use language to share experiences of their subjective lifeworlds, in the process of seeking mutual understanding in pursuit of action goals in the external world. In his critique of modernization, he cautions that the "progressively rationalized lifeworld" becomes "both uncoupled from and made dependent upon increasingly complex, organized domains of action" (Habermas 1987, 305).

Following on these same themes in *Moral Consciousness and Communicative Action* (Habermas 1990), he proposes "discourse ethics" as a further elaboration to establish the normative validity of rational argumentation as a basis for moral insights. In doing so, he posits that equal attention and weight should be given to the individual and the community. He states that

> they must emphasize the inviolability of the individual by postulating equal respect for the dignity of each individual. But they must also protect the web of the intersubjective relations of mutual recognition by which these individuals survive as members of the community. To these two complementary aspects correspond the principles of justice and solidarity, respectively. The first postulates equal respect and equal rights for the individual, whereas the second postulates empathy and concern for the well being of one's neighbors. (Habermas 1990, 200)

Discourse ethics, as an elaboration on the earlier deliberative procedures of communicative action, was especially interesting to us as a method to engage families and communities around the perspectives of researchers and participants in our ongoing research with children. For several years, starting in 1996, we employed discourse ethics to engage families, community social service agencies, and adolescents in extended deliberations on our social and biological research with infants, young children, and adolescents. This work was made possible with initial support from the National Science Foundation (Carlson and Earls 2001; Earls and Carlson 2002).[1] Beginning with the practical translation and application of communicative action and discourse ethics, we combined the capability model with communicative competencies in a diagram of the developmental components of deliberative capabilities (Earls and Carlson 2002). In a later section, we present a revised version of that earlier diagram, illustrating the measures of the components of achieved deliberative functionings.

Habermas's scholarship is in keeping with our criteria for selecting theoretical models as he strives for principles of universality and equity in public discourse. In spite of his penetrating critical appraisal of past and current social theory, he appears unwavering in his optimistic view of what is possible. His work is a statement of hope about better governance. We have labored to extract what would appear to be basic elements of communicative competency that we could target in children and adolescents to support and enhance their potential for communicative action. Four practical components that are operationalized from this work are (1) mutual trust as normative accord, sincerity; (2) perspective-taking as the ability to take the attitude of the other in practical discourse; (3) mutual understanding as achieved through symmetrical communication; and (4) shared social action through which a situation and a theme is identified and consensual understanding and action plans are realized. These components are discussed below in the description of the modules used in the YC Program in Tanzania along with the measures of individual elements of deliberative capability.

In addition to the foundational theories of Sen and Habermas, we have drawn on the work of three other scholars to complete our theoretical formulation for child citizenship. Bandura's (1986) work on social cognition is concerned with personal judgments of how well one can execute courses of action required to deal with intended outcomes. His close attention to measuring self-efficacy constructs in specific situations and with specific functions in mind is a tremendous advantage to our empirical orientation. It helps to link notions of capability and deliberation by creating new measures termed deliberative and communicative efficacy. These constitute competencies that are at the core of what it means to be a citizen.

All human development occurs in a context of relationships and resources. Bronfenbrenner's (1979) ecological systems theory captures the organizational complexity of the world in which children grow up. Each of four major systems—the microsystem (composed of family, peers, classroom), mesosystem (interactions of microsystems), exosystem (neighborhoods, workplaces), and macrosystem (the larger urban or rural context)—either directly or indirectly influences the child's development. The theory is captured in the name of our project, Child Health and Social Ecology (CHASE),[2] and in our use of multilevel research designs (Earls and Carlson 2001). A limitation of the theory is that it casts the child in a predominantly passive role. To be complete, an ecological theory needs to account for bidirectional influences. Our integration of self-efficacy and ecological theories permits the characterization of children as active citizens and as capable agents, acting in concert with other age groups to achieve collective well-being.

A method for public engagement is needed in which the skills of citizenship can be effectively and persuasively manifested in community settings. For this purpose, we adopt the work of Augusto Boal, the Brazilian theater practitioner and colleague of the educator and social theorist, Paulo Freire (Boal 1979). The creation of his "Theatre of the Oppressed" is based on the idea of dialogue between audience and performer. Using a method referred to as "simultaneous dramaturgy," methods of actor-audience interaction are developed in which actors stop a drama and ask the audience ("spect-actors" in Boals's parlance) for insights and solutions to their situation. We adopt this technique for children to use dialogue in community settings to break down the barrier that divides children and adults as citizens (Kamo et al. 2008). The integration of concepts and methods of self-efficacy, ecological systems, and community dramaturgy completes the theoretical synthesis needed to formulate and empirically test the concept of the child as citizen.

Measuring Community Context and Its Impact on Children—PHDCN

We became aware of the CRC while planning an interdisciplinary research project on urban violence in the United States. This planning process, involving dozens of scholars in law and the social sciences, began in the late 1980s and progressed over several years. The planning entailed a detailed exploration of approaches to measures of community context and developmental processes that would be used in a multilevel, longitudinal design (Tonry et al. 1991; Earls and Reiss 1994). From a demographic analysis of all large American cities, Chicago was chosen as the study site because it encompassed an impressive range of neighborhoods characterized by variation in socioeconomic statuses and races and ethnicities. Through extensive consultation and numerous workshops, the study objectives were broadened from an initial focus on crime and violent behavior to encompass a comprehensive range of outcomes, including public health conditions and educational achievement. To reflect this expanded mandate, the study was named the Project on Human Development in Chicago Neighborhoods (PHDCN) (Earls and Buka 1997).[3]

It was in this context that we started to think about how to interpret the CRC in terms of the theories, hypotheses, design, measures, and analyses that made up the PHDCN's research program. There were at least three ways in which the CRC informed this work. First, it shifted attention from predators of crime and violence to persons who were either directly or indirectly affected by violence. Second, it confirmed the importance of balancing the design so that the social context of human development was measured with as much theoretical and analytical confidence as were biological and psychological factors. Third, it revealed the importance of working directly with children about the concepts and measures used in the project. These modifications set in motion a systematic and enduring effort to establish the CRC as a framework for all our subsequent research with families and children.

The shift from exclusively thinking about perpetrators (or superpredators according to some) led to the development of improved measures of exposure to violence (Selner-O'Hagan et al. 1998; Brennan, Molnar, and Earls 2007). One of the more important uses of the data collected with this measure was the demonstration, using a propensity stratification analysis, that witnessing as well as being a victim of firearm violence increased the odds of engaging in serious violent behavior by a factor of three (Bingenheimer, Brennan, and Earls 2005). The exposure to violence issue had a significant impact on reframing the study. In its original conceptualization, the design weighed heavily on individual and family factors as the determinants of violent behavior. By expanding the agenda to include exposure to community influences, the door was opened to consider ecological determinants on par with individual factors in explaining health and behavioral outcomes. We considered this an affirmative step toward incorporating a child rights perspective (Carlson and Earls 2001).

Fundamental to this change in direction was the discovery of collective efficacy (Sampson, Raudenbush, and Earls 1997). Using a multilevel design and reliable measures of community attributes, we showed that after statistically controlling for social class, race/ethnic composition, and prior violence rates of neighborhoods, collective efficacy functioned as a protective factor. We were careful to define collective efficacy as a process that places primacy on the personal agency of group members. The specific manifestations of agency relate to one's willingness to assist others and supervise children. While the theory continues to be refined, three components of collective efficacy were delineated: (1) intergenerational closure (e.g., adults serving as role models), (2) reciprocal exchange (e.g., sharing resources), and (3) informal social control (e.g., willingness to intervene if children are skipping school) (Sampson, Morenoff, and Earls 1999). The social control component is of primary importance since it represents the key element of agency. As with Bronfenbrenner's ecological theory, a limitation of this attempt at refining the theory of collective efficacy is that it is conceived as a one-way flow from adults to children—thus the emphasis on supervision and role models. As our research progressed in line with rights-based thinking, the flow of collective action has been transformed to reflect a bidirectional process.

Subsequent to the demonstration that collective efficacy is a major determinant in controlling neighborhood violence (Sampson, Raudenbush, and Earls 1997), analyses have been extended to show it has a protective influence on birth weight (Buka et al. 2003), respiratory diseases (Sterndahl, Earls, and Wright forthcoming), child mental health (Xue et al. 2005), and age of sexual initiation (Browning, Leventhal, and Brooks-Gunn 2005). These findings shift attention away from deficit models of human development to one in which identification of assets and protective factors are fundamental to research and public action. These findings supported the plausibility of inferring a causal role of collective efficacy in health and behavioral outcomes.

Engaging Young Citizens in Deliberative Democracy

The importance of consulting children emerged in parallel with more traditional thinking in the PHDCN. The idea of exploring the relevance of child citizenship to collective efficacy and health promotion began as a pilot study with fewer than a dozen adolescents selected from public housing zones in Chicago. Residing in neighborhoods where street gangs, drug trafficking, easy access to guns, and police brutality dominate, the primary issue that concerned these adolescents was exposure to violence. Over a two-year period, the group focused on interpreting the relevance of child rights, as articulated in the CRC, to their own lives. Their skills in reasoned argumentation matured rapidly. Soon after the formation of the group, they were invited to participate in an international symposium on the rights of children.[4] This provided them with an early opportunity to deliberate in a public space. As they continued their critical discourse on the issues of gangs, drugs, and violence, they reached a consensus that Article 27, which addresses the standard of living, was most important. But rather than interpret the article in terms of material resources, their focus set out to examine the social relationships of adolescents to authority figures as the overwhelming determinant of their standard of living and a basis for the presence or absence of well-being. The three groups of authority figures that influenced their daily lives were parents, teachers, and police. To confirm their ideas, the group decided that they needed to assess the opinions of their peers. They designed a survey instrument to collect data, assessing the degree to which adolescents perceived adults as supportive. The evidence showed that authority figures were viewed as progressively less supportive of adolescents as they matured. This essentially translates into an explanation of how lowering levels of collective efficacy from the child's perspective leads to increasing rates of delinquency and violent behavior (Earls and Carlson 2002).

A second pilot study of the YC Program was conducted in Cambridge, Massachusetts, again with a small but diverse group of adolescents from the local high school. Using the same approach, this group analyzed the relevance of the CRC to their daily lives. They started by defining compromised well-being as a sense of detachment experienced by most adolescents in this progressive and relatively affluent community. This disturbing attitude pervaded both school and community contexts. Through extended discourse, they focused on the phenomenon of self-segregation as a mechanism that encouraged the detachment of subgroups defined by race/ethnicity. To investigate this, they elected to make a video to explore the theme of self-segregation. They made a documentary incorporating interviews that they conducted with fellow students. The video was widely shared locally and proved to be a persuasive source for change (Chan et al. 2003). At the same time, they realized that no matter how persuasive and probing, a video based on interviews with a few selected students was not equivalent to knowledge that could be generalized to the entire student body. To assess the broader school community, they decided to expand their analysis by conducting a survey on attitudes about self-segregation that sampled a large proportion of the student body.

The dynamic manner in which adolescents, with minimal prior experience in deliberation, displayed rational and critical thinking, reached mutual understanding, and arrived at a consensus on an action plan, is compelling proof of the concept for the YC Program. Children recognized the value of sharing egalitarian structures with adults and used these structures to become knowledgeable and persuasive agents of change in their communities and schools. While conducting the deliberative groups in the United States, we traveled extensively to other countries that, unlike the United States, had ratified the CRC. In places such as Brazil, Romania,[5] and Costa Rica,[6] we learned valuable lessons on how it was being used as a framework to redress violations of children's rights and to promote their well-being. We were now ready to devise a formal, standardized curriculum and evaluate the program in a rigorously designed experiment.

Building Deliberative Capabilities and Health Competence in Tanzanian Communities

Beginning in 2000, we challenged the gloomy and distorted characterization of Africa as a dying continent, paralyzed by HIV, and harboring legions of orphaned and vulnerable children. We had first visited Tanzania in the 1970s and again in the 1980s, never suspecting that we would return at the beginning of this millennium to witness this peaceful and politically stable country bearing the burden of a new, complex epidemic. After engaging in site visits with local government authorities, nongovernmental organizations, HIV consortiums, street children projects, and orphanages, we confirmed our guarded optimism and broadened our insights as to how adolescents, local residents, and elected leaders could act together to confront this devastating pandemic. We reasoned that young people could be the catalyst to mobilize their communities to confront the HIV pandemic, if provided with basic scientific knowledge and skills of deliberative citizenship. The challenge was to enable young Tanzanians to avoid the pessimism, charity, and helplessness conveyed by the expression "orphans and vulnerable children." Rather, if given the opportunity, we reasoned that they could become skilled, confident, and proactive citizens, even in the face of a serious epidemic and chronic poverty.

The theoretical framework that embraced the participatory rights of the CRC and synthesized the theories of capability, communicative action, self- and collective-efficacy, and social ecology into a formal curriculum was tested in a cluster randomized control trial (CRCT). The intervention was designed to create new opportunities for reciprocal interaction between young adolescents and their local residential communities in response to the crisis of HIV/AIDS. Fortunately, Tanzania has made considerable progress in its decentralization policies such that the devolution of decision-making and service delivery extends to ward and subward levels to promote a participatory system of governance. Roughly, every four thousand citizens live in a circumscribed jurisdiction where the formal structure of local government and informal organization of civil society are facilitated by democratically elected leaders at the ward and subward levels. The existence of these geopolitical units was ideal for configuring the YC Program as a potential influence on the local government and the health infrastructure. The aim was to test the YC Program as a structural intervention that, if successful, would integrate children and adolescents as participants in the civil and political activities in their local communities.

The Moshi municipality, in the Kilimanjaro region of northern Tanzania, was selected as the site for the YC Program. With funding from the National Institutes of Mental Health (NIMH), a seven-year research phase began in 2003.[7] The execution of a CRCT requires close attention to details and consistent monitoring of community partnerships, the execution of surveys, and the implementation of a complex and innovative intervention. The YC Program was conducted in fifteen *mitaa* (the smallest geopolitical unit in Tanzanian local government; *mtaa* is singular and *mitaa* is plural for subwards in KiSwahili) with fifteen matched *mitaa* serving as waiting controls. The sequence of events of the research program is outlined in Table 1. Broadly, there are four phases: preintervention, intervention, postintervention, and sustainability.

Preintervention. One of our first activities was to establish a relationship with local officials and community leaders. In a series of structured discussions between

TABLE 1
Phases of the Cluster Randomized Control Trial

Preintervention phase
Establish understanding with the community and gain support from municipal officials
Pilot study of concepts and measures
Baseline assessment of neighborhood characteristics, including demographics, collective efficacy, and other social norms related to HIV/AIDS (CS1)
Prerandomization cluster analyses of spatial and demographic features of all neighborhoods in the municipality (n = 60) to create nonadjacent matched *mtaa* pairs
Baseline assessment of physical and mental health (including measures of self-efficacy) of children, ages 10 to 14, randomly selected from each of the fifteen *mtaa* pairs (HA1)
Randomization of fifteen pairs to treatment and waiting control arms
Intervention phase
Implement YC curriculum in fifteen treatment *mitaa* (YC1) (see Table 2)
Surveillance of treatment and control groups by a Data Safety Monitoring Board
Postintervention phase
Repeat community survey (CS2) for evaluation of community-level outcomes
Repeat health assessment (HA2) for evaluation of individual-level outcomes
Implement the curriculum in the fifteen control *mitaa* (YC2)
Achieving sustainability
Endorsement of the YC project by full Moshi Municipality Council
YCs join with local health facilities to plan and execute HIV VCT health fairs
YCs collaborates with the Safer Cities Project
Moshi YC Program becomes demonstration site, with YCs hosting site visits from national and international groups

the CHASE staff and ward officers of the municipality, we explored the facts and perceptions about the resources needed and challenges encountered to improve children's health and well-being. We wanted these authorities to understand the ideas and research design that we were proposing and to see in it the added value of studying children as citizens. Open houses were organized at which parents and community members were invited to meet the research staff and discuss the project. The first data were collected in a baseline community-level survey and in a separate health assessment of adolescent participants.

Intervention. The scripted YC intervention comprised twenty-nine sessions divided into five modules that were implemented in two-hour sessions with children in the fifteen treatment communities (YC1), while an equal number of children in the control *mitaa* (YC2) waited to learn if the intervention proved effective. A brief description of the five modules of the YC Program is shown in Table 2 and includes reference to specific articles of the CRC and the components of capability (CAP) and communicative action (COM) theories adapted to each module. Young adult Tanzanians supervised and facilitated the groups.

TABLE 2
Contents of Modules and Sessions of YC1 Curriculum

Module One—5 sessions: Group Formation

(CRC: # 15 right to association; CAP: egalitarian; COM: good communication; trust; perspective-taking, health themes for deliberation; citizenship, group identity) The activities are designed to introduce CHASE intervention and full CRCT design, which children and their families have been randomly selected (and consented) to join. Other topics focus on the structure of local government, citizenship, good communication, and sharing community hopes and fears.

Module Two—4 sessions: Understanding the Community

(CRC: # 12 right to expression and to be heard; CAP: exploring opportunities and possibilities for being a citizen; COM: exploring pubic sphere, social norms) The activities involve learning observation and interviewing techniques, cooperative learning roles, involving local *mtaa* leader in a session discussing health and social mapping of the community.

Module Three—5 sessions: Health and Your Community

(CRC: # 13 right to expression/information, # 17 right to information to promote well-being; CAP: being a health educator; community opportunities to achieve this role; COM: learning objective domains of biology and medical facts; social norms of HIV; learning critical thinking) Sessions begin by discussing the social aspects, transmission, and testing and treatment of malaria and HIV infection. To place this in an active, participatory learning mode, sequences of events are acted out in skits depicting the "MacroWorld" (social conditions that increase risk of becoming infected, denial and stigma, etc.) and the "MicroWorld" (biological bases of transmission and infection, blood and immune system responses, testing and treatment, etc.). In the final sessions of this module, YCs present these skits in the semipublic schoolyard to their parents and leaders

Module Four—8 sessions: Making Community Assessments and Taking Community Action

(CRC: # 14 right to freedom of thought; CAP: becoming a survey researcher, community showing interest in the actions of YCs; COM: public discourse, rational argumentation; reaching mutual understanding about themes, planning—and taking—shared social action; assessing social norms) YCs deliberate and rank priorities for issues to address. A skit on universal testing is added to their repertoire. The MicroWorld and MacroWorld dramas are performed in different public spaces over a 14-week period with the objective of building HIV community competence. They learn to record GPS coordinates of their skit sites and to photograph community scenes. They design, conduct, and analyze a community survey of residents' beliefs about the YCs' capacities to educate about AIDS, to promote prevention and testing, and to reduce the stigma.

Module Five—7 sessions: Inter-Acting in Our Communities

(CRC: # 12, 13, 14, 15, 17; CAP: achieved status of deliberative citizen and health educator, with support and endorsement of adult citizens; COM: communicated a deliberative competence, led local government in communicative approach, socialized for citizenship and fostered social integration in community through deliberation in the public sphere) Over these last seven weeks, the YCs perform MicroWorld and MacroWorld skits one to two times a week, which attract large and interested audiences from "spect-actors" (Boal 1979). The YCs used the skits as a mechanism to engage and to argue about their community's norms related to HIV/AIDS. They present the challenges of reducing stigma and mobilizing for universal testing. A second survey is conducted using the same questionnaire as in Module 4 to assess changes in the community's beliefs about YC's capacities to educate and mobilize. A newsletter, including photos and a summary of their seven-month experience, is published and distributed across each of the fifteen treatment *mitaa*.

Postintervention. At the end of the YC1 intervention, the CHASE staff organized the recruitment and random selection of a new cross-sectional sample of adult residents for the postintervention community survey in the intervention and control *mitaa*. Non-CHASE interviewers who were unaware of the random allocation were employed as data collectors. The content of the interviews repeated many of the questions addressed in the baseline survey. The interviews consisted of items reflected in the domains of collective efficacy derived from the PHDCN, with special attention directed to the protection and support of children (i.e., intergenerational closure and informal social control) and to adult perceptions of children's knowledge and skills as community health agents. Table 3 illustrates the correspondence between theory-based functionings derived from our interpretation of capability and deliberation and at least one kind of empirically based method to measure the manifestations of these functionings as influenced by the YC Program. The left-hand column lists the functionings in a roughly hierarchical manner. The cognitive and motivational domains must be established for the cognitive, motivational, social, communication, and deliberation functionings to develop. The right-hand column represents items that are intended to access the child's subjective evaluation concerning his or her achievement of these functionings. The middle column indicates three mechanisms—agency, choice, and reciprocity—through which the functionings can be achieved. To assess interpersonal or objective validities, there are other types of measures or indicators used in our research, including the perspectives of the child's caregivers; interviews with community residents; administrative and political authorities; as well as observable outcomes, such as an increase in the number of persons being tested for HIV or a reduction in the incidence of HIV infection.

On completion of the postintervention community survey, the postintervention health assessment was conducted with the adolescents and their caregivers in the treatment and control *mitaa*. Most of the content of these assessments was identical to the first health assessment, providing for repeated measurement of those scales most aligned with the goals of the intervention. Based on the successful implementation of the YC curriculum in the fifteen intervention communities, we were ready to move the intervention to the waiting control group. The primary aim in this second installment was to maintain the quality of implementation while reducing costs. Preliminary results of the study have been published, showing the positive responses of adult residents to witnessing children's agency in the HIV skits (Kamo et al. 2008). The definitive results for the intention-to-treat analysis are under review (Carlson, Brennan, and Earls n.d.). In this multilevel analysis, community- and individual-level outcomes are assessed, and all participants, regardless of their degree of exposure to the intervention, are included.

Sustainability. During the second installment of the intervention, the first group of adolescents and their *mtaa* leaders checked in with each other to register their strong interest in not losing momentum in the community engagements that they had initiated. A collective decision was made to permit spatially adjoining

TABLE 3
Components and Measures of Deliberative Capability

Sen—Valued Functionings Habermas—Discourse CHASE—YC Program		Sen—Achieved Functionings Habermas—Practical Discourse CHASE—Deliberative Self-Efficacy
Social and Behavioral Components		**Survey Measures**
I. Cognitive	AGENCY	
Rational		to use talking and reasoning to solve problems I have with others
Perspective-taking		to understand my friends and classmates
		to be helpful if someone is hurt, upset or feeling ill
Knowledge/information		to increase scientific knowledge about HIV infection
Application		to be willing to be tested for HIV
II. Motivational		
Confidence	CHOICE	to know that if I study hard, I can learn math
Agency		to know my strengths and talents
Emotional regulation		to manage those thoughts and feelings that are important to me
III. Social		
Affiliation		to be a good friend
		to be kind to younger children
Personal respect		to be liked generally by others your age
Egalitarian		to usually share with others
Active in public sphere		to reduce HIV-related stigma
IV. Communication		
Expressive	RECIPROCITY	to express my opinions to other children my age
Receptive		to make adults listen to me
		to talk with others about anything that troubles me
V. Deliberation		
Trust		to keep my friends even when pressured to do things I refuse to do
Discourse		to say NO to my friends who want to do things I don't want to do
		to say NO to people who try to get me to use alcohol
Mutual understanding		to make my ideas understood when others disagree with me
Shared social action		to get others to cooperate with me in doing activities
		to ask assistance from adults about how to solve any problems

groups to merge. The strong motivation underlying this decision was taken as a positive sign for the sustainability of the YC Program. While continuing to pursue their interests in promoting HIV community competence as described in the next section, activated groups of YCs have directed their skills and enthusiasm to other problems, for example, community safety (Morse 2008).

As the scientific phases of the CRCT were completed, an agreement was reached that the YC Program would continue as a demonstration site for as long as there were funds to support a CHASE office and small staff of facilitators. By this juncture, universal testing had become the most important target in building HIV/AIDS competent communities (Granich et al. 2009). The YCs decided to organize weekend HIV testing fairs, using their skills in teaching the microbiology and social realities of HIV infection in collaboration with the local health personnel. This decision was a joint one based on the YCs' own deliberations and the frequent requests that they received from the community residents during their public exchanges. During the weeks leading up to a fair, they mobilized their communities by designing and circulating posters, making house-to-house visits, and performing their skits in multiple locations, all to announce the forthcoming fair. All of these events were exercised in public spaces and stood in marked contrast to the more clandestine manner in which persons sought HIV testing in clinics. The challenge taken on by the YCs was to create an atmosphere in which stigma was overcome and community solidarity achieved. By all accounts, this goal was accomplished.

The first HIV testing fair, based in two adjacent *mitaa*, went beyond expectations with more than one hundred residents volunteering to be tested and dozens left waiting in line at the end of the second day. Over the past three years, the YCs have organized ten health fairs that took place over two to three weekend days. In these new fairs, the numbers attending were even greater than in the first fair, with more voluntary counseling and testing (VCT) counselors needed to provide confidential testing for the large numbers of residents coming forward. Surprisingly, the number of men volunteering for testing was equal to or greater than the number of females. When the YCs decided to give greater attention to Prevention of Mother to Child Transmission (PMTCT), many more children accompanied by parents were brought for testing.[8] The postfair evaluation indicated that nearly all persons tested had come from the same *mtaa* and that the majority of persons tested had done so because of the persuasive actions of the YCs.

The most important consequence of the health fairs is that they provided a learning experience for the whole community to recognize the importance of regular testing. The capacity of children as young as 10 and 11 to gain the respect and responsiveness of their parents, municipal officials, and the community at large is a testament to the achievement of the program. That such a dreaded and highly stigmatized disease as HIV could become the topic of child citizenship should encourage others to extend and to refine our theoretically guided, systematic approach to address challenges to community health and child well-being.

Concluding Thoughts

The YC Program has successfully engaged adolescents, in advantaged and disadvantaged communities, in sustained discourse, social analysis, and definitive actions that address the collective well-being of their local communities. Our concentration on theory development has been essential in guiding us through a spectrum of large-scale epidemiological studies and smaller-scale, but highly informative, discourse experiences to a formally designed and rigorously conducted CRCT. The extraordinary accomplishments of the YCs in Moshi show that the theory and methods apply in one of the poorest societies in the world. When our work began, Tanzania was categorized in the "low human development group" of the UNDP Human Development Index (UNDP 2002) and had an HIV prevalence rate of 8.8 percent (UNAIDS 2004). Yet it has a democratic, decentralized governing structure, a condition that was certainly favorable to the uptake and potential sustainability of the YC Program.

The essential accomplishment of the YC Program is the demonstration that children can participate in deliberative democracy as legitimate and competent citizens. Their legitimacy is achieved through the recognition and guidance of adults, and their competencies are revealed in actions that can be as thoughtful as they are decisive. The importance of engaging children as citizens within the structure and functioning of their local governments cannot be overstated. It is here that the respect and dignity implicit in the definition of citizenship is established. Because there is something fundamentally humane about the status of being a citizen, we would argue that the identity established locally for a child is readily transferred to national and international contexts. But of course, this is an empirical question. Based on 20 years of theory development and research in the post-CRC era, we do take the position that if given respect, opportunities to be critically engaged with their communities and schools, and access to accurate information about conditions that concern them, children anywhere can achieve the status of "worthy citizen."

Notes

1. Ethics and Values Studies Program (EVS) of the National Science Foundation (SBR-9602176, Community Participation and Child Rights: An Ethical and Scientific Analysis) provided funding. Mary Carlson, principal investigator (PI).

2. Child Health and Social Ecology (CHASE) is a research unit at Harvard Medical School that developed the Young Citizens curriculum. It is organized to explore the interface between socialization and social integration in human development.

3. Between 1990 and 2005, grants from the John D. and Catherine T. MacArthur Foundation, the National Institute of Justice, and the National Institute of Mental Health funded the Project on Human Development in Chicago Neighborhoods. Felton Earls was PI, Mary Carlson co-PI, on grants from the U.S. Department of Education and Child Care Bureau to examine the quality of early childhood education and care programs across the city.

4. "Exploring the Rights of the Child" was an international conference that St. Xavier University in Chicago organized in early 1997. It was one of the first conferences on the topic of child rights to be held

in the United States. The YC Program was invited to provide an example of how the participatory rights of children could be demonstrated. The YCs commanded the attention of a large audience in what turned out to be one of the more provocative and interesting sessions at the conference. The Turner Foundation, the Jules and Doris Stein Foundation, and Center for Child Well-Being supported the Chicago and Cambridge YC Programs with seed grants.

5. During the same period of the PHDCN when we were starting the YC Program, we journeyed to Brazil and Romania to witness how the CRC guided responses to children exposed to extreme forms of social deprivation. We were fortunate to obtain support from UNICEF headquarters and the country offices in guiding us to exemplary programs in both countries. During this era, UNICEF's mantra had become "Children in Especially Difficult Circumstances" (Black 1996). In Brazil, we visited the city centers and cathedrals that these children considered home. We witnessed the context of neglect, abuse, and exploitation in which these children worked and lived. In child development terms, we defined this as late deprivation since most of these children had been adequately socialized in their early years. Their existence on the streets was a consequence of family poverty and other adverse social conditions (Earls and Carlson 1999). At the same time that Brazil could be criticized for its tolerance of the serious deprivation and exploitation of millions of street children, its child rights legislation is among the most advanced in the world. We were particularly impressed with the Guardianship Councils, which the Constitution established, to provide local implementation of the protection and provision rights (Duarte et al. 2007). It was in this context that we first heard the expression "from minors to citizens" and actually met children who confidently articulated the meaning of citizenship in their lives. It took a visit to Romania to fully understand the distinction between early and late deprivation. Following the assassination of Ceausescu in Romania in 1990, the world learned of tens of thousands of infants living in profoundly deprived state-sponsored residential institutions. Here we engaged in an experiment to examine neuroendocrinological mechanisms that were associated with recovery from early deprivation (Carlson and Earls 1997, 1999). Witnessing profound early and late deprivation at the societal level prepared us for the challenge to create a rights-based research project for the work on HIV health promotion that we were to pursue in Tanzania.

6. In marked contrast to the examples of Brazil and Romania, our journeying has also taken us to states where efforts to integrate children in democratic processes and institutions are well established. The most remarkable of these excursions was to Costa Rica, where we established a long-term collaboration with the Omar Dengo Foundation, which has evolved into a national program, the Deliberative Capacities for School Age Children (CADE) (Carlson, Earls, and Fonseca 2002; also see Fonseca and Bujanda's article in this volume).

7. Between 2002 and 2009, a grant from the National Institute of Mental Health (R01 MH66801) funded the project, Ecology of HIV/AIDS and Child Mental Health in Tanzania, with Felton Earls, PI; Mary Carlson, co-PI. Administrative supports for the local activities in Tanzania were provided through subcontracts from Harvard Medical School to the Kilimanjaro Christian Medical College (KCMC) and the Tanzanian National Bureau of Statistics (NBS).

8. Following the initial success of the VCT health fairs, collaboration with the Elizabeth Glaser Pediatric AIDS Foundation in Tanzania (EGPAF) was established to incorporate a focus on Prevention of Mother to Child Transmission in the YCs' community education and mobilization activities. The YCs included the role of breastfeeding for HIV-positive mothers in their skits because they considered it important information that was not discussed in public. Over the course of several fairs, the proportion of children coming for testing increased from 1 to 19 percent.

References

Arrow, Kenneth J. 1963. *Social choice and individual values*. 2nd ed. New Haven, CT: Yale University Press.

Bandura, Albert. 1986. *Social foundation of thought and action: A social-cognitive theory*. Englewood Cliffs, NJ: Prentice Hall.

Bingenheimer, Jeffrey, Robert T. Brennan, and Felton Earls. 2005. Exposure to firearm violence and violent behavior. *Science* 308:1323–26.

Black, Maggie. 1996. *Children first: The story of UNICEF, past and present*. Oxford: Oxford University Press.

Boal, Augusto. 1979. *Theatre of the oppressed*. New York, NY: Uziden.

Brennan, Robert T., Beth Molnar, and Felton Earls. 2007. Refining the measurement of exposure to violence. *Journal of Community Psychology* 35:603–18.

Bronfenbrenner, Urie. 1979. *The ecology of human development*. Cambridge, MA: Harvard University Press.

Browning, Christopher, Tama Leventhal, and Jeanne Brooks-Gunn. 2005. Neighborhood context and racial differences in early adolescent sexual activity. *Demography* 41 (4): 697–720.

Buka, Stephen L., Robert T. Brennan, Janet Rich-Edwards, Stephen Raudenbush, and Felton Earls. 2003. Neighborhood support and the birth weight of urban infants. *American Journal of Epidemiology* 157:1–8.

Carlson, Mary, Robert T. Brennan, and Felton Earls. n.d. *Adolescents promoting HIV competent communities: A cluster randomized control trial*. Submitted manuscript.

Carlson, Mary, and Felton Earls. 1997. Psychological and neuroendocrinological sequelae of early social deprivation in institutionalized children in Romania. In *Integrative neurobiology of affiliation*, ed. C. Sue Carter, I. Izja Lederhendler, and Brian Kirkpatrick, 419–28. New York, NY: New York Academy.

Carlson, Mary, and Felton Earls. 1999. Social ecology and the development of stress regulation. In *Developmental science and the holistic approach*, eds. Lars R. Bergman, Robert B. Cairns, Lars-Göran Nilsson, and Lars Nystedt, 229–48. Mahwah, NJ: Lawrence Erlbaum.

Carlson, Mary, and Felton Earls. 2001. The child as citizen: Implications for the science and practice of child development. *International Society for the Study of Behavioral Development Newsletter* 38:12–16.

Carlson, Mary, Felton Earls, and Clotilde Fonseca. 2002. Children and democracy: Focus on Costa Rica. *ReVista: Harvard Review of Latin America*, 2 (1): 39–41.

Chan, Brian, Barbara Trickett, Mary Carlson, and Felton Earls. 2003. Youth participation: A critical element of research on child well-being. In *Developmental assets and asset-building communities: Implications for research policy and programs*, eds. Richard Lerner and Peter L. Benson, 65–96. New York, NY: Kluwer-Plenum.

Dickens, Charles. 2003. *Great expectations*. London: Penguin.

Duarte, Cristina, Irene Rizzini, Christina Hoven, Mary Carlson, and Felton Earls. 2007. Evolution of child rights councils in Brazil. *International Journal of Children's Rights* 15:269–82.

Earls, Felton, and Stephen Buka. 1997. *Project on Human Development in Chicago Neighborhoods: Technical report*. Rockville, MD: National Institute of Justice.

Earls, Felton, and Mary Carlson. 1995. Promoting human capability as an alternative to early crime prevention. In *Integrating crime prevention strategies: Propensity and opportunity*, eds. R. V. Clarke, J. McCord, and P.-O. H. Wikstrom, 141–68. Stockholm: National Council for Crime Prevention.

Earls, Felton, and Mary Carlson. 1999. Children at the margins of society: Research and practice. *New Directions for Child and Adolescent Development* 85:71–82.

Earls, Felton, and Mary Carlson. 2001. Social ecology of child well-being. *Annual Review of Public Health* 22:143–66.

Earls, Felton, and Mary Carlson. 2002. Adolescents as collaborators. In *Youth in cities: A cross-national perspective*, eds. Marta Tienda and William Julius Wilson, 58–83. New York, NY: Cambridge University Press.

Earls, Felton, Giuseppe Raviola, and Mary Carlson. 2008. Promoting child mental health in the context of the HIV/AIDS pandemic with a focus on sub-Saharan Africa. *Journal of Child Psychology and Psychiatry* 49:295–312.

Earls, Felton, and Albert J. Reiss. 1994. *Breaking the cycle: Predicting and preventing crime*. Washington, DC: U.S. Department of Justice, Office of Justice Programs, and National Institute of Justice.

Granich, Rueben M., Charles F. Gilks, Christopher Dye, Keven M. DeCock, and Brian G. Williams. 2009. Universal voluntary HIV testing with antiretroviral therapy as a strategy for elimination of HIV transmission: A mathematical model. *Lancet* 373:48–57.

Habermas, Jürgen. 1984. *The theory of communicative action*, vol. 1, *Reason and the rationalization of society*. Trans. Thomas McCarthy. Boston, MA: Beacon.

Habermas, Jürgen. 1987. *The theory of communicative action*, vol. 2, *Lifeworld and system: A critique of functionalist reason*. Trans. Thomas McCarthy. Boston, MA: Beacon.

Habermas, Jürgen. 1990. *Moral consciousness and communicative action*. Trans. Christian Lenhardt and Shierry Weber Nicholsen. Cambridge, MA: MIT Press.

Habermas, Jürgen. 1991. *The structural transformation of the public sphere: An inquiry into a category of bourgeois society*. Trans. Thomas Burger. Cambridge, MA: MIT Press.

Kamo, Norris, Mary Carlson, Robert Brennan, and Felton Earls. 2008. Young citizens as health agents: Use of drama in promoting community efficacy for HIV/AIDS. *American Journal of Public Health* 98:201–4.

Knutsson, Karl E., for UNICEF. 1997. *Children: Noble causes or worthy citizens*. Aldershot, UK: Ashgate.

Morse, Mika. 2008. Young citizens: A case study in institutionalizing children's participation in community decision-making. *Child Legal Rights Journal* 28:23–54.

Sampson, Robert J., Jeffrey Morenoff, and Felton Earls. 1999. Beyond social capital: Neighborhood mechanisms and structural sources of collective efficacy for children. *American Sociological Review* 64:633–60.

Sampson, Robert J., Stephen Raudenbush, and Felton Earls. 1997. Neighborhoods and violent crime: A multilevel study of collective efficacy. *Science* 277:918–24.

Selner-O'Hagan, Mary Beth, Daniel Kindlon, Stephen Buka, Stephen Raudenbush, and Felton Earls. 1998. Assessing exposure to violence in urban youth. *Journal of Child Psychology and Psychiatry* 39:215–24.

Sen, Amartya. 1985. *Commodities and capabilities*. Amsterdam: North-Holland.

Sen, Amartya. 1992. *Inequality reexamined*. Oxford: Oxford University Press.

Sen, Amartya. 1993. Capability and well-being. In *The quality of life*, eds. Martha Nussbaum and Amartya Sen. Oxford: Clarendon.

Sen, Amartya. 1999. *Development as freedom*. New York, NY: Knopf.

Sen, Amartya. 2009. *The idea of justice*. Cambridge, MA: Harvard University Press.

Sterndahl, Michelle, Felton Earls, and Rosalind Wright. Forthcoming. Community violence and urban childhood asthma: A multilevel analysis. *European Journal of Respiratory Diseases*.

Tonry, Michael, Lloyd Ohlin, Kenneth Adams, Felton Earls, David Rowe, Robert Sampson, and Richard Tremblay. 1991. *Human development and criminal behavior: New ways of advancing knowledge*. New York, NY: Springer.

UNAIDS (Joint United Nations Programme on HIV/AIDS). 2004. *Report on the global AIDS epidemic: 4th global report*. Geneva: UNAIDS. Available from www.unaids.org/bangkok2004/gar2004_html/GAR2004_00_en.htm (accessed 13 August 2010).

UNDP (United Nations Development Programme). 2002. *Human development report 2002: Deeping democracy in a fragmented world*. New York, NY: Oxford University Press.

Xue, Yange, Tama Leventhal, Jeanne Brooks-Gunn, and Felton Earls. 2005. Neighborhood residence and mental health problems of 5- to 11-year olds. *Archives of General Psychiatry* 62:554–63.

Promoting Children's Capacities for Active and Deliberative Citizenship with Digital Technologies: The CADE Project in Costa Rica

By
CLOTILDE FONSECA
and
MARIA EUGENIA BUJANDA

This article explains several core aspects of the experience of the Omar Dengo Foundation of Costa Rica in the development of the Deliberative Capabilities in School Age Children project, a set of citizenship education programs based on the conception of children as citizens and on a particular conception of the role of digital technologies in the promotion of children's high-order skills. It analyzes the outcomes of the program designed for elementary schools and presents the lessons learned in the process of scaling up the initiative from its inception as a pilot to its implementation as a regular after-school program within the Costa Rican National Program of Educational Informatics.

Keywords: citizenship education; participation rights; information and communication technologies; self-efficacy; after-school programs

The Deliberative Capabilities in School Age Children project (CADE, its Spanish acronym) emerged in 2001 as a research and development initiative of the Fundación Omar Dengo (Omar Dengo Foundation [ODF]) to (1) conceptually explore and operationalize children's deliberative capabilities by linking them to children's exercise of their participation rights, (2) develop an educational methodology that can promote these skills, and (3) explore the contributions of digital technologies to the development of these capabilities.

Clotilde Fonseca is Costa Rica's minister of science and technology. She is a founding director of the Costa Rican Program of Educational Informatics—created in 1988 in Costa Rica by the Omar Dengo Foundation and the Ministry of Public Education—a program that has reached more than 1.5 million children and teachers during its more than two decades of work. She was executive director of the Omar Dengo Foundation from 1987 (when it was founded) to 1994 and from 1996 to 2010.

Maria Eugenia Bujanda is research director at the Omar Dengo Foundation. From 2003 to 2009, she led the foundation's citizenship education projects. She holds a PhD in education from Complutense University of Madrid.

DOI: 10.1177/0002716210383657

The result of these efforts has been the creation of a set of citizenship education programs for children and youth, focused on the development of self-efficacy and deliberative capabilities, both mediated by the use of digital technologies. These programs have been implemented in Costa Rica and other Central American countries.

In Costa Rica, CADE is being implemented in schools that take part in the National Program of Educational Informatics, a joint initiative that ODF and the Ministry of Public Education (MPE) carry out. From 2004 to the present, the project has been executed in twenty-four schools and two high schools across the country and has benefited nearly 950 children. It is conceived as an after-school program under the supervision of the computer lab teacher and carried out over four hours per week from February to November.

Between 2004 and 2010, CADE has extended its area of influence. It has definitively affected the proposal of the National Program of Educational Informatics related to the use of digital technologies to promote citizenship skills. Moreover, with support from the United Nations Democracy Fund, the Democracy Builders initiative was launched in 2007. This project seeks to build capacities for active citizenship and personal fulfillment of youth by enriching the official high school curriculum's civic education, using CADE's methodology.[1]

Two Founding Premises

CADE's conception of citizenship education is based on two pillars. The first is the recognition of children's participation rights and the need to help them to develop the skills required to exercise these rights in the context of a participatory and deliberative democracy. The second pillar is the conviction that at the beginning of the twenty-first century, digital technologies must be present in citizenship education proposals.

Children as citizens

The first premise on which CADE was built is that the changes brought about by the Convention on the Rights of the Child (CRC) in the conception of children and their rights require rethinking the basis and justification of citizenship education. Such education can no longer be conceived exclusively as the preparation of our children and youth to assume future political and civic responsibilities but, rather, as a process that partly consists of facilitating the enactment of the participation rights that children and adolescents already possess (Bujanda 2007; Fundación Omar Dengo 2010).

The CADE approach to citizenship education has been strongly influenced by the extensive and insightful work that Earls and Carlson have done to promote the conception of children as citizens as well as children's capacities to participate in the framework of a deliberative democracy (Carlson and Earls 2001; Earls and Carlson 2002). Based on Sen's capability approach (Sen 1992, 1999), these authors advocate the need to promote children's emerging participative capabilities and to create opportunities for them to be perceived as agents of change, capable of actively contributing to their well-being and that of their communities.

Earls and Carlson have successfully applied their theory to child mental health research in extreme contexts, such as the HIV/AIDS pandemic in Tanzania (Earls, Raviola, and Carlson 2008; Kamo et al. 2008). In Costa Rica, they encouraged the launch of CADE to test the effect that their approach could have in a country that is acknowledged to have a sustained record of promoting children and their capacities (Carlson, Earls, and Fonseca 2002). Their collaboration was decisive for the project to lay solid theoretical and research bases. From these bases, the ODF team designed and validated a curriculum that took advantage of ODF's experience in innovative school settings and its particular vision of digital technologies as tools for high-order skills development.

Digital technologies as drivers for citizen competence

The second premise on which CADE rests has to do with the value of incorporating a digital dimension into citizenship. Digital technologies can hardly be dissociated from the way in which citizenship is being experienced in contemporary societies. They are a powerful educational tool as well; they have enriched and expanded the ways in which students can learn, understand the views and positions of others, spread their own ideas and proposals, and join different networks and spaces for communication and dialogue.

Since its inception in 1988, ODF has produced and implemented successful educational programs that use digital technologies in innovative ways to develop capacities related to logical-mathematical thinking, problem solving, innovation, teamwork, communication, and social participation (Fonseca 2005, 2009; Fundación Omar Dengo 2005, 2006, 2009). At a still early time in the development of learning technologies—even for the developed world—ODF took on the challenge of massively introducing digital technologies in the educational system in conjunction with the Costa Rican MPE. Moreover, ODF's team adopted a radically new approach—at least in its regional context—about how technology can support learning. They developed a methodology that combined project-based learning, construction and manipulation of digital objects using programming languages, and the use of games as tools for the development of cognitive and digital skills.

CADE's proposal regarding technology use has tried to benefit from these new perspectives and resources to allow children to strengthen their rights and responsibilities as active citizens and to better understand the digital dimension of participatory processes and governments.

This article has two main purposes. After synthesizing the theory behind our proposal with two founding premises, we show how a curriculum, intertwined with the innovative use of digital technologies, was articulated to promote children's participation rights. Second, we examine some characteristics of the learning outcomes that children obtain in CADE's program for elementary schools.

The article concludes with three major lessons learned in the process of scaling up the initiative from its inception as a pilot to its implementation as a regular after-school program.

The Curriculum

In this section, we present the curriculum that the CADE project designed and disseminated, specifically its learning objectives, methodology, and the way technology is incorporated into the learning process.[2]

The objective: Develop children's self-efficacy and deliberative capacities

CADE claims that children should be able to exercise their rights to participate in the framework of a reflective, ethical, and dialogical citizenship characterized by the existence of opportunities for and the capacity to participate in public deliberations.

Deliberation takes shape as a social and political action within the framework of deliberative democracy theories. In a deliberative democracy, the legitimacy of political decisions requires giving the same attention to the reasons of all citizens in the process of debate on public issues (Bohman 1997; Feres 2000). It represents democratic practices in which citizen participation is not restricted to the act of voting but also includes taking part in public discussions and socially shared actions aimed at improving collective life.

CADE's definition of deliberation is founded on the proposals of Earls and Carlson (2002; Carlson and Earls 2001), as derived from a synthesis based on the theories of Sen (1992, 1999), Habermas (1984, 1987), and Bohman (1996, 1997). Burkhalter, Gastil, and Kelshaw (2002) and Gastil and Dillard (1999) have further articulated notions of deliberation as a political process. In CADE, deliberation is viewed as a cooperative dialogue on public issues in which participants carefully consider the available information, take into account the perspective of others, ensure everyone's equitable participation, and build agreements that integrate different contributions in search of the common good (Fundación Omar Dengo 2005).

For children to participate effectively in deliberative processes, they need opportunities to be part of them—in equitable terms—recognizing as well that a certain threshold of capabilities exists in children. Hence, the idea of producing a specific curriculum focused on the development of these capacities and the self-efficacy and sense of agency that will allow children to assume an active role in their communities.

Based on this definition of deliberation and on the four deliberation principles or traits (trust, perspective taking, mutual understanding, and social shared action) with which Carlson and Earls (2001; Earls and Carlson 2002) synthesized Habermas's related theory,[3] we formulated four broad deliberative competencies that helped us to organize the learning content and experiences along the curriculum:

- *Starting or getting engaged in public deliberations*. To participate in democratic processes, children must first see themselves as active members of the community, with valuable contributions to make for their own and others' well-being and whose voices should be taken into account. This is the trust and self-efficacy component.
- *Developing good dialogues*. Derived from Habermas's communicative ethics, good dialogue represents a form of communication in which participants understand that they all share a common goal—trying to reach the best idea or decision. Moreover, they must listen carefully to the ideas of others even if they do not share them, encourage everyone to participate equally, argue and assess ideas critically, try to put themselves in the others' places to understand their viewpoints, and build ideas with input from all.
- *Thoughtful inquiry*. Deliberating means thoughtfully discussing all sides of a question and carefully considering or weighing all the arguments. In the case of deliberations on public problems, it involves being able to research community problems, critically analyze available information, and build a rigorous and shared understanding of those problems and their possible solutions.
- *Undertaking cooperative and agreed-upon action*. In the context of citizenship, deliberation is concerned not only with discussion and dialogue but also with agreeing on and undertaking the best course of action in a given situation. This will usually require reaching agreements that integrate different perspectives and cooperating with others to carry out the plan of action.

This competence framework leads to the formulation of the program's learning outcomes (see Table 1).

The methodology: Five main ingredients

The devised methodology is a combination of different didactical strategies that have been proven to lead to effective learning and also to be consistent with citizenship education: (1) experiential learning, (2) cooperative learning, (3) thoughtful inquiry, (4) participatory theater, and (5) deliberation as the basis for group dynamics. These strategies have been explained extensively elsewhere (Fundación Omar Dengo 2010). Here, they are briefly defined.

- *Experiential learning*. The experiential approach to citizenship education (Koopmann 2002) entails creating learning strategies where children can act as citizens and experience their ability to become citizens. In CADE, this action component is structured around a process of investigation and intervention on community problems that affect them: children identify problem

TABLE 1
Expected Learning Outcomes in CADE

Dimensions	Children Should Get To . . .
Being able to start/engage in a public deliberation	See themselves as members of a local, national, and global community Be interested in the needs and problems of their local or national community Be aware of their rights to participate in the political and civic life and the responsibilities that they can assume Take the initiative to solve problems that affect them Develop trust in others
Being able to develop high-quality dialogues	Encourage everybody's participation from a symmetrical position Accept and value the ideas, beliefs, ways of being, or practices of others Provide reasoned explanations of their opinions using arguments, data, criteria, or facts to support that position Develop perspective taking Weigh all arguments, going beyond initial statements to achieve the integration of the ideas (integration of perspectives)
Being able to carry out thoughtful inquiry	Look for information and assess its usefulness Weigh the information and different points of view involved Look creatively for possible solutions to problems Evaluate different alternatives and their consequences
Being able to undertake cooperative and agreed-upon action	Participate with others to help to solve public problems Apply agreement-oriented decision-making procedures Reach agreements that integrate the perspectives of those involved Cooperate with others Assume responsibility for the agreements

areas in their community, select one to investigate, devise a solution, and carry out an action plan to gain support for their proposal or to put it into practice.

- *Cooperative learning*. Cooperative learning is one of the most useful and relevant approaches in education for active citizenship. Along with experiential learning, it offers a solid basis for effective learning. In CADE, special attention is paid to its techniques for making small group work more effective and truly collaborative (Johnson, Johnson, and Holubec 1994). For example, the use of roles makes it possible for each group member to be essential for the group to successfully perform the task and achieve the objective. Roles also allow children to take more control of the activities carried out and to promote concentration and self-esteem.
- *Thoughtful inquiry*. An environment is created in which citizenship is practiced and reflected upon. In CADE, children engage in inquiries about situations and dilemmas of civic life and about key concepts related to what they are experiencing, such as deliberation, citizenship, community, participation, agreement, consensus, justice, conflict, or democracy. To support this element of reflection, we use narrations, as in *Philosophy for Children*

(Lipman 1998). The curriculum includes a series of short stories about a group of children who feel affected by what happens in their community and want to do something about it. These stories help the children to imagine, understand the meaning of important concepts, explore feelings, and discover new ideas that would be otherwise too abstract.

- *Participatory theater*. In the 1960s, Brazilian dramatist Augusto Boal created the methodology of participatory theater as an instrument of political literacy and social transformation (Boal 2004). It consists of a series of exercises, games, and theatrical techniques that provide insights and alternatives for social and interpersonal problems. Using these techniques, children can express their views and ideas and deepen their understanding of the world not through verbal rational discourse but through more emotional dimensions of thought and communication. Moreover, participatory theater provides opportunities to promote crucial citizenship skills such as perspective taking and the ability to devise alternatives to the situations.
- *Deliberation as the basis for group dynamics*. Deliberative competence can only be developed if incorporated as part of the normal dynamics of work within the group, as the usual way of making decisions, managing relationships, and resolving personal conflicts. In CADE, deliberative procedures are present in all the activities.

The role of digital technologies

As stated above, the main purpose of integrating digital technologies into citizenship education programs is to offer students opportunities to broaden and enrich children's identities and actions as citizens. From this perspective, the curriculum that we developed considers the following uses of technology:

- *Problem solving and research*. Technologies and digital resources are used for researching and supporting problem-solving processes. Students can strengthen their inquiry strategies and expand the sources and means by which they obtain information. In CADE, technological resources play a critical role in every stage of the research and action process.
- *Participation in online deliberative processes*. The opportunity for interaction, collaboration, and deliberation among citizens is one of the main impacts that technologies are having in civic and political life. Children should be able to learn to interact effectively, responsibly, and safely in these new environments. On CADE's Web site, we incorporated the "online preferendum," a tool based on Newman and Emerson's (1997) developments, which allows geographically distant children to discuss and make decisions in a democratic manner on issues currently affecting their country. The participants decide what problem they want to discuss, propose solutions, argue about them, and reach an agreement on a plan of action. The discussion is based on the preferendum, a system for voting, conflict resolution, and decision-making, which

TABLE 2
Issues Addressed by Children Participating in CADE in 2009 (N = 26 Groups)

Topic	Frequency
Insecurity (crime)	14
Environmental pollution	10
Other	2

aims to generate the highest possible level of consensus among those called to take action.

- *Digital production and dissemination of proposals*. A key way that technologies can contribute to citizenship is by enabling children to create digital productions that reflect their proposals and ideas and allow the children to disseminate them to a variety of audiences. It is especially valuable for students to be able to use technological resources to express and systematize their own contributions and suggestions for improvement and to communicate to the public that has an interest or responsibility in the matter.[4]

An Approach to CADE's Learning Outcomes

This section presents data on three dimensions that enable a better understanding of the children's experiences and learning outcomes in CADE's programs for elementary schools. The information stems partly from a formative and impact evaluation carried out in 2009 (Moreno and Acon 2009). Among other things, this evaluation looked at the self-reported effects of the program in a group of students who graduated from CADE and at the perceptions of a sample of current, participating students.[5]

Children's main concerns

Since CADE became a program in 2004, public insecurity (crime) and pollution appear to be the main issues to which the participating children have devoted their attention. To explore this focus in more detail, the issues that the twenty-six groups of children who participated in CADE addressed in 2009 are examined.[6] Table 2 compiles, in three main categories, the problems that the groups of children selected after reaching consensus.

As shown in Table 2, the main concerns of children revolved around their experiences of insecurity (crime) in their communities,[7] expressed as

1. drug addiction among youth in the community (five groups),
2. fast-driving cars in front of the school (four groups),
3. abandoned and deteriorated areas in the community turning into dangerous places (two groups),

4. criminal activity of youth gangs in the community (two groups), and
5. fierce dogs loose in the community (one group).

It should be noted that crime is a concern that the adult population shares. The United Nations Development Programme's (UNDP's) 2005 National Human Development Report for Costa Rica presents fear as "a chronic feature" of Costa Rican society (PNUD 2006). According to the 2006 National Security Survey (Madrigal 2007), 33.1 percent of the population points to insecurity (crime) as the main problem that the country faces, ahead of the economic situation (28 percent). Between 75 and 76 percent of the population believes that insecurity poses a serious threat to the country's future welfare (PNUD 2009).

What is the basis for this concern? Although Costa Rica is considered a country with low criminality, at a considerable distance from other nations in the region (PNUD 2009), its inhabitants note with alarm the increasing crime rates and fear of losing their country's status and identity as peaceful and secure. Costa Ricans have the lowest homicide rate in Central America, comparable to Europe, but between 2000 and 2008 the rate almost doubled, from 6 to 11 per 100,000 inhabitants (PNUD 2009). The rate of robberies has also risen sharply, more than 30 percent between 1998 and 2003 (PNUD 2006). The victimization rates[8] have almost doubled in less than two decades, from 20 percent in 1986 to 38.7 percent in 2004. Theft on public roads increased by more than fifteen times in the past 15 years, reaching a level almost eight times the average in developed countries (PNUD 2006).

Similarly, there is a tendency to associate insecurity with the trafficking and consumption of illicit drugs; in the public imagination, the offender is a young, male drug addict (Madrigal 2007). Undoubtedly, this has to do with the illicit-drug offenses rate, which increased by 226 percent between 1998 and 2003 (PNUD 2006), as well as with the growing fear of homeless drug addicts on the streets.[9] The focus group survey conducted for the 2005 National Human Development Report captured the deep concern that parents have about the threat that the phenomenon of drug addiction poses, especially to their children (PNUD 2006).

Being part of this reality and being exposed to the adult and media discourses on these issues, it is perfectly understandable that children reflect these concerns as well. Of course, this does not mean that children's worries have no basis and that they are not suffering, in several ways, from the effects of these phenomena. For example, one of the main consequences of this atmosphere of fear is the limitation of opportunities for children to enjoy public spaces and recreational facilities. According to a special survey conducted for the 2005 National Human Development Report on the perceptions and the actual situations of crime experienced by children in marginalized urban communities (PNUD 2006), some groups of children in all of the surveyed schools said that they had stopped doing activities, such as going outside to play or run errands, due to fear.

On the problem of drug addiction among young people, the fears of children also have a real base. Although the data suggest that in Costa Rica, drug use is relatively low, there are concerns that the age at which drug consumption begins is decreasing. According to unpublished data from a 2003 study by the Institute on Alcoholism and Drug Dependence, drawing from a national sample of six hundred children in fourth grade, 7 percent smoked actively; 23.3 percent had, at some time, tried alcohol; and 14 percent had consumed alcohol in the last month. Two percent of respondents had used a drug other than alcohol and cigarettes at least once (PNUD 2006).[10]

In short, three main conclusions can be derived from the concerns that the children in CADE expressed. First, the children feel insecure in their communities, which should be a wake-up call for families, educational officials, and generally for adults, all of whom should encourage the entire community to think of ways to reduce children's vulnerability to real hazards and to the prevailing atmosphere of fear.

Second, there is a need to reflect, especially in the context of CADE, on children's dependence on the set of beliefs that are associated with the "popular perception" of insecurity, which quite often may rest on questionable evidence (PNUD 2009). Children show weak capacities to confront widely held assumptions, such as concerns that crime is primarily caused by young drug users or that crime can only be fought with an iron fist.[11]

Finally, problems related to the environment, another concern that the children address year after year, require greater attention. The specific environmental issues cited in 2009 by the participating children included

1. waste management in communities (four groups),
2. contamination of soils and rivers by industrial waste from intensive agriculture and livestock (four groups),
3. sewage collection (one group); and
4. pollution in general (one group).

The adult population does not share equally these environmental concerns. According to the Youth National Survey, only 0.6 percent of young people between 15 and 35 years old consider environmental problems to be the most severe (Fondo de Población de las Naciones Unidas 2009).[12] This disparity could be an indication of children's particular sensitivity toward nature, but it could also be a result of the program's emphasis on community diagnosis techniques based on touring and mapping exercises.

Children's community action plans

We now turn to an examination of the children's proposals and action plans and what they may reveal about children's understanding of their roles as citizens.

Table 3 shows the predominance of awareness-raising activities among children's action plans, such as giving talks, handing out brochures, or doing street drama aimed at providing information to and changing attitudes and behaviors of community members. This type of action shows up mainly in projects addressing

TABLE 3
Types of Actions Conducted by Children Participating in CADE in 2009

Action Type	Frequency
Contacting the authorities to request their support or intervention (by letter or email or in person in the case of the municipality or the school authorities)	11
Giving talks (children or experts), going to talk to neighbors house-to-house (for example, asking them to sign a commitment sheet and to provide a comment)	8
Distributing newsletters, brochures, or posters in the school or the community (for awareness or reporting), or in a school newspaper	7
Direct interventions in the community (collecting garbage, sharing towels and soap for washing hands, installing a waste collection center for recycling purposes, collecting money to fix the park, etc.)	3
Artistic activities (a mural, street drama, etc.)	2

issues related to crime—such as substance abuse or the presence of gangs—and waste management in the community.

In the case of drug abuse, children usually propose action plans that have to do with handing out information to other children and youth in the community to prevent them from adopting risky behaviors. The purpose of the waste management and water pollution activities is to sensitize the community to the importance of protecting the natural resources and to recommend recycling practices.

Children go to the authorities concerning more specific and defined problems for which the intervention requires a government body or when the solution involves reporting a complaint. For example, children have used this approach when they detect the need to install a traffic light or better road signs in the streets of their communities or when they confront pollution issues involving local companies or industries.

Especially when dealing with complex problems, such as crime, drug addiction, or pollution, groups of children sometimes find it difficult to undertake a deeper analysis of the causes and manifestations of these problems. The complexity of the problems could lessen their chances of raising plans of action that possibly have some sort of public impact. This difficulty is also partly due to the fact that some facilitators have conducted the children through rather superficial processes, limited to getting a general view of the problem and quickly moving into thinking about how to "make it known" in the community. Such a practice prevents children from deepening their understanding of and perspectives on such problems, thus limiting their chances of coming up with promising plans. This surface approach is reflected in the answer of a child, asked to summarize how his group addressed the research component of problem-solving: "We were looking for information on pollution and the teacher asked us how we could solve it and we answered not throwing garbage."[13]

In fact, though the impact of CADE's groups in their communities has not yet been studied, children and facilitators, consulted in the context of CADE's impact assessment, express doubts about their influence. For example, in the case of requests presented to the authorities, both children and facilitators report that most often, they get no response or follow-up.

In the case of community awareness-raising activities, it is difficult to estimate what their impact may have been. What can be observed is that, for some children at least, what remains of their passage through the program is the reflection about how to conduct themselves with regard to drugs or environmental protection. As discussed in the next section, when asking children about their learning in CADE, there are many references to the adoption of such practices on a personal level, while the possibility of engaging with others to generate a change in the community is mentioned less often than expected.

Interestingly, the children seem to have been more effective in the context of their own schools, as they often combine their action in the community with some type of collaboration in their educational context. Some examples of this include a plan to address violent and dangerous games among younger students during breaks, contributions to repair the toilets, talking to parents to avoid crowds at the entrance, or the launching of a recycling program. According to available reports, these actions were remarkably effective in and well appreciated by the school community.

With hope, the actions of children can have greater resonance in their communities, both to bring about an improvement in their well-being and in their sense of personal agency. The mere fact of their being actively involved in their community brings about positive changes for the children, especially in the sense of creating a stronger sense of community belonging and the development of the disposition to contribute to community development and welfare. In the words of one facilitator, referring to the importance of the children's community action, "[CADE] does not bring a solution because it takes a lot to solve a problem, but only the fact that they have a proposal for the community is very valuable."

The changes that participating children reported

Results of the children's participation are presented both for children currently enrolled in CADE as well as for graduates of the program. The question for the former group was, "Has being in CADE changed things for you?" For graduates, the question was, "Has participating in CADE generated changes in your life?"

As Table 4 shows, children's responses about the changes that they have experienced after passing through the program can be grouped into four main categories: less fear of speaking and interacting with others, increased interest and commitment toward community, increased ability to listen and participate in dialogue, and increased ability to relate and cooperate with others.[14]

TABLE 4
Major Changes Experienced by Graduate and Participating Students in CADE

	Participants (N = 101)		Graduates (N = 53)	
	Number	Percentage	Number	Percentage
Less fear of speaking and interacting with others	27	26.7	9	17.0
Increased interest and commitment toward community	11	10.9	19	35.9
Increased ability to listen and participate in dialogue	9	8.9	7	13.2
Increased ability to relate and cooperate with others	12	11.8	1	1.8
Other	10	9.9	8	15.1

Additional detail of the children's responses reveals the following:

- *Less fear of expressing themselves and interacting with others*. This is the most common response category among participating children (26.7 percent) and the second most common for graduate students (17.0 percent). For the former, the emphasis seems to be in having lost the fear or embarrassment of speaking to an audience: "I don't feel embarrassed to speak to classmates anymore"; "My fear of public speaking [changed]"; "[I changed] my way of thinking, and I am not afraid to speak my mind"; and "Before I was nervous, I felt embarrassed." In contrast, graduate students stress having overcome the shyness that hindered their relationships with other school children: "Being closer to peers, not being that antisocial anymore, meeting new people, before I was more lonely"; "Before I was very serious, it has helped me to open up, now I speak a little more and I can talk to all my classmates without feeling ashamed"; and "Before I was shy and now I'm not, I get along with anyone." For this latter group of students, it is not so much about being able to speak in public as being more capable of interacting with others and being part of a group. After the experience of CADE, overcoming shyness seems to have a major utility for them. Curiously, both groups refer to losing the fear to speak and interact primarily within the peer group, not so much with regard to adults. This outcome is due in large part to the creation by the facilitator of a "safe" environment for the participation of children, one in which acceptance, respect, and group self-regulation are promoted.
- *Increased interest and commitment to the community*. This is the most common category that CADE graduates mentioned (35.9 percent) and the second most common among participating children (10.9 percent). That the latter were interviewed before they had carried out their action plan may

perhaps explain in part their smaller number of responses related to this category. Both groups claim that they have increased their awareness and commitment to the welfare and development of their communities, especially on environmental issues: "I do not like to see things run, or the river polluted, I have changed"; "I think a little more on others and not only me, I worry about the community"; "Yes, thinking of taking care of the community, not damaging it"; "Now I collect garbage all the time; if someone throws something on the floor in front of me, I go and tell him to throw it in the trash"; and "I try to recycle now. Before I did not do it, I did not attach much importance, now I care more about the situations in the community." These statements suggest that the program may have had positive effects in terms of strengthening the children's sense of belonging and emotional attachment to their community, which is critical for the development of capacities for deliberation and active citizenship. Children's responses reveal a greater willingness to identify situations that affect the communities' general welfare and possibly also to contribute in various ways to the solution. It appears that for some of them, what has been reinforced is their sense of personal responsibility regarding the adoption of practices such as recycling at home or not littering in public places. Further research is needed to verify this. Stronger evidence of children's conscience of their capacity to participate together with others and have an impact on the community is expected.

- *Increased ability to listen and participate in dialogue*. This type of change is mentioned by 13.2 percent of graduate students and by 8.9 percent of currently participating children. The latter refer mainly to the ability to listen, respect, and participate in dialogue with others: "I learned to respect the verbal space of my teammates"; "I learned to discuss, to [participate in] dialogue, communicate"; "I learned to respect the opinions of others"; "I raise my hand before speaking and respect my teammates more"; and "If I have a conflict now, I [participate in] dialogue." Graduates are more profound in their responses. Their responses relate to the capacity not only to listen but also to value and take the perspective of others. For example, "Previously I had no tolerance, I did not have the capacity to listen to the views of others"; "It was like learning to listen to people, I learned that not only my opinion is worth [something]"; "I learned to value friends and others. You have to accept what they say, what they propose"; "Before I did not know to listen to other people, I only cared about myself, now I can understand people better"; and "I am more sociable, one has to adapt to people, not all are equal to one." It is noteworthy that it is this dimension of listening—valuing others—that children mention above other elements of the deliberative capacities.
- *Ability to relate better and cooperate with others*. Primarily participating children (11.8 percent) refer to this dimension. For example, "I have become more respectful and I learned to relate to my peers and others"; "Before I was very quarrelsome and I did not work well in groups"; "I have learned to be a better team member"; and "I have seen why it is important to work in teams, to respect, to help."

Main Lessons Learned

The importance of creating safe spaces for participation

The main effect of participating in CADE that children report is reduced fear, embarrassment, or shyness related to speaking in public, expressing their views, and addressing others. Moreover, this effect arises not only as something that children exclusively associate with their interactions within CADE groups, but it has an impact that lasts over time.

Such an outcome cannot be considered minor, if we consider the dominant patterns of interaction and socialization in traditional school settings. CADE creates a space for children to experience free expression, participation, and self-regulation and a new relationship with the educator. This type of environment ruptures the still dominant school culture—at least in Costa Rica—in which, for example, "no talking" is often a standard classroom norm.

Some children conveyed this difference during the interviews: "[CADE] means a time different to class time." In their responses, they mentioned two particularly important features:

- Having a voice ("In class, we could hardly give an opinion" and "I like that we are respected; we are taken into account").
- Generating relations of solidarity and camaraderie with others ("We all joined together as friends"; "I felt accepted, happy among friends, no one was despised, and we all treated each other well"; and "Whenever we had a problem, we talked about it and then we made up").

These perceptions, along with the main impacts reported, confirm the wisdom of the decision to base the program's initial activities on building trust, acceptance, and group dynamics. This approach has allowed for the creation of safe spaces for participation. In fact, often, the first stage of the CADE process is lengthened due to the difficulties that the groups experience in building this new environment—one that differs in several ways from their everyday environment. This finding suggests that it would be valuable for citizenship education programs to pay attention to the creation of relations among participants, based on trust and mutual understanding.

The importance of ensuring successful experiences of community participation

Children who have participated in CADE claim to have increased their concern for the community, which, we believe, reflects a strengthened social and political bond. To a lesser extent, they mention their capacity to participate in and have an impact on public life. We also observe that for some children, the experience has meant more learning to fulfill the duties attributed to good citizens than projecting themselves into the community as agents of change and subjects of rights. The discourse about the need to help the community—sometimes merely involving the adoption of personal habits and practices that contribute to its welfare or at least do not damage it—appears to be predominant. These children do not seem to have built this speech upon a conscious and rights-based identity as citizens.

Several factors may contribute to this result. First, certain limitations, related to the implementation of the program, result from not devoting sufficient time to the implementation of community action plans. Second, some facilitators exhibit inhibitions in leading groups toward more robust action plans with greater chances of having real impact.

The identity and experience of the educators as citizens could be the basis of these difficulties. It should be noted that CADE facilitators are recruited from teachers in educational computing who are not necessarily familiar with experiences of participation. Some may not see themselves as active citizens. Being introduced to a program such as CADE may also represent the first time that they have tried to have some political impact on a community problem. If the training offered to these facilitators does not compensate for this lack of familiarity and experience, some may find it difficult to pass on to children a more inclusive notion of citizenship and to help them to develop action plans that could have a real impact on the public life of communities.

Ensuring that children experience successful participation is undoubtedly difficult. It marks a break with visions and structures that are deeply rooted in society: "To some extent, child participation may be seen as more controversial, challenging or difficult to implement than measures supporting child survival, development and protection because it is based on presenting children as rights holders rather than as recipients of charity" (UNICEF 2009, 31–32). We have learned that ensuring that children know and fully understand their *rights* to participation is fundamental if we want them to experience successful participation. Recalling the participation rights of children and relating these to actions that are made as they move through the programs must be constantly reinforced.

The importance of helping children to develop critical problem-solving skills

When analyzing the issues that the children in CADE raise, a few of these issues dominated, as did the influence of adult popular discourse on children's ideas, particularly in their concerns about crime. While it is somewhat inevitable that children will participate in this discourse, CADE and other citizenship education programs provide children with opportunities to gather reliable information, practice evidence-based reasoning, and participate in critical discussion of claims that may be backed up with poor evidence or argued weakly.

This note is not meant in any way to question or minimize the concerns that the children raised. On the contrary, in a program such as CADE, it is especially important to pay attention to the concerns that are raised and to analyze what may be causing them, since the purpose is to give children the tools that can help them to cope with the situations that they worry about. But this has to be combined with helping children to overcome superficial and simplistic thought whenever it may be necessary.

There are a number of recommendations that citizen education programs may follow to improve children's thinking skills and dispositions, derived from the work that Harvard's Project Zero has done. These include increasing the use of precise thinking language (Tishman, Perkins, and Jay 1994), practicing effective thinking routines, and making thinking visible.[15]

However, it would also be important to check whether the methodology of the program is somehow encouraging the repetitive emergence of certain issues. For example, the fact that the community diagnosis carried out by the children relies largely on community tours and mapping exercises could be focusing children's attention on issues of high visibility. As a result, they may become focused on issues that are detected just by strolling through the streets of the community, such as garbage accumulation, polluted nearby rivers, concentrations of homeless people or drug addicts in some areas, the abandonment and deterioration of certain public places, and the lack of safe passages for pedestrians.

Final Thoughts

In the process of scaling up our initiatives, we have learned that defining a certain set of skills and devising a curriculum to teach these skills are only the first part of the challenge. The second and even more complex part lies in developing frameworks for and competencies of teachers or facilitators that will enable them to generate those learning outcomes in a reliable way in many settings, in dissimilar circumstances, and with little supervision.

Though there exist very interesting initiatives designed around peer learning strategies, the success of our educational initiatives still depends to a great extent on the performance of teachers as orchestrators of effective learning processes. That is why school-based citizenship education programs need to invest in evidence-based and thoughtfully designed teacher-development strategies. In this regard, we should ensure that our teacher training and development approaches allow for three things to happen at the same time: (1) teachers need to become aware of weaknesses in their own practices, (2) they need to have access to precise knowledge about best practices, and (3) they need to be motivated to adopt changes (Barber and Mourshed 2007). These elements have proven to be prerequisites for teacher change and can be achieved in the context of a school culture that enables teachers to learn from each other, engage in teamwork, and practice coaching on a regular basis. This sort of teacher development requires a well-focused school leadership, committed to taking on the promotion of a school ethos that allows children to experience participation and democracy. In CADE, we are highly aware of the necessity of working further in these two directions to lay the adequate structural conditions that can lead to more effective learning outcomes.

The age and gender differences in children who participate in CADE are issues that require closer attention. The data on these variables available to date do not allow us to draw any definitive conclusion. Such distinctions deserve to be explored in future studies.

Notes

1. The project's main publications, a citizenship education manual, and a guide for implementing active citizenship as a whole-school approach at the high school level can be downloaded for free from the project's Web site: www.fod.ac.cr/constructoresdemocracia.

2. The teaching guide for facilitators, as well as the theoretical and methodological documents, can be downloaded for free from www.fod.ac.cr/librocade.

3. Earls and Carlson (2002; Carlson and Earls 2001) identify four major principles that should be present in the deliberative process, based on Habermas's dialogical ethics. These four elements represent the pillars of the ideal speech situation and help to define more precisely the concept of deliberation: (1) *Trust*. The awareness of the possibilities and situations of the other and the opportunity to share an ethical framework for social action. (2) *Perspective-taking*. Understanding the feelings and emotions of others as well as the reasons for their behaviors. (3) *Mutual understanding*. A common knowledge based on an agreement held as valid, and therefore binding, reached thanks to the application of scientific thinking processes to determine the authenticity, precision, and value of information (critical thinking) as well as perspective taking. (4) *Social shared action*. A prosocial action oriented by norms and values that the group recognizes as valid and that involve cooperation, coordination, and regulation.

4. CADE has a web platform that integrates these tools and the possibilities for their use. See www.fod.ac.cr/cade.

5. Fifty-three graduate students from seven different schools were interviewed by telephone. The sample was made due to convenience, since data were available only for those who responded in time to take part in the evaluation. Their ages ranged between 12 and 17 years old, and 37.7 percent were men and 62.3 percent women. With regard to currently participating children, a questionnaire with open and closed questions was given to 101 students from eight schools that were part of the program in 2009.

6. In 2009, the size of the groups ranged between twelve and twenty-four children, with seventeen as the average. The program guidelines establish that groups should be made up ideally of twelve girls and twelve boys, but the final gender and number composition depended on the size of the school and the volunteers that participated (children join CADE voluntarily). Frequently, groups lose some of their participants as the school year draws on, due to a range of factors, including timetable incompatibility, the need to attend other commitments (schoolwork, housework), lack of interest, or even lack of parent's permission.

7. The same concern about problems facing the country was also reflected in the online preferendum carried out in 2009. From all the problems (corruption in public administration, lack of recreational spaces for children and youth, family breakdown, etc.), children finally selected public insecurity.

8. The percentage of households in which a family member was the victim of a crime in the 12 months preceding the interview.

9. According to PNUD (2006), mass media and the press reinforce this association. For example, *La Nación*, one of the most prestigious national newspapers in the country, published on August 26, 2009, the following headline: "San Jose Becomes Unsafe Due to Addict Indigents." See www.elcomercio.com/. In local newspapers, similar examples exist. A local newspaper from the area where two of the participating schools are located ran in 2007 this headline: "Drug Addicts and Robberies Frighten Neighbors." See www.sancarlosaldia.com/. It talks about the large number of assaults and the presence of drug addicts in the central park of the community during daytime hours.

10. Unpublished data included in PNUD (2006).

11. On the online preferendum, the solution that the children favored for public insecurity was to "be tough on criminals."

12. Insecurity is considered the country's main problem by 24.5 percent of the survey participants. Insecurity is followed by poverty (22.9 percent), drugs (10 percent), political corruption (9.2 percent), and lack of employment (8.9 percent). Environmental problems are among the least mentioned topics: only above "attitudes" (0.4 percent).

13. These quotes are taken from responses to interviews, in the case of graduate children, or to a questionnaire, in the case of currently participating children.

14. It is important to note that these results are consistent with the statements of the facilitators. When asked about CADE's impact on the children, their responses referred primarily to (1) losing the fear of public speaking, (2) projecting themselves to the community and strengthening their feeling of belonging, and (3) increasing capacities for dialogue and agreement reaching.

15. See www.pz.harvard.edu/vt.

References

Barber, Michael, and Mona Mourshed for McKinsey & Company. 2007. *How the world's best-performing school systems come out on the top*. Washington, DC: McKinsey & Company. Available from www.mckinsey.com (accessed 10 August 2010).

Boal, Augusto. 2004. *Theatre of the oppressed*. New York, NY: Theatre Communications Group.

Bohman, James. 1996. *Public deliberation: Pluralism, complexity and democracy*. Cambridge, MA: MIT Press.

Bohman, James. 1997. Deliberative democracy and effective social freedoms: Freedom, capacities, resources and opportunities. In *Deliberative democracy: Essays on reason and politics*, eds. James Bohman and William Rehg, 243–77. Cambridge MA: MIT Press.

Bujanda, Maria Eugenia. 2007. Los jóvenes como ciudadanos: Una nueva hoja de ruta para los programas de educación ciudadana. *Miscelánea Comillas, Revista de Ciencias Humanas y Sociales* 65 (126): 467–79. Available from www.fod.ac.cr/ (accessed 10 August 2010).

Burkhalter, Stephanie, John Gastil, and Todd Kelshaw. 2002. A conceptual definition and theoretical model of public deliberation in small face-to-face groups. *Communication Theory* 12 (4): 398–422.

Carlson, Mary, and Felton Earls. 2001. The child as citizen: Implications for the science and practice of child development. *International Society for the Study of Behavioral Development (ISSBD) Newsletter* 2 (38): 12–16.

Carlson, Mary, Felton Earls, and Clotilda Fonseca. 2002. Children and democracy: Focus on Costa Rica. *ReVista: Harvard Review of Latin America* 2:39–41.

Earls, Felton, and Mary Carlson. 2002. Adolescents as collaborators in search of well-being. In *Youth in cities*, eds. Marta Tienda and William Julius Wilson, 58–83. Cambridge: Cambridge University Press.

Earls, Felton, Giuseppe Raviola, and Mary Carlson. 2008. Promoting child mental health in the context of the HIV/AIDS pandemic with a focus on sub-Saharan Africa. *Journal of Child Psychology and Psychiatry* 49:295–312.

Feres, Claudia. 2000. El concepto de democracia deliberativa. Un diálogo entre Habermas, Cohen, y Bohman. *Metapolítica* 4 (14): 58–75.

Fondo de Población de las Naciones Unidas [United Nations Population Fund]. 2009. *Primera Encuesta Nacional de Juventud Costa Rica 2008, Informe integrado*. San José, Costa Rica: Fondo de Población de las Naciones Unidas; Consejo Nacional de Política Pública de la Persona Joven y Viceministerio de la Juventud.

Fonseca, Clotilde. 2005. From ICT to digital creation and productivity: Releasing the potential of technology for education and capacity building. In *Access, empowerment and governance: Creating a world of equal opportunities with ICT*, eds. Rinalia Abdul Rahim, Gabriele Siegenthaler Muinde, and Daniele Waldburger, 121–43. Kuala Lumpur, Malaysia: Global Knowledge Partnership (GKP). Available from www.fod.ac.cr (accessed 10 August 2010).

Fonseca, Clotilde. 2009. *Deepening understanding and addressing key challenges: Response to a dialogue on ICTs, human development, growth, and poverty reduction*. Available from http://publius.cc/dialogue_icts_human_development_growth_and_poverty_reduction/091109 (accessed 10 August 2010).

Fundación Omar Dengo. 2005. *Aprender a deliberar para una ciudadanía activa y democrática: Fundamentos teóricos y metodológicos y Guía didáctica para educadores*. San José, Costa Rica: Fundación Omar Dengo. Available from www.fod.ac.cr/publicaciones (accessed 11 August 2010).

Fundación Omar Dengo. 2006. *Educación y tecnologías digitales: Cómo valorar su impacto social y sus contribuciones a la equidad*. San José, Costa Rica: Fundación Omar Dengo.

Fundación Omar Dengo. 2009. *Estándares de desempeño de estudiantes en el aprendizaje con tecnologías digitales*. San José, Costa Rica: Fundación Omar Dengo.

Fundación Omar Dengo. 2010. *Manual de educación para la ciudadanía activa*. Vol. I: *Orientaciones teóricas y metodológicas*. San José, Costa Rica: Fundación Omar Dengo.

Gastil, John, and James P. Dillard. 1999. The aims, methods, and effects of deliberative civic education through the National Issues Forums. *Communication Education* 48 (3): 179–92.

Habermas, Jürgen. 1984. *The theory of communicative action*. Vol. 1: *Reason and the rationalization of society*. Trans. Thomas McCarthy. Boston, MA: Beacon.

Habermas, Jürgen. 1987. *The theory of communicative action*. Vol. 2: *Lifeworld and system: A critique of functionalist reason*. Trans. Thomas McCarthy. Boston, MA: Beacon.

Johnson, David W., Roger T. Johnson, and Edythe Johnson Holubec. 1994. *The nuts and bolts of cooperative learning*. Edina, MN: Interaction Book Company.

Kamo, Norifumi, Mary Carlson, Robert T. Brennan, and Felton Earls. 2008. Young citizens as health agents: Use of drama in promoting community efficacy for HIV/AIDS. *American Journal of Public Health* 98:201–4.

Koopmann, F. Klaus. 2002. Experiential civic learning by using "Projekt: Aktive Bürger." *OSD 2/2002: Civic and Economic Education in Europe*. Available from www.sowi-onlinejournal.de (accessed 11 August 2010).

Lipman, Matthew. 1998. El papel de las narraciones en la educación moral. In *Crecimiento moral y Filosofía para niños*, ed. Felix García Moriyón, 115–24. Bilbao, Spain: Desclée De Brouwer.

Madrigal, Johnny. 2007. *Resultados de la Encuesta Nacional de Seguridad Ciudadana 2006*. San José, Costa Rica: Programa de Naciones Unidas para el Desarrollo; Ministerio de Justicia y Gracia; Ministerio de Seguridad Pública. Available from www.pnud.or.cr/ (accessed 11 August 2010).

Moreno, Marjorie, and Siu Acon. 2009. Informe de resultados: Consultoría evaluación formativa y de impacto del proyecto CADE. Unpublished report.

Newman, D. R., and P. J. Emerson. 1997. *The on-line preferendum: A tool for voting, conflict resolution and decision-making*. Presented at International Conference on Voting, Rating and Annotation on the Internet, 21–22 April 1997. Austrian Academy of Sciences, Vienna. Available from www.qub.ac.uk (accessed 11 August 2010).

Programa de las Naciones Unidas para el Desarrollo (PNUD) [United Nations Development Programme (UNDP)]. 2006. *Venciendo el temor: (In)seguridad ciudadana y desarrollo humano en Costa Rica, Informe Nacional de Desarrollo Humano, 2005* [Overcoming fear: (In)security and human development in Costa Rica, National Human Development Report, 2005]. San José, Costa Rica: PNUD.

PNUD. 2009. *Abrir espacios para la seguridad ciudadana y el desarrollo humano. Informe sobre Desarrollo Humano para América Central 2009–2010*. San José, Costa Rica: PNUD. Available from http://hdr.PNUD.org/en/reports/regionalreports/ (accessed 11 August 2010).

Sen, Amartya. 1992. *Inequality reexamined*. Cambridge, MA: Harvard University Press.

Sen, Amartya. 1999. *Development as freedom*. New York, NY: Knopf.

Tishman, Shari, David N. Perkins, and Eileen Jay. 1994. *A thinking classroom: Learning and teaching in a culture of thinking*. Upper Saddle River, NJ: Allyn & Bacon.

UNICEF. 2009. *The state of the world's children, special edition: Celebrating 20 years of the Convention on the Rights of the Child*. New York, NY: UNICEF. Available from www.unicef.org/publications/ (accessed 11 August 2010).

Appendix

Time Line of Children's Rights

1919. The League of Nations establishes the Committee for the Protection of Children.

1924. The League of Nations adopts the Declaration of the Rights of the Child. The declaration addresses a child's right (regardless of race, nationality, or creed) to survival, nutrition, shelter, health care, humanitarian relief, protection from exploitation, and the right to grow up in an environment that fosters their development.

1946. The UN General Assembly creates UNICEF, expressly for addressing and alleviating the needs of children whom World War II affected.

1948. The UN General Assembly adopts the Universal Declaration of Human Rights. Although the declaration does not directly outline children's rights, these rights implicitly apply to children.

1959. The UN General Assembly unanimously endorses the Declaration of the Rights of the Child. This document builds upon the provisions in the 1924 declaration, adding provisions regarding a child's right to an identity, family, education, and freedom from discrimination.

1978. The Polish government drafts the precursory text for what eventually becomes the Convention on the Rights of the Child (CRC).

1979. The UN General Assembly proclaims 1979 as the International Year of the Child. The UN Commission on Human Rights establishes a working group to review and further build on the child rights treaty that the Polish government created.

1979–1989. Governmental representatives and NGOs work to draft the CRC. U.S. delegates

DOI: 10.1177/0002716210386336

insert provisions regarding a child's right to freedom of thought, speech, association, religion, and privacy at the request of President Reagan's administration.

1989. The UN General Assembly unanimously adopts the CRC.

1990. The CRC becomes international law. Heads of state and government and others gather in New York for the World Summit for Children to discuss how to translate the CRC into action. The event concludes with the signing of the World Declaration on the Survival, Protection, and Development of Children.

1990–1994. Resolutions are introduced in the U.S. Senate, calling for ratification of the CRC.

1995. On behalf of President Clinton, Madeleine Albright, the U.S. delegate to the UN, signs the CRC.

2000. The UN General Assembly adopts the Optional Protocol on the Sale of Children, Child Prostitution, and Child Pornography and the Optional Protocol on the Involvement of Children in Armed Conflict.

2002. The optional protocols become international law after ten countries ratify them. The U.S. Senate ratifies both protocols in December. The UN Special Session on Children meets to discuss how to improve the situation of the world's children. The event closes with the adoption of *A World Fit for Children*, a document that reaffirms leaders' obligations to promote and protect the rights of children that the CRC and its optional protocols established.

2009. One hundred ninety-three nations have ratified the CRC. The only two exceptions are the United States and Somalia.

Note: The dates and events contained in this appendix were gleaned from "Chronology: The Path to Promoting Universal Child Well-Being" compiled by the Campaign for U.S. Ratification of the Convention on the Rights of the Child (CRC)